THE FATHERS
OF THE CHURCH

A NEW TRANSLATION

VOLUME 41

THE FATHERS
OF THE CHURCH

A NEW TRANSLATION

SAINT JOHN CHRYSOSTOM

COMMENTARY ON SAINT JOHN
THE APOSTLE AND EVANGELIST

Homilies 48-88

Translated by

SISTER THOMAS AQUINAS GOGGIN, S. C. H.

THE CATHOLIC UNIVERSITY OF AMERICA PRESS
WASHINGTON, DC

Nihil Obstat:

JOHN M. A. GOODWINE

Censor Librorum

Imprimatur:

✠ FRANCIS CARDINAL SPELLMAN

Archbishop of New York

The *Nihil obstat* and *Imprimatur* are official declarations that a book or pamphlet is free of doctrinal or moral error. No implication is contained therein that those who have granted the *Nihil obstat* and *Imprimatur* agree with the contents, opinions, or statements expressed.

Library of Congress Catalog Card No.: 57-1545
ISBN 0-8132-1025-9
ISBN-13: 978-0-8132-1025-4 (pbk.)

CONTENTS

INTRODUCTION

THE EIGHTY-EIGHT HOMILIES comprising the *Commentary on the Gospel of St. John* were preached by St. John Chrysostom at Antioch in about 390. *Homilies* 48-88, which form the contents of this volume, continue the exegesis of St. John's Gospel from Chapter 7 to the end, with the exception of the episode of the adulteress (8.1-11). Since this is the only omission, it would appear that St. John Chrysostom was using one of the many Greek manuscripts of the New Testament which omit this section.

In the homilies of the present volume the commentary grows noticeably less detailed as the series progresses. This is a departure from what is to be observed in the early members of the group, where an entire homily often is centered around the elucidation of a single phrase or clause. In fact, so leisurely and thorough is the discussion that Homilies 1-20 embrace only Chapter 1 of the Evangelist. In striking contrast to this very detailed study, the four concluding chapters of the Gospel (18-21) have but six homilies (83-88) devoted to them.

The reason for this unevenness cannot be determined

definitively, but several possible explanations suggest themselves. The homilies follow the sequence of St. John's Gospel
very closely and seem to have been delivered consecutively
as a series. Internal evidence points to this continuity,
especially the frequent references recalling to the congregation
the text discussed in the homily immediately preceding. And
occasionally the preacher promises to complete the explanation of the day's text next time. Thus, it may have been the
limitation imposed by the necessity of completing the series
within a given period of time that constrained St. John
Chrysostom to develop the texts in a less detailed manner
towards the end of the Gospel.

It is more than likely, besides, that he felt it essential to
treat more exhaustively those portions of the Gospel that
particularly concern the doctrine of the divinity of Christ, and
yet might be somewhat obscure to the average listener. Exegesis of this type was especially timely since this fundamental
teaching was then so widely and persistently held in question.
Hence, of all the homilies St. John Chrysostom devoted to the
study of Scripture, these are the most controversial in tone,
for he used them as a means to anticipate and refute the
arguments of the Arians and other heretics who denied the
divinity of Christ and tried to quote Scripture to their purpose.

Or, possibly he was influenced, consciously or uncon-
sciously, by the example of the Evangelists themselves, who
exhibited reportorial terseness in narrating the events of the
Passion and those which took place after the Resurrection.

In any case, though the length of the Gospel text discussed in the individual homily varies, an identical pattern
is consistently followed in the form of each one of the eighty-
eight. As a preface the preacher quotes the text with which he
intends to begin his commentary. Then comes a brief intro-
duction, rather formal in tone, containing a few apt reflections suggested by the text of the day.

The commentary on the text follows, rambling in style, often repetitious, and wandering easily onto little by-paths opening out from the subject in hand. This part of the homily is not cast in any set form, but can be engagingly informal or relentlessly logical, as occasion demands. With the dramatic instinct of the born orator, St. John Chrysostom urges his audience to 'see' what is taking place as he graphically unfolds the Gospel story. He makes frequent use of the device of the dialogue in which he himself and an imaginary member of his audience parry question and answer with one another or with one of the Gospel personalities, such as Peter, or Pilate. Often he paraphrases the words of the Evangelist in order to clarify the meaning of a passage.

Though this commentary bulks large in each homily, a considerable part of each one is also devoted to the moral exhortation which directly follows the commentary. The teeming oriental city of Antioch furnished abundant matter calculated to be of grave concern to the shepherd of souls. Singling out a vice, or a virtue, or some excess or other, in each homily he drives home salutary moral lessons in a candid, homely style. Tactfully he makes his admonition inoffensive' by humbly including himself in the oft-recurring exhortation: 'Let us . . . '

All the capital sins are castigated in turn, in the form in which they were most prevalent. Covetousness, in particular, receives frequent mention, as he urges almsgiving, not only the rich to the poor, but also the poor to the poor, giving of what they have (59). He declares: 'Christ did not say, "I was sick and you did not cure Me," but merely "you did not visit Me." He did not say, "I was in prison and you did not get Me out," but "you did not come to Me" ' (60).

Conscious that he returned so often to this subject, he comments: 'Now, perhaps someone will remark with good reason, "Every day you preach about covetousness." Would that it were possible to speak of it every night also,' he adds drily (76).

Frequently, too, he suggests the thought of death, judgment, and future rewards and punishments as an incentive to the practice of virtue and the avoiding of vice (e.g., 77). He protests against the excessively demonstrative grief displayed by women on the occasion of the death of some close relative (62). He condemns the unbecoming extravagance so prevalent in burial and funeral arrangements in his day. 'These trappings,' he asserts, 'are an expression, not of sympathy for the departed, but of vainglory on the part of those left behind' (85).

From his pithy remarks on the contemporary scene much information can be gleaned, valuable to the historian of life and times; for example, regarding the theater and the races (58), or conditions in prisons (60), or the extravagant adornment of women (69).

Despite the fact that his words were addressed to his fourth-century congregation, much of what he said is remarkably timeless in character. For instance, 'Nothing is more potent,' he declares, 'than a good and prudent woman in molding a man and shaping his soul in whatever way she desires.' But, 'As a woman has great power for good, so she also has it for evil' (61). In urging respect for priests, 'Great indeed is the dignity of the priesthood,' he affirms.

Nearly every phase of human morality receives its share of praise or blame: the good use of time (58), the evil of adultery (63), bearing wrongs patiently (83), avoiding bad companionship (57), imitating Christ's meekness and gentleness (60), to mention but a few samples.

Finally, the homily always concludes with a brief prayer ending in a doxology. Though the latter is made up of stereotyped phrases, it is not always identical, but there are several recurring formulae.

Throughout the *Homilies,* St. John Chrysostom gives evidence of striking familiarity with sacred Scripture, both Old and New Testaments. He draws on them freely for apt quotations and pertinent illustrations, and his own deep reverence and respect for the Word of God shine brightly forth. He repeatedly recommends to his congregation careful study of the Scriptures and thoughtful meditation on their meaning. He notes with regret that in all too many cases attendance at the theater is preferred to listening to sermons in church. People who cannot identify Biblical characters, or even tell the number of the Apostles, can discourse eloquently of horses and charioteers and dancers, he declares (58).

The golden stream of the eloquence which earned St. John Chrysostom his name and his title to fame was not, if we may judge by the *Homilies* on St. John's Gospel, mere oratorical display. There is none of the exaggerated attention to form, at the expense of matter, characteristic of so much of the oratory of his day, as popularized by the sophists. However, he did not make the mistake of completely ignoring the taste of his refined and cultured audience by preaching in a plain style devoid of rhetorical embellishments. With unerring instinct he used his talent and education to best advantage in spreading the word of God, always careful not to compromise His interests. From the time he entered upon his apostolate in Antioch, the rhetorician humbly trod behind the preacher, lending his services as needed.

Perhaps the secret of the preacher's enduring appeal may lie in the golden thread of his sincerity that gleams with such genuine luster throughout these homilies. The tribute to the Evangelist, so gracefully expressed in the opening homily, might well be applied to St. John Chrysostom himself: 'There is no pretense in him, but with head uncovered he preaches the naked truth.' His eloquence was so well matched by his strict orthodoxy that it has been truly said that the Church

of the East has but a single Chrysostom and of the preachers
of the Western Church only Augustine compares with him.

On completing this translation of the *Homilies,* it is a
pleasure once again to acknowledge my indebtedness to
Sister Mary Eileen, S.C.H., for her generous assistance in
the preparation of the typescript of this volume; and to
Robert H. Haynes of the Widener Library of Harvard
University for many kind services, particularly for arranging
loans of texts.

SAINT JOHN CHRYSOSTOM

COMMENTARY ON SAINT JOHN
THE APOSTLE AND EVANGELIST

Homilies 48-88

Translated by

SISTER THOMAS AQUINAS GOGGIN, S. C. H., Ph. D.
Halifax, Nova Scotia

Homily 48 (John 7.1-8)

'Now after these things Jesus went about in Galilee, for he did not wish to go about Judea because the Jews were seeking to put him to death. Now the Jewish feast of Tabernacles was at hand.'[1]

Nothing is worse than jealousy and envy; by them death came into the world. When the Devil saw man being held in honor, since he could not endure the sight of his well-being, he did everything to cause him to lose it.[2] And in every instance one may see this same fruit developing from this root.

It was thus that Abel was slain,[3] and thus that David narrowly escaped being slain,[4] and so with many other just men; and it was by reason of this that the Jews became murderers of Christ. To show this the Evangelist said: 'After these things Jesus went about in Galilee, for he could not go about in Judea because the Jews were seeking to put him to death.' O blessed John, what are you saying? Is it that He who was able to do anything whatsoever He willed 'could not'[5] [go about Judea freely]; He who cast His hearers to the

---

1 John 7.1,2.
2 Cf. Wisd. 2.24.
3 Cf. Gen. 3.3-9.
4 Cf. 1 Kings 18.8.
5 'οὐκ εἶχεν ἐξουσίαν.' In the introductory text above, however: οὐκ ἤθελεν. Both are represented in the manuscript tradition for the passage. Cf. Merk 333, crit. app.

3

ground by saying: 'Whom do you seek'?[6] Was He, who could be present without being seen, powerless to act this time?

But how was it that later, going into their midst within the Temple, while the festival was in progress, before a congregation which included even His murderers, He discoursed of things that would annoy them still more? Indeed, they were amazed at this and kept saying: 'Is not this the man they seek to kill? And behold he speaks openly and they say nothing to him.'[7] What is the explanation of these riddles?

It was not in order that he might obtain the reputation of speaking in riddles that John spoke in this way. Perish the thought! On the contrary, he did this to make it clear that at one time Christ's divinity was being attested; at another, His humanity. When he said 'He could not' he was speaking of Him as a Man who did many things even in a human way; but when he asserted that He stood in their midst and they did not seize Him, he was, of course, proving the power of His Godhead. And this is so for in fleeing Christ was acting as a Man, and in making His appearance He was acting as God; in both cases, genuinely. The fact that He was not seized even though surrounded by those who were plotting against Him was proof of His invincibility and inviolability; while His withdrawal confirmed and strengthened the doctrine of the Incarnation, so that Paul of Samosata[8] might have nothing to say, or Marcion,[9] or those infected with the

---

6 Cf. John 18.4-7.
7 John 7.26.
8 Paul of Samosata in the third century denied the essential divinity of Christ and taught that He was merely a man, though born of a virgin and divinely inspired. See *Catholic Encyclopedia.*
9 Marcion (d. *c.* 170) taught, among other things, that the Old and New Testaments are opposed to one another. For a detailed treatment of his life and heretical teachings, see the article 'Marcionites' in the *Catholic Encyclopedia.*

disease of their teachings. By this means, then, He shut the mouths of all of them.

'After these things there was the Jewish Feast of Tabernacles.' The phrase 'after these things' can mean nothing else than that in the interest of brevity he had passed over without mention the considerable interval that elapsed between the two incidents he narrated. This is evident from the narrative itself, for, when Christ was sitting on the mountainside, the Evangelist stated, it was the Feast of Passover, while here he made mention of the Feast of Tabernacles.[10] Furthermore, he narrated no other incident that took place within the five months, and revealed to us nothing else beyond the miracle of the loaves and the discourse He addressed to those who had eaten.

Yet Christ Himself did not cease performing miracles and preaching, either during the day or in the evening, often even by night. Indeed, according to the statements of all the Evangelists, He acted in this way unceasingly while in the company of His disciples. Why in the world, therefore, did they omit that period of time from their story? Because it was not possible to recount everything. Besides, they endeavored to record those incidents which were later to give rise to accusation or opposition from the Jews. In fact, they had an abundance of that type of incident to recount.

I say this for they often merely recorded that He healed the sick and raised the dead, and that He was admired, but where they had something strange to tell or had to relate some accusation that seemed to develop against Him, they treated of such incidents in greater detail. The present instance, to be sure, is an example of this, because His brethren here did not believe in Him; therefore, the affair carried with

---

10 Cf. John 6.3,4. The Passover was celebrated in the spring (March or April) ; the Feast of Tabernacles took place at the end of September or the beginning of October, the time when the harvest was gathered.

it odium of no ordinary stamp. Indeed, the honesty of the Evangelists is worthy of admiration, since they were not ashamed to relate those details which seemed to bring opprobrium upon their Master, but on the contrary even strove to make these things known most of all.

Accordingly, in the present text, omitting to mention many signs and wonders and discourses, the Evangelist passed on at once to this incident. He declared: 'His brethren said to him, "Leave here and go into Judea that thy disciples also may see the works that thou dost; for no one does a thing in secret if he wants to be publicly known. Manifest thyself to the world." For not even his brethren believed in him.'

'Now what sort of incredulity have we here?' you will ask. 'For they besought Him to work miracles.'

Very great incredulity indeed, since their words and their boldness and the ill-advised familiarity of their manner toward Him were all evidences of incredulity. They thought that by reason of their kinship with Him it was permissible for them to address Him familiarly. Moreover, their demand was ostensibly that of friends, but their words betrayed their deep-seated envy, for by them they insultingly imputed to Him both cowardice and vainglory. Thus, the words, 'No one does a thing in secret,' show that they were accusing Him of cowardice, and at the same time that they held His deeds in suspicion, while the words that follow, namely, 'wants to be publicly known,' imply an accusation of vainglory.

Now, please notice the power of Christ. For, from the ranks of those who were making these remarks, one subsequently became first Bishop of Jerusalem: the blessed James.[11] It was he also about whom Paul said: 'But I saw none of the other apostles, except James, the brother of the

---

11 James the Less. St. John Chrysostom interprets 'His brethren' literally as the two Apostles, James the Less and his brother Jude, who were close relatives of Christ.

Lord,'[12] and Jude likewise is said to have become famous.[13] But now, though they had been present at Cana when the wine was miraculously made, they did not as yet derive profit from this. Whence, then, did they conceive such great incredulity? From jealousy and envy, for when some members of a family attain to greater excellence, this can somehow cause envy among those who do not succeed as well.

But whom did they call 'disciples' in this instance? All the crowd who were following Him, not just the Twelve. What, therefore, did Christ say? See how mildly He replied. For He did not say: 'Who are you to be giving Me this advice and to be instructing Me?' On the contrary, what did He say? 'My time has not yet come,' and here He seems to me to be implying something more. For perhaps through envy they were plotting to betray Him to the Jews. Therefore, it was with reference also to this that He said: 'My time has not yet come,' that is, 'the time for My crucifixion and death. Why, then, are you hastening to destroy Me ahead of time?'

'But your time is always at hand.' It was as if He were saying: 'Even though you continually associate with the Jews, they will not destroy you, since you are envious of the same things as they, but they will desire to do away with Me at once. So that your time is ever present, since you are in no danger. My time, on the contrary, is when the hour of the crucifixion is near, the time when I must die.' I say this for it is clear from what follows that He meant this.

'The world cannot hate you. How can it, since you have the same desires and pursue the same aims? But it hates me because I bear witness concerning it, that its works are evil.' That is, 'Because I upbraid and accuse it, for this reason I am hated.'

Let us learn from this to overcome our anger and not to

---

12 Gal. 1.19.
13 Cf. Jude 1.1, where he calls himself 'the brother of James.'

show indignation even if those who attempt to give us advice
are our inferiors. Christ tolerated it with mildness when the
incredulous offered Him counsel, though they not only gave
unseemly advice, but even gave it with evil intent. What
pardon, then, shall we obtain—we who are dust and ashes—
when we show ill will toward those who offer us advice, and
if our advisors are a little inferior to us, consider their gesture
unworthy of our dignity. Yet, see how He warded off their
charge with all mildness. When they cried: 'Manifest thyself
to the world,' He Himself replied: 'The world cannot hate
you but the world hates me,' in order to refute the implied
charge. 'Actually, I am so far from seeking glory from men,'
He meant, 'that I do not cease reproving them, and I do
so even though I know that hatred for Me is aroused by this
and death is being planned for Me.'

'But when did He reprove them,' you ask?

When, indeed, did He ever cease to do so? Did He not
say: 'Do not think that I shall accuse you to the Father.
There is one who accuses you, Moses.' Also: 'I know you,
that you have not the love of God.' And: 'How can you
believe who receive glory from men, and do not seek the
glory which is from the only God?'[14] Do you perceive how He
proved by all these statements that it was His fearless reproving of them that caused their hatred for Him, and not
His breaking the Sabbath?

'But why in the world did He send them to the feast,
saying: "Go up to the feast, but I do not go up just now"?'

To show that He had not spoken as He did out of any
need of the disciples or in the desire to curry their favor; on
the contrary, He was giving them permission to accomplish
the Jewish rites.

'How is it, then,' you will say, 'that He actually did go up,
though He had said: "I do not go up"?'

---

14 Cf. John 5.42-46.

He did not say with absolute finality: 'I do not go up,' but He meant: 'I do not go up now,' that is, 'with you, because my time is not yet fulfilled.' And in fact He was going to be crucified on the following Pasch.

'How is it, therefore, that He Himself did not go up now, too? For if it was because His time was not yet here that He did not go up, He ought not to have gone up at all.'

Yes, but it was not in order that He might suffer that He went up to the feast, but to give them a lesson.

'Well, why did He go privately? And I ask this for He had the power, if He did go up publicly, to remain in their midst and to make their lawless assault on Him ineffectual, as He often had done.'

However, He did not wish to do this repeatedly. For, if He had gone up publicly and had rendered them powerless once again, He would have caused His Godhead to shine forth still more brilliantly, a thing which was not required for the moment, and He was rather concealing it. And inasmuch as they thought it cowardly of Him to remain behind, He Himself proved the opposite, namely, that it was both courageous and wise. Likewise, He showed that since He foresaw the time when He was to suffer, when at a later date this time drew near, then He would especially wish to go up to Jerusalem.

Moreover, by saying: 'As for you, go up,' He seems to me to mean this: 'Do not think that I am forcing you to remain with Me, if you not wish to do so.' Further, by adding: 'My time has not yet come,' He seems to be making it clear that it was necessary for miracles to take place, and for groups of people to hear preaching so that more of the crowd might believe, and the disciples become more staunch as a result of witnessing their Master's fearless preaching and His sufferings.

From His words let us, then, learn meekness, gentleness—

'Learn from me, for I am meek and humble of heart,'[15]—
and let us reject every feeling of anger. Even if someone acts
arrogantly towards us, let us be humble; if someone is
domineering, let us give way; if he vexes and harasses us,
mocking and deriding us, let us not be overcome at this, lest
in warding off the attack we destroy ourselves.

Now I say this for anger is a wild beast, a ferocious wild
beast, eager for its prey. Therefore, let us chant to ourselves
incantations taken from the divine Scriptures, and let us say:
'You are dust and ashes,'[16] and 'Why is earth and ashes
proud?' Also: 'The wrath of his high spirits is his ruin,'[17]
And: 'A hot-tempered man is not seemly.'[18] Indeed, nothing
is more shameful than a countenance ablaze with anger,
nothing more disfigured. And if this is true of the countenance
much rather is it true of the soul. For, just as a noisome odor
is usually given off when mud is stirred up, so when the
soul is disturbed by anger great impropriety and unpleasant-
ness will result.

'But,' you will say, 'I cannot endure insult from my
enemies.'

Why is that, pray? For, if what is said be true, you ought
to show compunction even in his presence, and to be grateful
to him for the charges. If, on the contrary, it be false, treat
it with scorn. Does he call you poverty-stricken? Laugh at
him. Does he say you are low-born or foolish? Groan for his
future lot. For 'Whoever says to his brother, "Thou fool!"
shall be liable to the fire of Gehenna'[19] Therefore, when
he insults you, think of the punishment which he has in
store for him, and not only will you not feel angry, but you
will even shed tears for him. Indeed, one does not become

15 Matt. 11.29.
16 Cf. Gen. 3.19; 18.27.
17 Eccli. 10.9; 1.28,22.
18 Prov. 11.25 (Septuagint).
19 Matt. 5.22.

angry with a fever patient or someone suffering from inflammation, but one pities and grieves for all such unfortunates. The soul inflamed with anger is in truth like them.

However, if you do wish to retaliate, keep silence and you have dealt a mortal wound. On the contrary, if you parry reviling with reviling, you have kindled the blaze still more.

'But, if we remain silent, the bystanders will charge us with weakness,' you say.

They will not charge you with weakness; rather, they will marvel at your wisdom. Moreover, if, when insulted, you are vexed, you offer insult, also, and by showing vexation you force the bystanders to think that what is said is true. Tell me, why is it that the rich man laughs on hearing himself called a poor man? Is it not because he has no consciousness of poverty? So it is with us, also; if we laugh at insults we shall provide the strongest proof of not being consciously guilty of what is said.

Besides, how long shall we continue to fear the criticisms of men? How long shall we despise those of our common Lord and remain fastened to the flesh? 'For since there are strife and jealousy and dissensions among you, are you not carnal?'[20] Let us, then, become spiritual and let us curb this terrible beast.

There is no difference between anger and madness, but it is an evil spirit that comes and goes; rather, it is worse than demoniacal possession. For, the man possessed by a demon may even enjoy pardon, while he who indulges in anger will merit punishments without number, since he deliberately casts himself into the depths of ruin. Moreover, even before Gehenna that lies in store, he already begins to pay the penalty for his action, by introducing into his inmost thoughts a certain unceasing unrest and persistent distress all through the night and all through the day.

---

20 Cf. 1 Cor. 3.3.

Therefore, in order that we may free ourselves from punishments in the present life and from the penalty to be paid in the life to come, let us reject this passion and display all gentleness and meekness, so that even here we may find rest for our souls, and also in the kingdom of heaven.

May it be the lot of all of us to attain this by the grace and mercy of our Lord Jesus Christ. Through Him and with Him glory be to the Father, together with the Holy Spirit, now and always, forever and ever. Amen.

Homily 49 (John 7.9-24)

'When he had said these things to them he stayed on in Galilee. But as soon as his brethren had gone up to the feast, then he also went up, not publicly, but as it were privately.'[1]

The actions performed by Christ in a human way were so performed not merely for the purpose of confirming the Incarnation, but also that He might instruct us to virtuous living. For, if He did everything as God, whence would we be able to learn what we ought to do when faced with trials outside the realm of our experience?

I mean, for example, in this very instance, by proceeding right into the midst of the murderous Jews He checked their purpose. But, if He always acted thus, whence would we who are unable to do this know how we ought to act when we encounter difficulty? How would we know whether we ought to submit to death at once, or whether we, too, ought to make some provision so that our preaching might continue? Therefore, since we, who have not His power, would not know what we ought to do upon coming forth into the midst of our enemies, for this reason He gave us instruction in this regard.

'When Jesus had said these things,' the Evangelist says,

---

1 John 7.9,10.

'he stayed on in Galilee. But as soon as his brethren had gone up, then he also went up, not publicly, but as it were privately.' The words, 'His brethren had gone up,' are intended to show that He did not wish to go up with them. And therefore He stayed on in the place where He was and did not make Himself publicly known, though they were pressing Him to do so.

But why in the world did He who always preached publicly now do so 'as it were privately'? The Evangelist did not say 'secretly,' but 'as it were privately.' For, as I have said, Christ had to act in this way to instruct us how to conduct ourselves. Besides, it was not reasonable to put in an appearance rashly while they were angry and disturbed, but it was advisable to appear afterwards, when the feast was over.

'The Jews therefore were looking for him and saying, "Where is he?" ' What worthy conduct during the feast! Bent on murder, they wished to apprehend Him during the festival. To be sure, they also spoke like this elsewhere: 'What do you think, that he is not coming to the feast?'[2] Here they said: 'Where is he?' Because of their deep hatred and enmity they were not even willing to call Him by name. They were certainly showing great respect for the feast, great reverence! By means of the very feast they wished to hunt Him down.

'And there was much whispered comment among the crowd concerning him.' Now it seems to me that it was by very reason of the place where the miracle had been worked that they were excited and at the same time angry and afraid. They were not so much vexed because of His coming, as afraid lest He might again perform some such miracle. But everything turned out just the opposite of their wishes, and they themselves brought Him to public notice, without intending to do so. Now, 'Some were saying, "He is a good man." But others were saying, "No. Rather, he seduces the crowd." ' '

---

2 John 11.56.

Therefore, I think that the first opinion was that of the multitude, while the latter was that of the rulers and priests, for the slander was the work of their envy and wickedness.

'He seduces the people,' they said. In doing what, if you please? It was not because He was pretending and not really working miracles, was it? Indeed, experience bears witness to the contrary. 'Yet for fear of the Jews no one spoke openly of him.' Do you observe in every instance the corruption of the rulers and the sound judgment of their subjects, though these lacked the manly courage demanded by the occasion and which the common people particularly need to possess?

'When, however, the feast was already half over, Jesus went up and was teaching.' Because of the delay He made them more eager to hear Him. Those who had been seeking Him during the first days of the feast and saying, 'Where is he?'—upon seeing Him suddenly present, see how they drew near and how they would hang on His words: both those who said He was good, and those who denied it. However, the former did so in such a way as to obtain profit and to be moved to admire Him, whereas the latter were intent on laying hold of Him and restraining Him.

Accordingly, those who were saying 'He seduces the crowd' were saying it by reason of what His doctrine taught, whereas the others called Him 'good' because of His miracles. After allowing their anger to subside, then, He won out to such an extent that they attentively listened to His words, since wrath was no longer stopping up their ears. However, the Evangelist did not state His teachings, but said only that He taught in a wonderful way and that He captivated them and won them over, so great was the power of His words. Even those who had been saying 'He seduces the crowd' were won over and they marvelled. And therefore they kept saying: 'How does this man come by learning, since he has not studied?'

Do you perceive how he makes it clear here also that even their admiration was full of perversity? For, he did not say: 'They marvelled at His teaching,' or 'They accepted what He said,' but simply: 'They marvelled,' that is, they were moved with astonishment and were dumbfounded, saying: 'From what source has this Man come by this knowledge?' They did so despite the fact that they ought to have been aware, because of their very amazement, that there was nothing in Him that was merely human.

However, since they themselves were unwilling to aknowledge this, but were content merely to marvel at Him, listen to what He Himself said: 'My teaching is not my own.' Once more He was answering their suspicious thought by referring them to His Father, since He wished to refute them from that source. 'If anyone desires to do his will, he will know of the teaching whether it is from God, or whether I speak on my own authority.' Now, what He meant is this: 'Rid yourselves of wickedness: the anger, and the envy, and the hatred which have arisen in your hearts—entirely without provocation—against Me, and you will have no difficulty in realizing that My words are actually those of God. For, as it is, these passions darken your understanding and distort the sound judgment that shines there, while, if you remove these passions, you will no longer be thus afflicted.'

Yet He did not actually speak in this way, for He would have cut them to the quick. But He did imply all this by the words: 'He who does his will[3] will know of the teaching whether it is from God, or whether I speak on my own authority,' that is, 'whether I am saying something foreign and strange and in opposition to Him. Indeed, the expression "on my own authority" means essentially this: that I say nothing apart from what seems best to Him, but everything

---

3 That is, 'If anyone desires to do his will.' Cf. the Confraternity translation. St. John Chrysostom also uses this more accurate wording above.

that the Father wills I also will. If anyone does His will, he will know of the teaching.'

What is the meaning of 'If anyone does His will'? 'If a man loves a virtuous life, he will know the force of what I have said; if anyone is willing to pay attention to the Prophets, he will know whether I speak in fulfillment of them or not.'

'But how is His teaching His and yet not His own? For He did not say: "This teaching is not my own," but, after having first said, "It is mine," and having thus claimed it as His own, He added: "It is not my own." How, then, can the same thing be at the same time His and not His own?'

It was His, on the one hand, because He spoke without having been taught, but it was not His own because it was the teaching of His Father.

'Then how is it that He said: "All things that are the Father's are mine, and mine are His"?[4] For, if it was false to say that because it is the Father's it is therefore not Yours, it must be Yours for the very reason that it is the Father's.'

However, actually the expression 'is not my own' very clearly sets forth the doctrine of His and the Father's Oneness, as if He said: 'He has nothing different from Me in the way a thing belongs to another person. For, even if He is a different Person, I speak and act in such a way as not even to think a thought different from the Father, but to say and do the same thing as the Father.'

Then He went on to add an irrefutable argument, by setting before them an illustration drawn from human affairs and instructing them from familiar practice. And what is this? 'He who speaks on his own authority seeks his own glory.' That is, 'He who wishes to establish some teaching as his own wishes to do so for no other reason than to obtain glory as the fruit of this. But, if I do not wish to obtain glory as the

---

4 Cf. John 17.10.

fruit of My words, why should I desire to establish any teaching as My own?

'He who speaks on his own authority, that is, he who utters some personal and distinctive dictum does so for this reason: that he may make a reputation for himself. But, if I seek the glory of Him who sent Me, why should I prefer to utter teachings different from His?'

Do you perceive that there was a reason why there,[5] also, He said that He did nothing on His own authority? And what was it? That they might believe that He was not seeking after fame in the eyes of men. It was for this reason He spoke when He uttered the humble words: 'I seek my Father's glory,' since on every occasion He desired to persuade them that He did not love glory.

Accordingly, there were many reasons for His speaking in lowly vein of Himself: for example, that He might not be thought unbegotten or in opposition to God; that they might believe that He actually had assumed our flesh; also, because His listeners were so weak; and in order to teach men to act with moderation and not to be boastful with regard to themselves. But only a single reason can be discovered for His making laudatory statements about Himself, namely, the greatness of His nature. For, if they were scandalized when He said: 'I am before Abraham,'[6] what feelings would they have had if they were always hearing sublime statements made of Him?

'Did not Moses give you the Law, and none of you observes the Law? Why do you seek to put me to death?'

'Now how does this follow from what precedes it,' you will say, 'or what connection has it with what He had just said?'

They had brought forward two charges: one, that He was breaking the Sabbath; the other, that He called God His

---

5 At the Last Supper. Cf. John 17.4-9.
6 Cf. John 8.59.

Father, making Himself equal to God. From this passage it is indeed clear that His status was not in accord with their suspicious reasoning,[7] but in agreement with the literal sense of His statement, and that He was speaking, not as most men do, but in a distinctive way proper to Himself. Frequently, men have said that God is their Father,[8] for instance, that God alone has created us and is alone Father of us all, but they did not claim at the same time to be equal to God, so those who heard the statement did not take offense at it. Accordingly, just as, when they kept saying: 'He is not of God,' He corrected them and defended His breaking of the Sabbath, so also, if the truth were in accord with their suspicious reasoning and not in agreement with the literal sense of His statement, He would have corrected them and said: 'Why do you think I am equal to God? I am not equal.' Actually, however, He said no such thing, but quite the opposite. Furthermore, He proved He is equal by what followed.

His previous words: 'As the Father raises the dead and gives them life, so also the Son,' and 'that all men may honor the Son even as they honor the Father,' and 'Whatever He does, this the Son also does in like manner'[9]—all testified to His equality. But with regard to the Law He said: 'Do not think that I have come to destroy the Law or the Prophets.'[10] So, He also knew how to dispel the evil suspicions that were in their minds. However, in this place He not only did not dispel their suspicion that He was claiming to be equal to the Father, but even confirmed it. And elsewhere, too, when they were saying: 'You are making yourself God,'[11] He did not

---

7 That is, that He could not be equal to the Father.
8 Cf. Mal. 2.10.
9 Cf. John 5.21,23,20.
10 Matt. 5.17.
11 Cf. Matt. 9.4. 'This Man blasphemes.'

dispel the suspicion, but even confirmed it by saying: ' "But that you may know that the Son of Man has power on earth to forgive sins," he said to the paralytic, "Take up thy pallet and walk." '[12]

Accordingly, He here strengthened the previous contention that He was making Himself equal to God by showing that He was not opposed to God, but said the same words as He and taught the same doctrines. Finally, He proceeded to the question of His breaking the Sabbath by saying: 'Did not Moses give you the Law, and none of you observes the Law?' As if He said: 'The Law has said, "Thou shalt not kill," but you are committing murder [in desire], and do you accuse Me of transgressing the Law?'

'Why did He say, "None of you"?'

Because they were all seeking to put Him to death. Therefore, He meant: 'Even if I did break the Law it was in saving a man, but you transgress the Law for an evil end. Even if my action was a transgression, it was for the purpose of saving, and I ought not be judged by you who are committing grave transgressions. Your conduct, indeed, is an undermining of the whole Law.'

Then He went on to argue with them in this instance, though on the former occasion[13] He had likewise spoken in detail on the subject. At that time, however, it was on a more exalted level and in accordance with His dignity, but now in a more lowly strain. Why in the world was that? Because He did not wish to continue irritating them, for now their anger was roused to the limit and they were bent on murder. Therefore He waited, checking them by these two means: by accusing them of their bold purpose and saying: 'Why do you seek to put me to death?' adding meekly: 'a man who

12 Matt. 9.6.
13 Cf. John 5.19-30.

have spoken the truth'; and also by showing that murderers were not worthy to act as judges of another man.

Moreover, do you perceive both the humility of Christ's question, and the boldness of their reply? 'Thou hast a devil. Who seeks to put thee to death?' Words flowing from insane passion, and from a soul made shameless upon being unexpectedly reproved, and put out of countenance, as they thought, by these words of Christ! Even as certain robbers chant while engaged in hatching their plots, and then, desiring to put their victim off his guard, accomplish this by silence, so these men also acted. He Himself, however, omitting to charge them with this, so as not to provoke them to be still more brazen, once more undertook to make His defense of the charge regarding the Sabbath, basing His argument with them on the Law.

Now notice how prudently He did this. 'It is not remarkable,' He said, 'if you misunderstand Me, inasmuch as you misunderstand the Law, which you think you understand, and which you think was given by Moses. Therefore it is not at all strange if you do not pay attention to My words.' For, since they were saying: 'God spoke to Moses, but as for this man, we do not know where he is from,'[14] He proved that they also despised Moses, for, though he had given the Law, they did not hearken even to him.

'One work I did and you all wonder.'[15] Notice that where He had to defend Himself, and when some event caused Him to be accused of wrong-doing, He did not make mention of the Father, but laid stress on His own Person. 'One work I did.' He wished to show them that to fail to do it was to break the Law, and that there are many things superior to the Law, and that Moses had allowed himself to receive a precept in

---

14 John 9.29,30.
15 That is, the cure of the sick man at the pool of Bethsaida. Cf. John 5.1-18.

opposition to the Law and superior to the Law. For, circumcision had precedence over the Sabbath, though it was not from the Law but from 'the fathers.' 'And I also have done something superior to and better than circumcision.' He did not, in the next place, make mention merely of the precept of the Law, for example, that the priests transgress the Sabbath, as He had already said, but He spoke with even greater authority.

Further, the expression, 'you wonder,'[16] means 'you are amazed,' 'you are much disturbed,' for, if it were necessary for the Law to endure forever, circumcision would not have taken precedence over it. And though He did not say: 'I have done something greater than circumcision,' He refuted them authoritatively by saying: 'If a man receives circumcision. Do you perceive that the Law is then most of all confirmed, when a man breaks it? Do you perceive that the breaking of the Sabbath is observing the Law? Hence, if the Sabbath were not broken, it would have been necessary for the Law to be broken. So that I also have confirmed it.'

Moreover, He did not say: 'You are embittered at Me because I have done something greater than circumcision,' but, having merely mentioned what had actually taken place, He made it incumbent on them to decide whether restoring to health was more essential than circumcision, or not.

'Judge not by appearances.' What does 'by appearances' mean? 'Just because Moses has greater prestige among you than I, do not form your opinion in the light of your idea of the dignity of the persons, but rather in consideration of the nature of these matters, for this is what "give just judgment" means. Why, indeed, is it that no one has found fault with Moses? Why is it that no one has refused to obey him when he prescribes breaking the Sabbath by a precept that has been added on to the Law from a source outside of it? Yet he

---

16 Θαυμάζετε.

allows a precept to take precedence over the Law itself, a precept not introduced by the Law, but by a source outside of it—a thing which is most remarkable of all; while you, who are not law-givers, immoderately exact and defend the letter of the Law. However, Moses is more trustworthy than you, even though He bids the Law be broken by a precept which is not part of the Law.'

By saying 'a whole man' Christ was pointing out also that circumcision is but a partial restoring to health. Moreover, what is the restoration to health effected by circumcision? 'If any person shall not be circumcised, he shall be cut off from his people,' Scripture says.[17] 'I, on the contrary, have restored, not a man disfigured in part, but one that had been wholly diseased. Therefore, judge not by appearances.'

Let us think not that these words were addressed only to those then alive, but also to us, so that we may not corrupt justice in any matter but do everything in such a way as to secure it. Whether a man be poor or rich, let us not pay attention to appearances, but search out the facts. 'You shall not favor a poor man in his lawsuit,' Scripture says.[18] What, therefore, is the meaning of these words? 'Do not be overcome by pity or unduly influenced if the wrong-doer happens to be a poor man,' it means. And if we must not show favor to the poor man, much more must we not do so to the rich. Moreover, I address these words, not only to judges but also to all men, so that justice may nowhere be corrupted, but everywhere kept inviolate.

'The Lord loves justice,' Scripture says. 'He that loveth iniquity hates his own soul.'[19] Accordingly, let us not hate our own souls; let us not love iniquity. For the gain from so doing is little or nothing now, but there will be great harm resulting

17 Cf. Gen. 17.14.
18 Exod. 23.3.
19 Ps. 10.6,7.

from it in future. Rather, we shall enjoy no benefit at all from it here. For, when we live in luxury but with an evil conscience, is not this a punishment and chastisement?

Let us, then, love justice and let us at no time transgress this Law. Indeed, what fruit shall we be able to enjoy from the present life, if we depart from it without having acquired virtue? And what will plead for us there? Friendship or kinship or the favor of such a one? Yet why do I mention the favor of this or that man? Even if we have Noe or Job or Daniel as our father, that fact will not help us at all if we are betrayed by our own deeds. One thing, however, we do need: virtue in our soul. This will be able to save us, and free us from the everlasting fire. This will send us to the kingdom of heaven.

May all of us obtain this boon by the grace and mercy of our Lord Jesus Christ. Through Him and with Him glory be to the Father, together with the Holy Spirit, now and always, and forever and ever. Amen.

Homily 50 (John 7.25-36)

'Many therefore of the people of Jerusalem were saying: "Is not this the man they seek to kill? And behold, he speaks openly and they say nothing to him. Can it be that the rulers have really come to know that this is really the Christ? Yet we know where this man is from." '[1]

In the divine Scriptures there is not a word which has no purpose, for they have been completely inspired by the Holy Spirit. Therefore, let us examine every word with care. I say this, for it is sometimes possible to discover the entire meaning of the passage from a single expression, as we may do, to be sure, in the text now lying before us.

---

1 John 7.25-27.

'Many therefore of the people of Jerusalem were saying, "Is not this the man they seek to kill? And behold, he speaks openly and they say nothing to him." ' Now, why in the world did the Evangelist specify the people of Jerusalem? He was pointing out that, since they in particular had enjoyed the benefit of great miracles, they were most pitiable of all, because, though they had beheld a most convincing proof of His divinity, they were still entrusting this question entirely to the judgment of their rulers[2] who were utterly corrupt. Indeed, was it not a great miracle that those madmen and murderers, who were surrounding Him, and seeking to kill Him, and actually held Him in their power, suddenly grew calm?

What man, in truth, could have accomplished this? Who could have snuffed out their raging fury so completely? Nevertheless, even after such great miracles, see their madness and their folly. 'Is not this the man they seek to kill?' See how they incriminated themselves. 'The man they seek to kill,' they asserted, 'and they say nothing to him.' Further, not merely did they say nothing to Him, but that, even though He spoke openly. For, a man who was speaking openly and with entire freedom would be a greater source of irritation to them; yet they did nothing.

'Can it be that they have come to know that this is the Christ?' But what do you think? What opinion of Him have you?

'The opposite one,' they declared.

That is why they were saying: 'Yet we know where this man is from.' Oh, what wickedness! Oh, what perversity! They did not even follow the opinion of the rulers, but produced another, a completely corrupt one, worthy of their own stupidity.

---

2 That is, to the chief priests, who as members of the Sanhedrin may be called rulers, since they were the leaders of Judaism.

'We know where he is from; but when the Christ comes, no one will know where he is from.' Yet your rulers, when asked, said that He was born in Bethlehem.[3] Again, still others said: 'We know that God spoke to Moses; but as for this man, we do not know where he is from.'[4] Listen to the words of drunkards! And once more: 'Can the Christ come from Galilee? Is it not from the village of Bethlehem [that He will come]?'[5] Do you see that their reasoning is that of madmen? 'We know' and 'We do not know.' 'The Christ will come from Bethlehem' and 'When the Christ comes, no one will know where he is from.' What is clearer than this inconsistency? For they were intent on one thing only: namely, not believing in Him.

What, then, did Christ reply? 'You both know me, and know where I am from. Yet I have not come of myself, but he is true who has sent me, whom you do not know.' And again: 'If you knew me, you would then know my Father also.'[6] But how could He say that they knew Him and where He was from; and again, that they neither knew Him nor did they know His Father? He was not contradicting Himself—perish the thought!—but on the contrary was even being very consistent with Himself. He meant another kind of knowledge by the assertion: 'You do not know,' as when He said: 'The sons of Heli were children of pestilence, not knowing the Lord,'[7] and again: 'Israel hath not known me.'[8] Paul said in like manner: 'They profess to know God, but by their works they disown him.'[9] Surely, then, it is possible that one who 'knows' may also not 'know.' Therefore, this is what He meant: 'If you know Me, you know that I am the

---

3 Cf. Matt. 2.4-6.
4 John 9.29.
5 Cf. John 7.42.
6 John 8.19.
7 1 Kings 2.12.
8 Isa. 1.3.
9 Tit. 1.16.

Son of God.' For the words 'where I am from' do not refer in this context to a place.

This is clear, also, from what follows: 'Yet I have not come of myself, but he is true who has sent me, whom you do not know.' Here He meant the ignorance shown by their deeds, as Paul said: 'They profess to know God, but by their works they disown him.' Indeed, the sin was not one of ignorance, but of an evil and wicked will. Yet, though they knew this, they wished to appear to be in ignorance.

However, what kind of logic is used here? How is it that He used their own words to refute them? For, when they said: 'We know where this man is from,' He added: 'Yes, you know me.' Why, moreover, did some say: 'We do not know,' while these kept saying: 'We know'? Yet by declaring: 'We know where he is from,' they were implying nothing else than: 'He is of the earth,' and 'He is the son of the carpenter,' while He Himself conducted them up to heaven, by saying: 'You know where I am from,' that is, 'not from the place whence you insinuate but from the place where He who sent Me is.' And the words, 'I have not come of myself,' contain the implication that they knew that He had been sent by His Father, even though they did not admit it.

In two ways, therefore, He refuted them. In the first place, He voiced aloud and brought into the open the things which they were saying in private. And secondly, He revealed their thoughts, as if He said: 'I am not an outcast or one of those who come without a mission. But He is true who has sent Me, whom you do not know.'

'What is the meaning of: "He is true who sent Me"?'

'If He is true, He has sent Me with a view to the truth; if He is true, He that has been sent is therefore true.'

Further, He brought about their discomfiture in another way, also, confounding them out of their own mouths. For, inasmuch as they were asserting: 'When the Christ comes, no

one will know where he is from,' He proved from these words
that He Himself is the Christ. And I say this for it was with
reference to difference of location in place that they were
saying: 'No one will know,' and from this He proved that
He Himself is the Christ because He came from the Father.

Moreover, in every instance He bore witness that the
knowledge of the Father belonged to Him alone, as when He
said: 'Not that anyone has seen the Father except him who is
from the Father.'[10] These words greatly vexed them, for, to
say: 'You do not know him,'[11] and to charge that though they
actually did know Christ[12] they pretended to be in ignorance,
was sufficient to annoy and irritate them. 'They wanted
therefore to seize him, but no one laid hands on him because
his hour had not yet come.'

Do you perceive that they were held in check and their
anger was bridled in an invisible manner? However, why did
the Evangelist not say: 'He held them in check by an invisible
power,' but 'because his hour had not yet come'? He wished
to speak of Christ in a somewhat human and lowly way so
that He might be thought to be also Man [as well as God].
For, since He spoke of sublime things at all times, because
of this the Evangelist inserted these others occasionally.

When Christ said: 'I am from the Father,' He was
speaking, not as a prophet who acquires this knowledge, but
as One who sees Him and is in His presence. 'For I know
Him because I am from Him,' He declared. Do you perceive
how He kept confirming the words: 'I have not come of myself' and 'He is true who has sent me,' in order to refute the
contrary idea, so that He might not be thought in opposition
to God?

Moreover, notice how much good resulted from the

10 Cf. John 6.46,47.
11 The Father.
12 That is, that He is the Son.

humility of what he said. For the Evangelist asserted: 'After this many were saying: "When the Christ comes will he work more signs than this man works?"' What signs? There were as yet but three miracles: that of the wine, that of the paralytic, and that of the ruler's son, and the Evangelist has related no more. From this it is clear, as I have often said, that they omitted to mention most of the miracles, and have described to us only those because of which the rulers were plotting against Him.

'They wanted therefore to lay hands on Him and arrest Him.' Who? Not the multitude—since it was not desirous of power nor could it be overpowered by envy—but the priests. Some of the crowd, to be sure, were saying: 'When the Christ comes, will he work more signs?' Yet, their faith itself was not sound, but the type of faith that the vulgar crowd possesses. For the words, 'When he comes,' were not those of men who believed very firmly that this was the Christ. Therefore, either we may understand the words thus, or we may conclude that the statement was made by the crowds as they mingled, for, as the rulers were striving in every way to prove that He was not the Christ, they said: 'Let us suppose that He is not the Christ; will the Christ be superior to Him?' As I have already declared, the grosser sort of men are convinced not by teaching, nor by preaching, but by miracles.

'The Pharisees heard the crowd whispering and sent attendants to seize him.' Do you perceive that the breaking of the Sabbath was a mere pretext? What bothered them most of all was this. For in this instance, though they had no charge to make—either because of His words or because of His deeds—they wished to seize Him on account of the crowd. Now, they themselves did not dare to do so, since they anticipated danger, so they sent attendants to run the risk. Oh, what despotism, what madness and more than madness! Though they themselves had often held Him in their power,

yet had not prevailed against Him, they turned the task over
to servants, merely to vent their anger. Yet He had spoken
at length, also, near the pool, and they had done no such
thing, but merely asked questions and did not attack Him.
Here, however, they could no longer endure it, because the
people were on the point of flocking to Him.

What, therefore did Christ say? 'Yet a little while I am
with you.' Though He could have confounded and terrified
His hearers, He uttered words full of humility, as if He were
saying: 'Why are you striving to persecute Me and put Me
to death? Wait a little while and I will not refrain from
going to My death, even though some will try to hold Me
back.' Then, in order that no one might suppose that He
meant ordinary death by the words, 'Yet a little while I am
with you' (for some actually did think this)—in order, I
repeat, that no one might suppose this and that He would
accomplish nothing after death—He added: 'And where I
am you cannot come.'

But if He were going to be away from them in death
merely, they could go there, for we all shall depart thither.
Accordingly, His words won over His more unsophisticated
listeners, while they frightened the more daring, and caused
those who were eager for more details to hasten to listen to
Him because only a little time remained, and it would not be
possible always to enjoy his teaching.

Yet He did not simply say 'I am here,' but 'I am with you,'
that is, 'Even if you persecute Me, even if you drive Me off,
for a little while I shall not cease taking an interest in your
affairs, both by speaking of the things conducive to salvation
and by admonishing you. And I go to Him who sent Me.'
This was enough to frighten them and to plunge them into
anguish of mind. And I say this for He made it clear that
they would find themselves in need of Him, because He said:
'You will seek me'; not merely: 'You will not forget Me,'

but even: 'You will seek me and will not find me.'

Yet, where did the Jews seek Him? Luke said that women beat their breast on His account.[13] And it is likely that many others, both immediately after the crucifixion and after the city had been taken, remembered Christ and His wonderful works, and desired that He might be present among them again.

He added these words, of course, with the purpose of attracting them to Him. And I say this for the fact that there was but a short time remaining, and that after His departure He would be sought, and that they would not be able to find Him—all these facts were sufficient to persuade them to become His followers at once. For, if His presence were not going to be desired, they would think He was saying nothing noteworthy. Conversely, if it was going to be desired and it would be possible to find Him, not even thus would He have caused them to become concerned.

Once more, if He were going to be with them for a long time, in that case also they would have been unmoved. As it was, on the contrary, He alarmed and perturbed them from every angle. Besides, the words, 'I go to him who sent me,' are the assertion of One who is proving that He will receive no harm from the plots against Him and that His suffering will be by His own will. He was uttering two prophecies, then: that after a little while He would go away, and that they could not come to Him—making use of a power that certainly did not proceed merely from His human intelligence, in that He was foretelling His own death. Indeed, see even David saying: 'Let me know, O Lord, my end and what is the number of my days, that I may know how frail I am.'[14] Actually, however, there is no man who has this knowledge. And by this one power of His the other was made credible.

13 Cf. Luke 23.49.
14 Ps. 38.5.

Further, I think that He was subtly implying this fact to the attendants and that He was directing to them the argument by which especially He would win them over, showing that He Himself knew the reason for their coming, as if He said: 'Wait a little while and I will go away!'

'The Jews therefore said among themselves: "Where is he going?"' Yet it was not incumbent on those who desired to be rid of Him, those who were doing everything so as not to look upon Him, to ask this question. They should have said: 'We are glad, and when will this ever happen?' However, they were touched by His words and asked one another, in stupid suspicion, where He was going to go.

'Will he go to those dispersed among the Gentiles?' What is the meaning of 'those dispersed among the Gentiles'? The Jews gave this name to the other nations because of their being scattered far and wide and being mingled freely with one another. But they themselves had this ignominy in store for them in future, for they, also, were to be dispersed. Of old, indeed, the entire race had been welded together into a unified whole and it was not possible to find a Jew in any place other than in Palestine only. Therefore, because of this they called the Gentiles 'the dispersed,' taunting them and lording it over them.

What, then, is the meaning of 'Where I go you cannot come'? At that time, to be sure, all the Jews were intermingled with other races and were everywhere in the world. Therefore, if He meant the Gentiles, He would not have said: 'where you cannot come.'

Further, when they said: 'Will he go to those dispersed among the Gentiles?' they did not say 'and persecute them,' but 'and teach.' And so they had already desisted from their anger and believed His words. If they did not believe, they would not have asked one another what His words meant.

However, granted that He addressed these words to them,

we ought to fear lest He might have occasion to address them
to us, because we cannot go where He is on account of our
sinful lives. With reference to the disciples He said: 'I will
that where I am, they also may be with me.'[15] But with
regard to us, I fear lest He may say the opposite: 'Where I
am, you cannot come.' When we do the opposite to His commands, how can we go there? And I say this for even in the
present life, if some member of the army performs deeds unworthy of the king, he will not be able to see the king, but
after being stripped of his office he will pay the extreme
penalty.

Therefore, when we rob, when we are greedy, when we
deal unjustly, when we give blows, when we do not practice
almsgiving, we shall not be able to go there, but we shall
suffer the punishment that befell the foolish virgins. They
indeed were not able to go where He was, but withdrew, since
their lamps had gone out, that is, since grace had left them.[16]
If we will it, we shall make even brighter that light which we
received as soon as we received the grace of the Spirit, but, if
we are not willing to do so, we shall quickly lose it. When it
has gone out, there will be nothing else but darkness in our
soul.

Now, just as when the lamp is burning there is much light,
so when it has been extinguished there will be nothing but
darkness. Therefore, Scripture says: 'Do not extinguish the
Spirit.'[17] It will be extinguished when it does not have oil;
when some gust of wind, stronger than usual, blows on it;
when it is pinched and snuffed (for in this way is fire
extinguished). Moreover, it is pinched by the cares of this
life and extinguished by evil desire. And besides the things

---

15 John 17.24.
16 Matt. 25.1-13.
17 1 Thess. 5.19.

we have mentioned, nothing so effectually quenches it as un-
kindness, and cruelty, and rapacity.

Indeed, when in addition to not having oil we also throw
cold water on it—for this is avarice, chilling by its hard-
heartedness the souls of its victims—whence will it be able to
be kindled again? Well, then, we shall depart, bearing with
us dust and ashes, and with plenty of smoke to convict us of
having had lamps and of having extinguished them. Where
there is smoke a fire must have been extinguished.

However, may it not be our lot to hear those words: 'I
do not know you.'[18] But when may we hear them more
clearly than when on seeing a poor man we act as if we did
not see him? When we do not recognize the hungry Christ,
He also will not recognize us when we are without oil, and
rightly so. Indeed, if a man ignores a person in distress and
does not give him what he has, how will he expect to receive
in his turn what is not his?

Therefore, I beseech you, let us conduct all our affairs and
expend every effort so that the oil may not fail us, but we may
fill our lamps and go into the marriage with the Bridegroom.

May we all attain to this, by the grace and mercy of our
Lord Jesus Christ. Through Him and with Him glory be to
the Father, together with the Holy Spirit, now and always,
and forever and ever. Amen.

Homily 51 (John 7.37-44)

'Now on the last, the great day of the feast, Jesus stood and
cried out, saying: "If anyone thirst, let him come to me and
drink. He who believes in me, as the Scripture says, 'From
within him there shall flow rivers of living water.'"'[1]

---

18 Matt. 1.12.

---

1 John 7.37,38.

Those who come to the divine preaching and pay attention to it with faith must show the desire of the thirsty for it and stir up a similar longing in themselves. In this way, to be sure, they will be able very carefully to preserve what is said. And this is so for, when the thirsty receive a cup, they drain it very eagerly, and then their thirst is slaked. In the same way, also, then, if those who hear the divine words accept them thirstily, they will never cease until they exhaust them. Indeed, because we must ever be thirsty and hungry in this sense, Christ said: 'Blessed are they who hunger and thirst for justice.'[2]

Here, likewise, He says: 'If anyone thirst, let him come to me and drink.' Now, this means something like this: 'I draw no one to Me by compulsion or force, but I call the man who has a great desire and is on fire with longing.'

But why did the Evangelist note that it was 'on the last, the great day of the feast'? I ask this for both the first and the last were great days, and they spent the days between them largely in feasting. Why, then, did he say 'on the last'? Because on that day they were all assembled.

On the first day, of course, Christ was not present, and He mentioned the reason to His brethren. However, not even on the second or third day did He say any such words as those mentioned above, so that His words might not lose their effect, since His hearers were about to go to their feasting. But on the last day, when they were departing for home, He gave them supplies for their journey to salvation. Now, 'He cried out' partly to show His fearlessness, and partly on account of the size of the crowd. Moreover, to show that He was speaking of spiritual nourishment, He added: 'He who believes in me, as the Scripture says, "From within him there shall flow rivers of living water." '

2 Matt. 5.6.

Here the word κοιλίας means 'heart'[3] as Scripture says
elsewhere: 'And your law is within my heart.'[4]

'But where does Scripture say: "From within him there
shall flow rivers of living water"?'

Nowhere.[5]

'What, then, is the meaning of the words: "He who
believes in me, as the Scripture says"?'

Here we must place the punctuation so that the words,
'From within him there shall flow rivers of living water,' may
be part of Christ's words.[6] For, since many were saying:
'This is the Christ' and 'When the Christ comes, will he work
more signs than this man works?' He was showing them that
they must revise their ideas and believe in Him, not so much
from His miracles as from the Scriptures. Many, to be sure,
even when they saw Him working wonders, did not accept
Him as Christ. And they were even going to say: 'Do not
the Scriptures say that it is of the offspring of David that the
Christ is to come?'[7]

Moreover, He repeatedly returned to this subject, since He
wished to show that He was not avoiding the proof of His
identity based on the Scriptures; hence, He sent them to them
again and again. Now, I say this for before this He had said:
'Search the Scriptures'; and again: 'It is written in the

---

3 Literally 'belly'; Confraternity translation: 'within him.' The κοιλία
  is regarded in the Old Testament as the seat of man's emotional
  nature. Following the Semitic custom of expressing emphasis by
  mentioning some part of the body, the word is an emphatic way of
  saying: 'From him shall flow.' Cf. *ICC* 1.283.
4 Ps. 39.9.
5 This specific quotation cannot be identified, despite the fact that
  ἡ γραφή, as used here, always indicates a definite passage in the Old
  Testament. The idea expressed is scriptural and can be found in
  many texts; cf. Merk 336 for examples.
6 That is, 'He who believes in me as the Scripture says, from within
  him there shall flow rivers of living water'; an ingenious exegesis,
  though discarded by modern Scriptural criticism. Cf. *ICC* 1.281-283;
  Confraternity *Commentary* 322.
7 John 7.42.

prophets, "And they all shall be taught of God" '; and: 'Moses accuses you.'[8] And here, by saying: 'As the Scripture says, from within him shall flow rivers of living water,' He is alluding to the wealth and abundance of grace. He spoke in a similar vein elsewhere: 'A fountain of water, springing up unto life everlasting,'[9] that is ['He who drinks of the water that I will give him'] will have much grace.

In another context, then, He said 'life everlasting,' while here He speaks of 'living water.' And by 'living' He means 'ever-active.' For, when the grace of the Spirit enters into the soul and takes up its abode there, it gushes forth more abundantly than any fountain and does not cease, nor become exhausted, nor stand still. Well, then, to show at the same time its unceasing attendance upon the soul and its ineffable activity He called it 'a fountain' and 'rivers': not one river, but rivers without number. And in the other context He indicated its generous flow by the word 'springing up.'

Moreover, one may see clearly what is meant if one considers the wisdom of Stephen, the fluency of Peter, and the forcefulness of Paul, and notices how nothing could oppose them, nothing withstand them: whether popular fury, or violence of tyrants, or plots of demons, or daily deaths—but, like rivers borne along with rushing turbulence, they swept all aside and carried it off. 'He said this of the Spirit,' the Evangelist said, 'whom they who believed in him were to receive; for the Holy Spirit was not yet with them.'[10]

'Then how did the Prophets prophesy and work countless wonders?'

The Apostles, indeed, cast out demons, not by the Spirit,

---

8 John 5.39; 6.45; cf. 5.46.
9 John 4.14.
10 The Confraternity translation, following a strong manuscript tradition for the variant δεδόμενον, translates: 'had not yet been given.' Cf. Merk 336.

but by the authority of Christ, as He Himself asserted: 'If I cast out demons by Beelzebub, by whom do your children cast them out?'[11] He said this to make it clear that before the crucifixion they all cast out demons, not by the Spirit, but by His power. Accordingly, at the time when He was on the point of assigning their mission, He said: 'Receive the Holy Spirit'; and again: 'The Holy Spirit came upon them and then they did signs.'[12]

However, when He was sending them out during His public life the Evangelist did not say: 'He gave them the Holy Spirit,' but: 'He gave them power, and said: 'Cleanse lepers, cast out devils, raise the dead. Freely you have received, freely give.'' [13] In the case of the Prophets, to be sure, it is acknowledged by all that there was a giving of the Holy Spirit, but grace itself was retrenched and removed and altogether departed from the earth from the day on which the words were uttered: 'Your house is left to you desolate.'[14]

Yet the scarcity of grace actually began to be felt even before that day. For no longer was there a Prophet among them, nor did grace attend their sacred rites. Thus, the Holy Spirit had been withdrawn—though He was to be poured forth later in abundance—and the beginning of this renewed giving would be made after the crucifixion. Not only would the gift be more abundant, but it would be accompanied by greater gifts of grace. (And I say this for it was a more wonderful giving, as when He said: 'You do not know of what manner of spirit you are'; and again: 'Now you have not received a spirit of adoption as sons.'[15] For in truth

11 Matt. 12.27.
12 John 20.22; Acts 19.6.
13 Matt. 10.1,8.
14 Matt. 23.39.
15 Luke 9.55; Rom. 8.15.

those of old also possessed the Spirit themselves, but they did not provide others with It, while the Apostles filled innumerable others with It.)

Therefore, since they were going to receive this grace, though it had not yet been given, for this reason the Evangelist said: 'The Holy Spirit was not yet with them.' And therefore, too, in speaking of this grace he asserted: 'The Holy Spirit was not yet with them'—that is, not yet given—'seeing that Jesus had not yet been glorified,' calling His crucifixion 'glory. '

In truth, since we were enemies, and sinners, and lacking the grace of God, and hateful to God, grace was a proof of our restoration to favor. Morever, since a gift is usually bestowed, not on those who inspire dislike, but on friends and those who meet with approval, it was necessary for a sacrifice to be offered first on our behalf, and for man's unfavorable status to be destroyed and for us to become friends of God, and then to receive the gift. Indeed, if this was necessary in the case of the promise to Abraham,[16] much more was it so in the case of grace. To make this clear Paul said: 'For if they who are of the Law are heirs, faith is made empty, for the Law works wrath.'[17]

Now, what he meant is something like this: 'God promised to give the land to Abraham and his descendants.[18] However, his descendants were unworthy of the promise and could not obtain favor by their own works. Therefore faith came in, an easy condition, in order to attract grace, and that the promises might not fail of fulfillment.' And Paul said: 'Therefore the promise was the outcome of faith, that it might be a favor, in order that it might be secure.'[19] That is why it was

---

16 Cf. Gen. 15.6-20.
17 Rom. 4.14,15.
18 Cf. Gen. 17.8.
19 Rom. 4.16.

'a favor,' because they were not able to obtain it by the sweat of their brow.

But why, when Christ said 'as the Scripture says,' did He not add quotations from it? Because their understanding was thoroughly corrupt. For, some were saying: 'This is the Prophet.' Others were saying: 'The Christ is not to come from Galilee, but from the village of Bethlehem.' Still others were saying: 'When the Christ comes, no one will know where he is from.' Their opinion was divided, as it usually is in a disorderly crowd. And certainly they did not pay attention to His words, not even for the sake of acquiring information.

Accordingly, that is why He did not reply to them though they said: 'Can the Christ come from Galilee?' Yet, although Nathanael declared more vehemently and more contentiously: 'Can anything good come out of Nazareth?'[20] He praised him as a true Israelite. These men, however, and those who said to Nicodemus: 'Search [the Scriptures] and see that out of Galilee arises no Prophet,'[21] were speaking, not in the attempt to acquire information, but merely to destroy the reputation of Christ. Nathanael, on the contrary, said this because he was a lover of truth and well versed in ancient lore, while they were intent on one thing only: to deny that He was the Christ. And therefore He revealed nothing to them.

Surely those who contradicted themselves by saying at one time: 'No one will know where he is from,' and at another: '[He will come] from Bethlehem' clearly would have continued to contradict, even when they learned the truth. Granted, indeed, that they were in ignorance regarding the place—that He actually came from Bethlehem—because of His being brought up in Nazareth (though even this was

20 John 1.46.
21 John 7.52.

really not pardonable for He was not born there). Surely they were not ignorant, also, of His family, that He was of the house and family of David? How was it, then, that they said: 'Is it not of the offspring of David that the Christ is to come?' However, they wished to obscure this fact also by the question, since they said everything with evil intent.

Moreover, why did they not address Him and say: 'When we are perplexed about everything else, You bid us to believe in You according to the Scriptures. Tell us, how is it that the Scriptures say that the Christ is to come from Bethlehem, while you come from Galilee?' However, they said none of this, but uttered all their words maliciously. In truth, because they were not seeking to acquire information, nor did they desire to do so, the Evangelist at once added: 'Some wanted to seize him, but no one laid his hand on Him.' Actually, even if there were nothing else, this at least was enough to bring them to compunction. However, they were not moved, even as the Prophet said: 'They were separated and repented not.'[22]

Such as this, in truth, is malice. It is satisfied to stop at nothing; it is intent on one thing only, namely, to destroy the object of its machinations. However, what does Scripture say? 'He that diggeth a pit for his neighbor, shall fall into it.'[23] And this happened even then. For they wished to destroy Him in order to suppress His preaching, but just the opposite took place. His preaching flourished by the grace of Christ, whereas all their schemes have been snuffed out and have perished. Further, they have lost their fatherland, and freedom, and security, and worship, and have been deprived of all honor and glory, and become slaves and captives.

Accordingly, since we know these things, let us never plot against others, because we have learned that by so doing we

22 Ps. 34.16 (Douai).
23 Cf. Prov. 26.27.

are sharpening the sword against ourselves and wounding ourselves more deeply than others. But has someone offended you and you wish to pay him back? Do not pay him back, for you will not be able to repay him in this way. Indeed, if you take revenge, you are not revenged. Now, do not think that what I have said is a riddle; on the contrary, it is a true statement.

'How, and in what way?'

Because, if you do not take revenge, you make God the man's enemy, whereas if you do take revenge, that is no longer so. For, 'Vengeance is mine; I will repay, says the Lord.'[24] Now, if we have slaves and if, when they quarrel with one another, they do not submit their differences to us for judgment and punishment, but take care of them themselves, even if they submit to us a thousand times over, we are not requited but even are offended. 'Run-aways and knaves,' we say, 'you ought to have submitted everything to my judgment. But since you have anticipated and taken revenge, do not bother me in future.' Much more will God speak in this way, since He has exhorted us to yield to His judgment in everything.

Truly, how strange it is that we require of our servants so much virtue and obedience, while we do not yield to the Lord the submission which we wish our slaves to yield to us! And I am saying this because of your disposition to take revenge on one another, since the truly virtuous man ought not to do this, but ought to pardon and overlook offenses, even if there were not that great reward in store, namely, to receive forgiveness of sin in return.

If, indeed, you pass censure on the man who has committed a fault, why, may I ask, do you yourself offend and fall into the same faults? He has insulted you? Do not insult him in return, because in that case you have insulted yourself. He

---

24 Rom. 12.19; Deut. 32.35.

has struck you? Do not strike back, because in no way do you derive profit from that. Has he hurt your feelings? Do not hurt his in return, because there is no gain in that, but you have become in turn like him.

You will be able to make him ashamed in this way: if you suffer meekly, with gentleness; thus you will be able to discomfit him; thus you will be able to make him weary of his anger. No one cures evil by evil, but evil by good. Certain Greek philosophers reached this conclusion. Let us be ashamed, then, if, when there is such virtue among the pagans who lack divine wisdom, we should appear inferior to them. Many of them have been wronged and have borne it; many have been falsely accused and have not taken revenge; they have been plotted against and have shown kindness.

Moreover, it is not a little to be feared that some among them may be found superior to us in their way of life and so may cause our punishment to be more severe. For, when we who have shared in the Spirit, we who are in expectation of the kingdom, we who live virtuously for a heavenly reward, we who do not fear hell, we who are bidden to be angels, we who enjoy the benefit of the Mysteries, when, I repeat, we do not overtake them in practicing the same degree of virtue, what pardon shall we have? Indeed, if we must surpass the Jews (for, 'Unless your justice exceeds that of the Scribes and Pharisees,' Scripture says, 'you shall not enter the kingdom of heaven'),[25] much more so the heathen; if Pharisees, much more so unbelievers. For if, when we do not surpass the Pharisees' way of life, the kingdom will be closed to us, if we show ourselves inferior to the heathen how shall we be able to attain to it? Let us, then, cast out all bitterness and anger and passion.

'To say the same things is not irksome to me, but it is

---

25 Matt. 5.20.

necessary for you.'[26] Now this is true, for physicians also repeatedly make use of the same remedy. Similarly, we shall not cease shouting the same cries, giving the same reminders, teaching the same lessons, making the same exhortations. And we shall do so for the importunity of the affairs of this life is great and makes us forgetful, so we need unceasing instruction.

Therefore, in order that we may not gather in this place fruitlessly or in vain, let us show forth the fruits by our works in order that we may attain to the blessings of the life to come, by the grace and mercy of our Lord Jesus Christ. Through Him and with Him glory be to the Father, together with the Holy Spirit, now and always and forever and ever. Amen.

Homily 52 (John 7.45-8.19)

'The attendants therefore came to the chief priests and Pharisees; and these said to them, "Why have you not brought him?" The attendants answered, "Never has man spoken as this man." '[1]

Nothing is clearer than truth, nothing more simple to grasp, if we ourselves do not act perversely. Similarly, therefore, there is nothing that causes us more trouble than when we act perversely. For, see, the Pharisees and the Scribes who seemed, in truth, to be more learned, who were continually in Christ's company for the sake of plotting against Him, who even witnessed miracles and read Scripture, derived no benefit from all this, but even suffered harm thereby.

The attendants, on the other hand, though they could lay claim to none of this, were captivated by a single sermon, and

26 Cf. Phil. 3.1.

1 John 7.45-47.

despite the fact that they had gone to seize Him, they returned overwhelmed with admiration. Not only may we admire their wisdom, because they did not need miracles but were won over by His teaching alone (for they did not say: 'Never has man worked miracles as this man,' but what? 'Never has man spoken as this man')—well, then I repeat, not only may we admire their wisdom, but also their courage, because they said this to the Pharisees, to those who were hostile to Him and who were doing everything in pursuance of their enmity.

'The attendants came,' the Evangelist declared, 'and the Pharisees said to them, "Why have you not brought him?"' Now, it was a much greater thing to come back than to have stayed away. For in the latter case they would have escaped the fault-finding of the Pharisees, while actually they became heralds proclaiming the wisdom of Christ, and so displayed their courage the more. Moreover, they did not say: 'We were unable to bring Him because of the crowd, since they listen to Him as to a prophet.' On the contrary, what did they say? 'Never has man spoken as this man.' Though they could have uttered that defense of themselves, they yet disclosed their own real opinion.

Indeed, this was the opinion not of His admirers only, but even of these accusers, because they had sent them to seize Him, when they ought rather to have gone themselves to hear Him. Yet they did not hear a lengthy discourse, but, on the contrary, a short one. For, when the mind is open to conviction, there is no need of long speeches. Truth is like that.

What, then, did the Pharisees do? Though they ought to have shown compunction, they did just the opposite and found fault with them, saying: 'Have you also been led astray?' Up to this point they had been coaxing them along by blandishments, and had not spoken harshly lest they might end by becoming estranged. Now, however, they showed their feelings, yet spoke with caution. For, though they ought to have asked: 'What did He say?' and then ought to have shown admiration at His words, they did not do so, because they felt that they, also, might be won over. And so they argued with them from a very foolish premise. 'Why has no one of the rulers believed in him?' they asked. Do you blame this on Christ, then, rather than on those who have failed to believe?

'But this crowd, which does not know the Law, is accursed,' they declared. Actually, this is a greater indictment of you: that the crowd has believed, while you have not. The former are acting the part of those who know the Law; why, then, are they laid under a curse? You, rather, who do not keep the Law, are the ones who are laid under a curse, not those who obey the Law. Moreover, they ought not to have made a false accusation of Him in whom they did not believe, basing their charge on the evidence of unbelievers. For this is not the right way to act. In that case you have also not believed in God, as Paul says: 'For what if some of them have not believed? Will their unbelief make void the fidelity of God? By no means.'

Indeed, the Prophets repeatedly charged them saying: 'Hear, ye rulers of Sodom' and 'Thy princes are faithless.'[2] And again: 'Is it not your part to know judgment?'[3] In fact, everywhere they vehemently upbraided them. What, then? Will someone on that account find fault with God? Perish the thought! The fault, in truth, is with them. Moreover, what better proof could one offer that you do not know the Law, than that of your failure to obey it?

Now, when they said: 'Has anyone of the rulers believed in him?' and '[This crowd,] which does not know the Law,' Nicodemus in consequence attacked them and spoke as follows: 'Does our Law judge a man unless it first give him

2 Isa. 1.10,23.
3 Mich. 3.1.

a hearing?' He was proving, to be sure, that they neither knew the Law, nor carried out the Law. For, if it prescribed that no one put a man to death without first giving him a hearing, and if these men had striven to do this before giving a hearing, they were transgressors of the Law.

Moreover, since they asserted that not even one of the rulers believed in Him, for this reason the Evangelist made note of the fact that Nicodemus 'was one of them,' to prove that there were rulers, also, who did believe in Him. Not yet, to be sure, did they admit it as openly as they ought; nevertheless, they were followers of Christ. And see how cautiously he made his accusation. For he did not say: 'you wish to kill Him, yet are merely condemning the Man as a seducer.' No, he did not address them in this way, but less harshly, to hinder their unspeakable purpose, and their ill-advised and murderous design.

For this reason he directed the discussion to the Law by saying: 'Unless it give a careful hearing and know what he does.' Hence, there is need not merely of a hearing, but even of a careful one. This is the meaning of 'And know what he does': what His aim is, and why, and what His intention is, whether He wishes to overthrow the state and is acting as an enemy. Discomfited, then, because they had said; 'No one of the rulers has believed in him,' in their reply to his words they upbraided him, neither violently nor yet sparingly.

For how did it follow, when he had said: 'Our law does not judge anyone,' for them to reply: 'Art thou also a Galilean?' In fact, though they ought to have proved that they had not sent, without a trial, to summon Him, and that they were not obliged to give their reasons to him, they made their reply more roughly and angrily: 'Search and see that out of Galilee arises no prophet.'

But what was it that Nicodemus actually said? That He was a Prophet? He said that He ought not to be sentenced

without a trial. And they insolently added these words as
though to one knowing nothing about the Scriptures, as if one
were to say: 'Come now, learn,' for that is the meaning of
'Search and see.'

What, therefore, did Christ do? Inasmuch as they kept returning on every occasion to the subject of Galilee and the
Prophet, to remove all suspicion that might arise from these
hostile remarks, and to show that He was not merely one of
the Prophets, but is the Lord of the world, He declared: 'I
am the light of the world'[4]—not merely of Galilee, or of
Palestine, or of Judea.

What, then, was the comment of the Jews? 'Thou bearest
witness to thyself. Thy witness is not true.' Oh, what madness!
He sent them again and again to the Scriptures, and they
said: 'Thou bearest witness to thyself.' But what testimony
did He give?

'I am the light of the world.' What He said was great, truly
great; however, it did not disconcert them much, because He
was not now making Himself equal to His Father, or declaring that He is His Son, or that He is God, but merely
'light.' Nevertheless, they wished to discredit this, also, because
this was a much greater claim than to say: 'He who follows
me does not walk in the darkness,' meaning 'light' and 'darkness' in a spiritual sense, that is, 'He does not remain in error.'

By His words here He was spurring on and encouraging
Nicodemus, because he had spoken up bravely, and also
praising the attendants who had done this. Moreover, to cry
out[5] His message as He did was the action of one who wished
to cause others also to listen. At the same time, His words

---

4 St. John Chrysostom omits altogether the episode of the adulteress
(John 8.1-11), apparently following one of the many Greek manuscripts in which it is omitted. Cf. the Confraternity *Commentary* 323.
5 The expression τὸ κράξαι is St. John Chrysostom's. The Greek New
Testament has ἐλάλησεν; Confraternity translation: 'spoke.'

subtly implied that though they[6] were contriving their schemes both in darkness and in error, they would not vanquish the Light. Besides, He was reminding Nicodemus of those words which He had formerly said to him: 'Everyone who does evil hates the light, and does not come to the light, that his deeds may not be exposed.'[7] And since they were saying that no one of the rulers believed in Him, it was for this reason that He declared: 'He who does evil does not come to the light.' He was showing that the failure to come was caused, not by the weakness of the Light, but by their perverse dispositions.

They answered, and said to Him: 'Thou bearest witness to thyself.'

What did He reply? 'Even if I bear witness to myself, my witness is true, because I know where I came from and where I go. But you do not know where I came from.' These men were bringing up what He had previously said,[8] as if it were especially applicable here. What, then, did Christ now answer? To refute that opinion and to show that He had made those statements as if addressed to them and to their suspicion that He was merely man, He said: 'Even if I bear witness to myself, my witness is true, because I know where I came from.'

What does this mean? 'I am from God, and I am God and I am the Son of God. Furthermore, God himself is a trustworthy witness to Himself. But you do not know Him. You wish to do evil,' He meant, 'and though you know, you pretend not to know, but speak of everything in a human sense because you are unwilling to consider anything more than what appears to the senses. You judge according to the flesh. Just as to live according to the flesh is to live wickedly, so to judge according to the flesh is to judge unjustly. I judge no

---

6 The Pharisees.
7 John 3.20
8 That is, regarding the veracity of a man's own testimony in his own behalf.

one. And even if I do judge my judgment is just.' What He meant is something like this: 'You judge unjustly.'

'But if we judge unjustly,' you will say, 'why do You not accuse us? Why do You not punish us? Why do You not condemn us?'

'Because I did not come for that,' He replies. For, that is the meaning of the words: 'I judge no one. And even if I do judge, my judgment is true. Besides, if I wished to judge, you would be of the number of the condemned. Now I am saying these things, not yet as judge,' He says. 'And on this account I have not spoken [to condemn you]. I am not yet speaking as judge, as if I were not confident that if I judged I should convict you (and I say this for if I judged I should justly condemn you). However, the present is not the time for judgment.'

Moreover, by saying: 'I am not alone, but with me is he who sent me, the Father,' He was referring indirectly to the future judgment. And He was here alluding as well to the fact that it was not He alone who would condemn them, but also the Father. Next, however, He caused them to lose sight of this fact entirely by focusing their attention on His own testimony: 'And in your Law it is written that the witness of two persons is true.'

What, then, would the heretics say to this? They would cry: 'How is He in any way superior to other men, if we are to accept His words on their face value? For, in the case of men this ruling has been laid down because no man is considered a reliable witness in behalf of himself, but in the case of God how could this statement be valid? How is it, then, that He said "two"? Surely it was not because there are two Persons, or because They are men and for that reason there are two witnesses. Indeed, if He said this because there are two witnesses required, why did He not resort to John's testimony? And why did He not say: "I bear witness to myself and John bears witness to me"? Why did He not take refuge in the angel? Why did He not take refuge in the Prophets? And I say this for He could have found other witnesses without number.'

However, He did not wish to show merely that there were two witnesses, but that there were two who were even of the same substance. They said to Him: 'Who[9] is thy father?' He then replied: 'You know neither me nor my Father.' Actually they did know, but, since they were talking as if they did not know, and in order to try Him out, He therefore did not consider them worthy of a reply.

Henceforward, because the crucifixion was drawing near, He would say everything more explicitly and with more freedom, and place more reliance on the evidence of His miracles and of those who followed His teaching. Thus, He declared: 'I know where I came from.' This statement did not disturb them very much, but He would alarm them more by adding: 'and where I go,' since He was not going to remain dead. Yet, why did He not say: 'I know that I am God,' but: 'I know where I came from'?

He continually interspersed statements of lowly tenor among sublime ones and even cloaked over the latter. For, after He had said: 'I bear witness to myself,' and had proved this, He proceeded to something more lowly, as if He said: 'I know by whom I have been sent and to whom I shall return.' In this way, to be sure, they could not contradict Him, since they heard that He had been sent by Him and would return to Him. 'I have not said anything false,' He was asserting, 'inasmuch as I have come from the true God and shall return to Him. You, on the other hand, do not know God; therefore, you judge according to the flesh. For, though you have heard so many proofs and arguments you still say:

---

9 τίς; the Greek New Testament has ποῦ; Confraternity translation: 'where.'

"His witness is not true." Yet you considered Moses a reliable witness both with regard to what he said of others and with regard to what he said of himself. But you do not have the same opinion of the Christ. This is what "judging according to the flesh" means.'

'I judge no one.' Now, He had asserted: 'The Father does not judge any man.[10] How was it, then, that He now said: 'And even if I do judge, my judgment is true, because I am not alone'? Once again He was addressing Himself to their thoughts. That is, He meant: 'My judgment is also that of My Father. The Father in judging would not pass a judgment different from Mine, nor would I voice one different from His.' Moreover, why did He make mention also of the Father? He did so because they would not think that the Son was to be believed, unless He had received the witness of the Father. However, in other respects the saying does not hold good. For, in the case of men, when two persons bear witness in another man's affair, then the testimony is considered true; that is what 'the witness of two persons' means. But, if a man is going to bear witness to himself, there are no longer two persons.

Do you perceive that He spoke as He did for no other reason than to demonstrate His consubstantiality with the Father, and likewise to show that of Himself He did not need any other witness, and also to prove that He was no less powerful than the Father? See, then, His autonomy. 'It is I who bear witness to myself, and he who sent me, the Father, bears witness to me.' Further, if He were of inferior substance, He would not have made this declaration. But now, that you may not think that the Father was brought in for the sake of the number,[11] notice that His power is in no way different from the Father's.

---

10 John 5.22.
11 That is, two.

A man acts as witness when he is on his own merits a reliable witness. But this holds good in the affair of another man, and not when he is in need of testimony himself. In his own affair, on the contrary, when he is in need of witness coming from someone else, he is no longer considered a reliable witness. Here, however, it is just the opposite. And I say this for, though Christ is bearing witness in His own affair and though He asserts that witness is being borne Him by Another, He also declares that He is a reliable witness, to show His complete autonomy.

Why is it, indeed, that after saying: 'I am not alone, but with me is he who sent me, the Father,' and 'The witness of two persons is true,' He did not end with that, but added: 'It is I who bear witness to myself'? It is evident that it was to make clear His autonomy. Moreover, He put Himself in the first place: 'It is I who bear witness to myself.' Here He was pointing out both that He was equal to the Father in honor, and that it was of no profit to them if they maintained that they knew God the Father, while they did not know Him.[12] Further, He was saying that the fact that they did not desire to know Him was responsible for this. He therefore asserted that it is not possible to know the Father apart from Him, that He might thus perhaps draw them to know Him. For since, though they scorned Him, they continually were seeking to know the Father, He said: 'You cannot know the Father apart from Me.' Consequently, they who blaspheme the Son blaspheme not Him alone, but also His Father.

Let us avoid these errors, and let us give glory to the Son. Indeed, if He were not of the same nature as the Father, He would not have spoken as He did. If He were merely a teacher and actually was of a different substance, it would be possible for a man to know the Father without knowing Him, and, again, it would be possible for a man who knew

12 That is, God the Son.

Him not to know the Father at all. For he who knows a man does not thereby know an angel.

'Yes,' you will object, 'but he who knows creation knows God.'

By no means. There are many who know creation—nay, rather, all men do (for they see it), yet they do not know God.

Let us, then, give glory to the Son of God, not alone by this glory, but also by that of our works. For it is nothing without them. See, Scripture says: 'Thou art called Jew, and dost rely on the Law, and dost glory in God. Thou therefore who teachest another, dost thou not teach thyself? Thou who dost glory in the Law, dost thou dishonor God by transgressing the Law.'[13]

See to it that we, also, while we glory in the true Faith, do not dishonor God by failing to give the example of a life in accordance with our faith, and so cause Him to be blasphemed. And I say this for He wishes the Christian to be a teacher of the world, its 'leaven,' and 'light,' and 'salt.'[14]

Now, what is the 'light'? A shining life with no shadow of evil. Light is not useful to itself, nor is salt, nor leaven, but each is of service to others. Thus, not merely our own advantage is required of us, but also that of others. For if the salt is not salty it is not salt. Further, He showed something else besides; namely, that, if we ourselves live good lives, others will follow our example, while as long as we ourselves do not live good lives, we shall not be able to help others to do so.

Let there be no vanity, no softness among us. Worldly pursuits, to be sure, have this kind of nature, and such a nature the cares of this life have. That is why the foolish virgins were so called, because they were preoccupied with

13 Rom. 2.17; 21.23.
14 Matt. 13.33; 5.13-16.

vain trifles, worldly pursuits—gathering possessions here, but not where they ought to store them.

It is to be feared, therefore, that we may suffer the same fate; it is to be feared that we also may depart, clad in soiled garments, to that place where all have bright and shining ones. In truth, there is nothing more defiling than sin, nothing more impure. For this reason the Prophet cried out, to reveal its nature: 'Noisome and festering are my sores.'[15] And if you wish to learn the foulness of sin, think of it after it has been committed, when you are rid of the evil desire, when its fires no longer cause disturbance, and then you will perceive what sin is.

Think of anger when you are in a state of calm; think of avarice when you become free from that passion. There is nothing more shameful, nothing more defiling than rapine and greed. We repeat this frequently, not out of a desire to annoy you, but to gain a great and wonderful advantage for you. Moreover, he who does not begin to live righteously after hearing me the first time will, perhaps, do so after hearing me the second time; and he who disregards the second, will perhaps reform his life after the third time.

Thus, may we all get rid of all wickedness and possess the good odor of Christ. Glory be to Him, together with the Father and the Holy Spirit, now and always, and forever and ever. Amen.

---

15 Ps. 37.6.

Homily 53 (*John 8.20-30*)

'Jesus spoke these words in the treasury, while teaching in the temple. And no one seized him, because his hour had not yet come.'[1]

Oh, the insanity of the Jews! Before the Pasch they were seeking Him; then they found Him in their midst and repeatedly tried to arrest Him, both by their own efforts and through those of others, and were unable to do so. Yet they were not dumbfounded at His power, but persisted in their evil designs and did not cease from them.

Now, to indicate that they kept trying unceasingly, the Evangelist said: 'He spoke these words in the treasury, while teaching in the temple. And no one seized him.' He was speaking in the temple, and in the office of teacher, a thing that was enough to rouse them still more. Further, He was saying things that angered them, things because of which they censured Him, on the ground that He was making Himself equal to the Father. I say this for that is the meaning of the words: 'The witness of two persons is true.' Nevertheless, 'He spoke these words in the temple,' the Evangelist recorded, and in the guise of teacher, 'and no one seized him, because his hour had not yet come;' that is, because it was not yet the fitting time at which He willed to be crucified.

Hence, even when that time came, it was not a work accomplished by their power that took place, but one of His own planning. In truth, they themselves wished to accomplish it before that, but were not strong enough. They would not even then have been strong enough, therefore, if He Himself had not allowed it.

'Again, therefore, Jesus said to them, "I go, and you will seek me." ' Why in the world did He keep saying this repeatedly? To upset and terrify their minds. Notice, indeed,

---

1 John 8.20.

how much fear this caused. For, though they wished to kill Him in order to be rid of Him, they sought to find out where He was going, so great were the implications of what He said.

Now, He wished to teach them something else, namely, that His departure would not be the result of their use of force, but He was foretelling it ahead of time, and was prophesying the Resurrection by these words.

'Therefore they kept saying, "Will he kill himself?" '

What, then, did Christ reply? To remove that suspicion of theirs and to show that such an action is a sin, He said: 'You are from below.' And what He meant is something like this: 'It is no wonder that you have such thoughts—earth-bound as you are—and that you are not spiritual-minded, but I will do no such thing, for I am from above. You are of this world.' Here again He was referring to their worldly and earthly thoughts. From this it is clear that the words, 'I am not of this world,' do not mean that He did not become incarnate, but merely that He was completely divorced from their wickedness. This is the correct meaning, for He also said that His disciples were not of this world; nevertheless, they did have human bodies.

Accordingly, just as Paul, by saying 'You are not carnal,'[2] did not mean that they were without bodies, so by saying that His disciples were not of this world, Christ was testifying nothing else of them than their virtuous lives.

'Therefore I said to you that if you do not believe that I am he, you will die in your sins.' Now, if He came for the purpose of taking away the sins of the world, and it is not possible for them to be removed except by baptism, anyone who does not believe must still possess 'the old man.' Moreover, he who does not will the latter's death and burial by faith will perish with him, and will go to the next world to pay the penalty for his sins of the past. That is why Christ

2 Rom. 8.9.

said: 'He who does not believe is already judged'[3]—not only because of his unbelief, but also because he departs, still keeping possession of his sins of the past.

'They therefore said to him, "Who art thou?"' Oh, what stupidity! After so long a time, and miracles, and teaching, they asked: 'Who art thou?'

What did Christ reply? 'Why do I speak to you at all?'[4] What He meant is something like this: 'You do not deserve to hear My words at all, much less to learn who I am, for you speak with a skeptical attitude toward everything and pay attention to nothing I say. Furthermore, I could now refute all these statements of yours'—for that is the meaning of 'I have many things to speak and to judge'[5]—'nay, I have power not merely to refute, but even to punish, but he who sent me'—that is, the Father—'does not will this. For I have not come to judge the world, but to save the world. For God did not send his Son in order to judge the world, but in order to save the world.'

'If, then, He sent me to this end, and He is true, it is with reason that I do not judge anyone now. But I am speaking these things which are conducive to salvation, not to condemnation.' Now, He said this in order that they might not think that, though He heard such things as they were saying, through a want of strength He did not assail them, or else that He was unconscious of their attitude and scoffing.

'They did not understand that he was speaking to them about the Father.' Oh, what insanity! He spoke to them unceasingly about Him, yet they did not understand.

Next, since He did not succeed in attracting them by working many miracles, and by His teaching, He finally

3 John 3.18.
4 The Greek is ambiguous here. This free rendering, found in the Confraternity translation, best fits in with the explantion of St. John Chrysostom as given below.
5 John 12.47; cf. 3.17.

spoke to them of the cross, saying: 'When you have lifted up the Son of Man, then you will know that I am he, and that of myself I say nothing; and that he who sent me is with me and the Father has not left me alone.' He proved that it was right for Him to have said: 'Why do I speak to you at all?' so little attention did they pay to His words.

'When you have lifted up the Son of Man, will you not then, most of all, expect to be rid of Me and to do away with Me? However, I tell you that then, most of all, you will know that I am he, both because of the signs that will take place, and because of My resurrection and the destruction [of Jerusalem].' All these things were, in truth, adequate proof of His power.

Still, He did not say: 'Then you will know who I am.' But He affirmed: 'When you see that I am not affected permanently by death, then you will know that I am He, that is, the Christ, the Son of God, who both creates and directs all things, and is not in opposition to God.' That, of course, is why He added: 'And of myself I say nothing.' You will indeed know both things: both My power and My oneness with the Father. For the words: 'Of myself I say nothing' make clear Their identity of substance and that He uttered nothing at all that was foreign to the Father's sentiments.

'When in truth you have lost your religion, when it no longer is of profit for you to worship Him as before, then you will know that He is doing this to avenge Me and out of indignation towards those who did not listen to Me.' It was as if He said: 'If I were an enemy and a stranger to God, He would not have been roused to such anger against you.'

Isaias also said this: 'He shall give the ungodly for his burial';[6] and David: 'Then in his anger he will speak to them.'[7] He Himself said: 'Behold your house is left to you

---

6 Isa. 53.9.
7 Ps. 2.5.

desolate.'[8] Moreover, the parables make the same thing clear, as when He said: 'What will the owner of that vineyard do to those vine-dressers? He will utterly destroy those evil men.'[9] Do you perceive that at all times He spoke in this tenor because they did not yet believe?

But, if He will destroy them, as He actually did destroy them (for He said: 'Bring those men here and slay them, since they do not wish me to be king'),[10] why did He say that it was not His work, but referred to what happened as the work of the Father? He was adapting His words to their weakness and at the same time giving honor to His Father. That is why He did not say 'I am leaving your house,' but 'It is left,' for He said it impersonally. However, because He had said: 'How often would I have gathered thy children together, but thou wouldst not,' and then added: '[Your house] is left [desolate],' He showed that He Himself was the author of the desolation.

To resume: 'Since, though you have received benefits and have been cared for, you have been unwilling to know Me,' He said, 'you will know who I am in consequence of your being punished. And the Father is with me.' In order that they might not think that the words 'He who sent me' were those of an inferior, He said 'is with me,' since the first clause refers to His Incarnation; the second, to His Godhead. Further, 'He has not left me alone, because I do always the things that are pleasing to him.'

Once again He brought the discourse down to a lowlier level, since He was continually presenting arguments against that statement which they kept making, namely, that He did not come from the Father and did not keep the Sabbath. In answer, He said: 'I do always the things that are pleasing

8 Matt. 23.38.
9 Matt. 21.40,41.
10 Cf. Luke 19.27.

to him' to show that even the breaking of the Sabbath was pleasing to Him. Likewise, He spoke in this way just before the crucifixion: 'Dost thou suppose that I cannot entreat my Father?'[11] Yet when He merely said: 'Whom do you seek?' He caused them to fall back prostrate. Why, then, did He not say: 'Do you suppose that I cannot destroy you?' since He had proved this by what He did? He was condescending to their weakness, for He made every effort to prove that He did nothing in opposition to the Father.

Similarly, then, He was speaking in a somewhat human fashion here also. And just as He declared: 'He has not left me alone,' so also He said: 'Because I do always the things that are pleasing to him. '

'When he was speaking these things, many believed in him.' When He brought the discourse down to a lowlier level, then many believed. Do you still inquire, therefore, why it was that He spoke in a lowly tenor? Yet the Evangelist was clearly referring indirectly to this when he asserted: 'When he was speaking these things, many believed in him,' as much as crying out by this means: 'Do not be struck with astonishment, dear listener, if you hear something said in a lowly vein. For, some men had not yet been persuaded that He had come from the Father, even after such teaching as His. Therefore, it was with good reason that they heard something less sublime, in order that they might be convinced.' Besides, this was a justification of those who would in future speak in a lowly terms of Him.[12]

They did believe, then, yet not as they ought, but infrequently and sporadically, when they were pleased and were soothed by the humility of His words. The Evangelist showed that they did not have perfect faith by the words that immediately followed, since by these they insulted Him

---

11 Matt. 26.53.
12 For example, the Evangelists.

once more. And he made it clear that it was those very same men who did this when he said: 'Jesus therefore said to the Jews who had come to believe in him, "If you abide in my word" '—proving that they had not yet accepted His teaching but merely were giving attention to what He said. Therefore, He spoke even more forcefully.

Before, He had declared: 'You will seek me,[13] but this time when He said it He added something greater: 'in your sins you will die.' Moreover, He showed how this would take place: 'Because, on coming there, you cannot call Me to your aid any longer.

'These things I speak in the world.' By these words He indicated that He would at length go over to the Gentiles. And since 'they did not yet understand that He was speaking to them about the Father' before this, He once more spoke of Him. Moreover, the Evangelist was thus suggesting an explanation of the lowly tenor of His words.

Now, if we are willing to examine the Scriptures in this way, carefully and systematically, we shall be able to obtain our salvation. If we unceasingly are preoccupied with them, we shall learn both correctness of doctrine and an upright way of life. Even if a man be very hard, and stubborn, and vain, even if he gain no profit at other times, he will derive benefit at least during this period. He will receive some help —even though it may not be sufficient to be noticed—yet he will, nonetheless, receive it.

Now, if a person visits a perfume factory or remains near those engaged in this business, he is scented by the fragrant smell, even though he does not wish to be. Much more is this the case with a man as he departs from the church. For, just as sloth is the fruit of laziness, so also zeal develops from activity. Even if you are full of evil traits without number,

---

13 That is, a few days before this; cf. John 7.36.

even if you are impure, do not avoid spending time in this place.

'But, then,' you will object, 'what if, though I listen, I do not act on it?'

There is no small profit in bewailing your wretchedness. This is not a useless fear. This alarm is not ill-advised. If only you lament because 'though I listen, I do not act on it,' you will surely arrive sometime at practicing what you hear. For it is not possible for a man to talk with God and to listen to God speaking, without deriving profit.

First, as you know, we compose ourselves and wash our hands, when we wish to hold the book. Do you perceive how much piety we thus show even before the reading? Accordingly, if we continue with like exactitude, we shall derive great profit. For, unless the action makes our soul pious, actually we should not have washed our hands. Furthermore, if a woman is unveiled, she at once dons her veil as an indication outwardly of the piety she has within. And if a man has his head covered, he bares his head. Do you perceive how the external appearance becomes a token of the piety within? And then, upon sitting down to listen, one frequently utters deep sighs and decries his present life.

Let us, then, pay heed to the Scriptures, beloved, and if we study no other part, let us at least earnestly ponder the Gospels and let us keep them in our hands.

On opening the book you will at once see the name of Christ lying within, and will hear the Evangelist saying: 'Now the origin of Jesus Christ was in this wise. When Mary his Mother had been betrothed to Joseph, she was found to be with child by the Holy Spirit.'[14]

He who hears these words will straightway be filled with love for virginity, he will marvel at the birth, he will be set free from things of earth. And it is no trifle when you see the

---

14 Matt. 1.18.

Virgin deemed worthy of the Spirit and the angel conversing with her. These things, of course, are apparent from a casual reading. But, if you continue studying the text to its fullest meaning, you will at once scorn all the things of this life; you will despise everything here. If you are wealthy, you will not rejoice in your wealth, because you have heard that she who was the wife of a carpenter and born of a humble family became Mother of your Lord. Moreover, if you are poor, you will not be ashamed of your poverty, because you have learned that the Creator of the world was not ashamed of a very poor dwelling.

In the light of these considerations, you will not rob, you will not be covetous, you will not steal the possessions of others; rather, you will be desirous of poverty and despise wealth. And if this happens, you will banish all evil.

Once more, when you see Him lying in a manger you will not strive to surround your child with golden adornment, or to cause a couch to be decorated with silver for your wife. And if you are not striving for these things you will not be guilty of greed and rapine because of them.

It is possible to gain many other advantages, also, which I cannot mention individually at present, but those who have made trial of them will know them. Therefore, I beseech you to acquire these books and, along with the books, to preserve the thoughts derived from them and engrave them in your minds. For, when the Jews did not pay attention to them they were bidden to hang the books from their hands.[15]

---

15 The 'Tephillim,' a term derived from the Hebrew word for 'prayer,' and applied to the phylacteries worn on the forehead or arm. It was so called because it was a small case containing four inscriptions from the Old Testament which the sacred writer prescribed to be kept in the hand, before the eyes, etc. This was meant in a figurative sense, but interpreting it literally and wearing the Tephillim formed a part of the exaggerated attention given to outward marks of religion by the Pharisees. Cf. H. Lesêtre, 'Phylactères,' *Dictionnaire de la Bible* 15 (1912) 349-353.

We, on the contrary, place them not in our hands, but in our homes, when we ought to inscribe them on our hearts.

Indeed, by purifying the present life in this way we shall attain to the blessings to come. May all of us obtain these by the grace and mercy of our Lord Jesus Christ. Through Him and with Him glory be to the Father, together with the Holy Spirit, now and always, and forever and ever. Amen.

Homily 54 (John 8.31-47)

'Jesus therefore said to the Jews who had come to believe in him, "If you abide in my word, you shall be my disciples indeed, and you shall know the truth, and the truth shall make you free." '[1]

In our affairs, beloved, we have great need of perseverance. And perseverance is the fruit, when [Christ's] teachings become deeply rooted in us. No assault of the wind will be strong enough to uproot the oak which has sent its roots deep down into the depths of the earth and has become firmly encompassed by them. Similarly, no one will be strong enough to overpower the soul that is nailed down by the fear of God, because to be nailed down is to be more securely fastened than to be rooted. In fact, the Prophet prayed for this, when he said: 'Nail my flesh with thy fear.'[2]

Do you, also, nail your flesh with it and fasten it as if pierced by a nail. For, just as those who do so are difficult to ensnare, so those who do the opposite are easily caught and readily vanquished. This is the affliction which the Jews suffered at that time. Though they had heard Christ and had come to believe in Him, they once more became incredulous. In the desire, therefore, to deepen their faith so that it might

1 John 8.31-33.
2 Ps. 118.120.

not be merely superficial, He penetrated their souls with more forceful words. Now, though it is to be expected of those who believe that they be tolerant even of reproaches, these men immediately became indignant.

How was this? First, He promised: 'If you abide in my word you shall be my disciples indeed, and the truth shall make you free,' He was as much as saying: 'I am going to wound your pride, but do not be disturbed.' Or, rather, by these very words He placed a check on their vain thoughts. Of what, then, would He set them free? Of their sins. But what did they reply in their conceit?

'We are the children of Abraham, and we have never yet been slaves to anyone.' Their thoughts at once turned down to the earth, and this happened because they were clinging to the things of this world.

The words, 'If you abide in my word,' were those of One who was revealing what was in their hearts and who knew that, on the one hand, they had believed, but, on the other, they did not persevere in faith. Moreover, He was making an important announcement to them, namely, that they would become His disciples. Inasmuch as some had recently defected from Him, He was indirectly referring to them when He said 'If you abide,' because they also had heard Him and come to believe and had gone away, since they did not persevere in their belief.[3] 'For, many of his disciples turned back and no longer went about freely with him.'[4]

'You shall know the truth.' That is, 'You shall know Me, for I am the Truth. All the Jewish teachings were figures, but you will know the truth from Me, and it will free you from your sins.' Indeed, just as He had said to the others: 'You will die in your sins,' so also He said to these: 'It will make

---

3 That is, did not 'abide in His word.'
4 John 6.67.

you free.' Actually, He did not say: 'I will rid you of slavery,' but He left it to them to conclude this.

What, then, did they reply? 'We are the children of Abraham, and we have never yet been slaves to anyone.' Yet, if it were incumbent on them to wax indignant, they should have done so at the first part of what He said: 'You shall know the truth.' They should have said: 'What's that? Do we not now know the truth? Is our Law false, then, and our knowledge, too?' However, they were not concerned about any of this, but were vexed because of worldly considerations, and because their notions of slavery were based on these.

Truly there are, there are now, I repeat, many who are filled with shame because of things that should not matter, and because of this kind of slavery, but who no longer blush because of the slavery of sin. They would prefer a thousand times to be called slaves to the latter slavery rather than even once to be considered slaves in the other sense. Such were those men also and they did not know any other kind of slavery. They asked: 'Did You call slaves the descendants of the race of Abraham, nobly born as they are, and therefore not to be called slaves? For we have never yet been slaves.'

Such, to be sure, was the proud boast of the Jews. 'We are the children of Abraham; we are Israelites.' But never did they make mention of living an exemplary life. That is why John cried out against them, and said: 'Do not think to say, "We have Abraham for our father." '[5] Why, then, did Christ not refute their words? And I say this for they had often been slaves: to the Egyptians, and to the Babylonians, and to many others. He did not refute them because His words were uttered, not to satisfy His own ambition, but for their salvation and benefit, and He strove zealously to achieve this end.

He could likewise have mentioned the four hundred years;

5 Matt. 3.9.

He could have mentioned the seventy years; He could have mentioned what took place in the time of the Judges, now the twenty years of bondage, again the two years, once more the seven; in fine, He could have told how they had never left off being slaves. However, He did not try to prove that they were slaves of men, but, rather, that they were slaves of sin, for this is the harshest slavery and God alone can free us from it. The forgiveness of sin, indeed, belongs to no one else, and they themselves ackowledged this.

Therefore, since they had acknowledged that this is the work of God, He directed their thoughts to this acknowledgment by saying: 'Everyone who commits sin is a slave of sin,' and showed that it was this freedom of which He was speaking, freedom from this slavery.

'The slave does not abide in the house; the son abides there forever.' From this statement, also, He was quietly putting aside the prescriptions of the Law by His veiled reference to bygone times. It was in order that they might not appeal to them and say: 'We have sacrifices which Moses enjoined on us; those can free us from sin,' that He added these statements. Otherwise, what logical sequence is there in what He said?

'All have sinned and have need of the glory of God. They are justified freely by his grace'[6]—even the priests themselves. And therefore Paul said of the priest: 'He is obliged to offer for sins, as on behalf of the people, so also for himself, because he himself also is beset with weakness.'[7] Now, He made this clear by saying: 'The slave does not abide in the house.' Here He was pointing out both His own equality to the Father and the difference between a slave and a free man, for the parable indicates this: that is, the slave has no power, for that is the meaning of 'does not abide.'

---

6 Rom. 3.23,24.
7 Heb. 5.3.2.

But why, in speaking of sins, did He make mention of a 'house'? To indicate that just as a lord and master has complete authority in his house, so He Himself has power over all things. The expression, 'does not abide,' also means this: he has no power to bestow favors since he is not master, but the son is master. And this, indeed, is the meaning of 'abide there forever.' He was using a metaphor based on human relations, to forestall their saying: 'Who are you?' 'All things are mine, for I am the Son, and abide in the house of My Father.' Here He was calling His sovereignty His Father's 'house': 'In my Father's house there are many mansions.'[8] Since the discussion concerned freedom and slavery, it was with good reason that He used this metaphor, telling them that they did not have power to grant forgiveness of sin.

'If therefore the Son makes you free.' Do you perceive His consubstantiality with His Father and how He was showing that He has the same power as His Father? 'If the Son makes you free, no one will in future call your freedom in question, but you will have secure freedom. It is God who justifies! Who shall condemn?'[9] In these words He both made clear His own freedom from sin and referred indirectly to the freedom which is so only in name, for men also grant the latter kind, while God alone gives freedom from sin. By this He was urging them not to be ashamed because of the other kind of slavery, but only by reason of the slavery of sin.

Moreover, in the desire to point out that even if they were not slaves in the literal sense, because of their failure to repudiate the slavery of sin, they had become more truly enslaved, He at once added: 'You will be free indeed.' By this addition He also showed them that their freedom was not true freedom. Next, to prevent them from saying: 'We have no sin' (for they probably would have asserted this), see how

8 John 14.2.
9 Rom. 8.33,34.

He neatly included them in the category of sinners. For, omitting to mention everything else of which their life accused them, He brought to light this deed which they had in hand and were now intending to do, and said: 'I know that you are the children of Abraham; but you seek to kill me.'

Gradually and little by little He was weaning them from that well-known relationship to Abraham and teaching them not to pride themselves on it. For, just as freedom and slavery are contingent on one's deeds, so it is with nobility of race. Moreover, He did not say directly: 'You who are murderers of the Just One are not sons of Abraham'; on the contrary, He even agreed with them for the moment and said: 'I know that you are the children of Abraham.' However, this was not the point in question, so He continued with that other statement, calculated to disconcert them. For it is here, as so often, to be observed that when, in order to make an important point, He was somewhat more outspoken, He spoke thus only after performing some striking deed, so that the evidence of what he had done might confound his critics.

'But you seek to kill me.'

'What of it, then, if we are doing so justly?' they might ask.

But this was not the case; therefore He also stated the reason: 'because my word takes no hold among you.'

'How it is, then, that the Evangelist asserted that they had come to believe in Him?'[10]

They did, but as I have said, they changed again; therefore He sharply upbraided them. 'For if you boast of that relationship of yours with Abraham, you ought also to show it forth in your life.' Further, He did not say: 'You do not take hold of My word,' but 'My word takes no hold among you,' to point out the sublimity of His teachings. Yet they ought not to kill Him because of this, but rather to honor and cherish Him that they might learn His doctrine.

---

10 Cf. John 8.31.

'But why,' someone might ask, 'do You say these things of Yourself.'

In view of this He added: 'I speak what I have seen with my Father; and you do what you have heard with your father.' He meant: 'Just as I reveal My Father both by My words and by their truth, so you also reveal yours by your deeds. For I have not only the same substance but also the same truth as the Father.'

'They said to him, "Abraham is our father." '

'Jesus said to them, "If you are the children of Abraham, do the works of Abraham. But as it is, you are seeking to kill me." ' Here He repeatedly returned to their murderous design and reminded them of Abraham. Furthermore, He did this because He wished to detach them from this racial pride and to deflate their excessive conceit, and to persuade them no longer to place their hope of salvation in Abraham, or in nobility of race according to nature, but in that according to free will. For, this was the thing that prevented them from coming to Christ; namely, that they thought that the fact of their descent from Abraham sufficed for their salvation.

'But what truth did He speak? '

That He is equal to the Father. Indeed, it was on this account that the Jews were seeking to kill Him, and He declared: 'You are seeking to kill me, because I have spoken the truth to you which I have heard from my Father.' To prove that these things are not opposed to the Father He once again referred what He said to Him.

'They said to him, "We have not been born of fornication; we have one Father, God." '

What are you saying? You have God for your Father, yet do you censure Christ for saying this? Do you realize that it was in a special way that He declared that God is His Father?

Well, then, since He had stripped them of their claims based upon their relationship to Abraham, and there was nothing left for them to say, they ventured something else, greater still, by quickly resorting to calling God their Father. However, He deprived them of this prerogative, also, by saying: 'If God were your Father, you would surely love me. For from God I came forth and have come; and I have not come of myself, but he sent me. Why do you not understand my speech? Because you cannot listen to my word. You are of your father the devil, and the desires of your father it is your will to do. He was a murderer from the beginning, and has not stood in the truth. When he tells a lie he speaks from his very nature.'

He had stripped them of their claims based upon their relationship to Abraham, and, when they ventured to make a bolder claim He finally dealt another blow by saying not only that they were not true sons of Abraham, but even that they were sons of the Devil. He inflicted the stroke proportioned to their impudence, and did not administer it without establishing proofs, but gave it the support of accusations. 'To commit murder,' He declared, 'is a part of the wickedness of that scoundrel.' Moreover, He did not mention merely his deeds, but said: 'His desires it is your will to do,' to show that both the Devil and they were very strongly inclined to commit murder and that the reason for this was envy. For, though the Devil was unable to accuse Adam of any evil deed, he destroyed him only because he envied him.

Therefore, this is implicitly declared here. 'And he has not stood in the truth,' that is, 'in a righteous life.' For, since they frequently charged that Christ was not of God, He asserted that this statement also came from that source.[11] Indeed, it was the Devil who told the first lie, when he said: 'On whatever day you eat of it, your eyes will be opened.'[12] Moreover, he himself was the first one to use a lie. Men, to be

---

11 That is, the Devil.
12 Gen. 3.5.

sure, use a lie, though not as belonging to their own nature, but as the device of another; he, on the contrary, employs it as his very own.

'But because I speak the truth you do not believe me.' How does this follow? 'Though you do not charge me with any crime, you wish to destroy me. Since you are the enemies of the truth, for this reason you persecute Me. If this is not the reason, state the accusation.' Indeed, that is why He added: 'Which of you can convict me of sin?'

Then they said: 'We have not been born of fornication.' Yet many actually had been born of fornication; I say this for they were the issue of unlawful intercourse. However, He did not accuse them of this, but pursued the other line of argument. Since He had shown by all these statements that they were not of God but of the Devil (and He had done so truly, for to murder is diabolical and to lie is diabolical, and 'Both of these you have done'), He made it evident that to love Him is a sign that one is of God.

'Why do you not understand my speech?' In truth, they were always in a state of doubt and had been saying: 'What is this statement that He has made, "Where I go you cannot come"?' That is why He said: 'You do not understand My speech because you have not the word of God. And this is your plight because your thoughts cling to earth and so My teachings are much too great for you.'

'But suppose they were unable to understand them?'

When He here said they were unable, He meant that they were unwilling: 'You have schooled yourselves to be earthly-minded; you entertain no lofty thoughts.' For, since they kept asserting that they were persecuting Him because, as they said, they were zealous for the cause of God, He continually sought to show that to persecute Him was the work of those who hated God. And, contrariwise, to love Him is the mark of those who know God.

They declared: 'We have one Father, God.' They vaunted themselves on this, but it was because of the honor [of being God's children], not because of their own virtuous living.

'The fact that you do not believe is not, therefore, a proof that I am foreign to God; rather, your unbelief is a sign that you do not know God. Further, the cause of this is that you are willing to lie and to do the works of the Devil.' And it is meanness of soul that brings this about, as the Apostle said: 'For since there are jealousy and strife among you, are you not carnal?'[13]

'Further, why are you not able to understand my word? Because it is your will to do the desires of your father: you endeavor, you strive to do them.' Do you understand now that by the words 'you cannot' He meant 'You are unwilling'? Because 'This Abraham did not do.'[14]

'But what were his works?'

'Gentleness, meekness, obedience; while you are just the opposite: harsh and cruel.'

'Still, how was it that they came to resort to the protection of God? '

He had proved that they were unworthy of Abraham; therefore, in the desire to escape from this cloud, they ascended to the greater prerogative.[15] Since He had imputed murder to them, they made this statement as if making a kind of defense in that they were avenging God. Therefore, He made it clear that this very statement was indicative that they were at enmity with God.

Now, the words 'I came forth' signify that He is of God. And He said: 'I came forth,' to imply His coming to us. Further, since it was probable that they would declare: 'You are speaking of strange and novel things,' He said that He had

13 1 Cor. 3.3.
14 Cf. Gen. 18.
15 Namely, that they had God as their Father.

come from God. 'Therefore, with good reason you do not
listen to these things,' He averred, 'since you are of the Devil.
Why, indeed, do you wish to kill Me? What charge can you
make? If there is none, why do you not believe in Me?'

Accordingly, by thus demonstrating by their lies and intent
to murder that they were of the Devil, He proved also that
they were estranged from Abraham and from God, both
because they hated One who had done no wrong and because
they did not listen to His teaching. Moreover, He showed
conclusively throughout that He was not in opposition to God,
nor was it on this account actually that they did not believe
in Him, but because they were estranged from God.

If, despite the fact that He had not commited sin, and
though He said that He had come from God and had been
sent by Him, and though He spoke the truth, and spoke so
truly that in proof all were won over to Him, nevertheless they
did not believe in Him, it is clear that they did not believe in
Him because they were carnal. Indeed, habitual sin is wont, is
wont, I say, to debase the soul. That is why Scripture says:
'You have grown dull of hearing.'[16] Truly, when one cannot
despise the things of earth, how will he ever wisely value the
things of heaven?

Therefore, I beseech you, let us perform all our actions in
such a way that our life will be virtuous, our mind will be
purified, and nothing ignoble will be a hindrance to us.
Kindle the lamp of knowledge in yourselves and do not sow
among thorns. For, will he who does not know that covetousness is wicked ever attain to the knowledge greater than this?
How will he who does not refrain from things of earth ever
obtain the possession of the things of heaven? It is a good
thing to take by violence: not, however, perishable things,
but the kingdom of heaven. 'They seize it by force,' Scripture

---

16 Heb. 5.11.

says.[17] It is not possible, then, to obtain possession of it by laziness, but by exerting effort.

And what is the meaning of 'by force'? There is need of much strength (for, narrow is the way), and there is need, too, of a vigorous and noble soul. Plunderers wish to get ahead of everybody. They do not give heed to anything: not to unfavorable criticism, or to accusation, or to punishment; they are preoccupied with one thing only, namely, with getting possession of what they want to steal and they sweep aside all who get in their way.

Let us, then, steal the kingdom of heaven, for in this case plundering incurs praise, not blame, and it is a fault not to plunder. Here our wealth does not cause loss to someone else. Let us, therefore, strive to plunder it. If anger disturbs us, or evil desire, let us do violence to our nature, let us become more gentle, let us toil for a little while, that we may rest perpetually. Do not seize gold, but seize a wealth that makes gold seem mud by comparison.

Tell me, please, if lead and gold were both lying before you, which would you seize? Is it not very obvious that you would take the gold? Do you, then, recognize as valuable a substance the theft of which is punished, but pass up the more valuable thing in the case where he who seizes it is given honor? If, indeed, there were punishment in store for both kinds of plunder, would you not rather go in quest of the latter kind? However, such is not the case here; actually a blessed reward is in store.

'Still, how is it possible to plunder the kingdom of heaven]?' you will ask.

Scatter abroad the things you have in your hands. As long as you keep them, you will not be able to seize those other

17 Matt. 11.12: 'The kingdom of heaven has been enduring violent assault, and the violent have been seizing it by force.'

things. Consider, if you will, the case of a man who has his hands full of silver. As long as he keeps this, he will not be able to steal gold, will he, unless he casts it aside and becomes empty-handed? For, the robber must be unencumbered so as not to be prevented from his work.

I say this for there are at this very moment hostile powers besetting us, in order to rob us. But let us flee from them, let us flee and leave them no means of access to us from outside. Let us sever the cords that bind us; let us become unencumbered by the things of this life. What use is there in silken garments? To what end do we pass our time in the pursuit of such ridiculous trifles? To what end do we hide gold in the ground?

I should like to stop continually talking in this way, but you do not permit me to do so, because you are always furnishing me with occasions and reasons for sermons of the kind. However, let us now at least leave off, in order that, after instructing others also by our good example, we may obtain the promised rewards by the grace and mercy of our Lord Jesus Christ. Through Him and with Him glory be to the Father, together with the Holy Spirit, now and always, and forever and ever. Amen.

Homily 55 (John 8.48-59)

'The Jews therefore in answer said to him, "Are we not right in saying that thou art a Samaritan, and hast a devil?" Jesus answered, "I have not a devil, but I honor my Father." '[1]

Envy is a base passion and a bold one as well, and, just when it ought to remain hidden, that is the time when it flares up fiercely instead. Thus it was in the case of the Jews.

---

1 John 8.48,49.

Though they ought to have been moved to compunction by Christ's words, out of admiration for the frankness and the logic of what He said, on the contrary they insulted Him, calling Him a Samaritan and saying He was possessed by a demon. 'Are we not right,' they asked, 'in saying that thou art a Samaritan, and hast a devil?'

Indeed, whenever He said anything sublime it seemed foolishness to those who were completely lacking in understanding. And even though the Evangelist did not mention before this that they called Him a Samaritan, it is probable, in the light of this speech, that they often used this epithet. 'You have a devil,' they declared. Yet, who was it that really had a devil: He who honored God, or he who insulted Him who gave that honor?

What, then, did Christ reply, He who is gentleness and meekness personified? 'I have not a devil, but I honor my Father who sent me.' Where, on the other hand, it was necessary to teach them, and to deflate their great conceit, and to school them not to be vain because of Abraham, He used forceful language, but where it was needful to endure being insulted, He showed great gentleness. When they had said: 'We have God for our Father, and Abraham,' He had sharply upbraided them. But when they called Him a demoniac, He used a quiet manner of speaking, to instruct us to exact punishment in offenses relating to God, but to overlook those pertaining to ourselves.

'I do not seek my own glory.'

'I have said these things,' He meant, 'to show that it is not fitting for you to call God your Father, since you are murderers. And, so it is because of the honor that belongs to Him that I have said these things; on His account I hear these insults, and because of Him you are dishonoring Me. However, I do not care about these insults, for you owe an accounting for your words to Him on whose account I now hear them. I do not seek my own glory. Therefore, refraining from punishing you, I concentrate on encouraging you, and advise you to do those things by means of which you will not only escape punishment, but will even attain to everlasting life.

'Amen, amen, I say to you, if anyone keep my word, he will never see death.' Here He was speaking not only of faith, but also of purity of life. Moreover, He previously had said: 'He will have everlasting life,'[2] while here He said: 'He will never see death,' and at the same time He was indirectly declaring that they could do nothing to Him. For, if he who kept His word would not die, much more would He Himself not do so. As a matter of fact, because they themselves also were conscious of this, they said: 'Now we know that thou hast a devil. Abraham is dead, and the prophets are dead.' That is, 'Those who have heard the word of God are dead, yet will those who hear Yours not die? Art thou greater than our father Abraham?'

Oh, what vainglory! Once more they took refuge in the fact that they were descendants of Abraham. Yet it was more logical to say: 'Are You greater than God? Or are those who have listened to You greater than Abraham?' However, they did not say this, because they thought He was even inferior to Abraham. Therefore, first He showed that they were murderers and by this means depreciated the value of their relationship [to Abraham]. But when they persisted, He once again dealt with the same question by another method, namely, by showing that their efforts to kill Him were vain. Yet He did not discuss this 'death'[3] with them, nor did He reveal, nor explain, what kind of death He meant, but merely persuaded them that He is superior to Abraham in order that He might disconcert them by this fact.

'Surely,' He meant, 'even if I were just anyone at all, I still

---

2 John 5.24; 6.47.
3 'If anyone keep my word, he will never see death.'

ought not to die if I have done no wrong. But, inasmuch as I speak the truth, and have no sin, and am sent by God and am greater than Abraham, are you not mad and are not your efforts vain, when you strive to destroy Me?'

What, then, did they reply? 'Now we know that thou hast a devil.'

The Samaritan woman, on the contrary, was not like that, for she did not say to Him: 'Thou hast a devil,' but only this: 'Art thou greater than our father Jacob?'[4] These Jews, of course, were insolent men and hecklers, whereas she really wished to learn from Him. Therefore, though she was perplexed, she replied with befitting moderation, and called Him 'Sir.' Indeed, it was fitting for Him who made much greater promises [than Jacob or Abraham] and merited their credence not to be insulted, but to be admired; yet they said He was possessed by a devil. Truly, those words of the Samaritan woman were the words of one in doubt, but these latter were the words of unbelievers and perverts.

'Art thou greater than our father Abraham?' And so this dominion over death makes Him greater than Abraham. Therefore, when you see Him lifted up on the cross you will acknowledge that He is greater. That is why He said: 'When you have lifted me up, then you will know that I am the Son of God.'[5] Furthermore, see His prudence. After having first cut them off from the relationship they claimed, He showed that He was greater than Abraham, in order that they might realize that He was also greater than the Prophets by a wide margin.

In fact, because they were always saying that He was a prophet, that is why He declared: 'My word takes no hold among you.' On a previous occasion He asserted that He would raise the dead,[6] while here He said: 'He who believes

---

4 John 4.12.
5 John 8.28.
6 John 8.37; cf. 5.25-30.

will never see death.' This was something much greater than not permitting believers to remain under the dominion of death; therefore they were the more indignant. What, then, did they say?

'Whom dost thou make thyself?' Moreover, they said this insultingly, meaning: 'You are singing Your own praises.'

Therefore, Christ replied: 'If I glorify myself, my glory is nothing.'

What do the heretics say here? They declare: 'He heard, "Art thou greater than our father Abraham?" and did not have the courage to say "Yes" to them, but He did so in an enigmatic way. What then? Was His glory really nothing?'

It was nothing in their opinion. For, just as He said: 'My witness is not true,'[7] meaning not true according to their suspicious reasoning, so also here He said: 'There is one who glorifies me.' Yet, why did He not say: 'My Father who sent me,' as He had previously done, but: 'of whom you say that he is your God, and you do not know him'? He spoke in this way because He wished to make it clear that not only did they not know the Father Himself, but they did not know God at all.

'But I know him. And, so, it is not boasting for Me to say: "I know him," but it is a lie for Me to say: "I do not know Him"; whereas, when you say you know Him you are lying. Therefore, just as you are lying in asserting that you know Him, I should also be lying if I were to say that I do not know Him.'

'If I glorify myself.' Since they were saying: 'Whom dost thou make thyself?' He replied: 'If I make myself anyone my glory is nothing. Therefore, just as I have exact knowledge of Him, so you are ignorant of Him.' Accordingly, even as He had not stripped them of all their claims in the case of Abraham, but agreed: 'I know that you are the children of

---

7 John 5.31,32.

Abraham,' in order to make His arraignment of them the greater—so here He did not destroy their pretensions entirely, but what did He say? 'Of whom you say [that he is your God].' By giving the boast in their own words He made the accusation against them the greater.

'And how is it that you do not know Him? Because you are insulting the One who is saying and doing everything for His sake, so that He may be glorified, and you are doing so even though He has been sent by Him.' Though this statement was not yet supported by factual evidence, what followed confirmed its truth: 'And I keep his word.' Moreover, if they had any contrary evidence at all, they could have raised objection here, for this statement was a very strong proof that He had been sent by Him.

'Abraham your father rejoiced that he was to see my day. He saw it and was glad.' Once again He proved that they were estranged from Abraham, if they were displeased by things that caused him to rejoice. Further, 'my day' in this context seems to me to mean the time of the crucifixion which Abraham had prefigured in the offering of the ram and in that of Isaac.[8]

What, then, did they reply? 'Thou art not yet forty[9] years old, and hast thou seen Abraham?'

And so Christ was then almost forty years old. 'He said to them: "Before Abraham came to be, I am." And they took up stones to cast at him.' Do you see how He proved that He was greater than Abraham? For, since Abraham rejoiced that he was to see His day and considered it much to be desired, it is clear that he considered that it would be for his

---

8 Cf. Gen. 22.1-14.
9 Merk: πεντήκοντα; so also the Confraternity edition: 'fifty.' Merk 343 notes a variant τεσσεράκοντα with a weak manuscript tradition. St. John Chrysostom was apparently using a version of the New Testament in this tradition, for the Benedictine editor notes that this reading is found in all the manuscripts and editions of St. John Chrysostom at his disposal.

advantage and that it belonged to One greater than he. Moreover, since they were calling Him 'the son of a carpenter' and
thought that He was nothing greater than that, He was
gradually bringing them to a more exalted conception of Him.

Now, when they heard: 'You do not know God,' they did
not become offended, but when they heard: 'Before Abraham
came to be, I am,' they became wildly indignant and began
to stone Him, as if their nobility of family were being belittled.

'He saw my day and was glad.' Christ was showing that
not unwillingly did He come to His Passion if He actually
praised the one who rejoiced at the vision of the cross. This,
indeed, was the salvation of the world. The Jews, on the contrary, began to stone Him, so prone were they to commit
murder, and they acted in this way of their own accord, with
no one bidding them do so.

But why did He not say: 'Before Abraham came into
being, I was,' but, 'I am?' He did so in the way in which His
Father used this expression: 'I am.' For it meant that He has
always existed, since it is free from all limitations of time.
And therefore the phrase seemed to the Jews to be blas-
phemous. Now, if they resented the comparison to Abraham,
though it was a trifling matter, if He had often declared Himself equal to the Father, surely they would not have ceased
from stoning Him.

Next, once more acting in a human fashion, He fled and
hid Himself. Since He had given them sufficient instruction
and had fulfilled His task, He went from the Temple and
proceeded to the healing of the blind man, to give a guarantee
by His works that He is truly greater than Abraham.

But perhaps someone will say: 'Why did He not destroy
their power? For, if He had, they would have believed.'

He had cured the paralytic, and they did not believe;
furthermore, He worked countless miracles, and during His
very Passion cast them prostrate on the ground and spread

darkness over their vision, yet they did not believe. How would they believe if He destroyed their power? For there is nothing worse than a soul confirmed in sin. Even if it see miracles or wonderful works, it persists in the same disgraceful condition. I say this for, though Pharao had received many chastisements, he learned wisdom only while he was being punished, and remained obdurate up to his last day when he pursued those whom he had allowed to depart.

That is why Paul said repeatedly: 'Let no one of you be hardened by the deceitfulness of sin.'[10] For, even as the vital organs of the body, [beset by disease,] finally die and have no feeling, so also the soul, when it is in the grip of many passions, dies to virtue. No matter what argument you place before it, it does not comprehend it; even if you threaten punishment or anything else whatsoever, it remains unaffected.

Wherefore, I beseech, as long as we have hope of salvation, as long as we are able to be converted, let us do all things necessary. Indeed, like pilots who give way to despair and put their ship at the mercy of the wind, contributing nothing by their own efforts, those who have become hardened in vice cease to struggle against it in the end. For, the envious man looks only to one thing, namely to fulfill his desire. Whether he is going to be punished, or even to be carried off by death, he becomes obsessed by his passion only; so it is also with the intemperate and the covetous.

Moreover, if the compelling force of the passions is so great, that of virtue is much more so. And if we despise death for those things, we do this much more fittingly for the sake of virtue. Further, if those others despise their own life, much rather should we do this for the sake of our salvation. In truth, what defense shall be ours if, while those who are perishing put forth such efforts for their own destruction, we

10 Heb. 3.13.

do not display as much zeal for our own salvation, but remain ever consumed by envy? Indeed, nothing is worse than envy; in order that it may destroy another, it even brings about its own destruction.

The eye of the envious man is wasted away by grief; he lives always in ceaseless death; he thinks all men his enemies, even though they have done him no wrong. He grieves because God is honored, rejoices for the reasons for which the Devil rejoices. Is a certain man honored by men? But this is not honor; do not envy him. However, is he honored by God? Vie with him and become like him. But you do not wish this?

Well, then, why are you also destroying yourself? Why are you casting aside even what you possess? Why are you unable to become his equal or at least to get some good? Why, besides, do you choose the evil course, when you ought to rejoice with him in order that, even if you are unable to share in his good works, you may merit a reward for rejoicing with him? Indeed, even a good intention frequently suffices to accomplish a great good. At least, Ezechiel said that the Moabites were punished for this reason, namely, because they rejoiced at the misfortunes of the Israelites, and that certain others were saved because they mourned over the misfortunes of others.[11]

But, if those who mourn over the evil that befalls others have some reward, much more do those who rejoice at the honor won by others. He blamed the Moabites because they rejoiced over the misfortunes of the Israelites, even though it was God who was punishing the latter. However, not even when He himself inflicts punishment does He wish us to exult over those who are punished, for even He Himself does not wish to punish them.

Now, if we ought to grieve in sympathy for those who are punished, much more ought we not envy those who are

11 Ezech. 25.8-11.

honored. It was in this way, to be sure, that Core, Dathan, and their followers perished.[12] They caused the objects of their envy to be still more highly esteemed, and gave themselves over to punishment. Indeed, envy is a poisonous wild beast, a vile beast and willful wickedness, undeserving of pardon, a vice altogether lacking excuse, the cause and mother of all evils.

Therefore, let us tear it up by the roots, that we may be free from the evils of this life, and attain to the blessings of the life to come, by the grace and mercy of our Lord Jesus Christ. Through Him and with Him glory be to the Father, together with the Holy Spirit, now and always, and forever and ever. Amen.

Homily 56 (John 9.1-5)

'And as he was passing by, Jesus saw a man blind from birth. And his disciples asked him, "Rabbi, who has sinned, this man or his parents, that he should be born blind?" '[1]

'And as he was passing by, Jesus saw a man blind from birth.' Because He was exceedingly kind and concerned about our salvation, and desired to silence the tongues of the impious, He left nothing that He could do undone, even if there was no one who heeded. Indeed, the Prophet, on seeing this, said: 'That you may be justified in your sentence, vindicated when you condemn.'[2]

For this reason, accordingly, in this instance, also, because they did not accept the sublimity of His words—but even called Him possessed by a devil, and likewise strove to kill Him—as He went from the Temple, He healed a blind man.

---

12 Num. 16.1-15.

1 John 9.1,2,
2 Ps. 50.6.

His purpose was to soothe their wrath by His departure, and to soften their hard-heartedness and harshness by working the miracle, and also to give them guarantee of the truth of what He had said. Moreover, He worked a miracle that was not an ordinary one, but one that then took place for the first time. 'Not from the beginning of the world has it been heard,' the man declared, 'that anyone opened the eyes of a man born blind.' Perhaps someone had opened the eyes of a blind man, but not yet those of a man born blind.

Now, on departing from the Temple, He went expressly to perform this miracle, as is clear from the fact that it was He who saw the blind man, not the latter who came to Him. So intently did He look at him that His disciples also noticed the man. Because of this, at least, they began to question Him. For, when they observed Him intently looking at the man, they formulated a question and asked: 'Who has sinned, this man or his parents?' The question was a blundering one, for how could he have sinned before he was born? And how could he have been punished, if his parents had committed the sin?

How, then, did they come to ask this question? Previously He had said, as He healed the paralytic: 'Behold, thou art cured. Sin no more.'[3] Well, then, His disciples, thinking that he had been paralyzed on account of sin, reasoned: 'Evidently that other man suffered paralysis as a result of his sins. Has this man sinned? However, it is not possible to say whether he has or not, for he has been blind from his birth. But have his parents sinned? This does not account for it either, for a child does not pay the penalty for his father.' Thus, it was just as when, on seeing a small child suffering, we say: 'What explanation can one give of this? What has this little child done?' and are not so much asking for information as expressing our perplexity.

---

3 John 5.14.

What, then, did Christ reply? 'Neither has this man sinned, nor his parents.' Now, he said this, not to absolve them of having committed sins (for He did not make the unqualified statement: 'Neither has this man sinned, nor his parents,' but added by implication: 'that he should be born blind'[4]), but 'that the Son of God should be glorified in him.' He meant that this man had sinned, of course, as also had his parents, but his disability did not result from that.

Further, when He said this, He did not mean that though it was not so in the case of this man, certain others have suffered blindness for this reason, namely, because of the sins of their parents. It is not possible, if one man has sinned, for another to be punished. Besides, if we grant this, we shall assent to that other supposition as well, namely, that he committed sin before his birth. Therefore, just as by saying 'Neither has this man sinned' He did not mean that it is possible for anyone to sin before birth and be punished for this; so by saying 'nor his parents' He did not imply that it is possible for any man to be punished on account of his parents.

Now, I say this for He removed this erroneous suspicion through Ezechiel: 'As I live, saith the Lord, if there is this parable which says, The fathers have eaten sour grapes, and the teeth of the children are set on edge, [let it be no more a proverb.]'[5] Moreover, Moses said: 'A father shall not be put to death for his child.'[6] And regarding a certain king he said that it was for this reason that he did not do this,[7] namely, because he was observing the Law of Moses.

But, if someone say: 'How is it, then, that this statement is made, "[I am a jealous God] inflicting punishments for their fathers' wickedness on the children to the third and

---

4 This clause does not actually occur in Christ's words, but is found only as part of the previous question of the disciples.
5 Cf. Ezech. 18.3.2.
6 Deut. 24.16.
7 Namely, put to death the children of murderers; cf. 4 Kings 14.6.

fourth generation"?"[8] I should make this reply: that the declaration is not to be universally applied, but was made with regard to those who were going out of Egypt. And what it means is something like this: Inasmuch as those who were going out of Egypt, even after the signs and wonders vouchsafed to them, became worse than their forefathers who had seen none of these things, they would suffer the same punishments as their ancestors had suffered, since they dared to commit the same sins. And anyone who examines the context will see more clearly that the statement was actually made with regard to them.

'Why, then, was the man born blind?'

'That the glory of God might be made manifest,' He said. See still another difficulty, namely, whether without this man's affliction it was impossible for the glory of God to be made manifest. Certainly He did not assert that it was impossible, for in fact it was possible, but He meant: 'that it might be made manifest in the case of this man.'

'What, then,' you will say, 'was the man wronged for the sake of the glory of God?'

What wrong was there, pray, even if He had willed not to bring him into existence at all? Moreover, I maintain that he even benefited by the blindness, for he recovered spiritual vision. Indeed, what benefit did the Jews derive from their eyes? Truly they merited greater punishment, since they were blind in the act of seeing. What harm, on the contrary, did this man receive from blindness? Actually, because of it he received his sight.

Therefore, evil does not consist in the misfortunes of this life, as also good does not consist in the blessings of this life, but sin is the only evil, and blindness is in reality not an evil. He who had brought the man into being from nothingness could also have left him in that state.

---

8 Deut. 5.9.

Furthermore, some maintain that this conclusion[9] was stated, not in a causal sense, but because of what resulted, as when He said: 'For judgment have I come into this world, that those who do not see may see, and they who see may become blind.'[10] Now, of course, He did not come with this purpose: that those who saw might become blind. And again, Paul said: 'What may be known about God is manifest to them so that they may be without excuse.'[11] Yet it was not on this account that He manifested it to them, namely, that they should be deprived of excuse, but that they should obtain it. Once more, in another place: 'Now the Law intervened that the offense might abound.'[12] Yet it intervened not for this end, but that sin might be prevented.

Do you perceive that in every instance the conclusion refers to the result? For, even as some very able architect may complete part of the house and leave a part unfinished, so as to prove to the skeptical that the whole building is his work, when he supplies what has been left incomplete, so it is with God. He repairs and restores our body, as if it were an unsound house, when He heals the withered hand, gives strength to paralyzed limbs, straightens crooked ones, cleanses lepers, restores the sick to health, makes sound those with crippled legs, calls back corpses from death, opens diseased eyes, or supplies eyes where they do not exist. Since all these afflictions are infirmities proceeding from the weakness of nature, when He remedies them He displays His power.

However, when He said: 'That the glory of God may be made manifest,' He was speaking of Himself, not of His Father, for the glory of His Father was already manifest. Since they had heard that God made man by taking dust

---

9 That the glory of God should be made manifest.
10 John 9.39.
11 Cf. Rom. 1.19-21.
12 Rom. 5.20.

from the ground, it was for this reason that He also made clay in this way. In truth, if He said: 'I am the One who took dust from the ground and fashioned mankind,' it would seem offensive to His hearers, while if this was demonstrated by a concrete example, it would no longer give offense in future.

Accordingly, therefore, He Himself also took earth and mixed it with spittle, and thus made manifest His glory that had been concealed until then. Indeed, it was no small glory for Him to be regarded as Creator of the world. For by this miracle the rest of His claims were also substantiated, and from the part the whole was likewise established, since belief in the greater matter confirmed that in the lesser. Man is more honorable than all the rest of creation, and the eye is more honorable than the other members in our body. Because of this He created [the blind man's] vision; not out of nothing, but in the way He did.

The eye is, to be sure, a small organ in size, but it is more important than all the rest of the body. Paul showed this in the words: 'If the ear says, "Because I am not an eye, I am not of the body," is it therefore not of the body?'[13] Actually, of course, everything in us is a proof of the wisdom of God, but the eye is so more than any other organ. In truth, it governs the entire body; it adorns the countenance; it is a lamp for all the members. What the sun does in the world, this the eye does in the body. If you should extinguish the sun, you would destroy everything and create chaos; if you should extinguish the light of the eyes, the feet would also be useless, and the hands, and even life.

Now, if the eyes have been disabled, wisdom also departs, because by them we know God. 'For since the creation of the world his invisible attributes are clearly seen, being understood through the things that are made.'[14] Surely, then, the eye is

13 1 Cor. 12.16.
14 Rom. 1.20.

the light not merely of the body, but also of the soul more than of the body. Wherefore it is, as it were, established in a royal stronghold, after being allotted to its high station and holding precedence over the other senses. This, then, is what He formed out of clay.

Next, He took care that you might not think that He was in need of material when He created, and in order that you might learn that not even from the start did He need clay (for, since He had produced greater beings from nothing, much more easily could He make this one without using any substance). In order, then, that you might learn that it was not of necessity that He did this,[15] but to teach that He Himself was the Creator in the beginning of the world, after anointing the man's eyes with clay, He said: 'Go, wash, that you may perceive that I do not need clay in order to make eyes, but I used it that My glory might be made manifest by this means.'

Now, it was because He meant Himself when He said: 'that the glory of God be made manifest,' that He added: 'I must do the works of him who sent me.' That is, 'I must manifest myself and do things that have the power to prove that I do the same works as the Father—not 'similar' works, but 'the same' ones, a proof of closer identity, and a fact predicated of those who differ from one another not even in a small way. Who, then, will in future oppose Him, on seeing that He is able to do the same things as the Father?

Furthermore, not only did He fashion eyes, not only did He open them, but He also endowed them with power to see. And this is a proof that He also breathed life into them. Indeed, if this vital principle should not operate, even if the eye were sound, it could never see anything. And so He both bestowed the power to see by giving the eyes life, and also gave the organ of sight completely equipped with arteries,

---

15 That is, used clay in working the miracle.

and nerves, and veins, and blood, and all the other things of which our body is composed.

'I must work while it is day.'

'What do these words mean? And of what importance are they?'

Of great importance. For what He meant is something like this: 'While it is day, while it is possible for men to believe in Me, while this life lasts, I must work. Night is coming,' that is, 'the time to come, when no one can work.' He did not say: 'When I cannot work,' but 'when no one can work,' that is: 'When there is no longer faith, or works, or repentance.'

Now, in proof that by 'work' He here meant 'believe'—when they said to Him: 'What are we to do in order that we may perform the works of God?'—He replied: 'This is the work of God, that you believe in him whom he has sent.'[16] How is it, then, that no one can do this work at that time?[17] Because there is no faith there, but willingly or unwillingly, all will obey. In order that no one might say that He performed this miracle out of vainglory, He was pointing out that He did everything out of consideration for them, since they had the power to believe in this world only, and no longer would be able to gain any merit in the next.

Therefore, though the blind man did not come to Him, yet He did what He did because indeed he was worthy to be cured, and if he had seen Him, he would have believed and come to Him. Moreover, if he had heard from someone that He was present, he would not have ignored Him as he did. This is clear from the sequel: from his courage and from his faith itself. I say this for he could have thought things over and said: 'What in the world is this? He made clay and anointed my eyes and said to me, "Go, wash." Could He not

16 John 6.28-30.
17 That is, when night comes.

have healed me and then sent me to Siloe? I have often
bathed there with many others and have obtained no favor.
If He possesses any power, He would have healed me when I
was in His presence.'

Naaman did speak in this way to Eliseus. And he did so
for, when he had been bidden to go and wash in the Jordan,
he was in doubt, even though the reputation of Eliseus was
so great.[18] The blind man, on the contrary, did not hesitate,
or contradict, or reason with himself: 'What in the world is
this? Should He have put clay on my eyes? This is likely to
blind them more. Who has ever received his sight in this way?'
However, he framed none of these arguments. Do you perceive that his faith and good will were strong?

'Night is coming.' By this He was pointing out that even
after the crucifixion He would be concerned for the wicked
and would attract many over to Himself, for it would still be
day. But after this time had been completely finished, He
would cut them off. To make this clear He said: 'As long as
I am in the world I am the light of the world,' as He said also
to others: 'Believe, while you have the light.'[19]

Why is it, then, that Paul called the present life 'night,'
while Christ called it 'day'? He was not contradicting Christ,
but saying the same things, even though not in his words but
in his ideas. For he said: 'The night is far advanced; the day
is at hand.'[20] Moreover, he called the present time 'night'
because of those sitting in the darkness or because he was
comparing it with the 'day' of the life to come. Christ, on the
other hand, called the future life 'night' because of the
inability of sinners to effect a reconciliation then.

Paul called the present life 'night' because those spending
it in wickedness and unbelief are in darkness. In speaking

18 Cf. 4 Kings 5.11.
19 John 12.36.
20 Rom. 13.12.

to the faithful, then, he said: 'The night is far advanced; the day is at hand,' on the ground that they were on the point of enjoying that light, so he called the present life 'night.' He went on: 'Let us therefore lay aside the works of darkness.' Do you perceive that he was telling them that it was then night? Wherefore he added: 'Let us walk becomingly as in the day, in order that we may enjoy that light.'

Now, if this light in this world is so beautiful, think what sort that other will be. For it will be as much brighter than this, as the sunlight is more radiant than lamplight—and even more so. Moreover, to make this clear Christ said: 'The sun will be darkened,'[21] that is, by reason of the surpassing brightness of that brilliance, the sun will not be apparent.

Furthermore, if now we expend boundless wealth in order to possess well-lighted and airy houses, building them with painful toil, reflect how we ought to spend our very bodies in building shining mansions for ourselves in heaven where that ineffable light is. Here, indeed, there are strifes and contentions about boundaries and walls, while there, there will be nothing of this: no envy, no malice, and no one will contend with us about the setting of boundaries. Moreover, we must leave behind completely this home here, while that other will remain with us forever. Then, too, this one must deteriorate in course of time, and must be the prey of countless destructive agencies, while that one must remain forever incorrupt. Besides, the poor man cannot build this one here, while it is possible to build that one for two oboli, as that well-known widow did.[22]

Therefore, I seethe with indignation because, when so many blessings lie in wait for us, we are lazy, we make little account of them, and make every effort to have splendid homes in this world. On the other hand, we are not con-

21 Matt. 24.29.
22 Cf. Mark 12.41-44.

cerned, we take no thought as to how we may possess even a little abode in heaven. And, tell me, please: Where do you wish to have your home in this world? In a desert or in one of the small towns? I think not; but in great royal cities, where there is more trade, where the ostentation is more lavish.

I am leading you, on the contrary, to a city the architect and builder of which is God. I am urging you to occupy it and build there at the expenditure of less wealth, less toil. The hands of the poor build your home there and this is the truest kind of construction, whereas those that are being made in the present life are works of utter madness. Now this is actually so, for if someone should bring you to the land of Persia to see things there and then to return, and if he thereupon bade you to build a home there, would you not think it altogether foolish for him to urge you to make such an ill-advised expenditure? How is it, then, that you are doing this same thing on the earth which you are to leave in a short time from now?

'But I shall leave the house to my children,' you say.

However, they also will depart from it a short time after you—nay, frequently even before you—and those who come after them, in their turn. Further, the matter becomes a cause of disquiet to you even in this life, when you do not see heirs surviving you. In the next life, on the contrary, there is nothing like this to anticipate, but your possessions will remain undisturbed, both to you, and to your children and your grandchildren, if they imitate you in practicing the same virtue.

Christ claims that building; he who builds it does not need to set caretakers over it, or be concerned or anxious about it. Since God is sponsoring the project, what need is there of worry? He brings all the materials together and builds up the house. And not only is this fact wonderful, but also the fact that He builds it as is pleasing to you; or, rather, exceeding what pleases you and beyond what you desire. For He is the best of architects and is most solicitous for what is of benefit to you.

Even if you are a poor man and wish to build this house, it does not stir up envy against you, or cause jealousy of you. Indeed, no one capable of envy will see it, but only the angels who excel in rejoicing at your good fortune. No one will be able to encroach on its boundaries, for no one addicted to such conduct will dwell near it. There you will have as neighbors the saints—Peter and Paul and their followers—all the Prophets, the martyrs, the multitude of the angels, the archangels.

Accordingly, in the light of all this, let us pour out our possessions to the poor, that we may obtain possession of those dwellings in the next world. May we all be so fortunate as to obtain them by the grace and mercy of our Lord Jesus Christ. Through Him and with Him glory be to the Father, together with the Holy Spirit, forever and ever. Amen.

Homily 57 (John 9.6-16)

'When Jesus had said these things, he spat on the ground and made clay with the spittle, and spread the clay over the eyes of the blind man and said, "Go, wash in the pool of Siloe." '[1]

Those who are to gain any profit from what they read must not skim over even the smallest part of the words. Indeed, it is for this reason that we have been bidden to 'search the Scriptures,'[2] because it seems that many texts, though their literal meaning is easy to comprehend, actually have a great deal of meaning concealed in their depths. Notice, in fact, how true this is in the present instance, also.

---

1 John 9.6.7.
2 John 5.39.

The Evangelist said: 'When he had said these things, he spat on the ground.' To what words was he referring? 'That the glory of God may be made manifest' and 'I must do the works of him who sent me.' Now, the Evangelist did not merely record His words for us and then casually add: 'He spat'; He said this to make it clear that Christ was lending credence to His words by what He did.

Moreover, why did He not use water, but spittle, for the clay? He was going to send him to Siloe; therefore, He spat on the ground in order that no efficacy might be attributed to the pool, but that you might learn that it was truly the power proceeding from His mouth which both formed and opened the man's eyes. In fact, it was with this meaning that the Evangelist said: 'And made clay with the spittle.' Next, in order that the cure might not seem to come from the earth that He used, He bade him to bathe himself.

'Why, then, did He not perform the cure at once, instead of sending him to Siloe?'

He did this that you might learn the faith of the blind man, and also that the perversity of the Jews might be checked. For it was likely that they would all see him going off with the clay spread over his eyes. Indeed, by this strange behavior he would attract the attention of all of them to himself: both those who knew him and those who did not, and they would observe him closely. Since it is not easy to have it acknowledged that a blind man has received his sight, Christ first of all made certain by the long[3] journey to Siloe that there would be many witnesses, and by the strangeness of the sight He made those who witnessed it keenly attentive, so that, by becoming more observant, they might no longer be able to say: 'This is he; this is not he.' Besides, He wished also to establish this fact: that, because He sent the man to Siloe, He

---

3 That is, he would be obliged to walk through the crowded streets, drawing attention to himself by the unusual appearance of his clay smeared eyes. The pool was on the outskirts of the city.

was not an enemy of the Law and of the Old Testament.

He had no reason to fear that Siloe would afterwards receive the credit for the cure. And I say this for, though many often bathed their eyes there, they received no such benefit from doing this, since there also it was the power of Christ which accomplished everything. Further, that is why the Evangelist added the interpretation of the name for us. When he had said: 'to Siloe,' he added: 'That is, "sent," ' so that you might learn that there also it was Christ who healed the man, as Paul declared: 'They drank from the spiritual rock which followed them, but the rock was Christ.'[4]

Therefore, just as the spiritual rock was Christ, so also He was a spiritual Siloe. Moreover, it seems to me that the suddenness with which He mentioned the water hints to us of an ineffable mystery.

'What, then, is this?'

The unexpectedness of the manifestation of His power, something which was altogether unhoped for.

But notice that the judgment of the blind man was completely submissive. For he did not say: 'If it is wholly the clay, or the spittle, which is restoring my eyes, why do I have to go to Siloe? And if I need Siloe, why do I need the clay? Why did He spread it on my eyes? Why did He bid me wash?' However, he did not voice any of these thoughts, but occupied himself with one thing only, namely, to give complete obedience to the One who was giving him orders and nothing that happened gave him any offense at all.

But, if someone should say: 'How then, did he receive his sight when he removed the clay?' he will hear no other reply from us than that we do not know the way this happened. And why is it strange if we do not know? For, neither the Evangelist knew this nor the man who was healed. But he did

---

4 1 Cor. 10.4.

know that the cure had taken place, though he was unable to detect the method. Moreover, when he was questioned about this, he declared: 'He put clay on my eyes, and I washed, and I see.' But he was unable to tell how this took place, even if they asked ten thousand times.

'The neighbors therefore and those who were wont to see him before as a beggar, began saying, "Is not this he who used to sit and beg?" Some said, "It is he." ' The strangeness of the event, to be sure, made them incredulous, though so many details had been arranged so that they might not fail to believe.

'Some said, "Is not this he who used to sit and beg?" ' Bless us, how great is God's mercy! How low He condescended, when He so graciously healed even beggars. By this means He silenced the Jews, because it was not only the famous, or the prominent, or the ruling class, but even the ignoble, that He deemed worthy of His solicitude. And this is so for He came for the salvation of all. Moreover, what took place in the case of the paralytic happened in this instance, also. For the paralytic did not know who had healed him, nor did this man. And this happened because of the fact that Christ withdrew.

Now, Christ always withdrew after effecting a cure, so that His miracles might be protected against all suspicion. For, how could those who did not know Him—that is, who He was —fawn on Him and connive with Him in bringing about what took place? Indeed, this man was not even one of Christ's followers, but one of those beggars who sat near the Temple gates.

But when all were in doubt about him, what did he say? 'I am he.' He was not ashamed of his former affliction, nor did he fear the anger of the crowd, nor did he hesitate to appear in public in order to proclaim his Benefactor. 'They said to him: "How were thy eyes opened?" '

'He said to them: "The man who is called Jesus . . . " '

'What are you saying? A man did such a thing?'

However, he knew nothing noteworthy of Him as yet. 'The man who is called Jesus made clay and anointed them.'

Notice how honest he was. He did not say from what source Christ made the clay, for he did not state what he did not know. Actually, he did not know that He spat on the ground, but he was aware that He anointed his eyes because of the feeling and His touch. 'And he said to me, "Go, wash in the pool of Siloe." ' His hearing testified to this.

'But how did he recognize His voice?'

From the conversation with the disciples. However, even though he made all these statements, and accepted the evidence furnished by what Christ did, he was unable to tell the method He used.

But, if there is need of faith in regard to things that are perceived and felt, much more so is there in regard to things that are unseen. 'They said to him, "Where is he?" He said, "I do not know." ' Now, they said 'Where is he,' intent already on murdering Him.

On the other hand, see Christ's lack of vanity—how He did not remain with those who had been healed. In truth, He did not wish to enjoy the benefit of fame, or to win applause, or to show off. Notice, also, how truthfully the blind man gave all his answers.

They wished, then, to find Jesus so as to bring Him to the priests, but, since they did not succeed, they brought the blind man to the Pharisees, to question him more closely. Indeed, the reason why the Evangelist points out that it was the Sabbath is to show their wicked purpose and the charge on which they were seeking Him, as if they actually had found a hold on Him, and were able to discredit the miracle because it seemed to be a transgression of the Law.

Furthermore, this is evident from the fact that on seeing the man they straightway said nothing else than: 'How did He open your eyes?' Now, notice how they spoke. They did not say: 'How did you receive your sight?'[5] but 'How did He open your eyes?' giving him occasion to calumniate Him on the score that He had performed work. But he spoke laconically, as if to people who had already heard the answer. Without mentioning His name, or saying: 'He said to me, "Go, wash," ' he declared at once: 'He put clay upon my eyes, and I washed, and I see.' It was as if a great deal of slanderous talk had already taken place, and they had said: 'See what sort of work Jesus is doing on the Sabbath; He is anointing with mud.'

But please note that the blind man was not perturbed. To be sure, when He was being questioned in comparative safety and was speaking to the Jews merely, it was not a great thing that he told the truth; but now it was wonderful that, though he was in greater peril, he neither denied nor contradicted his previous statements. What, then, did the Pharisees say? Yes, and the others, also? They had brought him so that he might make a denial, but they met with just the opposite of what they wished and received more accurate information instead. Furthermore, this was to be their experience with miracles on every occasion, and we shall show this more clearly in what follows.

What, then, did the Pharisees say? Some—not all, but the more contentious—said: 'This man is not from God, for he does not keep the Sabbath.' Others asked: 'How can a man who is a sinner work these signs?' Do you perceive that they were being educated by the miracles? For, though they had, before this, sent agents to arrest Him, listen to what

---

5 Apparently an inaccuracy. Both Merk and the Confraternity translation record this as the question actually put by the Pharisees here. 'How did he open your eyes?' are the words of the Jews at the first interrogation of the man, and also later, in the second questioning by the Pharisees.

some were now saying, even though not all were doing so. And not all of them were, for as they were rulers, they fell into incredulity because of vainglory. Yet, even among the rulers many believed in Him, but did not acknowledge it.[6]

On the one hand, then, the opinion of the multitude was held of little account, inasmuch as the common people contributed nothing of moment to their synagogue; the rulers, on the contrary, since they were more prominent, experienced more difficulty in confessing their belief. Love of power prevented some; cowardice and fear of the majority, others. That is why Christ said: 'How can you believe who receive glory from men?'[7] Yet the very men who were seeking unjustly to kill Him were saying that they were of God, but that He who cured the blind could not be from God because He did not keep the Sabbath.

In answer to this, some replied that a sinner could not work such signs. Therefore, the others, maliciously remaining silent about the deed itself, stressed the fact that it seemed a transgression. For they did not say: 'He healed on the Sabbath,' but 'He does not keep the Sabbath.' These, on the contrary, made a weak reply, for, though they ought to have proved that He was not breaking the Sabbath, they drew their arguments only from His miracles, and with reason, for they still thought Him to be merely Man.

In fact, if this were not the case, they could have defended Him for another reason: namely, because He was Lord of the Sabbath and had made it Himself, but they did not yet have this idea of Him. However, no one of them dared to express his opinion openly, or by a decisive assertion, but only in the form of a doubt: some because of timidity, others because of the love of power. Therefore, 'There was a division among them.' This division first began among the people, then later

---

6 Cf. John 12.42.
7 Cf. John 5.44; 12.42-43.

among the rulers. 'And some were saying, "He is a good man." But others, "No, rather he seduces the people." '[8]

Do you see how much more lacking in wisdom the rulers were than the people, since they became divided in their opinion later? And even after they were divided, they did not show their finer feelings because they saw the Pharisees threatening. Thus, if they had broken away entirely from them, they would quickly have recognized the truth. For, it is possible for a division to occur with a happy result. Therefore, Christ Himself said: 'I have come, not to send peace upon the earth, but a sword.'[9]

There is indeed agreement that is wicked and disagreement that is good. And this is so for those who were building the tower [of Babel] were in agreement to their own disadvantage; whereas these same men later were in disagreement, unwillingly to be sure, yet to their advantage.[10] Furthermore, Core and his followers were in agreement for evil; therefore, it was well that they were cut off.[11] And Judas, too, was in agreement with the Jews for an evil end.

It is possible, therefore, for dissension to be a good thing and agreement to be an evil one. Therefore, Christ said: 'If thy right eye is an occasion of sin to thee, pluck it out; if thy foot, cut it off.'[12] But, if we must be separated from a member of our body that has become an accomplice in evil, ought we not much rather be separated from friends that are our confederates in evil-doing? So that agreement is not always a good thing nor is dissension always bad.

I am saying these things in order that we may avoid wicked men and seek the companionship of the good. For, if

8 John 7.12.
9 Cf. Matt. 10.34.
10 Cf. Gen. 11.1-9.
11 Cf. Exod. 16.1-35.
12 Matt. 5.29; 18.8.

we cut off the limb that has become gangrenous and incurable, lest the rest of the body may also contract the same disease, and we do this, not out of contempt for the limb, but in the desire to protect the rest, how much more necessary is it for us to do this with regard to evil companions? To be sure, if we can cause them to mend their ways, while we ourselves suffer no harm, we ought to make every effort to that end. But, if they should remain incorrigible and should have a harmful influence on us, we must cut them off and cast them from us. Often, indeed, they will rather derive profit from this procedure.

Therefore, Paul also urged us to this and said: 'Expel the wicked man from your midst' and 'so that he who has done this deed might be put away from your midst.'[13] Indeed, bad companionship is a terrible thing, a terrible thing! A pestilence does not infect, and scabies corrupt, those tainted—as quickly as the wickedness of evil men does those affected by this malady. For 'Evil companionships corrupt good morals.' The Prophet also said: 'Go out of the midst of them and separate yourselves from them.'[14]

Let no one, then, have an unworthy man as friend. For if, when we have good-for-nothing sons, we disinherit them and do not show respect for nature or her laws or her ties, much more ought we to avoid companions and acquaintances who are evil. Further, even if we receive no harm from them, we shall not be able to avoid the ill repute, for outsiders do not examine our lives closely, but judge us by our company. This advice I give both to young ladies and to young men, for 'Providing good things not only in the sight of the Lord, but also in the sight of men,' Scripture says.[15]

Let us, then, do everything so that our neighbor be not

13 1 Cor. 5.13,2,
14 1 Cor. 15.33; cf. Jer. 51.45.
15 Cf. Rom. 12.17.

scandalized. Even if our own lives be upright, by giving offense to others everything has been destroyed.

'How is it possible for an upright life to give scandal?'

When the companionship of those who have doubtful morals surrounds it with ill repute. For, whenever we boldly associate ourselves with evil-doers, even if we ourselves suffer no harm, we give scandal to others.

I address these words both to men and to women and also to young people, leaving it to their conscience to know clearly how great are the evils that spring from this source. Now, to be sure, I for my part do not suspect anything wrong—nor, perhaps, does any other of the more virtuous. But the more ordinary brethren are disedified in the light of the fact that you are practicing a life of perfection, so you must also take their weakness into consideration. And even if they be not harmed, the Gentiles suffer harm. Paul bade us be above reproach both 'to Jews and Gentiles and also to the Church of God.'[16]

I entertain no evil suspicion regarding the virgin (for I love virginity and 'Charity thinks no evil').[17] I am a great admirer of this way of life and cannot think anything unseemly of it. But how shall we persuade those outside the faith, for we must take them also into consideration? Let us, then, so regulate our conduct that no unbeliever may be able to find a just charge against us. Indeed, just as those who give example of an upright life glorify God, so those who do the opposite cause Him to be blasphemed.

However, may no such persons be among us, but may our deeds so shine that our Father in heaven may be glorified and we may enjoy good repute in His eyes. May we all obtain this by the grace and mercy of our Lord Jesus Christ. Through Him and with Him glory be to the Father, together with the Holy Spirit, forever and ever. Amen.

---

16 1 Cor 10.33.
17 1 Cor. 13.6.

Homily 58 (John 9.17-35)

'Again they said to the blind man, "What dost thou say of him who opened thy eyes?" But he said, "He is a prophet." The Jews therefore did not believe.'[1]

The Scriptures must be read, not merely casually or superficially, but with all care, so that one may not be confused. And I say this for even now one might with reason be perplexed at this text as to how it was that, though they had said: 'This man is not from God, for he does not keep the Sabbath,' they then said to the man: 'What dost thou say of him who opened thy eyes?' They did not say: 'What do you say of him who has broken the Sabbath,' but now substituted defense for accusation.

What, then, is to be said? These were not the ones who stated: 'This man is not from God.' But these were the ones who differed with them and declared: 'A sinner cannot work such signs.' Indeed, in the desire to refute them still more, but also in order that they themselves might not seem to be speaking in Christ's defense, they brought forward the man who had had experience of His power and questioned him. Note, therefore, the wisdom of the poor man, for he spoke more prudently than all these men. At once he declared: 'He is a prophet,' and did not quail before the opinion of the perverse Jews who had contradicted this and said: 'How can He be from God, if He does not keep the Sabbath?' On the contrary, he declared: 'He is a prophet.'

'And they did not believe that he had been blind and had got his sight until they called his parents.' Moreover, notice in how many ways they tried to hide and discredit the miracle. Yet the nature of truth is such that it becomes stronger by the very schemes by which men seem to be undermining it; it becomes resplendent by the means intended to obscure it. For,

---

1 John 9.17,18.

if these efforts to discredit the miracle were not made, its authenticity might have been doubted by many. But as it was, they did everything as if they were trying to reveal the truth. They would not have brought about a different result if they had been actually doing everything in Christ's behalf.

Now, I say this for they were trying to cast aspersion on Him because of the method He had used, when they said: 'How did he open your eyes?' that is, 'Was it by some kind of sorcery?' Elsewhere, indeed, when they were unable to indict Him, they tried to discredit the way in which He healed by saying: 'He does not cast out devils except by Beelzebub.'[2] And here once again, since they could assert nothing derogatory, they took refuge in the time [as a pretext for accusing Him] and said: 'He breaks the Sabbath,' and again: 'He is a sinner.'

Indeed, it was you who were envious and ready to cast aspersion on what was done by Him that He was questioning in very precise terms, when He said: 'Which of you can convict me of sin?'[3] Moreover, no one spoke in reply, nor did anyone say: 'You blaspheme when You say that You are without sin.' Yet, if they could have said it, they would not have remained silent. For they attempted to stone Him and said that He was not from God, because they heard that He was before Abraham. On the other hand, they boasted that they themselves—who were murderers—were from God, while they declared that He who worked such signs was not from God, when He healed, because He did not keep the Sabbath. Certainly, if these men had the shadow of a charge against Him, they would not have neglected to mention it.

But, if they called Him a sinner because of the fact that He seemed to be breaking the Sabbath, even this charge appeared ineffective, since their very associates remarked its great

2 Matt. 12.24.
3 John 8.46.

cold-bloodedness and meanness. Frustrated on all sides, then, they finally arrived at another more shameless and immoderate procedure. What was this? 'They did not believe,' the Evangelist says, 'that he had been blind and had got his sight.' How could they make the accusation that He did not keep the Sabbath, then, otherwise than as clearly believing it? And how is it that you do not believe the numerous crowd? The neighbors who know him?

However, as I have said, falsehood is always caught in its own snare. It makes the truth shine more brightly by means of the very devices by which it seems to threaten the truth, and this surely happened in this instance. In order that no one might have it to say that the statements made by neighbors and eye-witnesses were not accurate, but based on a fancied resemblance, they brought forward his parents, unwittingly proving by what they were doing that the cure was authentic. And this is so for the parents were the ones who would best of all recognize their own child.

Since the Jews were unable to overawe the man, but, on the contrary, beheld him proclaiming his Benefactor with great courage, they expected to discredit the miracle by means of his parents. And see the malice of their interrogation. What was it they said? Placing them in the midst of the assembly so as to cast them into an agony of terror, they conducted the questioning with great vehemence and anger. 'Is this your son?' They did not say: 'who was once blind,' but how did they put it?—'Of whom you say that he was born blind,' as if the parents were evil-doers, and conniving at the advancement of the interests of Christ.

O impious and worse than impious men, what father would choose to tell such lies of his son? Indeed, it was as if they were saying: 'Whom you made out to be blind, and not only that, but you have even published the statement abroad everywhere. How, then, can he now see? Oh, how stupid,' they meant, 'is your trickery and scheming!' For, they were trying by these two statements to cause them to make a denial, that is, by saying: 'of whom you say,' and 'How then does he see?'

Well, though there were three questions asked—whether he was their son, whether he was blind, and how it was that he had got his sight—they answered the first two only, but did not grant a reply to the third one. This took place in the interests of the truth, so that no other than the man who had been cured and who was a trustworthy witness should give this answer. How, indeed, could the parents have been currying Christ's favor, when out of fear of the Jews they had remained silent regarding some of the things they really knew? What was it they actually said?

'We know that this is our son, and that he was blind; but how he now sees, or who opened his eyes we ourselves do not know; he is of age, let him speak for himself.' By vouching for his trustworthiness they were begging off from answering themselves. 'He is not a child,' they meant, 'or immature, but able to testify about himself.'

'And they said these things out of fear of the Jews.' Notice how the Evangelist once again brings to the fore the sentiments and opinion of the latter. I mention this to throw further light upon that statement which they had made before, when they said: 'He makes himself equal to God.'[4] If that, also, were merely the notion of the Jews, and not in agreement with the verdict of Christ, the Evangelist would have added the statement that this was a notion of the Jews.

Therefore, when the parents had referred them to the man that had been cured, they called him again a second time. Now, they did not say to him openly and brazenly: 'Deny that Christ healed you,' but they wished to compass this result by a pretense of piety. 'Give glory to God!' they said.

4 Cf. John 5.18.

In truth, it would have seemed very ridiculous to say to his parents: 'Deny that this is your son, and that he was born blind.' And it likewise would have been obviously shameless to tell him to make this denial.

Therefore, they did not say this, but used another approach by saying: 'Give glory to God!'; that is, 'Confess that this man has done nothing. We ourselves know that this man is a sinner.'

Why, then, did you not upbraid Him when He said: 'Which of you can convict me of sin?'[5] How do you know that He is a sinner?

Yet, though the man made no reply to their words: 'Give glory to God!' when Christ met him, He praised him and did not find fault with him or say: 'Why did you not give glory to God?' On the contrary, what did He say? 'Dost thou believe in the Son of God?' He said this that you might learn that this is giving glory to God. But if He were not equal to the Father, this would not be glory. Since, on the contrary, he who honors the Son is also honoring the Father, it was with reason that the blind man was not reprehended .

To resume: as long as they expected the parents to dissent and utter a denial, they said nothing to the man himself. But when they perceived that they had no success from this approach, they came once more to him, and asserted: 'This man is a sinner.'

He said in reply: 'Whether he is a sinner, I do not know. One thing I do know, that whereas I was blind, I now see.' Surely the blind man was not afraid? Not at all! But why was it that he who had declared 'He is a prophet' said 'Whether he is a sinner I do not know?' He was not fearful, nor was this his conviction.[6] On the contrary, he wished Christ to be freed of the charges against Him, by reason of the evidence

---

5 John 8.46.
6 That is, that Christ was a sinner.

of the miracle, rather than by his words, and to make the defense of Christ credible when the evidence of the favor he had received should refute them.

Indeed, after further discussion, when he said: 'If this man were not a worshiper of God, he would not be able to work such signs,' they became so indignant that they replied: 'Thou wast altogether born in sins, and dost thou teach us?' If he had spoken in this way from the start, what would they not have done? And what would they not have said?

'Whether he is a sinner, I do not know,' as if he said: 'I am not now speaking on this Man's behalf, and for the moment I refrain from expressing my opinion. However, I do know clearly and can strongly affirm this: that, if He were a sinner, He could not perform such a miracle as this.' Moreover, by this means he placed himself above suspicion and made his testimony appear unbiased, on the ground that he was not trying to curry favor but was arguing from the fact of the miracle itself.

Since, therefore, they were unable to negate or remove the fact of the miracle, they once more returned to their former point and began to agitate about the method used in the cure. They were acting as people do who are running about—now here, now there—searching everywhere for a wild beast that is roaming in safety. Furthermore, they returned to his former words, that they might weaken him and his parents by continous questioning, so they said: 'What did he do to thee? How did he open thy eyes?'

What, then, was his reply? Because he had defeated them and laid them low he finally ceased speaking mildly. As long as the matter required examination and proof, he provided the explanation, speaking with restraint. But when he had once caught them and had won a splendid victory, taking courage at length he took the offensive against them. What did he say? 'I have told you once, and you have heard. Why would you hear again?' Do you perceive the courage of the beggar shown in the face of Scribes and Pharisees? So strong is the truth, so weak is falsehood. The former, indeed, even if it takes possession of merely ordinary men, makes them splendid characters; while the latter, even if it be in the company of the powerful, makes them weaklings.

Further, what he meant is something like this: 'You do not pay attention to what is said; therefore, I shall no longer speak to you. And I will not continue replying to you because you are asking captious questions. You wish to hear the answers, not to get information, but to discredit what is said. Would you also become his disciples?' Now he was including himself in the band of the disciples, for the words, 'would you also,' are those of one who is pointing out that he himself is a disciple. Then he had sufficiently ridiculed and discomfited them.

In truth, it was because he knew that this would exceedingly annoy them, and because he wished to upbraid them as severely as possible, that he said it. Now, this was certainly the act of a soul courageous in speech, lofty of ideals, and disdainful of their anger; a soul pointing out that this was a great dignity[7] and that from it he derived great confidence. He made it clear that they were being insolent regarding a Man actually worthy of admiration, while he himself was not insulted, but took as honor what they proffered as insult.

'Thou art his disciple,' they declared, 'but we are disciples of Moses.' However, this would not be reasonable, for you are disciples neither of Moses nor of this Man. For, if you were disciples of Moses, you would also be this Man's. For this reason Christ had said to them previously: 'If you believed Moses, you would believe me, for he wrote of me,'[8]

---

7 That is, to be a disciple of Christ.
8 John 5.46.

since they were always taking refuge in the words of Moses. 'We know that God spoke to Moses.' Who told you? Who proclaimed it?

'Our ancestors,' they declared.

Then he replied: 'Is not He more deserving of belief than your ancestors, since He has confirmed by miracles the fact that He came from God and that He has spoken heavenly things?'

Further, they did not say: 'We have heard that God spoke to Moses,' but 'We know.' Do you strongly maintain that you know things that you have heard, O Jews, and do you think that things that are seen are less convincing than things that are heard? Yet you have not indeed seen those things, but have heard them; while these you have not heard, but seen.

Accordingly, what did the blind man say? 'Why, herein is the marvel, that you do not know where he is from, though he works such miracles; that a man not outstanding among you, or famous, or illustrious, can do such things. Hence, it is completely clear that He is God, since He needs no human assistance at all. We know that God does not hear sinners.' Since they had first said: 'How can a man who is a sinner work these signs?' he afterwards seized upon their verdict, reminding them of their own words. 'This opinion,' he asserted, ' is common both to you and to me; hold to it, then.'

Now, notice his wisdom, please. He kept continually reviewing the miracle—since they could not do away with it— and based his arguments on it. Do you perceive that when at the start he said: 'Whether he is a sinner, I do not know,' he was not in doubt about the matter? Away with that idea! On the contrary, he knew that He was not a sinner. In fact, now that he had the opportunity, see what a defense he made.

'Now we know that God does not hear sinners; but if anyone is a worshipper of God, and does his will, [him he hears].' By these words he not only freed Him from the imputation of sin, but even showed that He was very pleasing to God and that all His deeds were those of God. For, since his questioners alleged that they themselves were worshipers of God, he added the words: 'and does his will.' He meant: 'It is not enough to be conscious of God, but we must also do His will.'

Next he spoke in praise of the miracle, in the words: 'Not from the beginning of the world has it been heard that anyone opened the eyes of a man born blind. Well, then, if you acknowledge that God does not hear sinners, and this Man has worked a miracle, yes, such a miracle as no one else has ever worked, it is altogether clear that He has surpassed all the rest in merit and that His power is greater than merely human power.'

What reply, then, did they make? 'Thou wast altogether born in sins, and dost thou teach us?' As long as they continued to expect him to make a denial, they thought him trustworthy, and called on him not once only, but a second time. I should like to say to them: 'But if you do not think he is to be believed, why did you summon him a second time and question him?' Since he spoke the truth, in no way intimidated by them, they condemned him at the moment when they ought most of all to have held him in admiration.

Moreover, what is the meaning of: 'Thou wast altogether born in sins?' In this they were harshly reproaching him with his blindness, as if to say: 'From the beginning of your life you have been in sin,' intimating that it was on this account that he had been born blind, which was an unreasonable assumption. Indeed, Christ said, in order to console him with regard to this: 'For judgment have I come into the world, that they who do not see may see, and they who see may become blind.'[9]

'Thou wast altogether born in sins, and dost thou teach us?' What was it that the man had actually said? Surely he did

---

9 John 9.39.

not express merely his own personal opinion? Did he not set forth a common belief in the words: 'We know that God does not hear sinners'? Was he not bringing to the fore what you yourselves had said?

'And they turned him out.' Are you taking note of the messenger of Truth, how his lack of learning acted as no deterrent to him? Do you see how much he had to listen to from the start, and how great sufferings he endured, and yet how he bore witness to Christ by word and deed?

Now, these things have been recorded in order that we also may imitate him. For, the beggar, the blind man, he who had never seen Christ, showed the greatest of courage at the outset, even before Christ's heartening words. Withstanding the whole crowd—murderous, devilish, furious—that wished to condemn Christ by what he said, he did not yield or give way, but very boldly refuted them. He chose to be turned out, rather than to betray the truth.

By contrast, we have lived for so long a time in the faith. By our faith we have seen countless miracles. We have received greater benefits than the blind man and, gazing with our inward eyes, have beheld ineffable mysteries. Since we have been called to such great honor, how much more than the blind man ought we to show the staunchest courage in behalf of Christ against those who are trying to indict Him and who are maligning Christians? We ought to silence them, and not make allowance for them at all.

Moreover, we shall be able to do this if we are brave, and also if we pay attention to the Scriptures and do not listen merely cursorily to them. If a man should come here with earnestness—even though he does not read the Scriptures at home—and if he pays attention to what is said here, within the space of even one year he will be able to obtain a considerable acquaintance with them. For we do not read these Scriptures today, and tomorrow others that are quite different, but always the same section and consecutively.

However, in spite of this, many have such an apathetic attitude that after such reading they do not even know the names of the books. And they are not ashamed, nor do they shudder with dread, because they have come so carelessly to the hearing of the word of God. On the other hand, if a musician, or a dancer, or anyone else connected with the theater should summon them to the city, they all hurry eagerly, and thank the one who invited them, and spend an entire half-day with their attention fixed on the performer exclusively.[10] Yet, when God addresses us through Prophets and Apostles, we yawn, are bored, become drowsy.

Furthermore, in the summer the heat seems to be oppressive, so we seek out the market-place; and in winter, on the other hand, the wet and mud are obstacles, so we sit at home. But at the race-track,[11] though there is no roof to keep off the moisture, most men foolishly stand enduring the heavy showers, while the wind whips the water into their faces, and they make no account of cold and wet and mud and a long journey. Nothing keeps them home or prevents them from going there, while they delay and do not assemble here where there is a roof over their heads and the temperature is admirable. Yet this is for the profit of their own soul.

How is this state of things tolerated, I ask you? Because we are more conversant with worldly pursuits, while we are more ignorant than children in those that are essential to salvation. Furthermore, if someone calls you a charioteer or dancer, you say you are insulted and do everything to avert the insult from

---

10 For a good picture of the fourth-century preoccupation with the theater as an amusement, see Puech, *St. Jean Chrysostome et les moeurs* 266-287.

11 Enthusiasm for racing as an amusement was widespread in the Roman Empire to the end of antiquity. The races were one of the attractions for which both Antioch and Constantinople were very famous. See Bussemaker and Saglio, 'Circus,' *DS* 1² (1887) 1187-1201.

yourself.[12] But if, on the contrary, he invites you to the show in which the charioteer or dancer appears, you do not refuse, and you patronize almost in its entirety that art the name of which you shun. But where you ought to cherish both the state and the name—that is, both to be a Christian and to be called such—you do not even know what in the world it is all about. What could be worse than this ignorance?

I should like to make these remarks frequently to you, but I fear that I should be making myself unpleasant to you in vain and without profit. For, I see not young men only, but even aged ones making fools of themselves. I am especially ashamed, with regard to the latter group, when I see a man, respected for his gray hairs, bringing shame on them, and dragging his son down with him. What indeed is more ridiculous than this? What deed more disgraceful? The child is taught by his father to lead a corrupt life.

Do my words prick you? I want them to do so; I want to place a restraint on you by means of the compunction aroused by my words, that you may reform your bad conduct in these matters. Now I say this for there are some, much less responsive than this audience here, who do not become ashamed at my words, but even speak at length in defense of their behavior. And if you ask: 'Who is Amos, or Abdias, or what is the number of the Prophets or of the Apostles?' they cannot even open their mouth. But with regard to horses and charioteers, they can compose a discourse more cleverly than sophists or rhetors.

Furthermore, after all this they say: 'What harm, now?' and 'What loss?'

Indeed, it is for this reason that I am groaning, namely, be-

12 Despite the enthusiasm generally felt for racing and the theater as amusements, the profession of charioteer, as well as that of dancer, was held in low esteem. Cf. Bussemaker and Saglio, *loc. cit.* 1196; L. Gougaud, 'Danse,' *DACL* 4 (1920) 248.

cause you do not know that the thing is harmful, and have no perception of the evil. God has given you a limited period of life to serve Him, and if you squander it vainly, and fruitlessly, and to no purpose, do you still seek to learn what the loss is? If you completely squander a little money, you deem this a loss, but when you squander your days entirely on Satan's pomps, do you consider that you are not doing anything wrong?

Though you ought to spend your entire life in prayers and supplications, while actually you waste your life, fruitlessly and for your damnation, in shouting and tumult and base words and quarreling and unlawful pleasure and deeds of sorcery—even after all this do you ask: 'What loss is there?' You are not aware that time must be expended more sparingly than anything else. If you spend gold, you will be able to replenish your supply, but if you lose time you will repair the loss with great difficulty, for a small amount has been dispensed to us in the present life. Therefore, if we do not use it as we ought, what shall we say when we depart to the next life?

Moreover, tell me this: If you bade one of your sons to learn a craft, and then he remained always at home, or spent his time somewhere else, would the master not entreat him to act differently? Would he not say to you: 'You made a written agreement with me and specified a limited time. Well, then, if your son is not going to spend this period of time with me, but elsewhere, how shall we present him to you as our pupil?'

Now, we also must say this, and God likewise will speak in this way to us. 'I have given you time,' He will say, 'to learn this art of piety; why have you spent this time vainly and fruitlessly? Moreover, why did you not unceasingly accompany your master, and why did you not pay attention to his words?'

Indeed, in proof that piety is an art[13] listen to what the Prophet says: 'Come, children, hear me; I will teach you fear of the Lord.' And again: 'Happy the man whom you instruct, O Lord, whom by your law you teach.'[14] Therefore, when you expend time fruitlessly, what defense will you have?

'Still, why is it,' you will say, 'that He has dispensed to us only a small amount of time?'

Oh, what stupidity and ignorance! You ought most of all to be grateful for this: namely, that He has cut short your toils and lessened your labors and has made your rest long— yes, everlasting. In return for this do you find fault and complain?

However, I certainly do not know how we have prolonged our sermon to this point and made it so long. Therefore we must now bring it quickly to an end. And we must do this, for it is characteristic of our wretched nature that while we are here in this place, if the sermon is long, we all grow bored, while there [in the theater], though they enter it at midday, they leave only under the guidance of torches and lamps. Yet, in order that we may not always be finding fault we beg and beseech you in closing: Grant this favor both to us and to yourselves and getting rid of all the rest, let us devote ourselves to spiritual things.

If you do this, we shall receive the favor of joy and happiness, and commendation by reason of you, and recompense for these efforts of ours. On the other hand, you will reap the entire reward because, though previously such a devotee of the stage, influenced by the fear of God and our exhortation, you have rescued yourselves from that plague and broken your bonds and hastened to God. Moreover, not only will you receive your reward in the next life, but even in this life you will enjoy genuine happiness. Indeed, virtue is like that;

---

13 That is, a skill to be learned from a teacher.
14 Ps. 33.12; 93.12.

besides the crowns made ready in the next life, it makes our life sweet even here.

Let us, then, be won over by what has been said, in order that we may attain to the blessings both in this life and in that to come, by the grace and mercy of our Lord Jesus Christ. Glory be to Him and to the Father, together with the Holy Spirit, forever and ever. Amen.

Homily 59 (John 9.35-10.13)

'And they turned him out. Jesus heard that they had cast him out, and when he had found him, said to him, "Dost thou believe in the Son of God?" He answered and said, "Who is he, Lord, that I may believe in Him?" '[1]

Those who endure some terrible suffering and are insulted for the sake of truth and the confession of Christ are the ones particularly held in honor by Him. For, just as the man who loses his wealth for His sake is the one who finds it before all others, and the man who hates his life is the one who especially loves it, so also the man who suffers insult is held in honor most of all. And this also happened in the case of the blind man.

Therefore, the Jews turned him out of the Temple and the Lord of the Temple found him. He was rid of the disease-ridden assembly and attained to the saving Fountain. He was dishonored by those who dishonored Christ and was honored by the Lord of the Angels. Such are the rewards of truth.

Similarly, if we also dispense our wealth here, we shall find ease in the next world. If we give to the needy, we shall have rest in heaven. If we are insulted for God's sake, we shall be honored both in this world and in the next. Furthermore, since they had turned him out of the Temple, Jesus found

1 John 9.35-37.

him. The Evangelist pointed out that He came there for the purpose of meeting him. And what reward He conferred on him: the best of blessings. And I say this for He made Himself known to him who before did not know Him and included him in the company of His own disciples.

Moreover, notice how the Evangelist told of His solicitude. For when Christ said: 'Dost thou believe in the Son of God?' he answered: 'Who is he, Lord?' Not yet, to be sure, did he know Him, though he had been cured by Him. He was blind before coming to his Benefactor, and after the cure he was maltreated by those dogs. Therefore, like some judge of the games, He welcomed him as an athlete who had been through many hardships and had been crowned.

Yet, what did He say? 'Dost thou believe in the Son of God?' What is this? After such refutation of the Jews, after such words as his, does He ask whether he believes? He did so, not out of ignorance, but in the desire to make Himself known and to show how much He esteemed the man's faith. He meant: 'So many people have insulted Me, but I make no account of them. I am concerned about one thing only: namely, that you believe in Me. For, one man who does the will of God is better than thousands who transgress it.

'Dost thou believe in the Son of God?' He was asking the question of him, as it might be asked by one who had been present and had heard his words and first He awakened in the man the desire for Himself. He did not say at once: 'Believe in Me,' but addressed him in the form of a question. What, then, did the other reply? 'Who is he, Lord, that I may believe in him?' These were the words of a loving soul that was earnestly seeking Him. He did not recognize Him whose cause he had so valiantly espoused, in order that you might learn his honesty. For, actually, he had not seen Christ before this moment.

He said to him: 'Thou hast both seen him, and he it is who

speaks with thee.' He did not say: 'I am he,' but was as yet restrained and ambiguous in what He said. The words, 'Thou hast both seen him,' were still not clear; therefore, He added more explicitly: 'He it is who speaks with thee.'

He replied: 'I believe, Lord,' and at once 'he worshiped him.'

Now, Christ did not say: 'I am the one who healed thee and said to thee, "Go wash in the pool of Siloe," ' but without mentioning all those details He said: 'Dost thou believe in the Son of God?' Then, the man at once worshiped Him with a display of deep feeling. This was something that few of those who were healed did; for example, the lepers, and perhaps others. By this action the man showed his belief in Christ's divinity, for he added the prostration in order that no one might think that what he said was merely words.

When he had worshiped Him, Christ said: 'For judgment have I come into this world, that they who do not see may see, and they who see may become blind.' Paul, too, said this: 'What then shall we say? That the Gentiles who were not pursuing justice have secured justice, but a justice that is from faith in Jesus; but Israel, by pursuing a law of justice, has not attained to the Law of justice.'[2] Further, by saying: 'For judgment have I come into this world,' Christ was both causing the man to be more earnest with regard to his faith, and stirring up the faith of those who were then accompanying Him, and He did so for there were Pharisees with Him.

Moreover, by the words 'for judgment' He meant 'for greater punishment,' pointing out that those who condemned Him were themselves condemned, and those who sentenced Him as a sinner were sentenced themselves. Here He was speaking of two kinds of sight and blindness: one physical, the other spiritual. Some of those who were with Him said

---

2 Rom. 9.30,31.

to Him: 'Surely we are not blind?' Just as they had said on another occasion: 'We have never yet been slaves to anyone; we have not been born of fornication,'[3] so here also they prated only of the things of sense and were ashamed of physical blindness.

Next, to show that in their case it was better to be blind than to possess sight He said: 'If you were blind, you would not have sin.' Since they thought that this misfortune was something to be ashamed of, He turned it back upon their own heads by telling them: 'This would make your punishment less severe.' As always, He was putting an end to human reasoning and leading them on to a great and wonderful consideration. 'But now you say, "We see." ' Here He was speaking as He had on that other occasion, when he declared: 'Of whom you say that He was your God.'[4]

'But now that you say that you see, you do not see.' By these words He pointed out that the power of sight, which they considered a creditable thing, actually could be for them a cause of punishment. Moreover, after He had consoled the man blind from birth for his former blindness, then He discussed the question of their blindness. Indeed, He confined Himself altogether to the subject of blindness in what He said, in order that they might not claim: 'It is not because we have the defect of blindness that we do not come to You but we avoid You as we would a false teacher.'

Accordingly, it was not merely casually that the Evangelist mentioned: 'Some of the Pharisees who were with him heard this and said, "Are we also blind?" ' He noted this fact deliberately, to remind you that these were the ones who had before turned from Him and then attempted to stone Him.[5]

---

3 John 8.33,41.
4 Cf. John 8.54.
5 Cf. John 8.33-59.

They were typical of those who followed Him indifferently, and who were easily influenced to turn against Him.

How, then, did He prove that He was not a false teacher, but a true shepherd? He set forth the well-known marks of each—both of the shepherd, and of the deceiver and despoiler —and from these gave them the means of discovering the truth. First of all, He made it clear who the false teacher and thief is, giving him these names with reference to Scripture, and saying: 'Amen, amen, I say to you, he who enters not by the door into the sheepfold, but climbs up another way, is a thief and a robber.'

See the marks of the robber: first, that he does not enter openly; second, that his approach is not in accordance with Scripture, for this is the meaning of 'not by the door.' Further, by these words He was making veiled reference both to the false teachers before Him and to those who would be after Him, both to Antichrist and to false Christs: Judas, and Theodas[6] and many others like them.

With good reason did He call Scripture a 'door.' For it leads us to God and opens to us the knowledge of God; it makes us His sheep; it guards us; and it does not permit the wolves to enter. Indeed, just as a door provides security, so Scripture prevents the entrance of heretics, places us in safety with regard to all our desires, and does not permit us to go astray. If we do not remove it, we shall not easily be overcome by our enemies. By means of it we shall be able to discriminate between all men: both the true shepherds and those who are not.

'But what is the meaning of "into the sheepfold"?'

It refers to the sheep and their care. For he who does not use the Scriptures, but climbs up another way to the sheep, that is, opens up another—and not legitimate—way for him-

---

6 He cannot be identified with absolute certainty; cf. Acts 5.34-36 and Confraternity *Commentary* 378.

self is a thief. Do you perceive from these words that Christ
was in complete agreement with the Father, since He brought
the Scriptures to the fore in support of what He said? Furthermore, that is also the reason why He had said to the Jews:
'Search the Scriptures,' and had cited Moses, and had called
him and all the Prophets to bear witness [to Himself]. 'For
all who listen to the Prophets will come to me,' He declared.
And 'If you believed Moses you would believe me also.'[7]

In the present passage, too, He was expressing the same
idea metaphorically. By saying 'climbs up another way' He
was referring indirectly to the Scribes, because they were
'teaching for doctrines precepts of men' and were transgressing the Law.[8] Therefore, to reproach them with this,
also, He said: 'None of you observes the Law.'[9] Moreover,
He did well to say 'climbs up,' instead of 'enters,' since this
is typical of a thief who wants to get over a wall and who
runs very great risk in all he does. Do you see how accurately
He described the robber? Notice, also, the distinguishing traits
of the shepherd.

What, then, are they? 'He who enters by the door is
shepherd of the sheep. To this man the gatekeeper opens,
and the sheep hear his voice, and he calls his own sheep by
name and when he has let out his own sheep, he goes before
them.' Thus, He set forth the marks both of the shepherd and
of the robber. Let us see once more how He applied the
parable to them.

'To this man,' He said, 'the gatekeeper opens.' Now, He
kept to the metaphor in order to make His words more
effective. And if you wish to interpret the parable word by
word, nothing prevents from considering Moses as the gate-

---

7 Cf. John 5.39-47.
8 Cf. Matt. 15.9, quoting Isa. 29.13.
9 John 7.19.

keeper, since it is he who has been entrusted with the words of God.

'The sheep hear his voice, and he calls his own sheep by name.' They were continually saying that Christ was a deceiver, and they lent assurance to this notion by their incredulity in asking: 'Has any one of the rulers believed in him?'[10] Consequently, He made it clear that He ought not be called dangerous and deceiving because of the unbelief of those men, but that they themselves ought to be so called, because they did not pay attention to Him, and as a result they ought to be cast quickly out of the sheepfold.

Now, if it is the part of a shepherd to enter by the customary door, and if He Himself did enter by it, all those who follow Him would qualify as sheep. On the other hand, those who are estranged from Him do not cast aspersion on the Shepherd, but deprive themselves of belonging to His flock. Yet, because He went on to say that He is 'the door,' once again you ought not to be disturbed, for He also said that He is 'Shepherd' and 'Sheepfold' and by these different appellations proclaimed the different manifestations of His providence. When He is conducting us to His Father, He calls Himself a door, but, when He is caring for us Himself, He calls Himself a shepherd. Indeed, that you may not think that His only function is to lead you to the Father, He calls Himself a shepherd, also.

'And the sheep hear his voice, and he calls his own sheep by name and leads them forth, and he goes before them.' Actually, shepherds do the opposite and follow their sheep from behind. However, He Himself, to show that He will lead all men on the road to the truth, does just the opposite to what other shepherds do; therefore, when He sent His disciples like sheep, He did not send them away from the

---

10 John 7.48.

wolves, but into the midst of wolves.[11] This 'shepherding' is in truth a much more remarkable one than ours.

Moreover, He seems to be referring indirectly also to the blind man. And I say this for after summoning him He led him forth from the midst of the Jews, and the man heard His voice and recognized it.

'But a stranger they will not follow because they do not know the voice of strangers.' Surely He here meant Theodas and Judas (and I think this for Scripture says: 'All who believed in them were dispersed'),[12] or else those who later would practice deception as false Christs. Indeed, in order that they might not assert that He was one of these, He differentiated Himself from them by many distinctions.

Now, the first distinction He made was that He taught from the Scriptures, for He Himself attracted His disciples by this means, while those others did not draw theirs after them by that agency. The second distinction He made was the obedience of the sheep, for all believed in Him not only during His lifetime, but also after His death; whereas they at once abandoned those others.

Further, in addition to these we can mention a third distinction—and no trifling one. For those others acted tyrannically and did everything with an eye to revolt, whereas He has so far removed Himself from suspicion of this that He fled from those who wished to make Him king. Moreover, when they asked whether it was permissible to give tribute to Cæsar, He bade them to pay it, and He Himself produced the didrachma.[13] Besides this, He came Himself for the salvation of the sheep 'that they might have life and might have it in abundance,' He declared; while they have deprived their followers even of the present life.

---

11 Cf. Matt. 10.16.
12 Acts 5.36,37.
13 Cf. Matt. 17.23-26.

Moreover, they have betrayed those who believed in them
and then have fled, while He was so faithful that He even
gave up His life. Then, too, they endured their sufferings
unwillingly and under compulsion, while He bore all willingly
and of His own free choice.

'This parable Jesus spoke to them, but they did not understand what he was saying to them.' Now, why did He speak
obscurely to them? Because He wished to make them more
attentive. Therefore, when He had effected this, He at length
put an end to the obscurity by speaking as follows: 'I am the
door. If anyone enter by me, he shall go in and out, and shall
find pasture.' That is, 'He will be in safety and security' (and
in the word 'pasture' He included the care and nourishment
of the sheep and supervision and guardianship over them),
and 'he will remain inside and no one will put him out.'
This, accordingly, actually happened in the case of the
Apostles who came in and went out freely as if they had
become masters of the whole world, and no one was powerful
enought to hinder them.

'All whoever have come are thieves and robbers; but the
sheep have not heard them.' Here He was not, as the heretics
claim, speaking of the Prophets (for whoever have believed
in Christ have heard them and have believed through them).
On the contrary, He meant Theodas and Judas and the other
fomenters of dissent. Furthermore, He was speaking in commendation of the sheep when He said: 'The sheep have not
heard them,' but nowhere can He be found praising those
who have failed to listen to the Prophets. On the contrary,
He very vehemently reproached and upbraided them. From
this it is clear that the words, 'have not heard them,' referred
to those dissenters. 'The thief comes only to steal, and slay,
and destroy'— as happened at that time since all were slain
and perished.

'I came that they may have life, and have it more abundantly.' Now what, I ask, is more abundant than life? The kingdom of heaven. However, He did not yet say this, but applied to it the name of 'life,' which was familiar to them.

'I am the good shepherd.' Here at length He was speaking of His Passion and making it clear that this would take place for the salvation of the world and that He would go to it not unwillingly. Then He again mentioned the example of the shepherd and the hireling. 'The shepherd lays down his life. But the hireling, who is not a shepherd, whose own sheep are not, sees the wolf coming and leaves the sheep and flees. And the wolf comes and snatches them.' Here He was pointing out that He was as powerful as His Father, if He Himself also was shepherd and the sheep were His own.

Do you perceive that when employing parables He spoke in a more sublime tenor, since there His words are shrouded in obscurity, and He was not providing His hearers with ready occasion for criticism? What, then, does this hireling do? 'He sees the wolf coming and leaves the sheep. And the wolf comes and snatches them.'

This is what those others have done, but He did the opposite. And I say this, for when He was arrested, He said: 'Let these go their way,' that the word might be fulfilled that no one of them should perish.[14]

Here it is also possible to interpret the 'wolf' as a spiritual one, for He did not permit him either to snatch the sheep. Indeed, he is not only a wolf, but also a lion, 'For our adversary the devil,' Scripture says, 'goes about as a roaring lion.' And he is likewise a serpent and a dragon: 'Tread upon serpents and scorpions.'[15]

Wherefore, I beseech you, let us remain in the care of the Shepherd, and we shall remain there, if we listen to His voice, if we obey Him, if we do not follow anyone else. Now,

14 Cf. John 18.8.
15 1 Pet. 5.8; cf. Luke 10.19.

what is His voice like? 'Blessed are the poor in spirit; blessed
are the pure of heart; blessed are the merciful.'[16] If we put
these beatitudes into practice, we shall remain in the care
of the Shepherd, and the wolf will be unable to come inside
the fold. However, even if he should attack, he will do this
for his own destruction, for we have a Shepherd who loves us
so dearly as to lay down His life for us. Therefore, since He is
powerful and loves us, what prevents us from being saved?
Nothing—unless we ourselves should put an obstacle in the
way.

How shall we do that? Listen to Him saying: 'You cannot
serve two masters, God and mammon.'[17] Therefore, if we
serve the one, we shall not be subject to the tyranny of the
other. I say this for the desire for money is more bitter than
any tyranny. Indeed, it brings no pleasure, but only cares,
and envy, and scheming, and hatred, and slander, and countless hindrances to virtue: laxity, licentiousness, greed, drunk-
enness. These make even free men slaves and worse than
slaves bought with silver; slaves, not of men but even
of the most serious of the passions and of the diseases of the
soul. Such a man dares to do many things displeasing both
to God and to men, lest someone may deprive him of this
slavery. Oh, bitter slavery and devilish tyranny, for this is
the harshest one of all because, though beset by such great
evils, we take pleasure in them; we cling to our bonds.
Though dwelling in a prison full of darkness, we do not wish
to go out into the light, but fasten the evils tightly to ourselves and revel in our disease.

Therefore, we cannot be rid of it, but are worse off than
those who dig mines: enduring toils and hardship, but not
enjoying the fruits of them. The worst thing of all is that if
someone wishes to free us from this bitter captivity, we do not

16 Matt. 5.3,8,7.
17 Matt. 6.24.

tolerate it, but are displeased and angry, no better disposed than madmen in this. Rather, we are even much more wretched than any of them, to the extent that we do not wish to be rid of our madness.

Surely it was not for this that you were brought into this world, O man? Surely it was not for this that you were created a man, namely, that you might work these mines and amass gold? Not for this did He form you in His image, but that you might be pleasing to Him, that you might attain to the blessings to come, that you might take part in the chorus of the angels.

Why, then, do you separate yourself from such kinship and thrust yourself into the lowest degree of dishonor and ignobility? He who has been born of the same birth-pangs as you, spiritual birth-pangs I mean, is perishing of hunger, while you are bursting with an abundance of wealth. Your brother has his body naked, while you add new raiment to your store of clothing, furnishing such an array for the worms.

Now, how much better to deck out the bodies of the poor? In this way your wealth remains incorruptible and you are free from all care and are preparing for yourself the life to come. If you do not wish these things to become motheaten, give them to the poor, because they are the ones who know how to shake out these garments well. I say this for the Body of Christ is more precious and safer than any chest. Indeed, not only does it preserve your garments, not only does it keep them from corruption, but it even makes them more beautiful.

Oftentimes, if the chest perishes together with the garments, you suffer the greatest loss, while not even death can injure this kind of safeguard. Here we have no need of doors and bolts or of watchful servants, or of any other such protection. And this is so for our possessions are free from every kind of treacherous attack and are kept carefully stored up, as is befitting things in heaven, for that place is altogether impregnable to every evil.

However, though we do not cease continually saying these things to you, you are not persuaded when you hear us. And the reason for this is that we mortals are possessed by an ignoble soul which clings to earth and grovels on the ground. Yet, may I not charge all of you with wickedness as if you were all sick of an incurable malady! For, even if those who are drunk with riches stop up their ears to my words, those who live their lives in poverty will be able to give attention to what I say.

'But what concern are these words to the poor?' you will ask. 'They certainly have no gold or such garments as these.'

Nevertheless, they have bread and cold water; they have two oboli and feet, so that they may visit the sick. They have a tongue and speech, so as to offer consolation to the afflicted. They have a house and roof, so that they may make the stranger welcome to their home. Indeed, we do not require such and such a number of talents of gold from the poor, but we expect these from the rich. Moreover, if a man be poor and come to the doors of the other poor men, our Lord is not ashamed to accept an obol, but will even say that He has received something greater from him than from those who have cast in much.[18]

How many men who are now living have envied the privilege of having lived at that time when Christ went about the earth in the flesh, that one might share one's home and one's food with Him! Behold, it is possible for this to take place now, and for us to extend to Him a more pressing invitation to a meal, and to dine with Him, and with greater profit. For, many of those who were then companions at table with Him have even been lost, as Judas also was, and others like him; while each one of those who now invite Him to

18 Cf. Mark 12.41-44.

their home and share with Him their table and roof will enjoy great blessing.

'Come, blessed of my Father,' He says, 'take possession of the kingdom prepared for you from the foundation of the world; for I was hungry and you gave me to eat; I was thirsty and you gave me to drink; I was a stranger and you took me in; sick and you visited me; I was in prison and you came to me.'[19] Therefore, in order that we may hear these words, let us clothe the naked, let us take in the stranger, let us feed the hungry, let us give drink to the thirsty, let us visit the sick, let us go to see the prisoner, in order that we may receive the fulfillment of His pledge and pardon for our sins, and may share in those blessings which are too great for speech or thought.[20]

May we all attain these by the grace and mercy of our Lord Jesus Christ. To Him be glory and power forever and ever. Amen.

Homily 60 (John 10.14-21)

'I am the good shepherd, and I know mine and mine know me, even as the Father knows me and I know the Father; and I lay down my life for my sheep.'[1]

A great thing, beloved, a great thing is the role of leader in the Church. It is one that requires much wisdom, and as great courage as Christ's words indicate: namely, sufficient to lay down one's life for the sheep; sufficient never to leave them unprotected and exposed to danger; and sufficient to stand firm against the attack of the wolf.

In this respect, indeed, the shepherd is different from the

---

19 Matt. 25.34-37.
20 Cf. 1 Cor. 2.9.

---

1 John 10.14-16.

hireling. The latter always looks out for his own safety, neglecting that of the sheep, whereas the shepherd ever cares for the safety of the sheep and pays no attention to his own. After pointing out the marks of the shepherd, then, He described two despoilers of the flock: the thief who slays and robs; the other who does none of these things, to be sure, but who does not pay any attention when they happen, nor does he prevent them.

By the first He was making a veiled reference to the followers of Theodas, and by the second He was exposing the teachers of the Jews who did not make provision for the sheep entrusted to their care or show any concern for them. Therefore, Ezechiel of old also reproached them with this and said: 'Woe to the shepherds of Israel! Surely shepherds do not feed themselves? Do not the shepherds feed their flock?'[2] On the contrary, they were doing the opposite, which is the greatest kind of wickedness, and cause of all the others. Indeed, that is why the Prophet added: 'They did not pay any attention to the sheep that had gone astray, nor did they seek that which was lost, nor bind up the one which was injured, nor heal the sick one, because they fed themselves and not the flock.'[3] Further, Paul also clearly stated this in another context when he said: 'For they all seek their own interests, not those of Jesus Christ'; and again: 'Let no one seek his own interests, but each one those of his neighbor.'[4]

However, Christ set Himself off from both types: from those who come to destroy, by saying: 'I came for this reason, that they may have life and have it more abundantly.' On the other hand, He showed that He was different from those who neglect the flock when it is being preyed on by wolves, since He did not neglect them and even laid down His life for them

2 Cf. Ezech. 34.2.
3 Cf. ibid. 34.4.
4 Phil. 2.21; 1 Cor. 10.24.

so that the sheep might not perish. That is why He said repeatedly: 'I am the good shepherd.'

Next, because His claims seemed unsubstantiated (for, though the words, 'I lay down my life,' would be fulfilled not long after, the others, 'That they may have life, and have it more abundantly,' would materialize only after their departure from this world, in the life to come), what did He do? He established the truth of one statement by the other: by laying down His life He showed that He also would give life. Moreover, Paul likewise said this: 'If when we were enemies we were reconciled to God by the death of his Son, much more, having been reconciled, shall we be saved'; and again: 'He who has not spared even his own Son but has delivered him for us all, how can he fail to grant us also all things with him?'[5]

But why did they not now reproach Him as before, when they said: 'Thou bearest witness to thyself. Thy witness is not true'?[6] Because He had often silenced them, and also because greater confidence in Him had been engendered in them by His miracles.

Then, since He had just said: 'The sheep hear his voice and follow him,' lest anyone might say: 'What, then, of those who do not believe?' listen to what He added: 'And I know mine and mine know me.' Paul also made this clear by saying: 'God has not cast off his people whom he foreknew.'[7] And Moses: 'The Lord knows who are his.'[8] 'I am referring to those whom I have foreknown,' Christ meant.

Next, lest you think that the extent of the knowledge [possessed by Shepherd and sheep] is the same, listen to how He corrected this idea by what He added. 'I know mine, and

---

5 Rom. 5.10; 8.32.
6 John 8.13.
7 Rom. 11.1.
8 2 Tim. 2.19.

mine know me,' He said. 'However, the knowledge is not the same.'

'But where is it the same?'

'In my Father and in Me. For in our case, even as the Father knows Me I also know the Father.' Moreover, if He did not wish to make this point, why did He add that statement?

Indeed, since He frequently placed Himself in the ranks of ordinary men, it was lest anyone might think that He possessed this knowledge merely as man that He added: 'Even as the Father knows me and I know the Father. I comprehend him clearly as he does me.' That is also why He said: 'No one knows the Son except the Father, and the Father except the Son,'[9] meaning a certain unique kind of knowledge, and such as no one else can possess.

'I lay down my life.' He kept saying this repeatedly to make it clear that He is not a deceiver. Similarly, when the Apostle wished to prove that his teaching was authentic, as he was delivering his discourse against the false apostles, he supported his case by referring to the dangers and mortal risks he had undergone: 'In lashes above measure, often exposed to death.'[10]

When Christ said: 'I am the Light' and 'I am the Life,' it seemed to the foolish to proceed from conceit. But to say 'I am willing to die' gave rise to no envy, no jealousy. That is why they did not reply to Him at this time: 'Thou bearest witness to thyself. Thy witness is not true.'[11] Great indeed was the solicitude evidenced by His words, if He was willing to give Himself for the sake of those who stoned Him.

For this reason, also, it was a propitious moment to introduce a reference to the Gentiles. And I say this for He asserted: 'Other sheep I have that are not of this fold. Them

---

9 Luke 10.22.
10 2 Cor. 11.23.
11 Cf. John 8.13.

also I must bring.' See, too, that the word 'must' as used here does not mean compulsive force, but that a thing is sure to take place, as if He said: 'Why are you surprised if these are going to follow Me, and the sheep are going to listen to my voice? For when you see others also following Me and listening to my voice, then you will be still more astonished.'

But do not be disturbed because He said: 'that are not of this fold,' for the distinction is merely in regard to the Law, as Paul, too, said: 'Circumcision does not matter, and uncircumcision does not matter.'[12]

'Them also I must bring.' He was pointing out that both groups had been scattered and mixed and had no shepherds— both the Jews and the Gentiles—because the Good Shepherd had not yet come. Then He foretold their union in the time to come: There shall be one fold.' Paul also clearly referred to this when he said: 'That of the two he might create in himself one new man.'[13]

'For this reason the Father loves me, because I lay down my life that I may take it up again.' Now, what could be more humble than this statement, if, indeed, our Master is going to be loved on our account, because He dies on our behalf? What, then, was He without the Father's love before that? Did the Father now begin to love Him, and did we actually become the cause of His love for Him?

Do you see how much He condescended to our lowliness? What was it that He wished to accomplish this time? Since they were saying that He was a deceiver, and was in opposition to the Father, and that He came to corrupt and destroy, He was telling them: 'If nothing else, at least this would impel me to love you: namely, that you are loved by my Father as I am, and I am loved by Him for this reason— because I am to die in your behalf.'

---

12 1 Cor. 7.19.
13 Eph. 2.15.

In addition to this, He wished also to establish the point that it was not unwillingly that He went to His death (for, if it were against His will, how would the deed evoke the Father's love?) and also that this was very much in conformity with His Father's will. If He worded this in a human way, do not be surprised, for we have frequently spoken of the reason for this, and to repeat the same things again would be superfluous and boring.

'I lay down my life that I may take it up again, and no one takes it from me. I lay it down of myself. I have the power to lay down my life and I have the power to take it up again.' Since, indeed, they had often wished to kill Him, He declared: 'If I do not will it, your effort is in vain.' And by the first part of what He said He confirmed the truth of the second point, that is, He attested His resurrection by means of His death. This, in fact, is the strange and wonderful truth. Indeed, both things happened strangely and contrary to the ordinary course of events, so let us examine His words more closely.

'I have the power to lay down my life,' He declared. Yet, who does not have power to lay down his own life? For it is possible for each one who desires to do so to destroy himself. However, He was not speaking in that sense. Then, how?

'I have the power to lay it down in the sense that no one can take my life, if I do not will it, and this is not possible in the case of ordinary human beings.' For we do not have the power to lay down our lives except by killing ourselves. And if we fall victim to conspirators who are in a position to kill us, we no longer have the power to lay down our life or not, as we choose, but even against our own will they will take away our life.

In His case, on the contrary, it was not so, but, even when others were conspiring against Him, He Himself had the power to refuse to lay down His life. Therefore, after declaring: 'No one takes it from me,' He added: 'I have the power to lay down my life'; that is, 'I alone can lay it down,' and this is not true in your case. And this is so because many others are able to take our life away from us. However, He did not say this from the start, for the statement would not have been credible, but when it had received confirmation from His deeds, and when, though they had often conspired against Him, they were not powerful enough to arrest Him (for He escaped from their hands times without number), then at length He said: 'No one takes it from me.' But, if this is true, it also follows that He went willingly to His death. Further, if the latter is true, it also confirms the fact that when He wished to take it up again, He could do so. For, if His death was more than merely human, do not doubt Him for the rest, since the fact that He alone was in control of the laying down of His life proves that He also was able to take it up again by His own power. Do you perceive how He confirmed the second point by the first, and by His death proved that the resurrection was beyond question?

'This command I have received from my Father.' What sort of command is this? To die in behalf of the world.

'Surely He did not first wait to hear it, and then consent; and surely He did not need to learn of it.'

Now, what man with sense would say this? But, just as in the former statement, 'For this reason the Father loves me,' He was making it clear that He willed the attack on His life and was removing the suspicion of His coming in opposition to the Father, so here, in speaking of a command received from His Father, He meant nothing else than 'I do what He wills.' He made this clear in order that, when they killed Him, they would not think that they prevailed over Him because He was abandoned and betrayed by His Father; also, that they might not have grounds for the insults they actually did hurl at Him: 'He saved others, himself he cannot save.' And:

'If thou art the Son of God, come down from the cross.'[14] Yet it was for this very reason that He did not come down, namely, because He is the Son of God.

Then, too, He took precaution lest, on hearing 'the command I have received from my Father,' you might think that His heroic action was merely dictated by another. To anticipate this mistaken idea, He had said: 'The good shepherd lays down his life for his sheep.' By these words He pointed out that the sheep were His and that all of what took place was His voluntary doing and that He did not need a command to compel Him to offer His life. Indeed, if He was in need of a command, how was it that He said: 'I lay it down of myself'? For, one who lays down his life of himself does not need a command.

Moreover, He set down the reason for which He did this. What was it? Because He is a shepherd; yes, the Good Shepherd. And a good shepherd does not need to be urged on to this[15] by another. But if this is so in the case of men, much more is it true as regards God. That is likewise the reason why Paul said: 'He emptied himself.'[16] Therefore the 'command' that is mentioned here has no other meaning than to serve as proof of His complete harmony with the Father. Furthermore, if He speaks so humbly and in human fashion, the reason is the weakness of His hearers.

'Therefore there arose a division among the Jews. Some of them were saying, "He has a devil and is mad. Why do you listen to him?" Others were saying, "These are not the words of one who has a devil. Can a devil open the eyes of the blind?" ' It was, to be sure, because His words were greater than those of an ordinary man and of uncommon quality that they said that He had a demon, after having already

---

14 Matt. 27.42,40.
15 That is, to lay down his life for his sheep.
16 Phil. 2.7.

addressed this insult to Him four times. (And I say this for before this they had said: 'Thou hast a devil. Who seeks to put thee to death?' And again: 'Are we not right in saying that thou art a Samaritan and hast a devil?'[17] And here: 'He has a devil and is mad. Why do you listen to him?') Or, rather, this was not merely the fourth time,[18] but He had heard this often. For the fact that they declared: 'Are we not right in saying thou art a Samaritan and hast a devil?' indicates that they had said this, not twice or three times, but often.

On the other hand, the Evangelist asserted: 'Others were saying, "These are not the words of one who has a devil. Can a devil open the eyes of the blind?" ' Since they were not able to silence His opponents by words, they finally had recourse to His deeds for proof. 'Certainly His words are not the words of one who has a devil. But even if you are not persuaded by His words, you are altogether confounded by His deeds.[19] If they are not the deeds of one who has a devil and are greater than those of an ordinary man, it is evident that they are the deeds of one who has divine power.' Do you follow the argument? For, from the fact that they said 'He has a devil' it is clear that His deeds were regarded as superhuman, but He proved by the character of His deeds that He did not have a devil.

What, then, did Christ reply? He made no answer to these remarks. Before, indeed, He had replied: 'I have not a devil,'[20] but now He did not do so. Since He had provided them with proof by His deeds, He now remained silent. In truth, they were not worthy of a reply, because they had

---

17 John 7.20; 8.48.
18 Though but three instances are actually mentioned, the Benedictine editor thinks the text is unmistakably τέταρτον.
19 Cf. John 10.38.
20 John 8.49.

called Him a demoniac by reason of those deeds because of which they ought to have admired Him and considered Him God. Further, what need was there of refutation by Him, when they were quarreling with one another and uttering recriminations against one another? Therefore, He remained silent and bore it all with meekness. He did so, not for this reason only, but also to teach us to be gentle and patient in all circumstances.

Let us, then, imitate Him. For He did not merely remain silent, but also pressed on again to the attack, and when asked a question, replied and showed the proofs of His foreknowledge. And though He was called a demoniac and a madman by men who had been the recipients of His benefits—not once only or twice, but often—He not only did not defend Himself, but even bestowed benefits upon them unceasingly. Why do I mention good works merely? He even laid down His life for them and by His crucifixion interceded with His Father for them.

Therefore, let us imitate these things. For, being a disciple of Christ means being meek and gentle. And from what source may we draw this meekness? If we are continually mindful of our sins, if we grieve for them, if we weep for them. A soul which habitually feels such contrition does not permit itself to become vexed and angry. In truth, where there is sorrow, anger cannot be; where there is compunction, anger is altogether out of place; where there is contrition of soul, there is no irritation. The soul that suffers the lash of contrition has no time to be aroused to anger, but it groans bitterly and weeps more bitterly.

Now, I know that many laugh when they hear these words, but I do not cease mourning for those who laugh. The present time is the time for mourning and grieving, because we commit many sins in word and deed. But gehenna will receive those who are guilty of such offenses as the above, and likewise the river flowing with a stream of fire, and, hardest of all, loss of the kingdom. With these threats hanging over you, then, do you laugh, and fare sumptuously? Though your Lord is angry and threatening, do you continue to be remiss? Do you not fear lest you may thus kindle for yourself the glowing furnace?

Do you not hear what He cries out every day? 'You saw me hungry and did not give me to eat; thirsty, and you gave me no drink. Depart into the fire which was prepared for the devil and his angels.'[21] This threat, indeed, He utters every day.

'But I did feed Him,' you will protest.

When, and on how many days? Ten or twenty? He wishes not merely that much time, but as long a time as you spend on the earth. The virgins, to be sure, had oil, but not enough for their salvation. And I say this for they lit their lamps, yet were shut out from the bridal chamber, and very rightly so. For they acted presumptuously in snuffing out their lights before the bridegroom came.[22]

Therefore, we need much oil and an abundant supply of mercy. Indeed, hear what the Prophet said: 'Have mercy on me, O God, according to thy great mercy.'[23] Well, then, we also must have mercy on our neighbors in this way: according to the great mercy shown to us. For, we shall obtain the kind of treatment from our Lord that we give to our fellow servants. And what is 'great mercy' like? When we give, not from superfluities, but from our necessities. But if we do not even give from our superfluities, what hope will there be for us? Whence shall we be rid of those sins of ours? Where shall we be able to flee and find salvation? For if the virgins, after such great and so numerous efforts found no encouragement

---

21 Cf. Matt. 25.42,41.
22 Cf. Matt. 24.10-13.
23 Ps. 50.1.

anywhere, who will intercede for us when we hear those fearful words of the Judge Himself as He speaks and reproaches us because 'you did not give me to eat when I was hungry.'

He said: 'As long as you did not do it for one of these least ones, you did not do it for me.'[24] In this He was not speaking only of His disciples, or of those who have adopted the life of monks, but of every one of the faithful. Any man who believes in God, even if he be a slave or a beggar in the market-place, has a right to enjoy all kindness. And if we neglect such a man when he is naked or hungry, we shall hear these words, and rightly so. In fact, what difficult or burdensome thing has He required of us? What that is not, on the contrary, very convenient and easy? For He did not say: 'I was sick and you did not cure me,' but merely: 'you did not visit me.' He did not say: 'I was in prison, and you did not get me out,' but 'you did not come to me.'

Well, then, the lighter the commands, so much the more severe will be the punishment for those who do not obey. What, indeed, is a lighter task than to go and visit the prison? And what task is sweeter? You will see some in fetters, others squalid; some with unkempt hair and clad in rags, others wasting away with hunger and running to your feet like dogs; some with their sides torn by lashes, others just returning, bound, from the market-place. Though they have begged all day, they have obtained not even the food they need; yet in the evening what they have collected painfully and toilsomely is demanded of them by their guards. After this, even if you be of stone, you will be at all events more merciful; even if you are living a soft and extravagant life, you will at least be wiser, because of having seen the condition of mankind in the light of the misfortunes of others. And this is so for you will be strongly reminded of that fearful day [of judgment] and its various punishments.

---

24 Matt. 25.42.40.

Furthermore, as you meditate and ponder over these things, you will completely discard anger, and carnal pleasure, and the love of things of this world, and will make your soul more tranquil than the smoothest of harbors. Also, you will reflect with wisdom upon that judgment, keeping in mind that if such minute planning, and arrangement of details, and inspiring of fear, and uttering of threats exist among men, much more is this so of God. 'For there exists no authority except from God.'[25] If, then, He allows earthly rulers to set up this order of things, much more will He himself do so.

Now, this is the case for, if the fear of the judgment did not exist, all would be lost, since, even though such great punishments do threaten, many men are deserters to the side of evil. If you wisely reflect upon these matters, you will be more readily inclined to show mercy and will enjoy great pleasure as a result—much greater pleasure even than those who return from the theater. For, those who rise from their seats there are on fire, burning with sinful desire. Indeed, when they have seen those lavishly decked out women on the stage, and have received innumerable moral injuries from the sight, they will be no more at peace than a billowy sea, as the impression of the faces, the clothing, the words, the gait, and all the other things, rises before their eyes and lays seige to their souls.

On the contrary, on coming from a visit to the prison, no such motions will affect them, but they will enjoy much tranquility and peace of soul as a result. For the compunction which results from the sight of the prisoners quenches that other fire altogether. Even if a licentious prostitute should meet a man as he is on his way from visiting the prison, it would do the latter no harm. For as one who has finally become immune, he will not thus be caught in the snare of that sight, since the fear of the judgment is at that moment

25 Rom. 13.1.

before his eyes, rather than that wanton face. That is the reason why he[26] who had experienced every kind of carnal pleasure declared: 'It is better to go to the house of mourning than to the house of laughter.' Moreover, in this life he will give evidence of such true wisdom as this, while in the next he will hear words worth innumerable blessings.

Let us not, then, neglect to practice deeds of this kind and to live such a way of life. Even if we should be unable to bring in food or to help by giving money, we still can cheer the prisoners by our words and hearten the soul that is discouraged, and assist in many other ways: for example, by conversing with the jailers, and making the guards more kind. In fine, we shall accomplish some good, whether little or great.

Moreover, if you say that there are not estimable, or upright, or well-mannered men in prison, but rather, murderers, and grave-robbers, and purse-snatchers, and adulterers, and libertines, and men weighted down with many crimes, even by this observation you are showing me the necessity for your visiting there. For we have not been bidden to show mercy to the good, and to punish the wicked, but to show this kindliness to all. Indeed, Scripture says: 'Be as your Father in heaven who makes his sun to rise on the good and the evil, and sends rain on the just and the unjust.'[27]

Well, then, do not bitterly denounce others, or be too severe a judge, but be gentle and kind. We ought to be so for, even if we have not become adulterers, or grave-robbers, or purse-snatchers, we ourselves are guilty of innumerable other offenses that are deserving of punishment. Perhaps we have often called our brother a fool, and this merits hell-fire for us. Or we have looked upon women with unchaste glances, and this amounts to the committing of adultery. Or, most serious of all, we have partaken unworthily of the Mysteries, and this

---

26 King Solomon; Eccle. 7.3.
27 Matt. 5.45.

makes us guilty of the Body and Blood of Christ. Let us not, then, be harsh judges of the rest, but let us reflect on our own guilt and thus we shall stop showing this merciless and cruel attitude.

Apart from this, we can also assert that even there we shall find many estimable men, who frequently are as good as anyone in the whole city. Even that prison where Joseph was contained many criminals; nevertheless, that just man cared for all of them, and his own identity was concealed among the rest. I say this for he was as good as anyone in the whole of Egypt; nevertheless, he lived in the prison, and no one of those in it knew him.[28]

At present, also, then, there are probably many upright and estimable men in prison, even if they are not recognized by all. The service you do to such as these gives you a return for your solicitude on behalf of all the rest. But, even if there be no one of this kind, even in this case you will have generous repayment.

Besides, your Master also did not speak only to the just and flee from the impure. On the contrary, He received even the Canaanite woman with much kindness, and also the Samaritan woman who was under a cloud, and impure besides.[29] Further, He received and restored to spiritual health another harlot, because of whom the Jews even reproached Him, and He allowed His feet to be washed by the tears of the impure woman, to teach us to show a kindly attitude to those who are in sin.[30] Indeed, this is the essence of mercy.

What is it you are saying? Thieves and grave-robbers live in the prison? Tell me, are all the inhabitants of the city just men? On the contrary, are there not many even worse than these, and who commit robbery with greater shamelessness?

---

28 Cf. Gen. 39.20.
29 Cf. Mark 7.24-30; John 4.1-26.
30 Cf. Luke 7.36-50.

The former, to be sure, shield themselves with solitude and darkness, if nothing else, and do these things in secret; while these, discarding false appearances, perform their evil deeds with unmasked faces, since they are men of violence, robbers, and misers. I say this for it is difficult to find a man who is innocent of unjust dealing.

But, if we do not actually rob of gold, or of such and such a number of plethra of land, we nevertheless do the same kind of thing by fraud and theft in lesser matters and in those where we can do so. Whenever, in contracts or in transactions involving buying or selling, we show greediness and try hard to pay less than the value, and do everything to obtain this result, is the deed not robbery? Is it not theft and avarice?

Do not tell me: 'I did not defraud anyone of a house or a slave.' Injustice is measured, not by the size of what is seized upon, but by the intention of the thief. Indeed, injustice means the same thing in great as in small matters, and justice does, also. Further, I call it equally purse-snatching whether a man takes gold by cutting off a purse, or if in buying from some huckster he takes off something fraudulently from the just price. And the man who breaks down the wall and steals something from within is not the only burglar, but also he who corrupts justice and wrongfully takes something from his neighbor. Let us not, then, overlook our own faults and sit in judgment on those of others. When it is the time for mercy, let us not search too closely into evil-doing, but, keeping in mind what we ourselves have been previously like, let us now become clement and merciful.

What, then, was our condition? Listen to Paul as he says: 'For we ourselves also were once unbelieving, unwise, going astray, slaves to various lusts and pleasures, hateful and hating one another.' And again: 'We were by nature children of wrath.'[31] But God, seeing us as it were confined in prison, and

---

31 Tit. 3.3; Eph. 2.3.

bound by cruel shackles, much more weighty than those of
iron, was not ashamed, but came and visited our prison.
Though we were deserving of innumerable punishments, He
brought us forth from there and led us into His kingdom and
made us more resplendent than the heavens, so that we also
might act in the same way according to our power. I say
this for He declared to His disciples: 'If, therefore, I the Lord
and Master have washed your feet, you also ought to wash the
feet of one another. For I have given you an example, that as
I have done to you, so you also should do.'[32] This precept He
recorded not merely with reference to the washing of feet, but
also with regard to all the other things in which He gave us
His example.

Is there a murderer living in the prison? Let us not, despite
this, be faint-hearted in doing him good. Is there a grave-
robber or an adulterer? Still, let us take pity, not on their
evil-doing, but on their misfortune. And frequently, as I have
said, one even will be found there who is superior to any
number of men. Moreover, if you continually visit those in
prison, you will not fail to come upon such a treasure. Just
as Abraham, in giving hospitality to any who chanced to
come, once happened upon angels,[33] so we also will at least
happen upon great men if we do this good work.

But if I may mention something besides: He who receives
a great man is not so much worthy of praise as he who wel-
comes a pitiable and wretched one. For the former presents in
his own life no little reason for treating him well, whereas the
man who has been cast off and put aside by all has but one
refuge, namely, the pity of his benefactor; so that this is un-
adulterated mercy without any admixture. Further, he who
does a service to the man who is esteemed and well known
frequently does it to make a show before the eyes of men,

32 John 13.14.
33 Cf. Gen. 18.

while he who serves the man who is cast aside and despised does this solely because of God's command.[34] That is why we are also commanded, if we make a banquet, to welcome to it the lame and the halt; and if we do a work of mercy we have been enjoined to show mercy to the least important and most ordinary. 'As long as you did it for one of these, the least of my brethren,' He said, 'you did it for me.'[35]

Well, then, since we are aware of the treasure that lies available in prison, let us visit there continually; let us busy ourselves there; and let us turn in that direction our enthusiasm for the theater. Even though you have nothing to bring there, bring the good cheer of your words. God rewards not only him who feeds the hungry but also him who visits those in prison. Indeed, when you go in and hearten the trembling and fearful soul, by offering encouragement, lending assistance, promising to defend, causing it to seek after true wisdom, you will receive no small reward for this, also.

In fact, if you were to speak in such a way outside the prison, many would laugh at you, since they are sated with excessive luxury. Those who are in misfortune, on the contrary, because their feelings are depressed, will pay attention to your words with much docility, and will praise you, and will be better men. When Paul also was preaching, the Jews frequently laughed him to scorn, but the prisoners listened to him in deep silence. In truth, nothing makes the soul so receptive to true wisdom as misfortune, and trial, and impending affliction.

Therefore, keeping in mind all these things—how many blessings we are instrumental in obtaining for those in prison, on the one hand, and how many for ourselves, if we continually spend time in their company—let us generously pass there the time wasted formerly in the market-place and in

---

34 That is, to love one's neighbor as oneself.
35 Matt. 25.40.

profitless pursuits, in order that we may both do benefit to them and prepare joy for ourselves.

Moreover, by bringing it about that God is glorified, we may thus obtain everlasting blessings by the grace and mercy of our Lord Jesus Christ. Through Him and with Him glory be to the Father, together with the Holy Spirit, forever and ever. Amen.

Homily 61 (John 10.22-42)

'Now there took place at Jerusalem the feast of the Dedication, and it was winter. And Jesus was walking in the temple in Solomon's porch. The Jews therefore gathered round him, and said to him, "How long dost thou keep us in suspense?" '[1]

All virtue is good, but especially that of meekness or gentleness. It proves that we are men; it distinguishes us from wild beasts; it makes us fit to dwell in the company of the angels. That is why Christ repeatedly spoke at some length about this virtue and bade us to be meek and gentle.[2]

Moreover, not only did He speak of it, but He also instructed us by His example. At one time He was struck and bore it patiently. At another, He was insulted and plotted against. Yet again, He went forth into the midst of those who were plotting against Him. For it was those who had called Him a demoniac, and a Samaritan, and who had often desired to kill Him, and had stoned Him, who now 'gathered round Him and asked, "Art thou the Christ?" ' Nevertheless, He did not put them off—despite the amount and extent of their treachery—but replied to them with great meekness.

However, we must review the entire context from the beginning. 'There took place at Jerusalem,' the Evangelist

---

1 John 10.22-24.
2 Cf. Matt. 11.29.

records, 'the feast of the Dedication; and it was winter.' This feast was a great and solemn one. For they commemorated with great fervor the day on which the construction of the Temple was completed, after they had returned from their long captivity in Persia.[3] On this day Christ also was in the Temple. For, since His Passion was near at hand, He was at last frequently visiting Judea.

'The Jews therefore gathered round him and said to him, "How long dost thou keep us in suspense? If thou art the Christ, tell us openly." ' Now, He did not reply: 'Why are you coming to Me for information? You have often called Me a demoniac and a madman and a Samaritan; and you have considered Me an enemy of God and a deceiver. Besides, you just now said: "Thou bearest witness to thyself. Thy witness is not true."[4] How is it, then, that you are asking Me questions and wish to get information from Me whose testimony you despise?'

On the contrary, He said nothing of this, though He knew that the intention they had in asking was an evil one. The fact that they 'gathered round him and said to him, "How long dost thou keep us in suspense," seemed to indicate that they had a desire to learn, but actually the intention which they had in asking was corrupt and insincere. Indeed, since His deeds did not allow of slander or contumely, but they were forced to rely on His words, they were repeatedly addressing questions to Him, asking them with a meaning different from the literal sense of their words, in the desire to confound Him by His own words. Because they were unable to make any accusation against Him, based on His deeds, they were in hopes of finding some pretext from what He said.

---

3 The Benedictine editor comments that St. John Chrysostom often calls Babylonia and Assyria 'Persia.' The Feast of the Dedication was celebrated in mid-December and lasted eight days. The event commemorated is recorded in 1 Mach. 4.36-59.

4 John 8.13.

That is why they urged: 'Tell us,' even though He had
often told them. I say this for He said to the Samaritan
woman: 'I who speak with thee am he,' and to the blind man
He said: 'Thou hast both seen him and he it is who speaks
with thee.'[5] Furthermore, He had also said this to these others,
even if not so explicitly, yet in other words. Still, if they were
reasonable, and if they were willing to question Him sincerely,
they would be obliged to acknowledge Him also because of
His words, for He Himself had often proved by His deeds the
point about which they were inquiring.

In actual fact, however, notice their perversity and contentiousness. For, when He preached to them and taught them
by His words, they said: 'What sign dost thou show us?'[6] But
when he furnished proofs by His works, they said to Him: 'If
thou art the Christ, tell us openly.' When His works proclaimed it, they sought for words; and when His words gave
them instruction, they took refuge in deeds, always inclining
to the opposite.

Indeed, the outcome proved that they were not asking for
the sake of getting information. For, though they apparently
considered Him to be so worthy of trust as to be acceptable
even when giving testimony of Himself; they at once stoned
Him when He had spoken even a few words. And so their
gathering about Him and pressing on Him were inspired by
an evil motive.

Besides, the manner of their interrogation of Him bristled
with violent hostility. For they said: 'Tell us openly, if thou
art the Christ, even though in His frequent appearances
during the festivals He had spoken all His words courageously
and had uttered none of them in secret. Yet they addressed
Him with words of doubt by saying: 'How long dost thou
keep us in suspense?' for this reason—that by provoking Him
they might again find some pretext for an accusation.

5 John 4.26; 9.37.
6 Cf. John 6.30.

Indeed, not here only, but also in other instances, and frequently, it is clearly evident that their questions invariably were put for this reason: not to get information, but to indict Him by reason of what He said. I maintain this for, when they came inquiring: 'Is it lawful to give tribute to Caesar or not?' and when they asked about putting away one's wife,[7] and when they inquired about the woman who they said had had seven husbands,[8] they were caught red-handed, since they were bringing up questions to Him, not through a desire for knowledge, but by reason of their evil purpose.

There, however, He reproved them and said: 'Why do you test me, you hypocrites?'[9] to show that He knew their unspoken thoughts. Here, on the contrary, He said nothing like that, to teach us not to reprove on all occasions those who scheme against us, but to endure many sufferings with meekness and gentleness.

Therefore, since it was a stupid thing for them to seek for the testimony of His words, when His works were proclaiming Him, listen to how He replied to them. On the one hand, He subtly conveyed to them that they were asking these questions in a captious spirit and not for the sake of getting information, and at the same time made it clear that He had already sent forth a voice clearer than that of His words, namely, that of His deeds. 'Often have I told you and you do not believe,' He said. 'The works that I do in the name of my Father, these bear witness concerning me.'

Those better disposed than these men were also continually saying this to one another: 'A man who is a sinner cannot work these signs'; and again: 'A devil cannot open the eyes of the blind'; and: 'No one can work these signs, if God is not with him.' Moreover, on seeing the miracles He performed, they said: 'When the Christ comes will he work

7 Matt. 22.17; cf. 19.3.
9 Cf. Luke 20.27-33.
9 Matt. 22.19.

more signs than this man works?' Further, these men themselves desired to believe on the basis of His works since they said to Him: 'What sign dost thou show us, that we may see them and believe in thee?'[10]

Since, then, they were pretending that they would believe merely on His word, though actually they did not believe in Him when He had performed such great works, He reproached them for their wickedness by declaring: 'If you do not believe by reason of My works, how will you believe in Me because of My words?' Therefore, their question was an empty one. 'However, I tell you,' He said, 'and you do not believe me because you are not of my sheep. I, indeed, have fulfilled on my part all the duties which a shepherd ought to perform, and if you do not follow me, it is not because I am not a true shepherd, but because you are not my sheep. For my sheep hear my voice and they follow me. And I give them everlasting life; and they shall never perish, neither can anyone snatch them out of my hand. Because my Father who has given them to me is greater than all; and no one is able to snatch them out of the hand of my Father. I and the Father are one.'[11]

Notice how in the way by which He gainsaid them He was encouraging them to follow Him. 'You do not listen to Me,' He meant, 'because you are not My sheep. Those who do follow Me are the ones who are of My fold.' He said this so that they would try to become His sheep. Then, after telling what rewards they would obtain, He said something startling in order to rouse them and to stir them to wish to follow Him.

'What, then? If no one is able to snatch them because of the power of the Father, have You no power? On the contrary, are You weak in protecting them?'

---

10 John 9.16; 7.31; cf. 2.18.
11 John 10.25-30.

Not at all. And that you may learn that the words, 'The Father who gave them to me' were said for their instruction, to prevent them from declaring once again that He was in opposition to God, after He had asserted: 'Neither shall anyone snatch them out of my hand,' He went on to show that His hand is one with the Father's. If this were not so, it would have logically followed for Him to say: 'My Father who has given them to me is greater than all, and no one is able to snatch them out of my hand.' However, He did not use these words, but: 'out of the hand of my Father.' Then, lest you might think that He Himself is weak, but that the sheep are in safety by reason of His Father's power, He added: 'I and the Father are one.'

It was as if He said: 'It was not because I myself lack power to protect the sheep that I declared that because of My Father no one snatches them, for I and the Father are one.' Here He meant that They are one in power, and I say this for His entire sermon on this occasion centered around this subject. But if Their power is the same, it is quite evident that Their substance also is the same. Since the Jews were engaged in innumerable activities—conspiring, putting people out of the synagogue—He meant that all their schemes were fruitless and in vain. For, 'The sheep are in the hand of my Father,' as the Prophet said: 'I have graven thy walls in my hand.'[12]

Besides, to show that the 'hand' is one, He referred to it at one time as His; at another, as the Father's. Moreover, when you hear the word 'hand' do not think of it as a visible hand, but as power or authority. And if no one could snatch the sheep for the reason that the Father had strengthened the Son, it was a vain gesture to make the statement that follows: 'I and the Father are one.' Indeed, if He were inferior to the Father, the statement would be a very rash one.

---

12 Cf. Isa. 49.16.

Actually, He meant nothing else than the equality of Their power, and the Jews, therefore, well aware of this, were ready to stone Him. However, despite this, He did not disillusion them of this idea, or dispel this suspicion. Yet, if they were entertaining an erroneous suspicion, He ought to have corrected it and said: 'Why are you doing this? I did not say these words to convey the meaning that the Father and I have the same power.' But, as a matter of fact, He did just the opposite, and confirmed their suspicion and offered proof in support of it, even though they were wildly enraged at this.

Indeed, He did not make apology for what He had said, on the ground that it had been badly stated, but, instead, He even reproved them because they did not have a fitting opinion of Him. For, when they asserted: 'Not for a good work do we stone thee, but for blasphemy, and because thou, being a man, makest thyself God,' listen to what He replied: 'If the Scripture called them gods to whom the word of God was addressed, how is it that you say that I blaspheme because I said, "I am the Son of God"?'

That is, He meant: 'If those who have received this prerogative by grace are not reproved when they call themselves gods, how would it be right to find fault with Him who possesses it by His nature?' However, He did not speak in this way as yet, but established this idea later, after first giving in to them and stooping to them in His language and saying of Himself: 'whom the Father has made holy and sent into the world.' After having thus calmed their wrath, He then added the clear-cut statement of fact. He spoke for the moment in a somewhat lowly tenor, so that His words might be accepted, but afterwards He raised them up to a more lofty level by speaking as follows: 'If I do not perform the works of my Father, do not believe me. But if I do perform them, and if you do not believe me, believe my works.' Do you perceive how, as I have said, He was establishing the idea that He is in no respect inferior to the Father, but equal in every respect? Since it was not possible to see His substance, by means of the sameness and identity of Their works He furnished proof of the equality of Their power.

'And what, pray, shall we believe?'

'That I am in the Father and the Father in Me. For I am nothing else than what the Father is, though still remaining the Son. He is nothing else than what I am, though still remaining the Father. If a person knows Me, he knows the Father, also, and has gained knowledge of the Son. But, if the power [of either one] were inferior, then what concerns the knowledge of Him would also be false. For it is not possible to gain knowledge of one substance or power by means of another.

'They sought, therefore, to seize him; and he went forth out of their hands. And again he went away beyond the Jordan where John was at first baptizing. And many came to him; and they were saying: "John indeed worked no sign. All things, however, that John said of this man were true." ' Now, whenever Christ made some great and sublime statement, He then quickly withdrew, giving way to their anger so that their passion was soothed and calmed by His withdrawal. And this, accordingly, He did at this time.

Why did the Evangelist mention the place? In order that you might learn that He went there for this reason: to recall to their minds what was said and done there by John and the latter's testimony to Him. In fact, on going there they did at once remember John, and that is why they said: 'John indeed worked no sign.' Otherwise, what logical connection was there in adding this remark? However, it was because the place brought to their minds the thought of the Baptist, and they had come to recall his testimony. Moreover, see how they wove together indisputable logical reasonings. 'John indeed worked no sign, but this Man does,' they declared. 'From this fact, then, His superiority is quite clear. Therefore, if we believed in John, even though he worked no sign, much more ought we believe in this Man.'

Next, because it was John himself who bore witness to Him, in order that John might not seem unworthy to bear witness because he had worked no sign, they added: 'Even if he worked no sign, nevertheless all things he said of Him were true.' No longer were they proving Christ worthy of belief because of John, but on the contrary they were showing that John was a reliable witness by reason of the things which Christ did. 'Many, therefore, believed in him,' for there were many things attracting them.

Now, I say this for they recalled the words which John had uttered when he called Him 'mightier than he,' and 'light,' and 'life,' and 'truth,' and all the rest. They also remembered the voice which came down on them from above, and the Spirit appearing in the form of a dove at that time, and pointing Him out to all.[13] Besides this, they recalled the proof afforded by His miracles in view of which they finally were convinced. 'For if we ought to have believed in John,' they declared, 'much more ought we to believe in this Man. If we believed in John without miracles, much more do we believe in this Man, after the testimony of John, and since we possess the proof afforded by His miracles.

Do you perceive how much profit they derived from their stay in this place, and from their isolation from wicked men? Because of this He repeatedly led them out and brought them away from evil companionship. And therefore He appeared to do this also in the Old Law, for He separated the Jews from the Egyptians, far away in the desert, and gave them instruction in all things. Moreover, He urged us to do this,

13 Cf. Matt. 3.11-17; John 1.6-34.

bidding us to shun market-places and noisy confusion and to pray in our room in secret.[14] And He gave this advice for a ship sails prosperously, if untroubled by a storm; and a soul likewise, if it is free from worldly cares, remains in a state of tranquility.

Therefore, too, women ought to be better able to live a truly Christian life since they remain, for the most part, closely secluded at home. It was thus, in fact, that Jacob was a plain man, since he dwelt at home and was not involved in the troubles of public life.[15]

'But,' you will say, 'there is much confusion at home, also.'

Yes, when you wish it so, and attract around yourself a host of anxieties. For the man who is greatly preoccupied with the affairs of the market-place and the law-court is completely swamped by worldly cares, as if by a kind of turbulent sea. Since woman, on the contrary, remains at home, as if in some school of asceticism, by keeping her thoughts recollected she will be able to fix her attention on prayer and reading, and the other practices of the Christian way of life.

Further, just as those who dwell in the desert have no one to bother them, so also, because she is always within the house, she can continually enjoy peace and calm. If it should ever be necessary for her to go out, not even then will there be cause for disturbance on her part. Indeed, there are necessary occasions for women to go abroad, whether for the sake of coming to this place,[16] or when the needs of the body must be cared for in the bath. However, she spends the bulk of her time at home, and so it is possible for her both to live as a good Christian herself, and, on welcoming her husband home, to soothe his cares, to mold his character, to cause him to cease from useless or angry thoughts. Thus, she can send

14 Cf. Matt. 66.
15 Cf Gen. 25.27.
16 That is, the church.

him forth again, completely rid of whatever evil effects he had acquired from the market-place, and bearing with him the virtues he has learned at home.

Indeed, nothing—nothing, I repeat—is more potent than a good and prudent woman in molding a man and shaping his soul in whatever way she desires. For he will not bear with friends, or teachers, or magistrates in the same way as with his wife, when she admonishes and advises him. Her admonition, in fact, carries with it a kind of pleasure, because of his very great love of the one who is admonishing him. Moreover, I could mention many men, formerly harsh and stubborn, who have become more tractable by this means. She shares with him his table and couch, the procreating of his children, his spoken words and secret thoughts, his comings and goings, and a great many other things as well. She is devoted to him in all things and as closely bound to him as the body is fastened to the head. If she chances to be prudent and diligent, she will surpass and excel all in her solicitude for her husband.

Therefore, I beseech women to carry this out in practice and to give their husbands only the proper advice. For, just as a woman has great power for good, so also she has it for evil. A woman destroyed Absalom; a woman destroyed Amnon; a woman would have destroyed Job; a woman saved Nabal from being murdered; a woman saved an entire nation.[17]

Furthermore, Debbora and Judith and innumerable other women directed the success of men who were generals.[18] And that is why Paul said: 'For how dost thou know, O wife, whether thou wilt save thy husband?'[19] In his day, too, we see Persis and Mary and Priscilla sharing in the Apostle's difficult trials.[20] You also ought to imitate these women, and mold the

---

17 Cf. 2 Kings 13; Job 2.9-10; 1 Kings 25; Esther 7-8.
18 Cf. Judges 4; Judith 14-15.
19 1 Cor. 7.16.
20 Cf. Rom. 16; 1 Cor. 16.19.

character of your husbands, not only by your words but also by your example.

'But how shall we teach them by our example?'

When your husband sees that you are not an evil woman, or a busybody and a fashion plate, and that you do not demand an extravagant expenditure of money but are content with what you have, then, then indeed, he will bear with you even when you give him advice. If, on the contrary, you show true wisdom in your words, while you do the opposite in practice, he will find fault with you for your very foolish talk.

But when you provide him with instruction, not only by your words but also by your example, then he will both show approval of you and be the more effectively convinced. For example, when you do not look for gold, or pearls, or a very extensive wardrobe, but seek in their stead modest and decorous behavior, and kindness, you both display these qualities in your own character, and in return receive them from his.

If, indeed, you must do something to please your husband, you ought to adorn your soul rather than to deck out—or rather, corrupt—your body. For golden raiment will not make you as lovable and desirable to him as decorum, and tenderness toward him, and willingness to give up your life for him. These are things that more surely captivate your husbands' hearts. In fact, that other kind of adornment is even a source of displeasure to him, since it depletes his wealth and causes him a great deal of expense and worry; while the things I have mentioned, on the contrary, cause the husband to become firmly attached to his wife. Love and affection and mutual attachment do not give rise to worry, nor 'do they make for expense, but quite the opposite. Further, that other kind of adornment begins to pall as it becomes familiar, while that of the soul grows more beautiful day by day, and enkindles a still greater flame of love.

So, if you wish to please your husband, adorn your soul with chastity, piety, and the careful management of your household. These qualities captivate him more and more, and never cease to do so. Old age does not destroy this beauty, or disease cause it to perish. In truth, a long period of time brings the body's beauty to an end and disease destroys it, as do many other things. Beauty of soul, on the contrary, is superior to all these influences. Beauty of body stirs up envy and kindles jealousy, while beauty of soul is immune from disease and altogether free from vainglory.

Thus, affairs at home will run more smoothly and the income will be more adequate, since the gold is not draped around your body, or bound about your hands, but is expended for necessary things, for example, for food for the servants, and the necessary care of the children, and other useful purposes.

But if this is not the case and the wife adorns herself with it for show, while her husband's heart is crushed with worry, what profit is there? What help? If his heart is heavy, this prevents him from even noticing her wonderful display of finery. Indeed, you are aware, you are well aware that even if a man sees his wife decked out as the most beautiful of all women, he cannot take pleasure in the sight if his soul is heavy with anxiety. A man who is to enjoy pleasure must first have a light heart and be in a relaxed frame of mind. If all his gold has been expended in large sums for the adornment of his wife's body, and there is financial difficulty at home, the husband enjoys no pleasure.

And so, if you wish to be pleasing to your husbands, you will put them in a pleasant frame of mind; and you will put them in a pleasant frame of mind if you do away with such adornment and aids to beauty. All these things, to be sure, seem to cause a certain pleasure at the very time of marriage, but at a later time they lose their attraction. Because of our familiarity with the sky, which is so beautiful, and with the sun which is so bright—though we cannot mention any heavenly body equal to them—we do not, nevertheless, marvel at them. How is it, therefore, that we marvel at a human body that has been decked out with finery?

These things I say in the desire for you to be ornamented with the true adornment, as Paul has enjoined: 'Not with gold, or pearls, or expensive clothing, but with good works such as become women professing godliness.'[21] But you wish to be agreeable to outsiders also and to be praised by them? This is certainly not the desire of a decorous woman. Still, if you do wish it, you will also have these as very enthusiastic admirers and extollers of your modest behavior, if you forego lavish adornment. Indeed, no one who is respectable and decent will admire that other type of woman, but only libertines and debauchees; rather, these will not really admire her, but will even revile her when their passions have been inflamed by the sight of the woman's wantonness..

Both kinds of men, on the contrary, will admire the virtuous woman of modest tastes, and all will approve her, since they receive from her no evil influence, but even instruction in the way to live a virtuous life. Moreover, while the praise of men, on the one hand, will be hers in abundance, the reward in store for her from God will be a generous one.

Let us, then, strive after this kind of adornment so that we shall live in this world in security, and may attain the blessings of the world to come. May we all obtain them by the grace and mercy of our Lord Jesus Christ. Glory be to Him forever and ever. Amen.

---

21 1 Tim. 2.9,10.

Homily 62 (John 11.1-29)

'Now a certain man was sick, Lazarus of Bethany, the village of Mary and her sister Martha. Now it was Mary who anointed the Lord with ointment.'[1]

Many men are scandalized when they see those who are pleasing to God enduring some terrible suffering, for example, falling into sickness or poverty or some such thing. They do not know that to have these sufferings is the privilege of those especially dear to God. For Lazarus was one of Christ's friends, and he was sick. Indeed, the messengers sent to Him stated this when they said: 'Behold, he whom thou lovest is sick.'

However, let us look at the account of his affliction from its beginning. 'A certain man was sick,' the Evangelist stated, 'Lazarus of Bethany.' It was not at random or by chance that he mentioned where Lazarus was from, but for a reason that will be explained later. Meanwhile, let us consider the text before us now. To aid us to identify Lazarus, the Evangelist mentioned the latter's sisters and noted besides the privilege Mary was to enjoy later, by saying: 'Now it was Mary who anointed the Lord with ointment.'

With regard to this some are in doubt. They ask: 'How was it that Christ allowed a woman to do such a thing?'

In the first place, they must understand this: that she was not the sinner mentioned in the gospel of Matthew,[2] or the one in the gospel of Luke,[3] for she was a different person.[4] Those others, indeed, were notorious sinners, reeking

---

1 John 11.1-2.
2 At the house of Simon the leper; cf. Matt. 26.6-13.
3 Cf. Luke 7.36-50.
4 Modern exegetes are agreed that she is not to be identified with the one in Luke. But they are of the opinion that Matthew, Mark, and John were all recounting an identical incident. John identifies the woman explicitly as Mary the sister of Lazarus and Martha. Cf. Confraternity *Commentary* 174.

with many vices, while she was devout and zealous. And I say this for she used to show much concern for the hospitable reception of Christ.

Now, the Evangelist pointed out both that the sisters loved Christ, and that He allowed Lazarus to die. But why was it that they did not leave their sick brother and go to Him, as the centurion and the royal official did, but sent messengers to Him? They had the highest confidence in Christ and were on terms of great familiarity with Him. But they were weak women, and were restrained also by their grief, for they made it clear later that they did not act in this way through any lack of respect. It is obvious, therefore, that Mary and that sinner were not the same person.

'But why did Christ receive that sinner?' you will ask.

That He might free her from her sinfulness; that He might show His mercy; that you might learn that there is no disease too powerful for His goodness. Do not, then, consider only the fact that He received her; rather, reflect on that other aspect of the incident: how she became a changed person.

And why did the Evangelist tell us this story[5] in detail? Or rather, what did he wish to teach us when he said: 'Now Jesus loved Martha and her sister, and Lazarus'? That we ought not to complain and bear it hard if those who are exemplary men and friends of God become sick.

'Behold, he whom thou lovest is sick.' They wished to arouse Christ's grief, for they were as yet looking on Him as Man. This is evident from what they said: 'If thou hadst been here, he would not have died'; and also from the fact that they did not say: 'Behold, Lazarus is sick,' but: 'Behold, he whom thou lovest is sick.'

What, then, did Christ reply? 'This sickness is not unto

---

5 That is, of the raising of Lazarus from the dead.

death but for the glory of God, that through it the Son of God may be glorified.' See how once again He spoke of His glory and the Father's as one. For, after saying 'the glory of God,' He added: 'that the Son of God may be glorified.

'This sickness is not unto death.' Since He intended to remain where He was for two days, He sent them back meanwhile to give this message. At this point the sisters are worthy of admiration, for the fact that, though they heard 'is not unto death,' yet saw him die, they did not lose confidence because the outcome was just the opposite, but even so came to Him and did not conclude that He had deceived them.

However, the word 'that' here is used not in a causal sense, but with the idea of result.[6] For the sickness developed from another cause, but He used it for the glory of God. When He had said this, 'He remained two days.' Why did He remain? In order that Lazarus might breathe his last and be buried, that no one might be able to claim that Christ revived a man who was not yet dead; that it was a coma, that it was a faint, that it was a seizure, but not death. And it was for this reason that He remained so long a time, so that corruption of the body might begin and the statement might be made: 'He is already decayed.'

'Afterwards He said to His disciples, "Let us go into Judea." ' Why in the world is it that though He nowhere else gave them notice beforehand [of moving from one place to another], in this instance He did so? They had been extremely fearful and, because they felt that way, He warned them of His intention lest it disturb them by its unexpectedness. But what did the disciples reply?

'Just now the Jews were seeking to stone thee, and dost thou go there again?' They were fearful, then, in His behalf, but more so for their own sake, because they had not yet been

---

6 That is, 'that the Son of God may be glorified.'

'made perfect.'[7] Therefore Thomas, quaking with fear, said: 'Let us also go, that we may die with him,' for he was weaker than the rest, and more lacking in faith.

However, see how Jesus encouraged them by what He said. 'Are there not twelve hours in the day?' He meant either: 'The man who is not conscious of having done any wrong will suffer no dreadful punishment, while he who does evil deeds will suffer it (so that we ought not to be afraid for we have done nothing worthy of death)'; or else: 'He who can see the light of this world walks in safety. And if the man who sees the light of this world is safe, much more is this true of him who is in My company if he does not separate from Me.'[8]

After uttering these words of encouragement, He went on to mention the reason that made it necessary for them to make the journey thither,[9] and He pointed out that they were not going to go to Jerusalem, but to Bethany. 'Lazarus, our friend, sleeps. But I go that I may wake him from sleep'; that is, 'I am not going for the same reason as before, to dispute and contend once more with the Jews, but to arouse our friend from sleep.'

'His disciples said, "Lord, if he sleeps, he will be safe." ' Moreover, they did not say this undesignedly, but in the desire to prevent His going there. They meant: 'You say that he sleeps? Well, then, there is no urgent need for Your departure.' Yet, it was for this reason that He said 'Our friend,' namely, to show that the journey was necessary.

Therefore, since they were somewhat reluctant, He then said: 'He is dead.' He had uttered the first statement as He did, because He did not want to be boastful, but when they

---

7 Cf. John 17.23.
8 See the interpretation placed on this brief parable by the Confraternity New Testament, namely, that in the divine plan Christ was safe until the hour appointed for His Passion.
9 Into Judea.

did not understand, He added: 'He is dead; and I rejoice on your account.' Why in the world 'on your account'?

'Because I have spoken of his death beforehand, when I was not there; and because when I raise him up there will be no possibility for doubt of what I have done.'

Do you see how imperfect His disciples were as yet and that they did not comprehend His power as they should have? And the fears that insinuated themselves were the cause of this, since they disturbed and confused their souls. Moreover, when He said: 'He sleeps,' He continued: 'I go that I may wake him.' On the contrary, when He declared: 'He is dead,' He did not now add: 'I go that I may raise him up.' For He did not wish to make known ahead of time by His words what He intended to affirm by His deeds. This was to teach us always to avoid vainglory and that we ought not to make promises too freely.

However, if He did this when He was appealed to in the case of the centurion (for He said: 'I will come and cure him'), He did so in order to show the faith of the centurion.[10]

Now, someone may say: 'How is it that the disciples conceived the idea that it was literally sleep He meant and did not understand that Lazarus was dead—I mean because He said: "I go that I may wake him"? And I say this for it was stupid if they thought that He was traveling fifteen stadia to wake him from sleep.'

In reply we should say this: 'They supposed that this was a riddle like many things He said.' Accordingly, they all feared the hostility of the Jews, and Thomas was more fearful than all the rest. Therefore he said: 'Let us also go, that we may die with him.'

Some maintain that Thomas himself wished to die, also, but this is not so, for the statement was rather one that proceeded from fear. However, he was not reproved, for

---

10 Matt. 8.7.

Christ still was making allowance for his weakness. Later, in fact, he became strongest of all and even swept all before him. It is indeed a wonderful thing that we see him who was so weak before the crucifixion becoming most fervent of all after the crucifixion, and after he came to believe in the Resurrection. So great is the power of Christ. For, the same man who did not dare to go into Bethany in company with Christ traversed almost the whole world, though he could no longer see Christ, and freely moved about in the midst of murderous people who even wanted to kill him.

'But if Bethany was fifteen stadia distant, and this is but two miles,[11] how was Lazarus dead for four days?'

He remained two days and on the day before these two the messenger had come,[12] that is, on the very day of Lazarus' death. Then, on the fourth day Jesus arrived in Bethany. Now, He waited to be summoned, and did not go uninvited, lest someone might hold in question what was to happen. Further, not even the beloved sisters came, but others were sent.

'Now Bethany was some fifteen stadia distant.' From this it is evident that it was likely that many people from Jerusalem were present there. In fact, the Evangelist immediately added that many of the Jews were comforting them. How could they offer comfort to those who were loved by Christ, despite the fact that they had agreed that, if anyone should confess Christ, he would be put out of the synagogue?

They were there either because of the grave misfortune that had occurred, or out of respect for the noble ladies or, at any rate, they were not of evil intent; and many of them, to be sure, believed in Christ. Further, the Evangelist mentioned these details to confirm the fact that Lazarus was really dead.

---

11 A stade was a measure of distance equivalent to about one-eighth of a Roman mile.
12 To say that Lazarus was ill.

But why in the world was it that the one who came to meet Christ was not accompanied by her sister? She wished to meet Him by herself and to inform Him of what had happened. And when He had inspired her with fair hopes, then she went off and called Mary and the latter went to meet Him, still sunk in the depths of woe. Do you perceive how ardent her love of Him was? She it was of whom He said: 'Mary has chosen the best part.'[13]

'How is it, then,' you will ask, 'that Martha seems more fervent?'

She was not more fervent, for it was not Mary who heard [His words about the resurrection] since Martha was the weaker. Indeed, though she had heard such sublime words, she said afterwards: 'He is already decayed, for he is dead four days.' Mary, on the contrary, though she had listened to no instruction, said nothing of the kind, but merely declared at once, with faith: 'Master, if thou hadst been here, my brother would not have died.'

Do you perceive how much true wisdom the women possessed, even if their understanding was weak? For on seeing Christ they did not immediately begin to lament or to cry or moan, as we are accustomed to do when we see some of our close friends coming in to us in time of sorrow. On the contrary, they at once expressed admiration of their Master. And so they both believed in Christ, but not as was fitting. For they did not yet understand clearly either that He was God or that He performed these miracles by His own power and authority, though He had instructed them regarding both these facts.

Moreover, it is evident from what they said that they did not know this: 'If thou hadst been here, our brother would not have died.' And this is likewise clear because they[14]

---

13 Luke 10.42.
14 Actually, it was Martha alone who said it.

added: Whatever thou shalt ask of God, God will give it to thee,' as if speaking of some exemplary and highly esteemed man. But notice, too, what Christ said. 'Thy brother shall rise.'

That reply answered for the moment the words: 'Whatever thou shalt ask,' for He did not say: 'I am making a petition that he will rise,' but what? 'Thy brother shall rise.' Therefore, if He had said: 'O woman, are you still casting your gaze down to earth? I do not need help from anyone else, but I do everything of myself,' it would have been very confusing and might have offended the woman. However, by now saying merely: 'He will rise,' He made the statement with the moderation which the situation required, and by His next words He hinted at what I have just now said. For when she declared: 'I know that he will rise on the last day,' He more clearly gave evidence of His own authority by saying: 'I am the resurrection and the life.' He made it plain that He did not need anyone to help Him, if He was in truth the life, for if He needed someone how could He Himself be the resurrection and the life? However, He did not yet say this explicitly, but merely hinted at it.

Again, because she said: 'Whatever thou shalt ask,' He Himself replied in turn: 'He who believes in me, even if he die, shall live,' to point out that it is He Himself who dispenses favors and it is necessary to ask them of Him. 'And whoever lives and believes in me, shall never die.' Do you perceive how He conducted her thoughts heavenward? For it was not merely restoring Lazarus to life that was His object here, but it was also necessary for her and those who were with her to learn of the resurrection. Therefore, before actually bringing the dead man to life, it was by His words that He instructed them in true wisdom. But if He is Himself the resurrection and the life, He is not restricted by place, and since He is present everywhere He can heal everywhere.

Therefore, if they had spoken as the centurion did: 'Only say the word, and my servant will be healed,'[15] He would have done this. But since they called Him to them and thought He ought to have come, for this reason He condescended to their wishes and came to the place, so as to raise them up from their lowly opinion of Him.

Nevertheless, though He condescended to them, He continued to show that He was able to heal, even when absent, and that is the reason why He delayed. For the favor would not have been so evident, if given at once and if the fetid odor had not preceded it. Furthermore, how did Martha know about the future resurrection? She had often heard Christ speaking of the resurrection; nevertheless she now had a great desire to see it take place.

Yet, see how confused she still was. For after hearing: 'I am the resurrection and the life,' she did not say, in keeping with this: 'Raise him up from the dead.' On the contrary, what did she say? 'I believe that thou art the Christ, the Son of God.'

What, then, did Christ reply to her? 'Whoever believes in me, even if he die, shall live'—He was referring to the death of the body. 'And whoever lives and believes in me shall never die'—referring to the death of the soul. 'Therefore, since I am the resurrection do not be upset if Lazarus is already dead, but have faith. For actually this is not death.'

He was, for the moment, offering her consolation for what had happened, and holding out hope to her, both by declaring: 'He shall rise,' and by saying: 'I am the resurrection,' and: 'After coming to life if he should die again, it would be no suffering. Hence, thou oughtest not to shudder at this kind of death.'

Now, what He meant is something like this: 'Neither is Lazarus dead, nor wilt thou be. Dost thou believe this?'

---

15 Matt. 8.8.

She replied: 'I believe that thou art the Christ, the Son of God, who hast come into the world.' It seems to me that the woman did not grasp the meaning of what was said. However, she did understand that it was something great, though she did not altogether understand it. That was why, when asked one thing, she replied another. Meanwhile, she gained enough profit so that she brought her grief to an end.

Such, indeed, is the power of Christ's words. That is why, when Martha had gone forth first, Mary followed. For her regard for the Master was not overcome by her strong feeling of grief when she was in His presence. So that, besides being loving, the minds of the women were truly virtuous.

At present, on the contrary, along with the rest of our vices there is one disorder especially prevalent among women. They make a show of their mourning and lamentation: baring their arms, tearing their hair, making scratches down their cheeks. Moreover, some do this because of grief, others for show and vain display. Still others through depravity both bare their arms and do these other things to attract the gaze of men.

What are you doing, O woman? Tell me, do you who are a member of Christ shamelessly strip yourself in the middle of the market-place, when men are present there? Do you tear your hair, and rend your garments, and utter loud cries, and gather a chorus around you, and act like a mad woman, and do you think you are not offensive to God? What great insanity is this?

Will not the heathen ridicule you? Will they not think that our teachings are myths? For they will say: 'There is no resurrection; the Christian teachings are jokes, lies, and tricks. The women among them, in fact, lament as if no one exists after this life. They pay no attention to the words inscribed in their books. And so they show that all those doctrines are mere fancies. For, if they believed that he who has died has not come to an end, but is transferred to a better life, they would not mourn him as one who no longer exists; they would not mutilate themselves so; they would not utter such words, completely lacking in faith, as "I will never see you again; I will never have you back again." All their teachings are fables. Moreover, if the most important one of their blessings is so thoroughly disbelieved, how much more must this be true of the rest of their piety.'

Pagans do not thus play the woman; many among them have lived according to the precepts of true wisdom. For example, a pagan woman on hearing that her son had fallen in battle, at once asked: 'But how are the fortunes of the city getting on?'[16] Furthermore, another true philosopher, who was crowned with a garland, took off the garland when he heard that his son had fallen in behalf of his native land, and asked which of his two sons it was. When he had learned the one who had fallen, he at once donned the garland again.[17]

Many, too, have given up sons and daughters to be sacrificed, to honor demons. Further, the Spartan women even exhort their sons either to bring their shield safely back from war or else to be carried back on it, dead.

Therefore, I am ashamed because the pagans practice such true wisdom, while we act so basely. They who know nothing of the resurrection perform the actions that should be performed by those who know about it, while those who do know about it act like those who are ignorant of it. Besides, many frequently do through human respect what they will not do for God's sake. The wealthier women, indeed, do not tear their hair or expose their arms; yet this is itself altogether blameworthy, not because they do not expose them, but

---

16 Cf. Plutarch, *Moralia* 241C 7.
17 Xenophon. That is, he calmly went on with what he had been doing. Cf. Diogenes Laertius 26, *Xenophon* 54.

because they act in this way, not through piety, but in order not to seem to disgrace themselves. So, then, human respect prevails over grief, while the fear of God does not prevail over it. Yet, is this not deserving of the utmost condemnation? In that case, then, poor women ought to do for the sake of the fear of God what wealthy women do on account of their wealth. However, actually it is just the opposite: the wealthy practice virtue for the motive of vainglory, while the poor act disgracefully because of their ignoble spirit.

What is worse than this discrepancy? We perform all our actions for human considerations; we perform all our actions with material ends in view. Moreover, we utter things full of stupidity and a great deal of nonsense. The Lord said: 'Blessed are they who mourn,'[18] meaning: 'who mourn for their sins,' yet no one mourns with that kind of sorrow or cares about the loss of his soul. But we were not enjoined to do this other thing and we do it.

'What, then,' you will ask, 'is a man not allowed to weep, though he is human?'

I do not forbid this, but I do forbid tearing yourself to pieces; I do forbid weeping without restraint. I am not brutal or cruel; I know that human nature is tried [by the death of dear ones] and misses their companionship and daily converse with them. It is impossible not to show grief. Christ also showed it, for He wept because of Lazarus. Follow His example yourself: weep, but gently, with decorum, with the fear of God. If you weep in this way, you do so, not as if you were without faith in the resurrection, but as one finding the separation hard to bear.

Besides, we also weep for those who are going away from home, or who are going on a journey, but we do not do this as if we were in despair. Weep in this way, then, at the death of a dear one, as if you were bidding farewell to one setting

18 Matt. 5.5

out on a journey. I am telling you this, not as an impersonal rule of conduct, but in consideration of your human nature. For, if the dead man is a sinner who has committed many offenses against God, you ought to weep, or, rather, not only to weep (for that is no help to him), but you ought to do what can give him assistance, namely, give alms and offer sacrifices. Furthermore, you ought to rejoice for this advantage, namely, that the opportunity to do evil deeds has been taken away from him.

On the contrary, if he was a just man, you ought to be still happier, because his fate now rests secure and he is free from uncertainty for the time to come. If he is a young man, you ought to be happy because he has been quickly freed from the evils of this life; if he is old, because he has departed this life after having received in its fullness what seems to be desirable. However, neglecting to consider these truths, you urge on your maid-servants to tear themselves to pieces, as if by this means honoring the departed, while actually it is a mark of the greatest dishonor. Truly, honor for the dead does not consist in lamentations and moanings, but in singing hymns and psalms and living a noble life. For the man who has departed this life will go on his way in the company of the angels, even if no one is present at his funeral; while he who has been corrupt will gain no profit, even if he has the entire city sending him off to the grave.

Do you wish to honor the departed? Honor him in other ways; namely, by giving alms, performing good works, taking part in the divine services. What good is done him by copious weeping? Moreover, I have heard also of another serious fault. I have heard that many women, forsooth, attract lovers by their mournful cries, gaining for themselves the reputation of loving their husbands because of the vehemence of their wailings. Oh, what devilish scheming! Oh, what diabolic trickery! What advantage for us who are but earth and ashes, for us who are but flesh and blood?

Let us look heavenward; let us reflect on spiritual considerations. How shall we be able to refute the heathen? How shall we be able to exhort them if we do such things? How shall we preach to them of the resurrection? How shall we discuss with them the rest of the Christian doctrines? How shall we ourselves live in security? Do you not know that death may be caused by grief? Darkening the soul's spiritual vision not only prevents it from perceiving what it should, but even causes it much harm. By showing excessive grief, therefore, we offend God and help neither ourselves nor the departed.

By restraining our grief, on the contrary, we both please God and conduct ourselves becomingly in the eyes of men. For, if we ourselves do not succumb unrestrainedly to grief, He will quickly take away the portion of grief we feel; whereas, if we give way to excessive grief, He will permit us to become entirely possessed by it. If we give thanks for it, we shall not be disheartened.

'Yet how is it possible for a man not to grieve,' you will ask, 'when he has lost his son, or his daughter, or his wife?'

I am not saying: 'Do not grieve,' but: 'Do not give way to unrestrained grief.' For, if we reflect that it is God who has taken him away, that it was a mortal husband or son we had, we shall quickly feel consoled. Excessive grief indicates that those who give way to it are seeking for something that is above and beyond nature. You were born a man, and therefore mortal; why, then, do you repine because something has happened in accordance with nature? You do not repine, do you, because you are nourished by eating food? You do not seek to maintain your life without this, do you? Act thus, also, in regard to death, and do not try to obtain immortality in the present life, though you are but mortal.

This doctrine has now been once and for all defined. Do not give way to excessive grief, do not tear yourself to pieces, but be resigned to the lot decreed for us all in common. Grieve, rather, for your sins. This is in truth the best kind of sorrow; this is the soundest practice of Christian teachings.

Let us, then, give way to this grief continually that we may obtain joy in the life to come, by the grace and mercy of our Lord Jesus Christ. Glory be to Him forever and ever. Amen.

Homily 63 (John 11.30-41)

'Jesus had not yet come into the village, but was still at the place where Martha had met him. When the Jews who were with her,' etc.[1]

Philosophy is a very good thing—I mean, of course our philosophy. Pagan philosophy, to be sure, is merely talk and fables, and not even the fables themselves possess any trace of true wisdom. In fact, all their teachings are uttered with a view to worldly repute.

Our philosophy, I repeat, is a very good thing and so is profitable to us even in this life. The man who despises wealth derives benefit even now from his philosophy, because it rids him of vain and useless cares. He who treads glory underfoot receives recompense even now from this, for he is a slave to no one, but is free with true freedom. He who desires heavenly things reaps a reward from this, since he counts as nothing all things present and easily prevails over all grief.

See, then, that when this woman[2] put the tenets of Christian philosophy into practice, she also was recompensed thereby. Now, I say this for, though all her consolers were gathered around her as she grieved and mourned, she did not

1 John 11.30,31.
2 Mary.

wait for the Master to come to her, nor did she stand on her dignity, nor was she held back by her grief. I mention this for women who are in grief have along with the rest of their misery this affliction, also: that they wish to be made much of because of their present sorrow. However, she was not affected in this way, but as soon as she heard that He was there she quickly went to Him.

'Jesus had not yet come into the village.' He was walking somewhat leisurely in order that He might not seem to be rushing precipitately upon the miracle, but that it might be evident that He was coming at their request. At least, it was either because the Evangelist wished to hint at this that he said: 'She rose quickly,' or else he was pointing out that she hurried in this way in order to go to meet Him as He came.

Moreover, she did not go alone, but was followed by the Jews who were in her house. Because of their presence her sister very prudently spoke quietly to her, so as not to cause disturbance among those who had gathered there. Mary did not mention the reason why she was going, for many would even have gone away if she had done so. But, as it was, they all followed her as she went, in order to weep with her, and perhaps the fact that Lazarus was really dead was confirmed once again by their presence.

'Now she fell at his feet.' She was more fervent than her sister. She was not embarrassed because of the crowd, or by their suspicious attitude towards Him (for there were even many of His enemies there, and some, to be sure, said: 'Could not he who opened the eyes of the blind have caused that this man should not die?'). However, she cast aside all human considerations, since her Master was present, and she was concerned about one thing only: showing honor to her Master. And what did she say? 'Master, if thou hadst been here, my brother would not have died.'

What did Christ reply? He made no reply to her for the

moment, nor did He repeat those words which He had also addressed to her sister (for the crowd was numerous and it was not the auspicious moment for such words). Instead, He merely asked a non-committal question and so condescended to their weakness. Further, in order to confirm the fact of His human nature, He wept a little and put off the miracle for the present. Indeed, it was to be a great miracle and such a one as He rarely performed, and because of it many were going to believe in Him. Therefore, lest, if it were done in the absence of the crowds, it might prove an obstacle to their faith and they might gain no profit because of its very greatness, He attracted many people as witnesses by means of His humility. And in order that He might not lose the quarry He even displayed a characteristic of human nature, for He wept and was troubled. For He knew that grief arouses sympathy.

Next, having curbed His own display of emotion (for the words: 'He groaned in spirit' mean this—that He outwardly restrained His troubled feelings), He asked the following question: 'Where have you laid him?' And so, the question was asked without any outward manifestation of His grief.

'But why in the world did He ask this question?'

Because He did not wish to force Himself upon them, but to get all His information from them, and to act at their request, so as to free the miracle from all suspicion of fraud.

'They said to him, "Come and see." and Jesus wept.' Do you see that He did not yet make any reference to the miracle of raising Lazarus from the dead, and that He did not approach the tomb as if he were going to raise him up, but as if to weep? For the Jews clearly indicated that He appeared to be going to the tomb to mourn, but not to raise the dead, when they said: ' "See how he loved him." But some of them said, "Could not he who opened the eyes of the blind have caused that this man should not die?" ' Not even in the presence of misfortune did they hold their malice in check. Yet what He was about to do was even more remarkable, for it is a much greater thing to dispel death that has come and conquered than to ward off death that is imminent.

Therefore, they were slandering Him by reason of the very things that should have caused them to marvel at His power. They were now admitting for the moment that He had opened the eyes of the blind, and, though they ought to have been in admiration of Him because of that, by reason of it they even criticized Him on another score, namely, on the ground that another miracle had not taken place.[3] Further, not only by this means were they all proved corrupt, but also because, though He had not yet come, though He had not yet done anything, they lodged their charges ahead of time, without waiting for the final outcome of the incident. Do you perceive how corrupt their judgment really was? He came, then, to the tomb and again He curbed His emotion.

'But why in the world is it that the Evangelist was at great pains to mention repeatedly that He wept and that He groaned?'

That you might learn that He truly did assume our nature. For, as he clearly asserted greater things of Him than the other Evangelists did, he also spoke here of Christ's human nature in a much more humble strain than they. He did not, to be sure, give the details of Christ's death in as humble a strain as the others did: for example, by asserting that He became very sad, that He was in an agony, but quite the contrary, for He said that He cast His enemies prostrate on the ground.[4] And so in this passage by mentioning His grief he made up for what was omitted in his account of the Passion.

In speaking of His death, indeed, Christ asserted: 'I have

---

3 That is, they criticized His not preventing the death of Lazarus.
4 Cf. Matt. 26.38; Mark 14.34; cf. Luke 22.43; John 18.6.

the power to lay down my life,'[5] and there He said nothing in lowly human fashion. That is the reason why, even in His Passion, the Evangelists attributed to Him much that is human, to prove by this means the genuineness of the Incarnation. Now, Matthew did so by means of His agony, and His becoming troubled, and by His [bloody] sweat, while John accomplished this by Christ's grief. If He were not truly possessed of our human nature, He would not have been overcome by grief once and then again a second time.

But what did Jesus do next? He did not defend Himself at all to them in answer to their charges. Why was it necessary to silence them by His words, when they were about to be refuted by what He did, and this was less likely to give offense and was better able to discomfit them? So He said: 'Take away the stone.'

But why in the world did He not remain at a distance when He called Lazarus forth and summoned him to His side? Or, rather, why did He not cause him to rise while the stone was still lying in place? I ask this for He who was able to move a corpse by His voice and to bring it back to life again would be still more capable of moving a stone by that same voice. He who could by His voice cause Lazarus to walk, when he was tied with bandages and bound hand and foot with them, would be much better able to move a stone. What am I saying? Even when absent He would have been able to accomplish this.

Why in the world, then, did He not do so? In order that He might make these people witnesses of the miracle, so that they might not say, as they had in the case of the blind man: 'It is he; it is not he.'[6] For their hands and their coming to the tomb attested the fact that it was actually he. Hence, if they had not been present, they might have thought it a figment of

5 John 10.18.
6 John 9.8,9.

the imagination, or that they were taking one person for another. However, they were actually present in the place and raised up the stone. And they were bidden to free the bound corpse from its bandages. Further, the friends who had [previously] carried him out for burial realized that it was really Lazarus himself, because they recognized the bandages. His sisters, also, had not been left behind; one even said: 'He is already decayed, for he is dead four days.' Accordingly, all these circumstances were sufficient to silence the unfair critics when they finally witnessed the miracle.

For this reason He bade them to take away the stone from the tomb: to show them that it was Lazarus whom He was bringing to life. That is also why He asked: 'Where have you laid him?' so that when they had said: 'Come and see' and had brought Him there, they might not have it to say that He had raised up another man. Thus, both their voice and their hands would bear witness to the miracle (their voice, since they said: 'Come and see,' and their hands which took away the stone and removed the bandages). Their sight and hearing also bore witness to it (the latter on listening to His words; the former, on seeing him come forth.) Likewise, their sense of smell, as it perceived the fetid odor, for Martha declared: 'He is already decayed, for he is dead four days.'

Rightly, then, did I say that the woman failed to understand the words of Christ, namely: 'Even if he dies, he shall live.' At least, see what she said here, as if the thing were impossible of fulfillment because of the length of time. She had this idea for actually, to bring to life a corpse that was of four days' standing and already in process of decaying was something foreign to her experience.

Further, while He said to His disciples: 'That the Son of God may be glorified,' a statement referring to Himself, He said to the woman, on the other hand, 'Thou shalt behold the glory of God,' referring to His Father. Do you see that

the weakness of His hearers was the cause of the difference
in what He said? Therefore, he was recalling to her mind
what He had said to her, all but rebuking her as if she were
forgetting it. Yet, because He did not wish, for the moment,
to terrify those present, He gently said: 'Have I not told
thee that if thou believe thou shalt behold the glory of God?'

Faith is a great blessing, a great one, and a cause of many
blessings, so that men are enabled to do the things of God in
His name. 'If you believe,' He declared, 'you will say to this
mountain, "Remove from here," and it will remove'; and
again: 'He who believes in me, the works that I do, he also
shall do, and greater than these he shall do.'[7]

'What sort of greater works?' you will ask.

The things which the disciples are found doing after this.
And I say this for the shadow of Peter brought a corpse to
life.[8] In this way the power of Christ was even more loudly
proclaimed. For, certainly it was not as remarkable a thing for
Him to work a miracle while He was still alive as for others
to be able to work greater miracles than He, in His name,
after His death. Indeed, this was an incontestable proof of
His resurrection. It would not have been believed in so
firmly, even if it had been seen by all men. For those others
could even have said that it was an apparition, but the man
who saw miracles being performed by means of Christ's
name only—greater ones than those worked when He was
dwelling among men—could not fail to believe in Him, unless
he were very dull of comprehension.

Faith is a great blessing, then, when it proceeds from a
fervent mind, from great love, and a zealous soul. It shows
that we are practical Christians, it conceals human worth-
lessness and, despising earthly reasoning, seeks after the
knowledge of heavenly things. Or, rather, it takes possession

7 Matt. 17.19: John 14.12.
8 Cf. Acts 5.15; but only the cure of the sick is mentioned as effected by
Peter's shadow.

of and rules by conquest that which the wisdom of men cannot discover.

Let us, then, have faith, and let us not entrust our own affairs altogether to reason. Why is it, may I ask, that the Greeks were able to discover nothing of God? Did they not know all the pagan wisdom? How is it, then, that they were unable to get the better of fishermen and tent-makers, and unlettered men? Was it not because the Greeks trusted everything to reason, while the latter placed all their confidence in faith? That is why these prevailed over Plato and Pythagoras and, in a word, over all who were in error:[9] those familiar with astrology, and mathematics, and geometry, and arithmetic. They surpassed all who had had a thorough and complete education, and became as far superior to them as true philosophers are to those who are actually dull and witless by nature.

Notice that [those of the Christian faith] assert that the soul is immortal, or, rather, they have not only asserted this, but have even argued in favor of this fact. The others, on the contrary, at first did not even know what in the world a soul is. But when they did discover it and had distinguished it from the body, they once more fell into error, some maintaining that it is incorporeal, others that it is a material body and fused with the body itself.

Once more, regarding heaven, some said that it was animated by a soul and was a god, while the fishermen both taught and argued that it is a work of God and part of His creation. However, it is not at all strange that the Greeks make use of reason, but it is a lamentable thing when those who seem to be of the faith are discovered to be concerned only with this life. Therefore, these, too, have gone astray, because some asserted that they knew God as He knows

---

9 On the attitude of the Church Fathers towards Plato, cf. R. Arnou, 'Platonisme des Pères,' *DTC* 12 (1929) 2258-2392.

Himself,[10] a statement which not even one of those others dared to make. Others declared that God could not beget without passion, since they did not agree that He is at all superior to men.[11] Still others maintained that neither an upright life nor carefully regulated conduct is of any profit.[12] However, there is not time to refute these errors now.

Indeed, both Christ and Paul, who were particularly concerned with regard to this matter, made it clear that orthodoxy of faith is of no profit if one's life is corrupt. Christ taught: 'Not everyone who says to me, "Lord, Lord," shall enter the kingdom of heaven'; and again: 'Many will say to me in that day, "Lord, did we not prophesy in thy name?" And then I will declare to them, "I never knew you. Depart from me, you workers of iniquity!" '[13] Those who are not on their guard will indeed easily slip into living an evil life, even if they have the true faith.

And when Paul was writing to the Hebrews he, too, spoke in this way and urged: 'Strive for peace with all men and for that holiness without which no man will see the Lord.'[14] Here by 'holiness' He meant chastity, so that each one ought to be satisfied with his own wife and not have relations with any other woman.[15] If a man is not satisfied with his own, he cannot attain salvation, but must be altogether lost even if he has innumerable good works to his credit; because it is impossible to enter into the kingdom of heaven if one is guilty of fornica-

---

10 The Anomoeans. Eunomius, founder of this sect, taught that there was nothing in divine teachings that might not be grasped by human reason. See art. 'Eunomianism' in *Catholic Encyclopedia*.
11 The logicial conclusion following from the fundamental error of the Arians. See art. 'Arianism' in *Catholic Encyclopedia*.
12 Following the erroneous views of Gnosticism, later to develop into the heretical doctrine of Antinomianism in modern times. See art. 'Antinomianism' in *Catholic Encyclopedia*.
13 Matt. 7.21-23.
14 Heb. 12.14.
15 Cf. 1 Cor. 7.2: 'Let each man have his own wife and let each woman have her own husband.'

tion. Moreover, this is true not only of fornication, but even more so, of adultery.

Indeed, just as when a woman who is married to one man has intercourse with another she commits adultery in consequence, so if a man who is married to one woman takes another wife he has committed adultery. Therefore, such a man will not be an heir to the kingdom, but will fall into hell. Listen to what Christ said of these: 'Their worm dies not, and the fire is not quenched.'[16] Indeed, a man is unpardonable if, though he has a wife and enjoys such consolation in her, he brazenly has an affair with another. His behavior surely is wantonness.

Yet, many men even refrain from intercourse with their wives when it is a time of fasting or prayer. Therefore, if a man is not even satisfied with his wife, but also has intercourse with another woman, how great a fire is he heaping up for himself! If it is not permitted for a man who has divorced his own wife and separated from her to have relations with another woman—for this is adultery—how great a wrong does the man commit who brings in another woman while his wife is still living with him?

Let no one, therefore, allow this evil to become implanted in his soul, but let him pull it up by the roots. He does not wrong his wife as much as himself. Indeed, this sin is so serious an offense, and so unpardonable, that if a wife separates from an idolatrous husband against his will God punishes the woman, but if she separates from a fornicator He does not do so. For Scripture says: 'If a believing woman has an unbelieving husband and he consents to live with her, let her not put him away.'[17]

It does not speak of the fornicator in this way, however, but what does it say? 'If anyone puts away his wife, save on

16 Mark 9.45; cf. 1 Cor. 6.9,10.
17 1 Cor. 7.13.

account of immorality he causes her to commit adultery.'[18] If cohabitation makes husband and wife one body, the man who lives with a harlot must become one body with her. How, then, can a chaste woman accept him, since she is a member of Christ? Or how can she join to herself the member of a harlot?[19]

Moreover, notice the striking difference.[20] On the one hand, the woman who lives with an unbelieving husband is not impure. (For Paul said: 'The unbelieving husband is sanctified by the wife.') But in the case of the harlot this is not so. What, then? 'Shall I then make the members of Christ members of a harlot?'[21] In the former instance the holiness remains, even though the unbeliever is dwelling with his wife, and it is not lost, but in the latter case it altogether departs.

Truly, immorality is a terrible thing, a terrible thing, and one that brings everlasting punishment. Even in this life it gives rise to innumerable evil effects. For the impure man is forced to live a wretched and burdensome life, and his condition is no better than that of those who are already suffering punishment. He enters another's house in great fear and trembling and holds all men equally in suspicion: both slaves and free men.

Wherefore, I beseech, hasten to rid yourselves of this disease. Moreover, if you do not obey my words, do not set foot within these sacred portals. I say this for it is not fitting that the sheep that are covered with mange and full of disease mingle with the healthy ones, but they should remain apart from the flock until they are free from the disease.

Moreover, we have become members of Christ; let us not, therefore, become members of a harlot. This place is not a

18 Matt 5.32.
19 Cf. 1 Cor. 6.15,16.
20 Between the evil of idolatry and that of immorality.
21 1 Cor. 7.14; 6.15.

house of ill fame, but a church. And if you have the members
of a harlot, do not stand in the church, lest you offer insult to
the place. Indeed, even if there were no hell, even if there
were no punishment, how do you dare to cleave to another
woman after the marriage vows made there, and the bridal
torches, after that lawful couch, after the begetting of your
children, after such intimate companionship? Do you not
know that those who, after the death of their wife, marry
another, are censured by many for this, even though the
procedure does not merit punishment? Yet you take another
wife even while yours is still living. What lust does this not
betoken? Learn what is said of such men as these. 'Their
worm dieth not.' Scripture says, 'and the fire is not
quenched.'[22]

Shudder at the threat; fear the punishment. The pleasure
experienced in this life is not as great as the punishment
exacted in the next. However, may no one here present be
subject to that penalty. On the contrary, by practicing
sanctity may we all deserve to behold Christ and to attain
the blessings promised. May we all enjoy these by the grace
and mercy of our Lord Jesus Christ. Glory be to Him and to
the Father, together with the Holy Spirit, forever and ever.
Amen.

Homily 64 (John 11.41-48)

'Jesus raised his eyes and said, "Father, I give thee thanks
that thou hast heard me. Yet I knew that thou always hearest
me. But because of the people who stand round, I spoke," '
etc.[1]

I have often said—and I now repeat—that Christ did not

22 Mark 9.45.

1 John 11.41,42.

have His own dignity in view as much as our salvation, nor was He thinking of how He might say something great, but how He could attract us. Therefore, sublime and great utterances from His lips are few, and these, obscure; while humble and ordinary ones are many, and are interspersed in His words in abundance.

Since men were attracted more strongly by the latter, He used them frequently. He did not utter the lofty ones exclusively, lest His hearers might be intimidated thereby, nor did He refrain altogether from them, lest the men of His day might in that case be disedified. Of course, those who have abandoned the earthly point of view would be able to grasp all His high dignity from even one sublime teaching; while men who are always earthly-minded would not have come to Him at all, if they did not frequently hear these ordinary and humble things of Him.

Yet, notwithstanding the fact that they did hear such things, they did not even then remain His followers, but stoned and persecuted Him, and tried to do away with Him, and called Him a blasphemer. Thus, when He made Himself equal to God, they declared: 'He blasphemes.' And when He had said: 'Thy sins are forgiven thee,' they still called Him a demon, as also when He asserted that he who hears His words is stronger than death. Moreover, when He said: 'I am in the Father and the Father in me,' they left Him. And they again took offense when He asserted that He had come from heaven.[2]

Now, if they could not bear such things though He said them so seldom, they would hardly have paid attention to Him if His discourse were always of lofty tenor and worded accordingly. At least, when He said: I speak as the Father has commanded me,' and 'I have not come of myself,' then they believed. Moreover, it is clearly evident that they did believe

---

2 Mark 2.7; Matt. 9.2; Luke 5.20; cf. John 8.51; 14.10; 6.41.

on that occasion, because the Evangelist took note of this and remarked: 'Because He said these things, many believed in him.'[3] Well, then, if speaking in humble tenor attracted people to believe, while lofty utterances frightened them away, is it not utter stupidity to fail to realize that the entire reason for the lowly ones was that He spoke for the sake of His hearers?

Besides, in another context, though He wished to say something noteworthy, He remained silent. In addition, He accounted for the reason for this by saying: 'That we may not give offense to them, cast a hook into the sea.'[4]

Accordingly, this is what He did in today's passage, also. After having said: 'I knew that thou always hearest me,' He added: 'but because of the people who stand round, I spoke, that they may believe.' Are these our words? Or is this merely a human supposition?

Therefore, perhaps a man will not allow himself to be persuaded by the written word, because it offends Him by the sublime things it records. However, when he hears Christ stating that the reason why He said humble things of Himself was in order that people might not take offense, how can he then persist in the suspicion that the ordinary words belong to Him by His nature and were not rather products of His condescension? Thus, in another context, also, when a voice was brought down from above, He said: 'Not for me did this voice come, but for you.'[5]

Now, though it is proper for the man of high dignity to say many humble things of himself, it is not right for the lowly man to say something great and lofty of himself. For the former conduct proceeds from condescension, and has for its excuse the weakness of those who are being instructed. Or,

---

3 Cf. John 14.31; 7.28-31.
4 Matt. 17.26.
5 John 12.30.

rather, the reason for it was to induce them to reflect on His humility, and His putting on of our flesh, and to instruct His hearers not to say anything great of themselves. It was also prompted by the fact that they thought Him an enemy of God, and did not believe that He came from God, and suspected that He was breaking the Law. Besides, there was the fact that His hearers envied Him and were hostile to Him because He asserted that He was equal to God.

On the other hand, there is no excuse—either reasonable or absurd—for someone who is of lowly station to make any sublime statement of himself, but this could only be stupidity and impudence and unpardonable boldness. Why, then, did He who is of that great and ineffable substance speak in ordinary terms of Himself? Both for the reason already stated and so that He would not be thought unbegotten. I say this for Paul seemed fearful of some such thing. Therefore he said: ['All things are subject to him], except him who has subjected all things to him.'[6] For even to think the contrary would be impious. And, if He were thought to be equal to the Father, though actually He was inferior to Him who had begotten Him, and of a substance other than His, would He not therefore have made every effort not to be considered so? As a matter of fact, however, He Himself did just the opposite, and said: 'If I do not perform the works of him who sent me, do not believe me.'

Moreover, by saying: 'I am in the Father and the Father in me,' He was also indirectly telling us of Their equality. But if, on the contrary, He were in truth inferior to the Father, He ought to have very forcefully denied it. Further, He ought never to have said at all: 'I in the Father and the Father in me' and 'We are one,' and 'He who sees me, sees the Father.'[7] I say this for, when the subject of His discourse was His

---

6 1 Cor. 15.27.
7 John 10.37,38,30; 12.45.

power, He said: 'I and the Father are one.' And when the subject concerned His authority, once again He said: 'For as the Father raises the dead and gives them life, even so the Son also gives life to whom he will.'[8] But He could not say this if His substance were different from that of the Father.

However, even if it were possible, He ought not to have made this statement, so that they would not conceive the erroneous idea that Their substance was one and the same. Indeed, if He frequently did not speak of Himself in fitting terms, lest they mistakenly think that He was in opposition to God, much more was this necessary in the above instance. But, actually, it was the deed of one who was making Himself equal to Him who begot Him—and thus to confirm their suspicion of this—for Him to say: 'That they may honor the Son even as they honor the Father'; and to assert: 'The works which he does, I also do in like manner'; and to declare that He is the resurrection and the life and the light of the world.[9]

Do you perceive how, on the one hand, He made such statements and defended Himself because He had not offended against the Law, while He not only did not remove, but even confirmed, the idea that He is equal to the Father? Thus, even when they said: 'Thou blasphemest, because thou makest thyself God,'[10] He proved His equality to the Father by pointing out the identity of His works with those of the Father.

Yet, why do I say merely that the Son has been spoken of in a manner below His dignity when, to be sure, the Father also, who did not assume our flesh, has had the same treatment? And this is so for He Himself also allowed many statements of humble tenor to be made of Himself ·for the sake of the salvation of those who would hear them. 'Adam,

---

8 John 5.21.
9 John 5.23,20.
10 Cf. John 10.33,36.

where are you?' and '[I will go down] to see whether they have done all that the outcry which comes to me indicates'; also: 'I know now that you fear God,'[11] and 'If so be they will hear'; likewise: 'Who shall give the heart of this people to be disposed in such a way?' and also the words: 'There is none like you among the gods, O Lord';[12] and many other similar texts which one might excerpt from the Old Testament will be found to be unworthy of the sublime dignity of God.

Further, in the case of Achab, God said: 'Who shall deceive Achab for me?'[13] In addition, there is also the fact that He always made Himself available for comparison with the pagan gods, and all this is below the dignity of God. However, viewed in another way, it becomes worthy of Him. I say this for He is so merciful that for the sake of our salvation He foregoes being spoken of in terms befitting His dignity. The very fact of His becoming Man and taking on Him the form of a slave is below His dignity, as is also the fact that He spoke humbly and lived in lowly circumstances— that is, if one looks to His intrinsic dignity; but it is worthy of His majesty if one considers the ineffable riches of His mercy.

But there is yet another reason for the humble tenor of His words. What is this? It was because they knew the Father and acknowledged Him, but they did not know the Son. Therefore, He repeatedly looked to the Father for support, because the Father was already accepted, while He Himself was not yet considered worthy to be accepted as God, not because His own worth was really inferior, but because of the stupidity and weakness of His hearers. Moreover, that is why He prayed and said: 'Father, I give thee thanks that thou hast heard me.' For if the Son gives life to whom He will, and if

---

11 Gen. 3.9; 18.21; 22.12.
12 Ezech. 3.11; Cf. Deut. 5.29; Ps. 85.8.
13 2 Par. 18.19.

He gives life as the Father does, why did He invoke the Father?[14]

However, it is finally time to resume our study of today's text itself. 'They therefore removed the stone where the dead man was lying. And Jesus, raising his eyes, said, "Father, I give thee thanks that thou hast heard me. Yet I knew that thou always hearest me; but because of the people who stand round, I spoke, that they may believe that thou hast sent me." '

Let us, then, ask the heretic: 'Did He receive from the prayer the power He needed to raise the dead man to life?'

If so, how did He perform the other works without prayer? For instance, when He said: 'Thou evil spirit, I command thee, go out of him'; and: 'I will; be thou made clean'; and: 'Take up thy pallet'; and: 'Thy sins are forgiven thee'; and to the sea: 'Peace, be still.'[15] Further, how was He at all superior to the Apostles if He Himself also performed His works by the help of prayer? Or, rather, not even they did everything through prayer, but often by calling on the name of Jesus, even without prayer. If His name had such great power, how was it that He Himself needed the help of prayer? But if He did need the help of prayer, His name would not have been powerful. In short, when He created man what prayers did He need? Was He not then held altogether equal in honor? For, God said: 'Let us make mankind.'[16] Actually, what greater weakness could there be than to need the help of prayer?

However, let us see what the prayer was. 'Father, I give thee thanks that thou hast heard me.' Who, then, has ever prayed in this way? Before saying anything else, He declared, 'I give thee thanks,' to point out to us that He did not need

---

14 Cf. John 5.22,21.
15 Mark 9.24; 1.41; John 5.9; Matt. 9.2; Mark 4.39.
16 Gen. 1.26.

the help of prayer. 'Yet I knew that thou always hearest me.' He said this, not because He lacked the power necessary for the miracle, but to show that He was of one mind with the Father.

'But why did He use the form of a prayer?'

Listen, not to me, but to Him as He explains: 'Because of the people who stand round, that they may believe that thou hast sent me.' He did not say: 'That they may believe that I am inferior, that I have need of assistance from above, that I can do nothing without prayer,' but: 'that thou hast sent me.' To be sure, prayer does imply all this, if we take it at face value, but He did not mean: 'That thou has sent me who am weak, who have recognized my subservience to You, who can do nothing of myself.' On the contrary, since He omitted to mention all of this so that you might not get the erroneous idea that anything of it is true, He declared that the true reason for His prayer was: 'Lest they think that I am an enemy of God, lest they say, "He is not of God," and in order that I may show that the miracle takes place in accordance with Your Will.' He was as much as saying: 'If I were an enemy of God, the miracle would not take place successfully.'

Now, the words, 'Thou hast heard me,' are used in the case of those who are both friends and equals. 'Yet I knew that thou always hearest me'; that is, 'I have no need of prayer to effect the accomplishment of My will,' but I am saying this in order to convince people that You and I have one will.' Why, then, do You pray? 'For the sake of those who are weak and somewhat stupid.'

'When he had said this, he cried out with a loud voice.' Why did He not say: 'In the name of My Father, come forth'? Why did He not say: 'Raise him up, Father?' On the contrary, even though He had assumed the attitude of one praying, why did He omit all this and display His authority by what He did? Because it was a mark of His wisdom to show condescension by His words, but authority by His deeds. They could find nothing else of which to accuse Him than that He was not from God, yet in this way they were deceiving many. For this reason, by what He said He proved this very point more than sufficiently, and in the way that their weakness required. Of course, He could have shown in another way His own dignity, as well as His harmony with the Father, but the crowd would not have been able to ascend so high.

So He said: 'Lazarus, come forth.' This was the fulfillment of what He had previously stated. 'The hour is coming in which the dead shall hear the voice of the Son of God, and those who hear shall live.'[17] Lest you think that He derived the power from someone else, He instructed you about this beforehand, and then fulfilled it by His deeds. Moreover, He did not say: 'Arise,' but 'Come forth,' addressing the dead man as if he were alive.

What power could match this? But if He did not perform the miracle by His own power, how was He at all superior to the Apostles who said: 'Why do you stare at us, as though by any power or holiness of our own we had made this man walk?' If, though He did not do it by His own power, He did not admit this, as the Apostles did of themselves, would they not be more virtuous, because of disclaiming the glory? They did this elsewhere, also: 'Men, why are you doing this? We also are human beings like you.'[18]

So, then, the Apostles, because they had done nothing by their own power, spoke in this way to convince people of that very thing; yet, when He acquired a similar reputation in His own regard, would He not have dispelled that suspicion if He did not indeed perform His works by His own power? Who would deny this?

---

17 John 5.25.
18 Acts 3.12; 14.14.

Actually, Christ did just the opposite and said: 'Because of the people who stand round, I spoke, that they may believe.' So that, if they did believe, there would have been no need of the prayer.

But if it was not below His dignity to pray, why did He ascribe to them the reason for doing it? And why did He not say: 'that they may believe that I am not equal to You'? For He ought to have come to this because of their suspicion. Yet, when He was suspected of breaking the Law, He made a pronouncement on that very subject, even though they had given no expression of their suspicion: 'Do not think that I have come to destroy the Law.'[19] Here, on the contrary, He confirmed their suspicion. In short, what need was there of such circumlocution and mystery? For it was enough to say: 'I am not equal,' and be finished with it.

What, then? Did He not say: 'I do not do my own will'?[20] However, He said this also obscurely, and with a view to their weakness, and for the same reason as that for which He offered the prayer.

But what is the meaning of 'Thou hast heard me'? He meant, that is, 'There is no opposition between Me and Thee.' Thus, the words, 'Thou hast heard me,' do not signify that He had not the power of Himself. (Indeed, if this were the case, it would mean, not a lack of power only, but also a lack of knowledge, at least if He did not know before He prayed that God was going to answer Him favorably. Morover, if He did not know this, how was it that He said: 'I go that I may wake him from sleep,' and did not say: 'I go that I may pray to the Father to wake him from sleep.')

In like manner, these words ['Thou hast heard me'] are not indicative of weakness on His part, either, but of His

---

19 Matt. 5.17.
20 Cf. John 8.30: 'I seek not my own will.'

complete agreement with the Father, as also are the words, 'Thou always hearest me.' Therefore, we must come to this conclusion, or else conclude that He was speaking in answer to their suspicion. Further, if He was, in truth, neither ignorant nor weak, it is quite evident that He spoke words of humble tenor for this reason: that you might believe in Him because of their very exaggeration, and might be forced to acknowledge that they stem, not from His true dignity, but from His condescension.

But what do the enemies of truth say as a result of these words? 'He did not say: "Thou hast heard me," because of the weakness of His hearers,' they assert, 'but to show the Father's superiority to Him.'

Yet, actually, His saying this was not a proof of the Father's greater excellence, but an abject humiliation of Himself and an assertion that as Man He was not above human nature. For, to pray is not in accord with the dignity of God the Father nor of Him who shares His throne. Do you see that no other reason than their unbelief prompted Christ to pray?

At any rate, notice that the miracle also testified to His authoritative power. He called, and he who had been dead came forth, still bound. Next, so that the deed might not appear to be an illusion (for it seemed no less wonderful for the man to come forth still bound, than to raise him from the dead), He bade them to unbind him, in order that, by touching him and coming close to him, they might see that it really was Lazarus.

Furthermore, He said: 'Let him go.' Do you perceive His lack of ostentation? He did not draw him to Himself, or bid him follow in His company, so as not to seem to any of them to be showing off—so well did He know to act with moderation.

But, when the miracle had taken place, some marveled

at it, while others went to tell the Pharisees. What did they do then? Though they ought to have been struck with amazement and to have marveled at Him, they plotted to kill Him because He had brought the dead man to life. Oh, what stupidity! They thought they could give over to death Him who conquered death in the bodies of other men. So they said: 'What are we doing? For this man is working many signs.' They still were calling Him a 'man,' though they had received such a great proof of His Godhead. 'What are we doing?' They ought to have been believing and worshiping and adoring and no longer calling Him a man.

'If we let him alone as he is, the Romans will come and take away both our nation and our city.' What is it that they were plotting to do? They wished to disturb the people profoundly, on the pretext that they were going to be in danger because of a vague threat of the imposition of a tyrannical government. 'For if the Romans learn that He is gathering the people together,' they declared, 'they will be suspicious of us and will come and take away our city.'

Why, may I ask? He has not taught them to revolt, has He? Did He not bid them to give tribute to Caesar? Did He not flee when you wished to make Him king? Did He not give evidence of an ordinary and unpretentious life, possessing no home or anything else of the kind? Therefore, they were saying these things, not because they anticipated danger, but out of envy. Yet, even though they did not really anticipate it, things turned out that way and the Romans did take away their city, when they themselves had killed Christ.

Now, I say this for His actions were far from being at all suspicious. Indeed, He who was healing the sick, and giving example of a life above reproach, and advising men to obey their rulers was not conniving at a dictatorship, but destroying it. 'But we are basing our suppositions on examples from the past,' they said. However, those men of the past did teach sedition, while He taught just the opposite. Do you perceive that their words were hypocrisy? For what proof had they of such a thing? Had He attracted to Himself swaggering satellites? Did He draw chariots in His train? Did He not seek after solitude?

However, lest they seem to be speaking because of their own feelings, they said that the whole city was in danger, and that plots were being hatched against the common good, and that they were fearful of the worst. This was not the cause of your being taken captive in the past, but quite the contrary: both as regards the present captivity [under Roman rule] and that in Babylon and the one under Antiochus that followed.[21] It was not the fact that there were worshipers of God among you, but that there were wrong-doers among you who angered God, that caused your betrayal.

But that is what envy is like. When it has once blinded the soul it does not allow it to see anything it should. Did He not teach men to be meek? When struck on the right cheek to turn the other, also? To bear wrongs patientl;? To be more eager to suffer injury than others are to inflict injury? Tell me, then, if you please, are these the deeds of a man who is conniving at dictatorship, or do they not rather belong to one who is destroying it?

However, as I have said, envy is a terrible thing and reeks with pretense. It has filled the world with innumerable evils. Because of this disease the law courts are thronged with cases. From it come vainglory and avarice. From it come ambition and pride. Because of it, the roads are beset by brutal robbers, and the sea is infested with pirates. Inspired by it, murders are committed throughout the world. By its influence our race is torn apart. Whatever you see that is evil you will find comes from this.

---

21 Cf. 4 Kings 26; 1 Mach. 1.

It has penetrated even the Church. From the start it has brought about terrible results without number. It has been a mother to avarice, a plague which has turned things upside down and has corrupted justice. (For, Scripture says: 'Gifts blind the eyes of the wise, and as a muzzle on the mouth, prevent them from correcting.'[22] Avarice makes us slaves instead of free men; we talk about it every day, yet accomplish no good.

We become worse than wild beasts; we rob orphans; we fleece widows; we are unjust to the poor; we pile up woe upon woe. 'Woe is me, because the holy man is perished out of the earth.'[23] Moreover, now henceforth we must mourn; or, rather, we ought to say this every day. We accomplish nothing by our prayers, nothing by our advice and exhortation; so, then, there remains but to weep. This Christ also did. When He had delivered many exhortations in Jerusalem, since they gained no profit, He wept for their blindness. This the Prophets likewise did; let us now do so as well. Now is the time to mourn and weep and lament. It is timely also for us to say now: 'Call for the mourning women, and send to them that are wise women, and let them speak.'[24] Perhaps we shall thus be able to drive the disease of avarice from those who are building elaborate homes, from those who are securing fields for themselves by fraud.

It is very timely to mourn, but you who have been fleeced and wronged take part with me in my mourning; join your tears to my laments. However, let us show our grief by mourning, not for ourselves, but for them, for they have not wronged you, but have destroyed themselves. You indeed will possess the Kingdom of Heaven in return for being wronged,

22 Eccli. 20.31.
23 Mich. 7.2.
24 Jer. 9.17.

while they will have hell in exchange for their unjust gain.
Therefore, it is better to suffer wrong and not to do wrong
to others.

Let us mourn for them not with human lamentation, but
with that from the sacred Scriptures by which the Prophets
also mourned. Let us mourn bitterly with Isaias and say:
'Woe to them that join house to house and lay field to
field that they may wrest something from their neighbor.
Shall you alone dwell in the midst of the earth? Great and
fair houses, and there will not be inhabitants in them.'[25]

Let us mourn with Nahum and let us say with him:
'Woe to him that buildeth up his house [by injustice].'[26] Or,
rather, let us mourn for them as Christ did in His day, when
He said: 'Woe to you rich, for you are now having your
reward and your comfort.'[27] Let us not, I beseech you, cease
mourning in this way, and if it be not unbecoming, let us
also bewail the apathy of our brethren. Let us not weep loudly
for him who is already dead, but let us weep for the robber,
the grasping, miserly, greedy man.

Why do we mourn for the dead for whom this does no
good for the future? Let us mourn for those for whom change
is still possible. However, if we mourn, perhaps they may
laugh. Yet, even this merits our grief, because they are
laughing about those matters for which they ought to mourn.
Of course, if they have been moved at all by our lamentations we ought to cease lamenting, because they are going to
reform. But, when they remain unmoved, let us persist in
weeping not merely for the rich, but also for the miserly, the
grasping, the rapacious.

Wealth is not an evil thing (for we can use it as we

---

25 Cf. Isa. 5.8,9.
26 Actually, the quotation is Jer. 22.13; cf. Nah. 3 for his prophecy
of the destruction of Nineve.
27 Cf. Luke 6.24.

ought, when we spend it for those in need); but avarice is an evil thing and brings everlasting punishment. Let us mourn, then. Perhaps there will be some reformation as a result; or, even if those who fall into this vice are not freed from it, others at least will not fall into it unawares, but will be on their guard.

Now, may they be set free from this affliction, and may we never be betrayed into it, that we may all in common attain to the possession of the blessings that have been promised, by the grace and mercy of our Lord Jesus Christ. Glory be to Him forever and ever. Amen.

Homily 65 (John 11.49-12.8)

'But one of them, Caiphas, being high priest that year, said to them, "You know nothing at all; nor do you reflect that it is expedient for us that one man die for the people," ' etc.[1]

'The nations are sunk in the pit they have made; in the snare they set, their foot is caught.'[2] This happened in the case of the Jews, for they were saying that Jesus ought to be slain, that the Romans might not come and take away both their nation and their city. But, when they did slay Him, then they suffered this very fate; and when they had taken the measures they deemed necessary to escape it, they did not escape it.

Moreover, He who was slain is in heaven, while they who killed Him have hell for their portion, even though they did not plan it that way. But what was their plan?' 'From that day forth their plan was to put him to death,' the

1 John 11.49,50.
2 Ps. 9.16.

Evangelist said. For they were declaring: ' "The Romans
will come and take away our nation." But one of them,
Caiphas, being high priest that year, said—because he was
more shameless than the rest—"You know nothing at all." '

The doubts which the others felt and had set forth for
discussion (for they said: 'What are we doing?'), this man
shouted out brazenly, without disguise, and querulously. What
was it he said? 'You know nothing at all; nor do you reflect
that it is expedient that one man die, instead of the whole
nation perishing. This, however, he said not of himself; but
being high priest, he prophesied.' Do you perceive how
powerful the authority of the office of high priest is? For,
since he had been deemed at all worthy of the office of high
priest—even though undeserving of the honor—he prophesied,
but without knowing what he was saying. Moreover, grace
merely made a mouthpiece of him but did not touch his
foul heart.

In fact, many other men also have predicted the future,
though they were undeserving the privilege—Nabuchodonosor, Pharao, Balaam—and the reason for them all is evident.
Further, what he meant is something like this: 'You are
deliberating; you are still attending to this affair too hesi-
tantly, and you do not know that the safety of one man must
be made of no account for the sake of the common good.'

See how great the power of the Spirit is! It was able to
bring forth from a malicious mind words full of wonderful
prophecy. Furthermore, the Evangelist called the nations
'the children of God,' because they would be so in the
future. Similarly, Christ Himself also had said: 'And other
sheep I have,'[3] and He also was calling them so because
they would be in future.

But what is the meaning of 'being high priest that year'?

---

3 John 10.16.

Along with the other Jewish customs, this one also was corrupt. For no longer did they hold the office of high priest for a whole lifetime, but for one year, from the time when the offices began to be purchased.[4] However, even so, the Spirit was still present. But when they raised their hands against Christ, He then abandoned them and went over to the Apostles. The torn curtain of the Temple made clear reference to this,[5] as also the voice of Christ, when He said: 'Behold, your house is left desolate.'[6] Further, Josephus, who lived a short time later, declared that certain angels, who still remained among them to see whether they would be willing to reform, abandoned them.[7] Indeed, as long as the vineyard remained loyal, everything went well; however, when they killed the Heir, no longer was this so, but they perished.[8] And God, taking from the Jews their place of predilection, as one takes a bright garment from an uncooperative child, gave it to the faithful slaves among the Gentiles, and left the Jews alone and unprotected.

However, it was not unimportant that Christ's enemy made this prophecy. This fact could even have attracted the others to Him. In fact, the matter turned out contrary to what Caiphas wished. For, when Christ had died, because of this the faithful were free from the punishment in the world to come.

What is the meaning of 'That he might gather into one those near and those far off'? He made them one body. He

---

4 St. John Chrysostom seems to be in error here. It is well authenticated that Caiphas had already been high priest for fifteen years when he said these words reported by the Evangelist. Therefore, by the words 'that year' the latter did not mean that the tenure was annual. For several possible explanations of his meaning, cf. E. Jacquier, 'Caïphe,' DB (1899) 45; also, Confraternity Commentary 335.

5 As mentioned by the Synoptics in describing the death of Christ.

6 Matt. 23.28.

7 See De bell. Jud. 1.6.31.

8 Cf. Matt. 21.38-41.

who dwells in Rome considers the natives of India his member. What could be equal to this gathering? And Christ is the head of all.

'From that day forth the plan of the Jews was to put him to death.' Now they had sought to do this before, for the Evangelist said: 'This is why the Jews were seeking to put him to death'; and 'Why do you seek to put me to death?'[9] Then, however, they were merely seeking to do so, while now they confirmed their purpose and treated the affair as a task to be accomplished. 'Jesus therefore no longer went about openly in Judea.' Once again He saved Himself in human fashion, as He frequently did. And I have explained the reason why He often went away and withdrew from public notice.

Further, He now took up His abode in Ephrem near the desert, and remained there with His disciples. Do you not think His disciples were disturbed on seeing Him saved by human means? No one else now followed Him to Ephrem, for, since the Feast of the Passover was at hand, the people were all hastening to Jerusalem. Jesus and His disciples, on the contrary, at a time when everybody was joyous and celebrating the feast, were in hiding and were in danger; nevertheless, they stayed on with Him.

I say this for they remained in hiding in Galilee when the Pasch took place and the Tabernacles, also. Again, later, during the feast, only they—of all the other followers— showed their loyalty by fleeing with their Master and remainin in hiding with Him. Because of this Luke asserted that He said: 'I have continued with you in time of trial.'[10] Further, He said this to show that they derived their strength from His assisting grace.

'Now many from the country went up to purify themselves.

---

9 John 5.18; 7.20.
10 Cf. Luke 22.28.

And the chief priests and Pharisees had given orders to seize him.' A fine kind of purification: accompanied by a bloody purpose, the intention to commit murder, and bloodstained hands! 'And they were saying, "Why do you think that he is not coming to the feast?" ' It was by means of the Passover that they were laying their schemes, and they were making the time of the feast an occasion for committing murder; that is, they reasoned: 'He must make His appearance here, because the feast calls for His presence.'

Oh, what impiety! At the time which required them to show more piety than usual, and to set free those imprisoned for the worst of crimes, at that time they sought to apprehend Him who had done no wrong. Yet, even though they were already embarked on this project, not only did they accomplish nothing, but they even became altogether ridiculous. That is why He frequently escaped when He fell in with them and held in check those who desired to kill Him, and caused them to be discomfited: because He wished to bring them to repent by the display of His power. And likewise it was in order that, when they should succeed in taking Him, they would learn that this happened, not by their own strength, but because He permitted it. Not even at this time, to be sure, were they strong enough to capture Him, even though Bethany was nearby; indeed, when they did finally capture Him, He cast them prostrate on the ground.

'Six days before the Passover, he came to Bethany where Lazarus was; and he shared a meal with them, and Martha served, while Lazarus ate.' Now this is a proof of the veracity of the resurrection of Lazarus, that many days later he was still alive and was partaking of food. From this passage it is also clear that the supper took place in Martha's home, and they welcomed Jesus because they were His friends and beloved by Him. But some assert that this took place in the home of someone else.[11]

However, Mary was not serving at table, for she was His disciple. In this case once again she was more deeply spiritual than Martha. For she was not lending her services as if called on to do so, nor did she minister to all the guests in common, but she paid honor to Him alone, and she approached Him, not as man, but as God. Indeed, that is why she poured out the ointment and wiped it dry with her hair, because she did not have the kind of opinion of Him which most people had.

Yet Judas rebuked her, with a pretense of piety in what he said. Therefore, what did Christ say? 'She has done a good turn for my burial.'[12] But why in the world did He not rebuke the disciple on account of the woman, or declare what the Evangelist asserted, namely, that he had found fault with the woman because of his own thievery?

By His great patience Christ wished to put him to shame. In fact, because He knew that Judas was a traitor He had previously rebuked him often, as when He said: 'There are some of you who do not believe' and 'One of you is a devil.'[13] Therefore, He made it evident that He knew he was a traitor, yet He did not charge him with this openly, but made allowance for him out of a desire to win him back.

How is it, then, that another Evangelist said that all the disciples were expressing indignation at the waste?[14] Yes, all of them, and he as well; but the others did so with a different intention.

Now, someone may ask: 'Why in the world did He entrust

---

11 At the house of Simon the Leper; cf. Matt. 26.6; Mark 14.3.
12 This wording of Christ's reply is not as recorded by John, but as in Matt. 26.11; Mark 14.7.
13 John 6.65,71.
14 Matt. 26.8.

the purse for the poor to one who was a thief, and why did He give the office of dispensing it to one who was greedy for money?'

In answer I should reply as follows: God knows the ineffable explanation; but if we must say something by way of conjecture, it is that He did this in order to deprive Judas of all excuse for the betrayal. For he could not say that he did it for love of money (and I say this for he had enough from the purse to satisfy his desire). Actually, on the contrary, he did it because of his great wickedness which Christ wished to check and so displayed much condescension toward him. Therefore He did not accuse him of being a thief—even though He knew he was one—in order to put an obstacle in the way of his evil purpose and remove all excuse.

'Let her be'—Christ said, 'she has done this for my burial.' Once again He was admonishing the traitor by speaking of His burial. However, the warning did not give him pause, nor did the words soften him, even though they were enough to plunge him into grief. It was as if He said: 'I am annoying to you and tiresome, but wait a little while and I shall go away.' I say this for He conveyed this idea by saying: 'But you do not always have me.'

However, nothing of this caused the bestial and crazed man to yield, even though He said and did much more than this, and both washed his feet on the night of the betrayal and shared with him His table and hospitality. This is a thing that usually places a restraint on the souls even of robbers (and besides He uttered other words as well, capable of softening even a stone). Further, these events took place, not a long time before, but on the very day, that the passage of time might not cause him to forget. However, he stood firm in his purpose, notwithstanding everything.

A terrible vice is covetousness, a terrible vice. It disables both eyes and ears, and makes men fiercer than wild beasts, not permitting them to consider conscience, or friendship, or association, or the salvation of their own soul. On the contrary, often it has weaned them away irrevocably from all these considerations, and like some harsh tyranny it makes its captives slaves. Moreover, the terrible feature of this very bitter slavery is that it even persuades them to feel grateful for it, and the more they become enslaved to it, so much the more will the pleasure they take in it be increased. As a result, the disease becomes especially hard to cure; as a result, the beast becomes hard to tame.

This vice made Giezi a leper instead of a disciple and prophet;[15] it destroyed Ananias and his followers;[16] it made Judas a traitor; it corrupted the rulers of the Jews, who accepted gifts and became partners of thieves. It has brought on innumerable wars, and filled the roads with bloodshed, and the cities with mourning and weeping. It has made banquets impure, and tables accursed, and has filled foods with unlawfulness.

Therefore Paul called it idolatry.[17] Yet, not even by so doing did he instill fear of it. Why did he say it is idolatry? Many possess riches and do not dare to make use of them, but they regard them as sacred, passing them on intact to their children and their children's children, not daring to touch them, as if they were something consecrated to God. And if ever they are forced to use them, they feel as if they were doing something sacrilegious. But, besides this, just as the pagan diligently cares for his idol, so you entrust your gold to barriers and bolts, putting your treasury in place of a temple, and storing up the gold in vessels of silver.

Yet you do not worship it as he does his idol? Yes, but you

---

15 Cf. 4 Kings 5.20-27.
16 Cf. Acts 5.1-11.
17 Cf. Col. 3.5.

show all the care that he does in its regard. Again, he would gladly give up his eyes and his life rather than his idol. And those who love gold would do this, too.

'But I do not adore the gold,' you will protest.

Neither does he adore the idol, but the evil spirit dwelling within it. Thus, you, too, even if you do not adore the gold, still adore the evil spirit that pounces upon your soul from the sight and the desire for the gold. Indeed, the vice of covetousness is worse than an evil spirit, and many people are more obedient to it than those others are to their idols. The latter, indeed, do not obey in many matters, but the slaves of avarice give way in everything and obey in whatever it says to do.

What does it say? 'Be hostile, inimical to all men; forget nature, spurn God, sacrifice yourself to me.' And they are completely obedient. Moreover, the pagans sacrifice oxen and sheep to the idols, so covetousness says: 'Sacrifice your soul to me,' and its slave obeys. Do you perceive what sort of altars it has? What kind of sacrifice it accepts? The covetous will not come to the possession of the kingdom of God;[18] still, not even on that account are they afraid. Yet, this tendency is weaker than all the rest, for it is not innate or natural. Surely, if it were, it would have been in man from the beginning. Actually, there was no gold at first, nor was anyone infatuated with gold.

However, if you wish, I shall explain whence this vice has entered the world. By striving in rivalry, each man with the one before him, they spread the disease, and a man's predecessor incited him to rivalry, even though he at first had no desire. For, when men saw beautiful homes, and extensive fields, and large numbers of slaves, and silver vessels, and a great accumulation of garments, they made every effort to get better ones, so that the first egged on the second, and these, those who came after. However, if they wished to act vir-

---

18 Cf. 1 Cor. 6.10.

tuously, they would not have given the rest this kind of example, yet neither have the latter any excuse for their covetousness. For there are others also who despise riches.

'Who does despise them?' you will ask.

Indeed, the great evil is that because vice is widespread this seems impossible to achieve, and it is not believed that anyone at all acts virtuously. Shall I mention, then, many in the cities and many in the mountains who do spurn riches? Yet what good would it do? For you will not be better because of them.

Besides, the subject of my discourse to you just now is not of these, so that you would give up all your possessions—though I wish you would— but, since the burden would be too great, I do not insist on this. But I do urge you not to covet the possessions of others and to share your own possessions. We shall find many of this type who are content with their own possessions, caring for their own families and providing a living for them by honest toil.

Why do we not emulate and imitate these? Let us think about our ancestors. Is not their property still standing, preserving only their names: the bath of this one, the surburban house and dwelling of that one? On seeing them do we not at once groan, thinking of how much toil he expended, how many frauds he perpetrated. Yet he is nowhere in sight, but others enjoy the fruits of his toil, people whom he never intended to enjoy them—perhaps even his enemies—while he suffers the extreme penalty.

This fate also awaits us. For inevitably we shall die, we shall meet with the same end. What angry rivalry, what expense, what enmity did they not undergo? Yet what fruit do they enjoy? Everlasting punishment, and never to obtain any consolation, and to be castigated by all men, not only while living, but even after death. What else? When we see the images of many men placed prominently in their homes, do we not mourn them more? Truly, the Prophet has well said: 'Surely every living man is disquieted in vain.[19] For, in reality, concern about such matters is disquiet—disquiet and unnecessary commotion.

However, this is not the case in the everlasting mansions, in the dwellings of the next life. In this life, indeed, one man toils and another enjoys the fruit, while in the next each one will be master of his own toils and will receive the reward for them, many times over.

Let us, then, strive for that type of possessions. Let us prepare dwellings for ourselves there, that we may find rest in Christ Jesus our Lord. Glory be to Him and to the Father, together with the Holy Spirit forever. Amen.

Homily 66 (John 12.9-24)

'Now the great crowd of the Jews learned that he was there; and they came, not only because of Jesus, but that they might see Lazarus whom he had raised from the dead.'[1]

Just as wealth is apt to cause the downfall of those who are not on their guard, so it is also with political power; for the former leads to covetousness, the latter to pride. Notice, for instance, that the ordinary people among the Jews, who were subject to authority, were possessed of sound health spiritually, while their rulers were corrupt.

Indeed, in testimony that the multitude believed in Him, the Evangelists repeatedly declared: 'Many of the people believed in him.'[2] Many of the rulers, however, did not believe. Moreover, they themselves—not the crowd—said:

---

19 Cf. Ps. 38.7.

---

1 John 12.9.
2 See, for example, John 7.31.

'Has any one of the rulers believed in him?' And what did they add? 'This crowd, which does not know the Law, is accursed.'[3] They meant that those who believed in Him were yet more accursed, while they themselves, His murderers, were impeccable. Now, in the present incident, many who witnessed the miracle believed, but the rulers were not only not satisfied with crimes performed for reasons personal to them, but also sought to put Lazarus to death. Granted that you seek to kill Christ because He broke the Sabbath, because He made Himself equal to God, and on account of the Romans, as you say, what charges can you lodge against Lazarus, that you seek to kill him? Surely the charge is not that he received a favor?

Do you perceive how murderous their purpose was? Even though Christ had worked many miracles, no one of them enraged them in this way: neither the paralytic, nor the blind. This one, indeed, was more remarkable by its nature and took place after many others, and it was a strange thing to see a man that had been dead four days walking about and talking. A fine way to keep the feast, by mixing murders with their celebration!

Furthermore, on one occasion they appeared to be accusing Him of breaking the Sabbath, and by this means they seemed to win over the people.[4] Here, on the contrary, since they could find nothing blameworthy in Him, they turned the attack against the one who had been healed. Here, indeed, they could not even say that He was in opposition to the Father, for His prayer refuted them. Therefore, since He had taken away the grounds for the charge they had so often trumped up, and as the miracle was a very evident one, they rushed headlong into murder.

Hence, they would have done this also in the case of the

3 John 7.48.
4 The cure of the man born blind; see John 9.1-41.

blind man, if they had not been able to accuse Him of breaking the Sabbath. Besides, the blind man was an obscure person, so they cast him out of the Temple. Lazarus, on the other hand, was a well-known personage, as is evident from the fact that many came to console his sisters. Further, the miracle took place before many eyewitnesses and was accompanied by much that was strange. Therefore, they all went hastily to see. Accordingly, it vexed the rulers that, though the festival was at hand, they were all paying no heed to it and going to Bethany.

Thus, they were trying to kill Him, yet did not consider that they were doing anything daring—so murderous were they. For this reason the Law at its beginning opens with this: 'You shall not kill,'[5] and the Prophet makes this charge: 'Their hands are full of blood.'[6]

How is it, then, that though He had not been walking about openly in Judea, but had withdrawn into the desert, He now once again entered Judea very openly? After quenching the fire of their anger by His withdrawal, He went back to them when they had calmed down. Besides, the large crowd that went before and came after Him was enough to precipitate His enemies into an agony of fear. For no miracle so effectually attracted people to Him as that of Lazarus.

Now, another Evangelist asserted that He entered Jerusalem with such a great display of honor that 'they kept spreading their cloaks under his feet' and 'All the city was thrown into commotion.'[7] Further, this was done to prefigure one prophecy and to fulfill another, and the same act was the commencement of one and the end of the other. For, the words: 'Rejoice, for thy king comes to thee meek,'[8] applied

---

5 Exod. 20.13; cf. Luke 18.20, where this commandment heads the list repeated by Christ to the rich young man.
6 Isa. 1.15.
7 Matt. 21.8,10.
8 Cf. Matt. 21.5.

to Him as He fulfilled this prophecy; while in the fact that He was seated upon an ass He was prefiguring the circumstance that in the future He would hold the unclean race of the Gentiles under His sway.

'But how is it that the other Evangelists said that He sent His disciples and said to them: "Loose the ass and her colt,"[9] while John did not say anything like that, but only: "He found a young ass and sat upon it"?'

Because it is likely that both things happened, and that after the ass had been set loose, while the disciples were leading it to Him, He found it and sat upon it. Further, they took the branches of palm and olive, and spread their cloaks on the road to show that they now had a more exalted opinion of Him than that He was merely a prophet. So they said: 'Hosanna! Blessed is he who comes in the name of the Lord.'

Do you perceive that it would particularly enrage the rulers that all were convinced that He was not opposed to God? And that the point on which, most of all, the people had divided opinions was that He said that He came from the Father?

But what is the meaning of: 'Rejoice greatly, daughter of Sion'? Because all their kings were, for the most part, unjust and covetous and had betrayed them to their enemies, and had perverted the people and made them subject to their enemies, the Prophet said: 'Take courage; this Man is not of that kind, but meek and humble,' and He proved this by the ass. For He did not enter with an army in His train, but only with an ass.

'This his disciples did not [at first] understand: that this thing was written about him,' the Evangelist asserted. Do you perceive that there were very many things that the disciples did not know about, because He Himself did not reveal them to them? I say this because when He said: 'Destroy this

---

9 Cf. Mark 11.3; Luke 19.30, 31; Matt. 21.2.

temple and in three days I will raise it up,' the disciples did not then understand this.[10] Further, another Evangelist asserted that His meaning was concealed from them and they did not understand that He must rise from the dead.[11] However, it was rightly concealed from them. Therefore, another Evangelist said that each time they heard about the subject they were sad and discouraged, and this happened because they did not comprehend the meaning of the Resurrection. But it was rightly concealed from them because it was too great a thing for them to grasp. Yet, why was the explanation of the ass not given to them? Because it also was a great thing.

Further, notice the virtue of the Evangelist; see how he was not ashamed to expose the fact that they were ignorant in the beginning. Accordingly, they knew that the prophecy was recorded, but did not understand that it was written with reference to Him. And this is so for it would have given them offense if they thought He was to endure such sufferings, even though He was a king, and if they heard that He was to be betrayed as He actually was. Besides, they would not have grasped at once the idea of the kingdom to which He referred. For, certainly, another Evangelist asserted that they thought He meant the kingdom of this world.[12]

'But the crowd bore witness that he had raised Lazarus from the dead.' So many would not have been at once won over, the Evangelist meant, if they had not believed in the miracle. 'The Pharisees therefore said to them,[13] "Do you see that you avail nothing? Behold, the world has gone after him." ' It seems to me that these are the words of men who reasoned soundly, on the one hand, but did not have the

---

10 John 2.19.
11 Cf. Mark 9.9.
12 Cf. Matt. 20.22.
13 πρὸς αὐτούς. The Greek New Testament has πρὸς ἑαυτούς and the Confraternity translation is 'among themselves.'

courage to speak openly, and then were attempting to hold them back on the ground that in the light of what had happened, they were attempting to do the impossible.

Moreover, here again they called the people 'the world.' Thus, Scripture habitually uses the expression 'the world,' with reference to creation and also to those living in wickedness. It used this term of the former when it said: 'Who bringeth out his world by number';[14] and the latter when it said: 'The world cannot hate you, but it hates me.'[15] Moreover, it is necessary to understand these things clearly lest we provide the heretics with some basis of argument from the meaning of the names.

'Now, there were certain Gentiles among those who had gone up to worship on the feast.' Since they were at length on the point of becoming proselytes, they went to the feast. Therefore, because His fame had been spread abroad, they said: 'We wish to see Jesus.' Philip stepped aside in favor of Andrew, since the latter was of higher rank than he, and communicated the message to him. However, not even Andrew acted with complete authority in the matter, for he had heard: 'Do not go in the direction of the Gentiles.'[16] For this reason, when he had conferred with the disciple, he brought him to the Master, for they spoke to Him together.

And what did He reply? 'The hour has come for the Son of Man to be glorified. Unless the grain of wheat fall into the ground and die, it remains alone.' What is the meaning of 'The hour has come'?

He had said: 'Do not go in the direction of the Gentiles,' to remove from the Jews every pretext for ignorance, and He had held His disciples back. Therefore, since the Jews had persisted in their unbelief, while the Gentiles wished to come

14 Cf. Isa. 40.26.
15 John 7.7.
16 Matt. 10.5.

to Him, 'It is at length time,' He said, 'to go to my Passion, since all things have been fulfilled. For, if we should adhere to the Jews, despite their unbelief, and not admit the Gentiles, even though they wish to come to us, that would be unworthy of our Providence.' Accordingly, since He was finally going to send His disciples to go to the Gentiles after the crucifixion, and since He saw that the latter were already coming eagerly to meet Him, He declared: 'It is time to go to the crucifixion.'

Moreover, before this He did not permit them to go to the Gentiles, in order that this might serve as testimony to the Jews. For, before they repelled Him by their deeds, before they crucified Him, He did not say: 'Go, therefore, and make disciples of all nations';[17] but: 'Do not go in the direction of the Gentiles'; and: 'I was not sent except to the lost sheep of the house of Israel'; and 'It is not fair to take the children's bread and cast it to the dogs.'[18]

But when they hated Him and hated Him so much as to kill Him, it was useless to adhere to those who were repelling Him. And I say this for they denied Him by saying: 'We have no king but Cæsar.'[19] Then at length He cast them off, since they had cast Him off. That is why He declared: 'How often would I have gathered thy children, but thou wouldst not.'[20]

What is the meaning of 'Unless the grain of wheat fall into the ground and die'? He was speaking of the crucifixion. Lest they be disconcerted at the thought that it was at the time when the Gentiles also came to Him that He was slain, He said: 'This very thing will be the cause of their coming to me, and will spread My preaching.' Next, because He was not convincing them effectively enough by His words, He illustrated this idea by an object lesson. 'This also happens in

17 Matt. 28.19; 10.5.
18 Matt. 15.24, 26.
19 John 19.15.
20 Matt. 23.37.

the case of grain: when it dies it brings forth fruit more abundantly. But if this is true of seeds, it is much more so of Me.' However, His disciples did not understand His words. The Evangelist repeatedly set forth this fact in order to make excuse for their subsequent flight. Incidentally, Paul, also, used this illustration in discoursing of the Resurrection.[21]

Therefore, what excuse will they have who do not believe in the Resurrection, since the phenomenon may be observed every day in seeds, and in plants, and in our birth process. For the seed must first undergo corruption, and then generation takes place. In short, when God makes something, there is no need of [human] reasonings. How, indeed, did He make us out of nothing?

I am addressing these words to Christians who say they believe in the Scriptures. And I shall add something else, drawing on human reasoning. Some men live in vice, others in virtue. Yet many of those who spend their lives in vice have come to extreme old age enjoying good fortune, while many virtuous men receive just the opposite. When, therefore, will each receive what he deserves? In what period of time?

'All the same,' they reply, 'there is no resurrection of the body.'

They do not listen to Paul saying: 'This corruptible body must put on incorruption.'[22] He was not speaking of the soul (for the soul does not suffer corruption). Moreover, resurrection is predicated of that which has fallen, and the body it is that has fallen. But why is it you do not wish resurrection of the body to take place? Is it impossible for God to achieve it? However, it would be utter stupidity to assert that. But it is not fitting? Why is it not fitting for the corruptible body that has shared hardship and death with the soul, also to share its crowns?

---

21 Cf. 1 Cor. 15.35-44.
22 1 Cor. 15.53.

Certainly, if it were not fitting, it would not have taken place from the start; He Himself would not have taken on His Body again. Yet, listen to what He said in testimony that He did assume it again and did raise it up: 'Put your fingers here,' and 'See that a spirit does not have bones and sinews.'[23] Further, why did He raise Lazarus up, if it were better for him to rise without his body? Why did He include the raising of the dead among His miracles and good works? And why did He generally give food [to those who had been raised up]?[24]

Well, then, beloved, do not be deceived by the heretics. I say this for there is a resurrection and a judgment. But those who do not wish to give a reckoning for their deeds deny this. Yet there must indeed be a resurrection such as that of Christ was. For He is the beginning and first-born of the dead. However, if the resurrection consists only in purification of soul and in becoming free from sin,[25] how did Christ rise from the dead, since He did not commit sin? How are we rid of the curse, if He did in truth commit sin? How could He say: 'The prince of the world is coming, and in me he has nothing'?[26] For, these words clearly refer to His sinlessness.

To sum up, then: according to our opponents, either He did not rise from the dead, or if He arose He must have committed sin before His resurrection. On the contrary, however, He did rise from the dead and He did not commit sin. Therefore, He did arise in the Body, and these wicked doctrines are nothing else than products of vainglory.

Moreover, let us avoid this nauseous error, for Scripture says: 'Evil companionships corrupt good morals.'[27] This error

---

23 Cf. John 20.27; Luke 24.39.
24 See, for example, the incident concerning the daughter of Jairus, Mark 5.43.
25 As the Gnostics claimed.
26 John 14.30.
27 1 Cor. 15.33.

is not the teaching of the Apostles; it is Marcion and Valentine[28] who have made this innovation. Well, then, beloved, let us avoid it. For purity of life is no benefit if one's doctrines are corrupt, just as, therefore, contrariwise, sound doctrines are no advantage if one's life is immoral. Greeks spawned these teachings; our opponents nurtured them, taking them from non-Christian philosophers and maintaining that matter is uncreated, and many similar errors. Therefore, just as they claimed that there could not be a Creator, unless elemental matter were uncreated, so they also denied the Resurrection.

However, let us not heed them, since we know the omnipotent power of God. Let us not heed them. I say this to you, for we, indeed, shall not beg off from the combat against them. But he who is unarmed and defenseless will easily be captured, even if he falls in with the weak and though he may be stronger than they. Indeed, if you had paid attention to the Scriptures and thus sharpened your powers each day, I would not be advising you to avoid battle against them, but would counsel you, on the contrary, to plunge into the fray. I say this for truth will prevail. But since you do not know how to use the Scriptures, I dread the struggle, lest they may find you unarmed and vanquish you. Indeed, nothing, nothing is weaker than those who are deprived of the help of the Spirit.

Further, if they cite pagan philosophy, you ought not to be in awe, but to laugh them to scorn because they are making use of stupid teachers. For those philosophers could discover no sound teaching either about God or about creation, but Pythagoras did not yet know things which even the widow among us understood.[29] On the contrary, they declared that

28 For their teachings see art. 'Marcionites' in *Catholic Encyclopedia*.
29 Cf. Mark 12.41-44.

the soul is a shrub or a fish or a dog.[30] Ought we, then, pay attention to them, do you think? Yet, how would that be reasonable? They are great men in their village, they wear their tresses long, they cast their cloaks about them. Their philosophy goes thus far. But if you look within, you see ashes and dust and nothing sound, but 'Their throat is an open grave,'[31] with everything reeking with foulness and ulcerous matter, and all their teachings worm-eaten. The first of them declared that God is water; his successor that He is fire; another, air; and all of them confined themselves to corporeal things.[32] Therefore, ought you to be in awe of them, do you think, when they did not even arrive at the idea of an incorporeal God? And if later they accepted it at all, it was after their contact with our co-religionists in Egypt.

However, lest we cause you too much disturbance, let us interrupt our discussion at this point. For, if we begin to set forth their teachings—what they said of God, what of matter, what of the soul, and what of the body—there will be much laughter in consequence. Besides, they are not in need of being accused by us, for they themselves have confounded one another. For instance, the one who in opposition to us wrote his work concerning matter[33] refuted himself. Wherefore, lest we keep you here longer to no purpose and unroll a veritable labyrinth of words, omitting these details we shall say only that one thing; namely, persevere in listening to the divine Scriptures and do not enter into argumentation where it is not necessary. Paul also urged Timothy to this course of action, even though he was already possessed of a great store of wisdom and had the power to work miracles.[34]

Well, then, let us obey him and, putting aside empty talk,

---

30 Cf. Empedocles Fr. 117D.
31 Ps. 5.10.
32 Thales; Empedocles; Anaximenes.
33 Not to be identified with certainty.
34 Cf. Tim. 2.14.

let us occupy ourselves in good works—I mean in brotherly love and hospitality. And let us make much account of alms-giving that we may attain to the promised blessings by the grace and mercy of our Lord Jesus Christ. Glory be to Him forever and ever. Amen.

Homily 67 (John 12.25-33)

'He who loves his life loses it; and he who hates his life in this world keeps it unto life everlasting. If anyone serve me, let him follow me.'[1]

Sweet is the present life and full of great pleasure—not for all, however, but only for those who feel an attachment for it. If a man has his eyes fixed on heaven and keeps looking at the beauties to be discovered there, he will quickly come to despise this life and will consider it of no account.

Bodily beauty does indeed inspire admiration, as long as none more fair puts in an appearance; but, when greater comeliness appears, the first is less esteemed. Well, then, in our case likewise, if we habitually keep our gaze fixed on the beauty of heaven, and closely observe the loveliness of the kingdom there, we shall quickly free ourselves of the bonds of the things of this life. For, a feeling of attachment to present things is a kind of manacle.

Moreover, listen to what Christ said to persuade us of this: 'He who loves his life loses it; and he who hates his life in this world keeps it unto life everlasting. If anyone serve me, let him follow me; and where I am there also shall my servant be.' These words seem to be enigmatic. Actually, however, they are not obscure, but are full of deep wisdom.

But how does 'he who loves his life' lose it? He does so who

---

1 John 12.25,26.

carries out its untoward desires; he who gratifies it more than he ought. That is why Scripture warns us in the words: 'Do not go in the desires of thy soul.'[2] If you do, you will lose it (because this conduct is off the road which leads to virtue), just as, contrariwise, therefore—'he who hates it in this world will save it.'

'And what does "he who hates it" mean?'

He who does not yield to it when it counsels something harmful. Yet He did not merely say: 'He who does not yield to it,' but: 'He who hates it.' For, just as we cannot bear even to listen to the voice of those we hate, and do not like to see their face, so it is also with our soul; when it enjoins on us things contrary to the good pleasure of God we must vehemently turn away from it. Since He was about to discourse to them of death—of His own death—and He foresaw that they would be dejected and downcast, He made a very strong statement: 'What do I say? Unless you bear my death with fortitude? Indeed, unless you yourselves die, there will be no fruit for you.'

Moreover, notice how consoling He made His words. It was very hard and depressing to hear that the man who loves his life must perish. Yet, why do I speak of the past, inasmuch as even now we shall find men gladly enduring every kind of suffering, for the sake of enjoying this present life, even though they have this belief in the life to come? When they see buildings, and works of art, and mechanical devices, they weep and cry out: 'What great things man devises, and yet will he become dust?' So strong is their attachment to the present life. To destroy these bonds, then, Christ said: 'He who hates his life in this world keeps it unto life everlasting.'

Now, to prove that He was speaking to hearten them, and to dispel their fear, listen to what He went on to say: 'If anyone serve me, let him follow me.' He was referring to His

2 Cf. Eccli. 18.30.

death and requesting that they follow Him by their deeds. For it is altogether necessary for the one who serves to follow the one served. Moreover, notice when He said this to them. It was not at the time when they were being persecuted, but when they were in good cheer, when they thought they were in safety, because of the honor and reverence shown by many toward Him. It was when they could even stand up and hear the words: 'Let him take up his cross and follow me,'[3] that is, 'Be always ready for danger, for death, for departure from this life,' He meant.

Next, since He had mentioned the tribulations, He also set forth the reward. What was this? To follow Him and to be where He is, and this means that resurrection succeeds to death. For 'Where I am,' He said, 'there also shall my servant be.' But where is Christ? In heaven. Well, then, even before our resurrection takes place, let us take our abode there, in spirit and thought.

'If anyone serve me, my Father will honor him.'

'Why did He not say "I"?'

Because they did not yet have the proper opinion of Him, but esteemed the Father more highly. Indeed, how could those who did not yet realize that He must rise again conceive a great opinion of Him? That is why He said to the sons of Zebedee: 'That is not mine to give, but it belongs to those for whom it has been prepared by my Father,'[4] even though, to be sure, it was He who would act as judge. But here He was also confirming the fact that He is true Son of God. For the Father will honor them as servants of His true Son.

'Now my soul is troubled. And what shall I say? Father, save me from this hour.'

'But surely these were no longer the words of One encouraging them to go to meet death?'

---

3 Matt. 16.24.
4 Mark 10.40.

On the contrary, they were those of One especially urging them to do so. Lest they might assert that He was altogether free from human pain and so found it easy to accept death, and that He gave us encouragement without Himself being in any danger of death, He showed that, even though He dreaded death, He did not refuse to undergo it, because of its efficacy for our salvation. And this is a manifestation of His human nature, not of His divinity. That is why He said: 'Now my soul is troubled' (for, if this were not so, what connection was there between this statement and the following one: 'Father, save me from this hour'?) and He was so deeply troubled that He even sought release if it were possible to escape.

This was the weakness of His human nature. 'However, I have no justification to offer for begging release from death,' He said. 'No, this is why I came to this hour.' It was as if He was saying: 'Even though we are disturbed, even though we are troubled, let us not flee from death. For, though I also am now troubled, I am not speaking so as to avoid it, for I must bear it when it comes upon Me. I do not mean: "Release Me from this hour," but what? Father, glorify Thy name. Even though My perturbation caused Me to speak as I just did, I mean the opposite: "Glorify Thy name"; that is, "lead Me henceforward to the cross." '

This very effectually shows that He was human and that His human nature did not wish to suffer death, but was clinging to the present life, and it proves that He was not without human feelings. Just as the fact that He suffered hunger was not held against Him, or that He slept, so the fact that He dreaded the separation from this present life ought not to be held against Him, either. Christ's Body was, to be sure, altogether free from sin, but it was not without physical needs; otherwise, it would not have been a real body. By these words, accordingly, He taught still another lesson. What, then, is it? That if we are ever in a state of distress and fear, we should not for that reason desist from our undertakings.

'Father, glorify thy name!' He was showing them that He would die for the sake of truth, and was referring to this as giving glory to God. Moreover, this effect would be evident after the crucifixion. The world would be converted and come to know the name of God and to serve Him, though not the name of the Father only, but also that of the Son. Nevertheless He remained silent about this as yet.

'There came therefore a voice from heaven, "I have both glorified it and will glorify it again."'

'When had He glorified it?'

'In previous events; and I will glorify it again after the crucifixion.'

'What, then, did Christ reply?'

'Not for me did this voice come, but for you.' However, they thought it was thunder, or that an angel had spoken to Him.

'Yet how was it that they thought this? Was the voice not clear and distinct?'

Yes, but it quickly sped past them, since they were somewhat unspiritual and carnal and immortified. Moreover, some merely detected the sound, while others knew that the voice was articulate, but they did not yet comprehend what it meant. What, therefore, did Christ say? 'Not for me did this voice come, but for you.'

'Why did He say this?'

To refute the statement that they were repeatedly making; namely, that He was not from God. For how was it possible that He was not from God if He was glorified by God whose name was also glorified by Him? It was for this reason, to be sure, that the voice came. And that is also why He Himself said: 'Not for me did this voice come, but for you. It was not that I might learn from it something of which I was ignorant (for I know all things that are the Father's),[5] but for your sake.' In fact, since they were saying that an angel had spoken to Him or that there had been thunder, and since they were not heeding the voice, He said: 'It came for your sake, that you might be induced by this means to inquire what was meant.'

But though they were amazed at the incident, when they heard that it had happened for their benefit, they did not inquire about it, even in the light of this. With good reason, indeed, did the voice not seem to be altogether clear, when the person who heard it did not know why it was speaking.

'For your sake did the voice come.' Do you perceive that the human touches always were added for their benefit, and that it was not because the Son was in need of assistance that they occurred?

'Now is the judgment of the world; now will the prince of this world be cast out.'

'What connection has this with the words: "I have both glorified it and will glorify it"?'

A close connection, and it is very much in harmony with them. For, since He had said: 'I will glorify it,' He was now pointing out the method of glorification.

'And what is this method?'

'[Satan] will be cast out,' He declared.

'But what is the meaning of "Now is the judgment of this world"?'

It was as if He said: 'There will be judgment and retribution.'

'How and in what way?'

'The Devil destroyed the first man when he caught him in

5 Cf. John 17.10.

the toils of sin (for "through sin death entered");[6] but he has not found this in Me. Why, then, did he leap upon Me and give Me over to death? Why did he put it into the mind of Judas to destroy Me? Now, do not tell me at this point that God planned this, for that is the result, not of the Devil's strategy, but of God's wisdom, and for the moment let it be the mental process of that evil one that we examine. How, then, is the world judged in Me?'

It is as if at a session of a court of justice the Devil should be addressed as follows: 'Granted that you destroyed all men because you found them guilty of sin; but why did you destroy Christ? Is it not very evident that you did so unjustly? Well then, through Him the whole world will be vindicated.'

Furthermore, in order that this may be still clearer I shall illustrate the point by an example. Suppose that there is a certain tyrant, given to violence, who inflicts evils without number on all who come into his hands. If, on coming to grips with a king, or the son of a king, he should destroy the latter unjustly, his death will cause retribution to be made for the others, also.

Suppose that some creditor is exacting with his debtors, and beats them, and casts them into prison. Then suppose that out of the same high-handedness he puts someone who owes nothing into the same prison. The creditor will pay the penalty for what he has done to the others, for that innocent man will destroy him.

Thus has it also happened in the case of the Son. For the Devil will have punishment demanded of him for what he has done to us, because of what he dared to do to Christ. Now, to prove that Christ was indirectly saying this, listen to what He said: 'Now will the prince of the world be cast out

---

6 Rom. 5.12.

by my death. And I, if I be lifted up, will draw all to myself,'
that is, 'even the Gentiles.'

Moreover, lest anyone might say: 'How will he be cast out
if he also overcomes you?' He declared: 'He will not overcome Me, for how could he overcome Me if I am drawing
the rest to Myself?' Further, He did not mention the Resurrection, but something greater than the Resurrection, namely:
'I will draw all to myself.' If He had merely spoken of the
Resurrection, it would by no means be clear that they would
also believe in Him, but by declaring: 'They will believe,'
He was asserting both things at once, and confirming the fact
that He would also rise again. For, if He had remained dead,
and so was just a man, no one would have believed.

'I will draw all to myself.'

'How is it, then, that He could say that the Father draws
them?'

Because when the Son draws them, the Father is drawing
them. And He meant: 'I will draw them as if they were
being restrained by a tyrant, and unable to come to me
merely by their own efforts, and without power to escape from
his hands while he opposes them.' But elsewhere He called
this 'plunder.' 'No one can plunder the goods of the strong
man, unless he first binds the strong man, and then he will
plunder his goods.'[7] Now, He said this to suggest his strength.
Accordingly, what He there called 'plunder' He here called
'drawing.'

Therefore, since we know these things, let us rouse ourselves, let us glorify God, not by our faith alone, but also by
our life; otherwise, it would not be glory, but blasphemy.
God is not so much blasphemed by an impure Gentile as
by a corrupt Christian. Wherefore, I beg you to do everything
so that God may be glorified. Indeed, He said: 'Woe to that
servant by whom the name of God is blasphemed' (and when

---

7 Cf. Matt. 12.29.

there is a 'woe' pronounced, at once every punishment and retribution follow); but 'Blessed is he by whom His name is glorified.'

Let us not, then, be in darkness, but let us avoid all sins, especially those which also bring harm to the general welfare, for by these in particular is God blasphemed. Indeed, what pardon shall we have when we who are exhorted to give to others plunder the goods of others? What hope of salvation shall we have? If you do not feed the hungry you will be punished, but, if you also strip him who is already clothed, what pardon will you obtain? We shall not cease saying these things repeatedly. For perhaps those who do not listen today will listen tomorrow; and those who do not pay attention tomorrow will be persuaded to do so the day after that.

However, if some should even continue to be obdurate, at least we shall be judged guiltless. For we have fulfilled our duty. But I hope that we may not have to be ashamed because of our words to you, and that you may not have to hide your faces. May we all be able to stand confidently before the tribunal of Christ, so that we ourselves may be able to be proud of you and to receive some palliation of our own misdeeds in your being found worthy of approbation, in our Lord Jesus Christ. Glory be to Him and to the Father, together with the Holy Spirit, forever. Amen.

Homily 68 (John 12.34-41)

'The crowd answered him, "We have heard from the Law that the Christ abides forever. And how canst thou say, 'The Son of Man must be lifted up'? Who is this Son of Man?" '[1]

Deceit is a thing that is readily detected and easily caught, even if it is camouflaged exteriorly by colors without number.

---

1 John 12.34,35.

And just as those who are repairing cracks in walls cannot make them sound by smearing on paint, so, too, liars are easily found out.

Accordingly, the Jews had this experience here. For, when Christ had said to them: 'If I be lifted up from the earth, I will draw all to myself,' they replied: 'We have heard from the Law that the Christ abides forever. And how canst thou say, "The Son of Man must be lifted up"? Who is this Son of Man?'

So, then, they knew that the Christ is an immortal Being and has life without end. Well, then, they also understood what He meant. I say this for the Resurrection is frequently mentioned by the Scriptures in the same passage as the Passion. For example, Isaias mentioned them together when he said: 'He was led as a sheep to the slaughter,' and all that follows.[2] David in Psalm 2 and elsewhere frequently linked both these things. Further, when the Patriarch [Jacob] had said: 'He crouched and couched as a lion,' he added: 'and as a lion's whelp, who will disturb him?'[3] He meant at the same time the Passion and the Resurrection. However, though these Jews in the present instance thought they were silencing Him, and proving by their reference to the Law that He was not the Christ, actually they were acknowledging that the Christ abides forever.

Yet see how ill-disposed they were. For they did not say: 'We have heard that the Christ will not suffer,' or 'will not be crucified,' but 'that he abides forever.' However, not even this statement was contradictory, for the Passion was not an obstacle to the Resurrection. From this incident it is possible to see that they did understand much that was likely to be in doubt and that they were deliberately persisting in error. Indeed, since in His previous preaching He had spoken of

2 Isa. 53.7.
3 Cf. Gen. 49.9.

His death, on hearing the words 'be lifted up' they suspected
He was referring to this. Next they said: 'Who is this Son
of Man?' and they said it maliciously. They meant: 'Do not
think that we are talking about You, yet You say that we are
contradicting out of hostility toward You. See, we do not
know about whom You are speaking; nevertheless, we are declaring our opinion.'

What, then, did Christ reply? To silence them and to prove
that His Passion was no obstacle to His abiding forever He
said: 'Yet a little while the light is among you,' making it
clear to them that His death was a change of state. And this
is so for the sunlight is not extinguished, but disappears for a
little while, and appears again.

'Walk while you have the light.' What period of time was
He referring to here? Was it the whole of the present life,
or the time before the crucifixion? I for my part think it was
both, for by His ineffable mercy many believed after the
Resurrection, also. And He said this to attract them to the
faith, as He had done previously, when He said: 'Yet a little
while I am with you.'[4]

'He who walks in the darkness does not know where he
goes.' What things, in truth, the Jews are doing in our day,
yet do not know what they are doing, but, as it were, are
walking in darkness! They think, to be sure, they are traveling the straight road, but they are really walking on the opposite kind: keeping the Sabbath, preserving the Law, observing the regulations regarding food. Yet they do not know
where they are walking. For this reason He said: 'Walk in
the light, that you may become sons of light,' that is, 'My
sons.'

Even though in the beginning the Evangelist said: 'They
were born not of blood, nor of the will of the flesh, but of
God,' that is, 'of the Father,' here He Himself is spoken of as

---

4 John 7.33.

begetting them, that you may learn that Father and Son have the same activity.

'These things Jesus spoke and he went away and hid himself from them.' Why did He hide Himself at this time? It was not, indeed, because they were taking up stones to cast at Him, nor had they uttered any such blasphemy as before. Why, then, did He hide Himself? Since He read their hearts, He knew that their anger was strongly aroused, even though they said not a word. He knew that they were seething and bent on murder, so He did not wait for them to proceed to the deed, but hid Himself in order to allay their ill-will.

In fact, see how the Evangelist hinted at this. At once he added: 'Now though he had worked so many signs, they did not believe in him.' What signs were these? The numerous ones which the Evangelist omitted to mention. Moreover, this[5] is evident from what followed. I say this for, when He had yielded to them and had gone away, and when He had returned again, He spoke to them gently in the following words: 'He who believes in me believes not in me but in him who sent me.' Now, see what course He followed. He began with humble and lowly words and referred them to His Father. Then He once more spoke in sublime terms. And when He perceived that they were becoming wildly indignant He withdrew, and then once more He restrained Himself and began again with words of humble tenor.

'Where else did He do this?'

Where, indeed, did He not do it? See, to be sure, what He said at the outset. 'As I hear, I judge,' then in a more lofty strain: 'For as the Father raises the dead and gives them life, even so the Son also gives life to whom he will.'[6] Again: 'I do not judge you; there is another who judges.'

---

5 That is, that Christ hid Himself in order to allay their ill-will.
6 John 5.30,21.

Then, He again withdrew. Also, when He went to Galilee, He said: 'Do not labor for the food that perishes.' And after asserting great things of Himself: that He had come down from heaven, that He would give everlasting life, He once again withdrew. Then, too, when He was at the Feast of Tabernacles, He did this same thing.[7] Further, one may continually observe that His teaching was thus given variety: by His coming, His going away, by using humble words, by using sublime ones. And this He did here.

'Now though he had worked so many signs, they did not believe in him,' the Evangelist said, 'that the word which Isaias spoke might be fulfilled, "Lord, who has believed our report, and to whom has the arm of the Lord been revealed?" ' And again: 'They could not believe,' he declared, 'because Isaias said: "Thou shalt hear with thy hearing and understand not."[8] Isaias said these things when he saw his glory and spoke of him.'

Notice again that the words 'because' and 'said' do not indicate cause, but refer to the final outcome. For it was not 'because' Isaias said this that they did not believe; it was because they were not going to believe that Isaias said it. Why, then, did the Evangelist not put it that way, but say that their unbelief came from the prophecy, not the prophecy from their unbelief? And why did he go on to declare this very thing more emphatically in the following words: 'This is why they could not believe, because Isaias said'? From this passage he wished to establish the veracity of the Scripture by several proofs, and to emphasize the fact that whatever it has prophesied turns out not otherwise than as it has said. For, lest anyone might ask: 'Why did Christ come? Did He not know that they were not going to pay attention to Him?' Scripture introduces the Prophets who also foreknew this.

---

7 Cf. John 8.50; 6.27; 8.59.
8 Isa. 53.1; cf. 6.9.

He came, in fact, that they might have no excuse for their sinfulness. For the Prophet foretold what He did, as altogether certain of fulfilment. Indeed, if it were not going to take place at all, he would not have foretold it. However, it was going to be completely fulfilled because the Jews were so incorrigible.

Further, if the words 'they could not' occur instead of 'they did not wish,' do not be surprised. I say this for elsewhere Scripture says: 'Let him accept it who can.'[9] Thus, it is apt frequently to say 'can' for 'will.' And again: 'The world cannot hate you, but it hates me.'[10] Moreover, one may observe this practiced in ordinary usage, as when a man says: 'I cannot like such and such a one,' referring to the compulsion exercised by his will; and again: 'Such a one cannot be good.'

Moreover, what did the Prophet say? 'If the Ethiopian changes his skin and the leopard her spots, this people will be able to do well, when it has learned evil.'[11] He did not mean that it was impossible for them to practice virtue, but that they did not wish to do so, therefore they could not. Now, what the Evangelist said means this: that though it was impossible for the Prophet to lie, it was not therefore impossible for them to believe. Indeed, it was possible, even if they did believe, for him still to be truthful. For he would not have this prophecy if they were going to believe.

'Then, why did he not say it in that way?' you will ask.

Because Scripture has certain modes of speaking peculiar to it and it is necessary to observe its rules.

To continue: 'Isaias said these things when he saw his glory.' Whose glory? That of the Father. How is it, then, that it was the Son of whom John spoke,[12] and the Spirit

---

9 Matt. 19.12.
10 John 7.7.
11 Jer. 13.23.
12 Cf. John 1.14; 'We saw his glory.'

of whom Paul spoke? Not because they confused the Persons, but to show that They have a single dignity. I say this for the attributes of the Father are those of the Son, and those of the Son are those of the Father.[13]

Even though God said many things by the agency of angels, no one asserted: 'As the angel said,' but what? 'God hath spoken.' For, the words uttered by God through angels would be those of God, yet these words of God would no longer belong to the angels. So, here John meant that the words uttered by Isaias are really those of the Spirit.

'And spoke of him.' What did he say? 'I saw the Lord sitting upon a lofty throne,' etc.[14] Therefore by 'glory' in this passage John meant that vision [which Isaias saw]: the smoke, the hearing of ineffable mysteries, the sight of the Seraphim, and the lightning flashing from His throne—the glory which those Powers could not look at.

'And spoke of him.' What did he say? That he heard a voice saying: ' "Whom shall I send? and who shall go for us?" And I said, "Lo, here am I, send me." And he said, "With thy hearing thou shalt hear and understand not; and seeing, thou shalt see and know it not. For he has blinded their eyes, and hardened their hearts; lest they should see with their eyes and understand with their hearts." '

See once again another puzzling passage, though it is not so if we study it correctly. For, just as it is not part of the normal functioning of the sun's nature when it hurts the eyes of those whose vision is weak, so it is likewise with those who do not study the words of God closely. Thus, in the case of Pharao, God is said to have hardened his heart, and so it is with those who contend against the words of God. Moreover,

---

13 According to the Benedictine editor, the majority of the manuscripts containing this homily have a variant reading: 'and those of the Son are those of the Spirit.'

14 Isa. 6, *passim*.

this is an expression peculiar to Scriptural usage, similar to that found in the words, 'He has given them up to a reprobate sense' and 'He has let fall to the lot of the nations [the adoring of false gods],'[15] that is, 'He has granted,' 'He has allowed.' For in no way does this imply that it was God who was responsible for these things, but it shows that these things took place as a result of the wickedness of those men.

Indeed, when we are abandoned by God, we are given over to the Devil; and when we have been given over to the Devil we are afflicted with innumerable dread consequences. Well, then, to frighten his hearers the sacred writer said: 'He has hardened' and 'He has given up.' In testimony that He Himself not only does not give us up, but does not abandon us, either, unless we wish it, listen to what He said: 'Have not your iniquities divided between me and you?' And again: 'They who withdraw from you perish.'[16] Furthermore, Osee declared: 'Thou hast forgotten the law of thy God, I also will forget thee.' And He Himself said in the Gospels: 'How often would I have gathered thy children together, but thou wouldst not!' Isaias, also, in another place: 'I came, and there was not a man: I called, and there was none that would hear.'[17]

Now, He said these things to show that it is we who start off the process of abandonment and become responsible for our destruction. For God not only does not wish to abandon or punish us, but, even when He punishes, does so with reluctance. Indeed, He said: 'I desire not the death of the sinner, but that he be converted and live.'[18] Christ even wept over the destruction of Jerusalem, as we do in the case of our friends.

---

15 Rom. 1.28; Deut. 4.19.
16 Cf. Isa. 59.2; Ps. 72.27.
17 Osee 4.6; Luke 13.34; Isa. 50.2.
18 Cf. Ezech. 18.32.

Therefore, since we know these things, let us make every effort not to be separated from God. On the contrary, let us take pains about the care of our souls and about showing love for one another. Let us not tear our members to pieces (for that is the conduct of madmen and insane persons), but, in proportion as we see that they have evil dispositions, let us give them greater care. I say this for it often happens that we see many people with difficult or incurable diseases in their bodies, and we apply remedies unceasingly. What, to be sure, is worse than feet afflicted with gout and what worse than gouty hands? Shall we, therefore, amputate the limbs? By no means. On the contrary, we make every effort to afford them some relief, since we cannot cure the affliction.

Let us do this also in the case of our brethren; even if they are incurably ill, let us continue applying remedies. And let us bear one another's burdens. In this way we shall both observe the precept laid down by Christ and attain to the blessings promised, by the grace and mercy of our Lord Jesus Christ. Glory be to Him and to the Father, together with the Holy Spirit, forever and ever. Amen.

Homily 69 (John 12.42-50)

'And yet, even among the rulers many believed in him; but because of the Pharisees they did not acknowledge it, lest they should be put out of the synagogue. For they loved the glory of men more than the glory of God.'[1]

We must flee from all the passions that corrupt the soul— all of them without exception—but much more from those that of their nature give rise to many sins: I mean, for example, avarice. This is in itself a fearful malady, but it

---

1 John 12.42,43.

becomes much more serious in that it is the root and mother of all evils. Such, also, is vainglory.

Notice, for instance, that these men were estranged from the faith because of their love of the glory of this world. For the Evangelist said: 'Even among the rulers many believed in him; but because of the Jews they did not acknowledge it, lest they should be put out of the synagogue.' Accordingly, Christ had spoken to them of this before. 'How can you believe who receive glory from one another, and do not seek the glory which is from the only God?'[2] Surely they were not rulers, but slaves in the lowest degree of slavery.

However, this fear was destroyed later on. For on no occasion do we see the Apostles held captive by this passion. I say this because in their case rulers and priests professed their belief. The grace of the Spirit came and made all of them more unyielding than adamant.

On this occasion, therefore, because this human respect was an obstacle to their belief, listen to what He said: 'He who believes in me, believes not in me but in him who sent me.' It was as if He said: 'Why are you afraid to believe in me? Faith in God comes through Me, as also, accordingly, does unbelief.' Notice how by every means He showed the complete identity of Their substance. Further, He did not say: 'He who believes Me,' lest someone might assert that He was merely referring to His words and so was saying what might be said of ordinary men. For he who believed the Apostles did not believe them, but God. However, that you may learn that He was speaking of belief in His substance, He did not say: 'He who believes My words,' but 'He who believes in me.'

'Yet why did He never state the opposite, namely: "He who believes in the Father believes not in the Father, but in Me"?'

---

2 John 5.44.

Because they would reply: 'Look, we believe in the Father, yet do not believe in You.' I say this for they were still very weak. In addressing His disciples, to be sure, He did speak in this way. 'You believe in God, believe also in me.'[3] However, because He perceived that these men were too weak to hear such words, He lead them on in a different way. Therefore, He showed them thát it is impossible to believe in the Father without believing in Him. Further, that you might not think that He was speaking as if of a man, He added: 'He who sees me sees him who sent me.'

'What is this, then, is God a body?'

By no means, for He was here speaking of mental vision, and by this means was making evident His consubstantiality with the Father. Further, what is the meaning of 'He who believes in me'? As one might say: 'He who bears water from the river takes not the water of the river, but really that of its source.' Yet, this illustration is still too feeble for the matter.

'I have come a light unto the world.' Since the Father is called by this name in the Old as well as the New Testament, He also used this name for Himself. That is why Paul likewise called Him 'brightness,'[4] since he learned from Scripture to do so. Christ was pointing out that His relationship to the Father is very close, or, rather, that there is no difference, if He said—as He did—that belief in Him is not belief only in Him but includes the Father. Moreover, He called Himself 'light' because He sets men free from error and so destroys the darkness of their minds.

'If anyone does not hear me, it is not I who judge him; for I have not come to judge the world, but to save the world.' Lest they might think that it was because of some lack of power that He failed to judge those who rejected Him,

---

3 John 14.1.
4 Heb. 1.3.

He therefore declared: 'I have not come to judge the world.'

Next, that they might not become somewhat lax for this reason, when they learned that he who believes will be saved, while he who does not believe will be punished, see how He threatened them with the fearful tribunal. He went on to say: 'He who rejects me and does not accept my words has one to condemn him.'

'If the Father judges no one, and You have not come to judge the world, who will judge him?'

'The word that I have spoken will judge him.' It was because they were saying that He was not from God that He spoke in this way, to point out that they will not then be able to say these things. On the contrary, 'The words which I have now spoken will stand in the position of accuser to convict them and deprive them of all excuse.'

'The word that I have spoken.' What sort of word? 'I have not come of myself, but he who sent me, the Father, has given me commandment what I should say and what I should declare,' and other statements similar to this. Accordingly, He was speaking in this way for their sake, in order that they might not have a shred of excuse. If this were not so, how would He be any better than Isaias? I say this for the latter said: 'The Lord hath given me a learned tongue that I should know when I ought to speak a word.' Further, what of Jeremias? When he was sent he then was inspired by God. And what of Ezechiel? For, when he had eaten the chapter of the book, he then spoke prophetically.[5]

Otherwise, also, those who were to listen to what Christ said would be found to have been responsible for His acquiring this knowledge. For if, when He was sent, He then 'received commandment what He should say,' you would have to admit that before He was sent He did not know what to say.

---

5 Cf. Isa. 50.4; Jer. 1.7; Ezech. 3.1.

Yet, what is more impious than these words, if someone should interpret them in this way, without understanding the reason for their humility? However, Paul declared that he knew, and the disciples did, also: 'What is the good and acceptable and perfect will of God.'[6] And did the Son not understand until He 'received commandment'? But how could this be reasonable? Do you perceive that Christ was bringing what He said down to an excessively low degree of humility for this reason: that He might attract them and might silence those to come afterwards?

Therefore, He spoke in human fashion for this reason: that He might thus compel them to get away from the commonplace meaning of what was said, since they knew that it proceeded, not from His nature, but from the weakness of His listeners.

'And I know that his commandment is everlasting life. The things, therefore, that I speak, I speak as the Father has bidden me.' Do you perceive the humility of His words? For He who receives a command is not His own master. Yet, to be sure, He had said: 'As the Father raises the dead and gives them life, so the Son also gives life to whom he will.'[7] Then, He has power to raise whom He wills, but has not power to say what He wishes? No, for what He wished to convey by His words was as follows: 'It would be contrary to Our nature for the Father to say one thing and for Me to say another.'

'And I know that his commandment is everlasting life.' He addressed these words to those who were maintaining that He was a seducer of the people and had come to destroy. However, when He said: 'It is not I who judge,' He was pointing out that He was not the cause of the destruction of such men. Indeed, by these words He was as much as

6 Rom. 12.2.
7 John 5.21.

testifying—since He was on the point of departing from them and of no longer dwelling with them: 'I have spoken to you as saying nothing of My own, but saying everything as from the Father.' And He therefore concluded His discourse to them on a humble note, that He might say: 'To the very end it is this kind of word that I have uttered to them.'

What sort of word was this, then? 'I speak as the Father has spoken to Me. But, if I were in opposition to God, I should say just the opposite, because I should say nothing pleasing to God, so as to secure the glory for Myself. As it is, however, so completely have I referred everything to Him that I say nothing of My own. Why, therefore, do you not believe Me when I say that I have received His commandment, and in this way effectually dispose of your malicious suspicion regarding My being in opposition to God?

'Now, when men have agreed to perform a mission, it is impossible for them to do or say anything not in conformity with the wishes of those who have sent them, as long as they continue to fulfill their mission and do not falsify it. Thus, it is likewise not possible for Me to do or say anything contrary to what the Father wills. What I do, to be sure, He does, because 'He is with me and the Father has not left me alone.'[8]

Do you see how He was constantly pointing out His close affinity with the Father and that there is no difference between them? I say this for, when He said: 'I have not come of myself,' He was speaking, not to become dispossessed of His own power, but to dispose of the idea that it is different from and opposed to that of the Father. For, if men are their own masters, much more so is the only-begotten Son. Moreover, listen to what Paul said in testimony to the truth of

---

8 John 8.29.

this statement: 'He emptied himself and delivered himself up for us.'[9]

However, as I have said, vainglory is a terrible thing, a terrible thing! It caused the Jews not to believe, and others to have faulty faith and to pervert to impiety those things which by His mercy He said for their sake. Let us, then, flee from this beast, above all. For it has many colors and shapes, and spreads its peculiar poison everywhere: in riches, and in luxury, and in beauty of body. Because of it we exceed what is necessary in all phases of our life. Because of it we go to excessive expense in clothing, and acquire numerous swarms of slaves. Because of it, the extent of our need is totally disregarded, and extravagance has its way in homes, in clothing and in food.

Do you wish to enjoy real glory? Practice almsgiving; then the angels will praise you; then God will give you approval. As it is, however, O woman, your admiration extends only to goldsmiths and weavers, so you depart this life uncrowned, and frequently aware that you have made yourself the target of cursing. If, on the contrary, you do not adorn your body with these ornaments, but pour them out to satisfy the hunger of the poor, you will receive great commendation on all sides, and generous praise. When you give those things to others, you will then possess them, whereas if you alone keep them, you will not possess them. Your home is not a secure storehouse, but the hands of the poor provide a safe one.

Why do you deck out your body, while you neglect your soul, enslaved as it is by impurity? Why do you not give as much thought to your soul as to your body? You ought, rather, to give it more care. Beloved, you ought at least to give it an equal amount of thought. Tell me, please, if someone should ask you which you would prefer: for your body to be glowing with health and to excel in beauty, but to be

---

9 Phil. 2.7; Eph. 5.2.

clad in mean clothing, or for your body to be crippled and full of disease, but adorned with gold and lavishly decked out—would you not choose by far to possess beauty as part of the very nature of your body rather than merely in the outward covering of clothes? Then, will you make this choice with regard to your body, but just the opposite one in the case of your soul? If it is foul and noisome and black, what fruit do you think you will enjoy from your golden ornaments? But what insanity is this?

Apply this adornment within yourself and place these necklaces around your soul. For the ornaments placed about the body do not contribute either to its health or its beauty, since they do not make what is black, white—or what is discreditable, beautiful or good-looking. If you place ornaments about your soul, on the contrary, they quickly make it white instead of black, beautiful and comely instead of foul and deformed. Moreover, this is not my statement, but that of the Lord Himself, who spoke as follows: 'If your sins be as scarlet, I will make them white as snow,' and 'Give alms and all things are clean to you.'[10]

Further, if you act in this way, you will not only make yourself beautiful, but also your husband. For, if husbands see their wives foregoing this worldly adornment, they will not be forced to undertake great expense. If they do not have expense they will refrain from all covetousness, and they will be better disposed to give alms. And so you will be able confidently to urge them to do as they ought. As it is, however, you have been deprived of such power as this. What sort of words will you find to say these things? With what kind of expression will you look at your husbands as you urge them to give alms, when you are spending the greatest part of their wealth on apparel for your body? When you forego adornment with golden ornaments, then you will be

---

10 Isa. 1.18; Luke 11.41.

able to speak confidently to your husband on the subject of almsgiving.

Even if you do not succeed at all, you have completely fulfilled your duty, or, rather, it is impossible for him also not to gain profit, since you are speaking to him by means of your very deeds. 'For how dost thou know, O wife, whether thou wilt save thy husband?'[11] Therefore, just as you will now give a reckoning both regarding yourself and regarding him, so, if you lay aside all this show, you will have a double crown. You will be crowned and glorious, together with your husband, for those endless ages, and will enjoy everlasting blessings.

May we all attain these by the grace and mercy of our Lord Jesus Christ. Glory be to Him forever and ever. Amen.

Homily 70 (John 13.1-12)

'Before the Feast of the Passover, Jesus, knowing that his hour had come, to pass out of this world to the Father, having loved his own who were in the world, loved them to the end.'[1]

'Be imitators of me,' said Paul, 'as I am of Christ.' That is why He took flesh from our clay, in order that by this means He might teach us virtue. Indeed: 'In the likeness of sinful flesh as a sin-offering, he has condemned sin in the flesh,' Paul declared. Moreover, Christ Himself said: 'Learn from me, for I am meek and humble of heart.'[2]

Now, He taught this, not in word only, but also by His deeds. I say this for they had been calling Him a Samaritan and a devil and a seducer, and were taking up stones to cast

11 1 Cor. 7.16.

1 John 13.1.
2 1 Cor. 11.1; Rom. 8.3; Matt. 11.29.

at Him. Now, the Pharisees sent servants to arrest Him, and again they despatched others to plot against Him, while they themselves continued frequently insulting Him, even though they had no grounds for accusation, but were, in fact, continually receiving benefits from Him. Nevertheless, even after such great rebuffs, He did not refrain from doing good to them both in word and deed.

Even when a certain servant struck Him, Christ said: 'If I have spoken ill, bear witness to the evil; but if well, why dost thou strike me?'[3] However, these were His relations with His enemies and those who were plotting against Him. Let us see, on the other hand, how He acted in the present instance toward His disciples, or, rather, how He treated His betrayer.

He had reason to despise him most of all, because, in spite of being a disciple, and a companion of His table and hospitality, and an eye-witness of His miracles, and so highly honored, he committed the most serious offense of all. He did not, to be sure, cast stones at Christ, or openly insult Him, but he betrayed Him and gave Him up. Yet see how kindly Christ received him and washed his feet. He did so, for He wished by this action to restrain the betrayer from that evil deed.

Even though it was possible for Him, if He had desired, to wither him, as He did the fig-tree; or to pierce him through, as He splintered the rocks; or to tear him, as He did the curtain of the Temple; yet He did not wish to force him, but to draw him away from the betrayal by his own free choice. And that is why He washed his feet. Yet that wretched and unhappy man was not even shamed by this.

'Before the Feast of the Passover,' the Evangelist said, 'Jesus, knowing that his hour had come.' He did not then only know it, but he meant that He acted as He did, having

---

3 John 18.23.

'known' long before. 'To pass out of this world': the Evangelist was euphemistically referring to His death as 'a passing.'

'Having loved his own, he loved them to the end.' Do you perceive that, when He was on the point of leaving them, He gave them stronger evidence of His love? For the words 'Having loved them, He loved them to the end,' mean this, that He omitted nothing that one who loves deeply usually does.

'But why in the world did He not act in this way from the start?'

He performed His greater deeds in the latter part of His life to increase their attachment to Him, and to store up for them ahead of time great courage for the frightful things that were to come upon them. The Evangelist called them 'His own' in the sense of 'His intimate friends,' though he had also called others 'His own' in the sense of 'His own creatures,' as when he said: 'His own received him not.'[4]

Further, what is the meaning of 'who were in the world'? He said this because the dead were also His own—Abraham and Isaac and Jacob and their followers and others like them —but they were not in the world still. Do you perceive that He is the God both of the Old and of the New Testaments? But what is the meaning of 'He kept on loving them without ceasing'? John made this statement as a proof of the greatness of Christ's love, though he had stated another proof of it elsewhere, namely, that He laid down His life for His friends.[5] This, however, had not yet taken place.

For what reason did He choose this moment to wash their feet? He did it because it was much more admirable to do so at a time when He appeared more estimable in the eyes of all; as He was on the point of departing from them, He thus

---

4 John 1.11.
5 Cf. John 15.14.

left behind no small consolation. For, since they were going to suffer very deep grief, to counterbalance it He was using this means of giving them consolation.

'And during the supper, the devil having already put it into the heart of Judas to betray him.' The Evangelist said this in amazement, and to make it clear that Christ washed the feet of this man who had already determined to betray Him. Furthermore, he was pointing out the exceeding wickedness of the man, because not even the sharing in Christ's hospitality prevented him—hough this is a thing that can most of all act as a check on wickedness—nor the fact that Christ remained his Master and continued to bear with him to the last day.

'But Jesus, knowing that the Father had given all things into his hands, and that he had come forth from God and was going to God.' Here the Evangelist was once more speaking in wonderment that He who is so great and so pre-eminent, He who had come from God and was going to Him, He who is the Ruler of all things, performed this action, and thus did not disdain to stoop to such an office.

I think that John was here speaking of the salvation of the faithful, when he mentioned 'giving over' [all things into his hands]. I say this for, when Christ said 'All things have been delivered to me by my Father,' He meant this 'giving over.' Elsewhere He also said, similarly: 'They were thine, and thou hast given them to me'; and again: 'No one can come to me, unless the Father draw him'; and: 'unless it is given to him from heaven.'[6] Therefore, either the Evangelist meant to say this, or else that Christ would be in no way depreciated by this action, since He had come from God and was going to God and possessed all things.

However, when you hear of 'giving over' do not understand it in a human sense, for he was making clear the honor Christ shows toward His Father, and His complete oneness with

---

6 Matt. 11.27; John 17.6; 6.44; 3.28.

Him. For, as the Father gives over to Him, so He Himself also gives over to the Father. Paul also made this clear by saying: 'When he gives over the kingdom to God the Father.'[7]

However, John was here speaking in a more human fashion to show Christ's great solicitude for them and to reveal His ineffable love for them, because, in short, He was concerned about them as 'His own.' He was teaching them that humility is the mother of blessings, since He declared that it is the beginning and end of virtue. Moreover, the words, 'He had come forth from God and was going to God,' do not occur merely by chance, but in order that we may learn that He was performing actions worthy of One coming from that Source and returning there, since He was trampling all vanity underfoot.

'And rose from the supper and laid aside his garments.' Notice how He showed humility not only by the fact of washing their feet, but in other respects, besides. For it was not before reclining to eat that He arose, but after they had all settled down to the meal. Then, too, not merely did He perform these ablutions, but He did so after He had laid aside His garments. And He did not stop with this, but girded Himself with a towel. Moreover, He was not satisfied with this, but He Himself filled the basin. He did not bid someone else to fill it, but did all these things Himself, to show that, when we do good, we must not do such things in a spirit of routine, but with enthusiastic zeal.

Now, it seems to me that He washed the feet of the traitor first, because the Evangelist said: 'He began to wash the feet of the disciples,' and added: 'He came to Simon Peter. And Peter said to him, "Dost thou wash my feet? With those hands with which thou didst open the eyes of the blind," he meant; "the hands with which thou didst cleanse lepers; the hands with which thou didst raise the dead?" ' His words

---

7 1 Cor. 15.24.

indeed are very emphatic. Therefore, he need not have said any more than the word 'Thou,' for of itself it was sufficient to convey all this meaning.

Further, someone will probably ask: 'How was it that no one of the others stopped Christ, but only Peter, though it was an action indicative of no small love and respect? What, then, is the reason for this?'

It seems to me that He first washed the traitor's feet, and came next to Peter, and that the rest were instructed by his example. It is clear, then, from the fact that John said: 'When he came to Peter,' that He washed someone else before the latter. However, the Evangelist was not very explicit, for the word 'began' merely hints at this. Besides, even if Peter was first in rank, it is likely that the traitor was forward and took his place at table ahead of the leader.

I say this for his forwardness was also shown later in the supper, when he dipped his bread with the Master, and when, after being reproved, he did not feel compunction. At that time Peter, on the contrary, because he had been rebuked once at the beginning of the supper, even though he was again speaking out of love, was so humbled that in fear and trembling he needed another to ask the question;[8] while Judas, after being repeatedly admonished, persisted in his brazenness. When Christ came to Peter, then, 'Peter said to him, "Lord, dost thou wash my feet?" '

'Jesus answered him, "What I do thou knowest not now; but thou shalt know hereafter." ' That is: 'Thou shalt know how great is the profit from this, how useful it is for instructing, and how it can lead us to complete self-abasement.'

What did Peter reply? He still opposed Him and said: 'Thou shalt never wash my feet!' What are you doing, Peter? Do you not remember what you said before? Did you not say: 'Far be it from thee'? And did you not hear: 'Get behind

---

8 That is, 'Is it I, Lord?'

me, Satan'?[9] And have you not yet become wise but are still impulsive?

'Yes,' he replies, 'but what He was doing took me completely by surprise.'

Therefore, because Peter was acting out of his great love, Christ also once again overcame him by that same means. Accordingly, just as on that occasion He had rebuked him sharply and said: 'Thou art a scandal to me,' He acted similarly here and said: 'If I do not wash thee, thou shalt have no part in me.' What, then, did His fervent and zealous disciple reply?

'Lord, not my feet only, but also my hands and my head.' He was vehement in his refusal, and even more so in giving consent: and in both cases he acted out of love. Why, indeed, did Jesus not explain for what reason He was doing this, but answer with a threat? Because Peter would not have obeyed. For, if He had said: 'Allow me to do this because by this means I am persuading you to practice humility,' Peter would have promised to do so ten thousand times, so that His Lord might refrain from doing this.

Actually, what did He say? A thing that Peter would dread and tremble at most of all: namely, that he would be estranged from Him. For it was Peter who frequently asked: 'Where art thou going?' Moreover, that is why he also declared: 'I will even lay down my life for thee.'[10]

Now, if on hearing: 'What I do thou knowest not now, but thou shalt know hereafter,' he did not even then acquiesce, much more would he not have done so if he had learned this.[11] Therefore Christ said: 'Thou shalt know hereafter,' because He realized that, even if Peter learned this now, he would still resist. Further, Peter did not say: 'Instruct me,

---

9 Matt. 16.22,23.
10 John 13.36,37.
11 That is, the true significance of the washing of the feet, namely, an act of humility on the part of Christ.

so that I may grasp what You are doing.' On the contrary, he said something much more vehement, and did not give himself the chance to learn, but again offered resistance by saying: 'Thou shalt never wash my feet.' But when he was threatened he at once relaxed his tone.

Now, what is the meaning of: 'Thou shalt know hereafter?' 'Hereafter'—when? He meant: 'When thou shalt cast out demons in My name; when thou shalt behold Me being taken up into heaven; when thou shalt learn from the Spirit that I am seated at the right hand of the Father—then thou shalt know what is now happening.'

What, then, did Christ reply? When Peter had declared: 'Not my feet only, but also my hands and my head,' He said: 'He who has bathed needs only to wash his feet, and he is clean all over. And you are clean, but not all. For he knew who it was that should betray him.'

'Yet, if they are clean why do You wash their feet?'

He did so in order that we might learn to act humbly. That is why He did not go to any other member of the body, but only the one which seems to be less honorable than the others.

'But what is the meaning of "He who has bathed"?'

He said this instead of 'he who is clean.'

'Surely they were not clean, since they were not yet rid of their sins, nor had they been deemed worthy of the Spirit, inasmuch as sin still prevailed, the handwriting of the curse still remained, the Victim had not yet been offered. How is it, then, that He said they were clean?'

On the contrary, lest you think, by reason of these words, that they were clean, because free from sin, He later added: 'You are already clean because of the word that I have spoken to you.'[12] That is: 'You are clean only to that extent. You

_____
12 John 15.3.

have already received the Light; you have already gotten rid of the Jewish error.' I say this for the Prophet asserted: 'Wash yourselves be clean, take away evil from your souls.'[13] So that such a man has been bathed and is clean.

Therefore, since they had rooted out all evil from their souls and were following Him with complete sincerity, for this reason He declared, in accordance with the Prophet's words: 'He who has bathed is already clean.' I say this for in the Prophet's words he does not mean bathing by water—the Jewish method of purification—but the purifying of the conscience.

Let us also, then, be clean. Let us 'learn to do well.' And what is the meaning of 'to do well'? 'Judge for the fatherless, defend the widow, and come and let us reason together, saith the Lord.'[14] In the Scriptures there is frequent mention of the widows and orphans, but we make no mention of this subject. Yet consider how great the reward. 'If your sins be as scarlet, I will make them as white as snow: and if they be red as crimson, I will make them as white as wool.' Now, this is so for the widow is without a protector. Therefore God exercises great solicitude in her behalf. And he does this for, though it is possible for them to enter into marriage for the second time, they are enduring the trials of widowhood by reason of the fear of God.

Let as all, then, men and women, stretch out our hands to them, lest at some time we may undergo the trials of widowhood. And, in case we do undergo them, let us first lay up for ourselves an abundant store of mercy. The power of the widows' tears is not small, but can open up heaven itself. Let us not, then, treat them harshly or make their misfortune worse, but aid them in every way.

If we help them thus, we shall be obtaining great security

---

13 Cf. Isa. 1.16.
14 Cf. Isa. 1.17,18.

for ourselves, both in the present life and in the time to come. For they will be our protectors, not here only but also in the next world, by cutting away the greater part of our sins because of our benefits to them, and so causing us to take our stand confidently before the tribunal of Christ.

May all of us obtain this by the grace and mercy of our Lord Jesus Christ. Glory be to Him forever and ever. Amen.

Homily 71 (John 13.12-19)

'And after he had put on his garments, and when he had reclined again, he said to them, "Do you know what I have done to you?" 'etc.[1]

It is a dangerous thing, beloved, a dangerous thing, to plumb the depths of evil. For the soul at length becomes incorrigible. Therefore we ought to make every effort not to be caught in its toils at the start. It is certainly easier not to become entangled at all than to retrieve oneself after having become entangled.

Indeed, see how much help Judas enjoyed when he began to be involved, yet even so he did not amend himself. Christ said to him: 'One of you is a devil.' He asserted: 'Not all of you believe.' He said: 'I do not speak of you all,' and 'I know whom I have chosen,'[2] yet Judas did not grasp the import of one of these statements.

'Now after he had washed their feet and put on his garments, when he had reclined again, he said, "Do you know what I have done to you?" ' No longer was He addressing Peter alone, but also all of them. 'You call me Master and Lord, and you say well, for so I am.'

'You call me'—He gave approval to their judgment. Then,

---

1 John 13.12,13.
2 John 6.71,65; 13.18.

lest the words might be thought merely an expression of their love, He added 'for so I am.' Therefore, by citing what was said by them He at once made His words inoffensive, while the fact that their words were corroborated by Him raised these above suspicion.

'For so I am,' He declared. Do you perceive that, when He was speaking to His disciples alone, He spoke more openly and revealed the truth about Himself? Therefore, just as He said: 'Call no one on earth Master; for one only is your Master,' so He declared: 'Call no one on earth your father.'[3] However, the word 'one' and 'one'[4] is predicated not of the Father only, but also of [the Son] Himself. For, if He was ruling Himself out when He spoke, how was it that He said: 'That you may become sons of light'?[5] And, again, if He meant that the Father only is Master, how was it that He said: 'For so I am'? and also: 'One only is your Master, the Christ'?

'If, therefore, I the Lord and Master have washed your feet,' He said, 'you also ought to wash the feet of one another. For I have given you an example, that as I have done to you, so you also should do.' Yet it is not the same, for He Himself is Master and Lord, while you are fellow slaves. Therefore what is the meaning of 'so'? He meant: 'with the same zeal.' That is why He selected His examples from matters of greater importance: namely, that we might at least accomplish the lesser ones.

I say this for teachers write the letters for children very beautifully, so that they may attain to at least an imperfect imitation. Where now are those who despise their fellow slaves? Where now are those who demand honor for them-

---

3 Cf. Matt. 23.8,9.
4 That is, 'One is your Master; one is your Father.'
5 John 12.36.

selves? Christ washed the feet of the traitor, a sacrilegious
wretch and a thief, and even at the time of the betrayal made
him a sharer in His table, even though he was beyond reconciliation. And do you give yourself airs and raise your eyebrows?

'Let us wash one another's feet,' He said.

'Those of slaves, too?'

And what great thing is it, even if we do wash the feet of
slaves? For in our case 'slave' or 'free man' is a distinction in
name only, while in that of Christ it was true in actual fact.
For He Himself was Lord by nature, while we were slaves, yet
He did not beg off from doing even this. As it is now, however,
it is considered praiseworthy if we do not treat free men as
slaves, as bondsmen bought for a price, Yet what shall we
then say,[6] we who have received the example of such great
forbearance, but do not imitate it ourselves even slightly, and
who, on the contrary, adopt the opposite attitude: both
magnifying ourselves unduly and not rendering to others
what we ought? For God has made us debtors to one another
—after He Himself had begun this process—and debtors in
regard to a smaller amount. He Himself, to be sure, was
Lord, whereas if we perform an act of humility we do it to
our fellow slaves.

Accordingly, He made an indirect reference to this very
thing, also, by saying: 'If, therefore, I the Lord and Master,'
and again: 'So you also.' Indeed, it would have followed
logically for us to say: 'How much rather we slaves,' and He
left this conclusion to the conscience of His hearers.

'But why in the world did He wash their feet at that
precise moment?'

They were presently going to enjoy honor: some of them
more, some less. Therefore, in order that they might not
magnify themselves at the expense of one another, and say
again what they said before this: 'Who is greater?' and that

---

6 Before the judgment seat of God.

they might not wax indignant toward one another, He took down the pride of all of them by declaring: 'Even if you are very great, you ought not to lord it over your brother.' Moreover, He did not mention a point that was even greater, namely: 'If I have washed the traitor's feet, what great thing is it if you wash the feet of one another?' But, after having made this clear by His deeds, He left the conclusion to the judgment of those who witnessed them. That is why He had said: 'Whoever carries out and teaches, he shall be called great.'[7] For teaching a thing is illustrating it by one's deeds.

Indeed, what conceit would this deed not purge out? What pride and vanity would it not dispel? He who is seated upon the Cherubim washed the traitor's feet, and do you, O man, who are but earth and ashes, and cinders, and dust, magnify yourself and act arrogantly? What hell would such conduct not deserve? Therefore, if you have a desire to be really high-minded, come and I will show you a way, for you do not know what it is at all. Well, then, if a man is preoccupied with present things, as if they were important, he is low-minded. So that there could be no humility without magnanimity, nor could there be puffed-up pride, unless it proceeded from pusillanimity.

For, even as small children become attracted to trifling objects, in open-mouthed admiration of balls and hoops and blocks, but cannot arrive at an understanding of great things, so also in this life the truly wise man considers present things as nothing (and therefore he will not himself choose to acquire them nor to take them from another), while the man who is not such will be affected in the opposite way and feel an attraction for cobwebs, and shadows, and dreams and things even more unsubstantial.

'Amen, amen, I say to you, no servant is greater than his master, nor is one who is sent greater than he who sent him.

---

7 Matt. 5.19.

If you know these things, blessed shall you be if you do them. I do not speak of you all. But that the Scripture may be fulfilled, "He who eats bread with me has lifted up his heel against me." ' Here He was repeating what He had said before, to put them to shame. 'For if the servant is not greater than his Master, nor is one who is sent greater than he who sent him, and this deed has been performed by Me, much more ought it be performed by you.'

Then, lest anyone say: 'Why are You saying these things, for do we not already know them?' He added this very thing: 'I am saying this to you, not because you are ignorant of it, but in order that you may exemplify My words by your deeds. For the knowledge is common to all, but not the doing.' Indeed, that is why He said: 'Blessed shall you be if you do them.'

Accordingly, that is why I, also, am frequently—indeed, always—saying the same thing to you, even though you know it, that I may spur you on to the deed. The Jews also had knowledge, but they were not blessed, because they did not carry it out.

'I do not speak of you all,' He said. Bless me, what forbearance! Not yet did He convict the traitor, but concealed his deed to give him, by this means, an opportunity to repent. He both convicted him and did not convict him by saying: 'He who eats bread with me has lifted up his heel against me.'

Further, it seems to me that the words, 'No servant is greater than his master,' were also said for this reason: that if men ever should be wronged by servants, or by persons still more inferior, they might not take offense, looking to the example of Judas who, after enjoying innumerable benefits, repaid his Benefactor with the opposite. And therefore Christ quoted the words: 'He who eats bread with me.' Omitting to mention all the rest, He spoke of the thing which should most of all have restrained Judas and changed his purpose.

'He who has been fed by Me, he who has shared My table,'
He meant.

He said this, besides, to teach them to do good to those who
injured them, even if the latter continued to be incorrigible.
After declaring: 'I do not speak of you all,' lest fear might
beset many of them, He ended by singling him out by saying:
'He who eats bread with me.' The words 'not of you all' did
not altogether restrict what He said to one person, and that
is why He added: 'He who eats bread with me,' to point out
to that wretched man that He would be arrested, not because
He was caught unawares, but even though He had complete
knowledge. And this was, most of all, calculated to hold him
in check. Moreover, He did not say 'betrays me,' but 'has
lifted up his heel against me,' because He wished to affirm
the treachery and deceit and covertness of the plot.

Furthermore, these details have been recorded that we may
not bear ill will against those who wrong us, but may
reproach them and weep over them. Indeed, not those who
are wronged, but those who do wrong deserve our tears. For
the covetous man and the slanderer, and the man guilty
of any other wrong-doing injure themselves most of all,
while they are of great benefit to us, if we do not avenge
ourselves. I mean, for example: has that fellow robbed you?
Have you given thanks and praised God for the injury? You
have reaped a reward ten-thousandfold by that thanksgiving;
just as the other has stored up for himself untold suffering by
fire.

If someone should say: 'What if I cannot avenge myself on
the wrong-doer, because I am weaker?' I should make this
reply: 'You could have shown annoyance or vexation, for
these were within your power: to curse your oppressor, to
utter ten-thousand imprecations upon him, to defame him
to all men. Well, then, if a man does not do these things,
will he not receive the reward for not avenging himself? For it

is clear that, even if he were able to do so, he would not have done so.'

Indeed, the man that has suffered injury uses the weapon available to him when, because of his contentiousness, he avenges himself on his aggressor with curses, insults, and treachery. Well, then, do you not only refrain from doing these things but also pray for your adversary. I say this for, if you not only refrain from doing these things, but also pray for him, you have become like God. For 'Pray for those who calumniate you,' He said, 'so that you may be like your Father in heaven.'[8]

Do you perceive what great profit we derive from the injury done us by others? Nothing so pleases God as not returning evil for evil. But why do I say merely 'not returning evil for evil'? We have been enjoined to return the opposite, in fact: namely, good works, prayers. That is why Christ repaid the man that was going to betray Him with just the opposite. For example, He washed his feet, reproved him in private, inspired him with fear sparingly, ministered to him, allowed him to share in His table and His kiss. Yet, though he did not become better because of these things, He Himself persevered in His course of action.

However, come, and let us instruct you by the example of slaves and by the abundant evidence offered by characters in the Old Testament, that you may understand that we have no semblance of excuse, when we bear ill-will because of injuries. Shall I mention Moses, therefore, or shall we bring our discussion to a still earlier time? The greater the antiquity of the examples cited, the more we are convinced by them. Why in the world is that? Because at that time virtue was harder to practice. For those who then were living did not have commandments written down, or the example of mens' lives, but nature engaged in the struggle, equipped only with

---

8 Cf. Matt. 5.44,45.

its own powers, and was forced to keep afloat at all times
without external assistance.

Therefore, in praise of Noe, Scripture not merely called
him 'blameless,' but added 'among the men of his day,'[9] to
make it clear that he was so at that time when the obstacles
to virtue were many. Besides, other men were illustrious after
him, yet he will have no less praise than they. For he was
blameless in his own time.

'Who, then, before the time of Moses was patient in the face
of injuries?'

The blessed and noble Joseph, who, though illustrious for
his chastity was no less illustrious for his patience. He was
sold, when he had done no wrong, but was only giving service,
acting as a slave, performing all the offices of a servant. Still
his brothers utttered malicious accusation against him, yet he
did not get back at them even though he had his father on
his side. On the contrary, he went to bring food to them in
desert. And when he did not find them, he was not plunged
into despair, nor did he turn back (even though he had good
reason to do so if he wished), but he stayed among wild beasts
and those savage men, continuing to act like a true brother.

Once again, when he was living in the prison and was
asked the reason, he said nothing of their wickedness, but:
'I have done nothing and was kidnapped from the land of the
Hebrews.'[10] And after this, when he again was in a position of
authority, he both fed his brethren and freed them from dreadful misfortunes without number. For, if we are vigilant, the
wickedness of our neighbor cannot deprive us of our own
virtue.

However, his brethren were quite different from him. For
they stripped off his tunic, and tried to kill him, and made

---

9 Gen. 6.9.
10 Gen. 40.15; cf. Gen. 37-44 for the following details of the well-known
  story of Joseph.

insulting remarks about his dream, and even though they had been provided by him with nourishment they tried to deprive him of his life and freedom. Moreover, they began to eat while they disregarded their brother cast down naked in a cistern. What could be worse than this savagery? Were they not worse than any murderers?

Furthermore, they afterwards drew him out of the cistern and betrayed him to ten-thousand deaths by selling him to savage and uncouth men, who were about to go away to foreign peoples. However, on becoming king, he not only failed to take revenge on them but even freed them from guilt, at least as far as he could, calling what had happened the providence of God instead of their evil-doing. Moreover, what he did against them was done, not out of revenge, but he was playing a part in all this for the sake of his brother.[11] Afterwards, to be sure, when he saw that they were devoted to the latter, he at once tore away his disguise, and wept, and embraced them as if his greatest benefactors, though he had been once destroyed by them. Further, he brought them all into Egypt and repaid them with innumerable benefits.

Therefore, what excuse shall we have, after being given the Law and grace and such true wisdom, if we do not even emulate him who came before the giving of grace and the Law? Who will save us from punishment? For there is not, there is not anything worse than continuing to remember injuries. The man who owed ten-thousand talents has made this clear, since at first he was not required to pay, and then was again required to do so.[12] He was not required to pay because of the mercy of God, but he was required to pay because of his own wickedness and the fact that he was unforgiving toward his fellow slave.

Since we know all this, let us forgive the trespasses of our

---

11 Benjamin, still with Jacob in Chanaan.
12 Cf. Matt. 18.24.

neighbors and repay them with the opposite that we may obtain the mercy of God, by the grace and mercy of our Lord Jesus Christ. Glory and power be to Him forever and ever. Amen.

Homily 72 (John 13.20-35)

'Amen, amen, I say to you, he who receives anyone I send receives me; and he who receives me receives him who sent me.'[1]

Great is the reward for services dispensed to the servants of God and the fruits of this redound to us. For 'He who receives you receives me; and he who receives me receives him who sent me,' He declared. And what benefit could be equal to that of receiving Christ and His Father?

Yet, what logical sequence is there between this statement and the words that precede it? What connection has it with the first assertion: 'Blessed shall you be, if you do these things,' for Him to add: 'He who receives you'? It does follow this closely and is very much in harmony with it. See how this is so. Since they were about to go forth to endure many frightful sufferings, He was encouraging them in two ways: one, with regard to Himself; the other, with regard to others.

For He meant: 'If you are truly wise and always remain mindful of Me and keep remembering what I have suffered and all that I have done, you will endure frightful things with ease.' And not only in this way was He encouraging them but also by the fact that they would enjoy much assistance from all men. He was making them aware of the first point by saying: 'Blessed shall you be if you do these things' and of the other by declaring: 'He who receives you receives me.' For He opened the doors of all men to them so that they

---

1 John 13.20.

might derive twofold encouragement: both from the virtue displayed in their own conduct and from the zeal of those who would minister to their needs.

Next, since He had delivered these injunctions to them because they were about to traverse the whole world, upon reflecting that the traitor would be deprived of both these advantages and would enjoy the benefit of neither of them—neither of patient endurance in his trials nor of the services of persons extending him hospitality—Christ was once more troubled. It was to reveal this, and to make it clear that He was troubled on account of the traitor, that the Evangelist added: 'When Jesus had said these things, he was troubled in spirit and said solemnly, "One of you will betray me." '

Once again He struck them all with terror by not mentioning the traitor by name. Moreover, some were in doubt, even though they were conscious of no wrong-doing, for they considered Christ's statement more to be trusted than their own reason. And that is why they looked at one another. Therefore, by limiting the entire matter of His betrayal to one man He reduced their fear, but by adding 'One of you' He disturbed them all. What, then, did they do?

Peter, always ready for action, beckoned to John, while the rest merely looked at one another. Since he had been rebuked before, and had tried to prevent Christ when He wished to wash his feet, and because on many occasions he found himself rushing in out of love, but being reproved, though he was fearful for this reason, he neither remained silent nor did he speak, but wished to get the information through the mediation of John.

Moreover, it is worth while to inquire into the reason why it was that when all were disquieted, timid, and their leader was fearful, John reclined at Jesus' bosom as if quite at ease, and not merely reclined, but even leaned on His breast. Besides, not only this merits careful study, but also what follows. What is this? The fact that he said of himself: 'He whom Jesus loved.' Why, indeed, did no one else say this of himself, even though the others also were loved?

They were, but John was loved more than the others. So, if no one else has spoken in this way of himself, but only John himself of himself, it is not at all strange; (Paul also did so, when the occasion called for it, and spoke of himself in the following words: 'I know a man who fourteen years ago . . .').[2] Indeed, not insignificant have been other praiseworthy facts related of John. Or does it seem to you insignificant that when he heard 'Follow me' he at once left his nets and his father and followed Christ? And that He took him alone, together with Peter, to the mountain? And that elsewhere again he alone entered a house with Christ, Peter and James?[3]

Further, he himself also told about as great a tribute of Peter and did not conceal it, but declared that Christ said: 'Peter, dost thou love me more than these do?' And in every instance he portrayed him as fervent and showing sincere affection toward Christ. Moreover, when Peter said: 'What of this man?'[4] he said it because of John's great love for Christ.

For this reason, therefore, no one else said of himself: 'He whom Jesus loved.'[5] However, John himself would not have said it if he had not become involved in this little incident. For if, after saying that Peter beckoned to him to ask the question, he had added nothing further, he would have caused much perplexity, and forced us to seek the reason. That is why he said: 'He was reclining at Jesus' bosom,' to explain this. Yet, do you think that you have learned a trifling thing when you have heard 'he was reclining at Jesus' bosom' and that the Master permitted him such great freedom? If you seek to learn the cause of this, the privilege was granted in

---

2 2 Cor. 12.2.
3 Matt. 4.20-22; 17.1; Luke 8.51.
4 John 21.15,21.
5 Namely, because Christ did love John more than the others.

consequence of His love; therefore he said: 'he whom Jesus loved.'

Moreover, I think that he did this for another reason, namely, in the desire to show that he himself was guiltless of the charge. That is why he was on terms of intimacy with Christ and was under no constraint. Why, then, did he not make this statement in any other place, but only when his leader[6] beckoned to him? It was, to be sure, that you might not think that he was beckoning as if to one greater than he that John explained that this incident took place because of the great love of Christ for him.

'But why did he lean on His bosom?'

They did not yet have any suspicion of His great dignity; besides, He was in this way soothing their troubled spirits. For it is probable that even their glances were then dejected. If they were troubled in their souls, much more would their faces reveal this. Well, then, to put them at their ease, He prepared the way both for His own statement, and for the disciple's question, by permitting him to rest on His bosom. And notice John's lack of pretension. For he did not mention his own name, but said merely: 'He whom Jesus loved,' even as Paul did, when he said: 'I know a man who fourteen years ago.'

Accordingly, Jesus then for the first time accused Judas, though not even then by name. How did He do so? 'It is he for whom I shall dip the bread and give it to him.' Even the method He used was calculated to shame the traitor, for, after sharing the same bread, he was dishonoring the table. Granted that his partaking of Christ's hospitality did not shame him, whom would it not win over to receive the morsel from Him? Yet it did not win Judas. Therefore 'Satan then entered into him,' deriding him for his shamelessness.

---

6 Peter.

As long as he was of the company of Christ's disciples, Satan did not dare to take possession of him, but attacked him from without. However, when Christ had exposed him and thus set him apart, Satan finally seized upon him with complete freedom. Indeed, since he was such as he was, and incorrigible besides, it was not fitting to keep him within the company any longer. And that is why Christ at last cast him out; then, when he had been cut off, Satan seized him. Leaving his companions, the traitor went out into the night.

'Jesus said to him: "Friend, what thou dost, do quickly." And none of those at table understood.' Alas, what great shamelessness! How is it that he was not softened, was not ashamed, but became more calloused and went out? However, the words, 'Do quickly,' were not spoken as a command or as advice, but in reproof, and to show that Christ Himself wished him to mend his ways. But since he remained incorrigible, He dismissed him.

'And none of those at table understood this,' the Evangelist said. Here, someone may be greatly perplexed because, when the disciples asked: 'Who is it?' He answered: 'It is he for whom I shall dip the bread, and give it to him,' and yet they did not understand, even so—unless He spoke privately so that no one else understood. I say this for John leaned back on His bosom for the purpose and asked the question practically in His ear, so that the traitor was not revealed. Furthermore, Christ replied in the same way, and so, not even then did He make him known. And though He said openly: 'Friend, what thou dost, do quickly,' the rest did not understand, despite this.

Moreover, He said this to show that what He had declared to the Jews about His death was true. For He had asserted to them: 'I have power to lay down my life, and I have power to take it up again, and no one takes it from me.'[7] In

---

7 John 10.18.

truth, as long as He prevented, no one was strong enough to
do so, but when he had at length consented, then the deed was
easy to achieve. Therefore, He was implying all of this when
He said: 'What thou dost, do quickly,' yet not even then did
He make him known. For perhaps they would have made
away with him. That is the reason why 'None of those at table
understood.'

'Not even John?'

Not even he, for he could not have supposed that a
disciple would come to such a pitch of wickedness. Indeed,
since they themselves were far removed from such evil-doing
they could not even suspect such things of others. Therefore,
even as He had just now said to them: 'I do not speak of
you all,' and He had by no means made His meaning clear,
so here also they thought He was speaking of something else.

'Now it was night when he went out,' the Evangelist
declared.

'Why, may I ask, do you mention the time?'

That you may learn his eager readiness for the deed,
because not even the time of day held him back from entering
upon it. However, not even this revealed him to them. They
were inhibited by fear and troubled with much anxiety at the
moment, and did not understand the true reason for His
words, but they supposed that Christ said this 'that he should
give something to the poor.' For He expended much care
on the poor to teach us, also, to be very zealous in that regard.

Now, it was not without reason that they supposed this, but
'because Judas held the purse,' although no one is recorded
to have contributed money for Christ; on the contrary, the
Evangelist declared that the women of the company ministered to His needs from their own resources.[8]

'But how is it that He who bade them to carry neither

---

8 Cf. Luke 8.3.

wallet, nor money, nor staff, provided a purse for the service of the poor?'[9]

He did so that you might learn that, though He was very poor and destined to be crucified besides, He had to concern Himself a great deal about this matter. Indeed, He did many things to provide for our instruction.

Thus the disciples thought that He was addressing these words also to Judas 'that he should give something to the poor.' Yet, the fact that up to the last day Christ was unwilling to expose him did not bend the traitor from his purpose. We, too, ought to act thus and not reveal the sins of our companions, even if they are incorrigible. And we should do this for even after this He gave a kiss to him who had come to betray Him and received in return such a monstrous wrong. Then He went on to something that demanded much more courage, namely, the cross itself, the most ignominious death, and there again He showed His merciful love.

Further, He here called the crucifixion 'glory' to teach us that there is nothing so base and ignominious that it does not make the one who endures it shine more splendidly—when he endures it for God's sake. In fact, after Judas had gone out to betray Him, He said: 'Now is the Son of Man glorified,' by this means dispelling the gloomy reflections of the disciples and persuading them not only not to be downcast, but even to rejoice. That is why He kept rebuking Peter from the start,[10] because it is a great glory for Him who has come into the power of death to win a victory over death.

Now, this is what He had said of Himself: 'When I have been lifted up, then you will know that I am he.' And again: 'Destroy this temple.' Once more: 'No sign shall be given to you but the sign of Jonas.'[11] Truly, was it not undoubtedly

9 Cf. Matt. 10.10.
10 When he protested at Christ's predictions of the Passion.
11 John 8.28; cf. John 12.31-33; 2.19; Luke 11.29.

great glory that even after death He could perform works greater than those before His death? For, in order that the Resurrection might win credence, the disciples did perform greater works. But, if He were not alive and if He were not God, how could they work such great miracles in His name?

'And God will glorify him.' What is the meaning of 'God will also glorify him in himself'? ['He will glorify him'], that is, 'by His own agency,' not by the agency of another. 'And will glorify him at once,' that is, at the same time as the crucifixion. 'Not by the long passage of time,' He meant, 'will He glorify Him, nor will He wait for the long period after the Resurrection, nor will He then only reveal His splendor, but will make His brilliance appear on the very cross.' In fact: 'The sun was darkened, the rocks were rent, the curtain of the Temple was torn in two, many bodies of the saints who had fallen asleep arose. The tomb had seals, and guards sat beside it, and though the stone lay over the body, the body arose.[12] Forty days passed by and the abundant grace of the Spirit came, and all the disciples at once preached Him. This is the meaning of 'He will glorify him in himself and will glorify him at once'—not by angels and archangels, or by any other power, but by His own agency.

But how did He glorify Him in Himself? By doing all things to the glory of the Son, although it was the Son who did all things. Do you perceive that He was attributing to the Father the things that He Himself did?

'Little children, yet a little while I am with you. You will seek me, and, as I said to the Jews, "Where I go you cannot come," so to you also I say it now.' Finally, after the supper, He entered upon His time of sorrow. For when Judas departed it was no longer evening, but night. Indeed, since they were going to be raised to positions of authority a

---

12 Cf. Luke 23.45; Matt 27.51.

little later, it was necessary to place all His teachings in their keeping, so that they would remember them; or, rather, the Spirit would recall all things to their minds. For it is likely that they would forget many truths that they were then hearing for the first time; besides, they were on the point of undergoing strong temptations.

In fact, they would be depressed to the extent of falling asleep, as another Evangelist declared, and would be oppressed by sadness, as Christ asserted: 'But because I have spoken to you these things, sadness has filled your heart.'[13] How, then, could they have remembered all these things accurately?

'Why in the world, then, did He tell them to them?'

They derived no small profit, to the glory of Christ—when they later knew these things more clearly—on remembering that they had heard them before from the lips of Christ.

'But why did He cause their spirits to become dejected ahead of time by saying: "Yet a little while I am with you"? He said this with reason to the Jews; but why do you place us equally in the same category as those ingrates?'

'By no means do I do so.'

Yet why did He say: 'As I said to the Jews?' He was reminding them that now He was no longer foretelling these events because of the presence of those wretches, but was merely stating He had previously foreseen them, and they themselves were witnesses who had heard Him saying these things to the Jews. That is why He added the words: 'Little children,' in order that, on hearing Him say: 'As I said to the Jews,' they might not think that what He said was addressed to them in the same way. It was not to cause them dejection, then, that He spoke thus, but to hearten them, in order that the dreadful things that were impending for them might not utterly disconcert them because of being unexpected.

'Where I go you cannot come.' He was pointing out that

---

13 Cf. Luke 22.45; John 16.6.

His death was a transition and change to a better condition—
to a place which does not admit mortal bodies. He said this
to arouse their love for Him and make it more ardent. For
you know that it is when we see loved ones leaving us
that we most of all have the deepest affection for them, and
more so when we see them departing for a place to which we
cannot go. He said these words, therefore, to frighten the
Jews, on the one hand, and, on the contrary, to stir up the
love of the disciples for Him.

'Such a place it is that not only is it impossible for those
others to go there, but it is even impossible for you, my best
beloved.' By these words He was likewise making evident His
own exalted dignity.

'To you also I say it now.'

'Why "now"?'

'In one way to them, and in another to you, that is, not
in common with them.'

'But where did the Jews "seek" Him? Where, the disciples?'

The disciples, when they fled; the Jews, when they
experienced unendurable and frightful sufferings and all
manner of things defying description, as the city itself was
captured and the wrath of God beset them on every side.
Therefore, He said this to them because of their unbelief, but
He now says it to you to prevent the frightful events of the
Passion from coming upon you without warning.

'A new commandment I give you.' Now, since on hearing
these things they were likely to become greatly perturbed,
because they were about to be left alone, He comforted them
by placing about them the protection of the root and guarantee of all blessings: charity. It was as if He said: 'Are you
grieving because I am going away? But if you love one another, you will be stronger.'

'How is it, then, that He did not say this?'

Because He said what was more helpful to them than this:

'By this will all men know that you are my disciples.' At the same time He was revealing by these words that their company would not be disbanded, inasmuch as He had given them its hallmark. Moreover, He said this after the traitor had been cut off from them.

'How is it, then, that He called the commandment itself "new," though it is found in the Old Testament?'

He Himself made it new by the way they were to love and to this end He added: 'as I have loved you. For in loving you I have not been discharging a debt to you for things already carried out by you, but it is I Myself who have initiated the process,' He meant. 'So you also ought to do good to those dearest to you, even if you are not indebted to them.'

Furthermore, He omitted to mention the miracles they were going to perform, and identified them by their charity. Why in the world was that? Because this is the virtue which is particularly the distinctive mark of saintly men. Indeed, it is the basis of all virtue. By means of it, most certainly, all of us are saved. 'This is in fact what it means to be My disciple,' He meant. 'Thus, all men will praise you, when they see you imitating My love.'

'What, then? Do not miracles show this much more plainly?'

By no means. For 'Many will say, "Lord, did we not cast out devils in thy name?" '[14] And again, when they were rejoicing because the demons were obedient to them, He said: 'Do not rejoice in this, that the devils are subject to you, but that your names are written in heaven.'[15] More than this: the power to work miracles would win over the world, when charity was first present; but, if the latter were not there, then the power of miracles would not have lasting value. It was

---

14 Cf. Matt. 7.22-23. 'And then I will declare to them, "I never knew you. Depart from me." '
15 Luke 10.20.

this, to be sure, that at once made them virtuous and good, namely, the fact that the hearts and souls of all of them were one. If, on the contrary, they were at enmity with one another, everything would have been lost.

Further, He addressed these words not to them only, but to all who would in future believe in Him. And now, too, nothing is so great a source of scandal to the pagans as a lack of charity.

'But they also find fault when miracles do not take place,' you will say.

However, not in the same way.

'But where did the Apostles show love for one another?'

'Do you see Peter and John, who were inseparable, going up to the Temple? Do you see Paul disposed towards them as he was, and are you still in doubt? Indeed, if they had come to possess the other virtues, much more did they possess the mother of all goodness. For this flower grows from a soul endowed with virtue, while where there is immorality this plant withers. Indeed, 'Because iniquity will abound,' Christ declared, 'the charity of the many will grow cold.'[16] Further, miracles do not influence the pagans so much as one's life; but nothing causes one's life to have this influence as much as charity. Indeed, they have often even called the workers of miracles seducers, but they would be unable to cast aspersion on purity of life.

Therefore, when the message of the Gospel had not yet been given, it was reasonable for miracles to be held in awe, but now admiration ought to be awakened rather by a man's life. In truth, nothing has such an influence on the pagans as virtue; nothing offends them as much as vice, and rightly so. For, if the pagan sees the miser or the robber advocating the opposite course of action, and if he observes the man, who has been bidden to love even his enemies, treating his fellow

---

16 Matt. 24.12.

men like wild beasts, he will declare that the words are nonsense. If he sees a man trembling with the fear of death, how will he accept the words spoken of immortality? When he sees us ambitious for power and enslaved by the other passions he will remain more firmly fixed in his own beliefs, since he entertains no exalted opinion of us.

Indeed, we, we are responsible for their remaining in error. For they have long since come to despise their own teachings and at the same time to admire ours, but are kept from them by our lives. It is easy, to be sure, to be virtuous in theory (for many, even among them, have done so), but they are seeking for the proof found in practice.

'Well, let them recall our ancestors.'

But they do not trust that proof; on the contrary, they look for evidence from those now alive.

'Show me your faith by your works,'[17] they say.

However, there is no such evidence; or, rather, when they observe us attacking our neighbors more savagely than any wild beast, they call us the plague of the world. These things hold the pagans back and do not permit them to come over to us. Consequently, we shall suffer punishment for this: not only for the evil deeds we commit, but also for the blasphemies uttered against the name of God. To what end shall we have given ourselves over to wealth and luxury and the other passions? Therefore, let us refrain from them in future.

Listen to what the Prophet said of certain foolish men: 'Let us eat and drink; for tomorrow we shall die.' But in the case of men of the present day it is not possible to mention only a certain few, so numerous are those who aim at the possession of all things. Thus, to censure them as well, the Prophet said: 'Shall you alone dwell in the midst of the earth?'[18] Wherefore, I fear that something hard to bear may

---

17 Cf. James 2.18.
18 Isa. 22.13; 5.8.

happen to us and we may draw down on ourselves the far-reaching vengeance of God.

In order that this may not take place, let us cultivate every kind of virtue, so that we may also attain to the possession of the good things of the life to come, by the grace and mercy of our Lord Jesus Christ. By Him and with Him glory be to the Father, together with the Holy Spirit, now and always, and forever and ever. Amen.

Homily 73 (John 13.36-14.7)

'Simon Peter said, "Lord, where art thou going?" Jesus answered, "Where I am going thou canst not follow me now, but thou shalt follow later." '[1]

A great love is a noble thing; it is more consuming than fire and ascends to the very heavens. Moreover, there is no barrier strong enough to check its impetuous course.

For instance, when Peter, who was aflame with love, heard 'Where I go you cannot come,' what did he say? 'Lord, where art thou going?' And he said this, not so much because he wanted to get the information as because he greatly desired to follow Him. Yet he did not for the moment dare to say explicitly: 'I am coming,' but asked: 'Where art thou going?'

Christ, on the other hand, replied not to the words, but to Peter's thought. For it is clear from what Christ said that Peter desired this. What, indeed, did He say? 'Where I am going thou canst not follow me now.' Do you see that Peter greatly desired to follow Him, and asked the question for that reason?

But when he heard 'Thou shalt follow later,' not even then could he hold his love in check, though given such fair promise, but rushed ahead so eagerly as to say: 'Why cannot

1 John 13.6.

I follow thee now? I will lay down my life for thee.' In fact, because he had shaken off the fear of being a traitor and appeared himself to be among those loyal to Christ, he now confidently put the question himself, while the rest remained silent.

What is it you are saying, Peter? Christ said: 'Thou canst not,' and do you declare: 'I can'? Well, then, you will learn by experience itself that your love is of no account unless grace from above is present. From this it is clear that Christ permitted that fall of Peter's because of His concern for him. For, even from the first He had been trying to teach him, but because he persisted in his stubborn zeal, He Himself did not continue to press him, nor did He force him to the denial, but left him alone so that he might learn his own weakness.

Christ had said that He must be betrayed, and Peter declared: 'Far be it from thee; this will never happen to thee.'[2] He was rebuked for this, yet did not learn the lesson. On the contrary, once again when Christ wanted to wash his feet, he said: 'Thou shalt never wash my feet.' Again, on hearing 'Thou canst not follow me now,' he declared: 'Even though all shall deny thee, I shall not deny thee.'[3] Therefore, since he who made a practice of contradicting Christ was likely to be puffed up with pride even to the point of foolishness, He instructed him not to resist Him in future. At least Luke was implying this when he asserted that Christ said: 'I have prayed for thee that thy faith may not fail,'[4] that is, 'that you may not perish in the end.' He was teaching him humility in all things and that human nature itself is worth nothing of itself.

Indeed, since Peter's great love had made him inclined to contradict Christ, He finally placed a curb on him, in order

2 Matt. 16.22.
3 Cf. Mark 14.28-31.
4 Luke 22.32.

that he might not also have this inclination in the later period when he would assume the control of the world, but that, on the contrary, being mindful of his past experience, he might recognize his own limitations.

Yet see how low he fell. For he did not fail once or twice, but so far departed from his senses as to say the word of denial three times within a short space of time, that he might learn that he did not love as much as he was loved. Nevertheless, Christ afterwards said to him who had thus fallen: 'Dost thou love me more than these do?'[5] Thus, his fall took place, not by reason of the cooling of his love, but because he had been deprived of aid from above. Therefore, He once again accepted Peter's love, but cut away the contradictory spirit that proceeded from it. For, if you love, you ought to submit to the one you love.

Moreover, Peter, He said to you and to your companions: 'Thou canst not.' Why did you dispute with Him? Did you not know what it means to gainsay God? 'But, since you do not want to admit in this way that it is impossible for My statements not to be fulfilled, you will learn it in your denial of Me,' Christ said, though this then appeared to you very much more incredible. You did not, indeed, understand this, but you did have the knowledge of that other in your soul. Nevertheless, it was the unexpected that happened.

'I will lay down my life for thee.' Because he had heard that no one has greater love than this,[6] he at once pounced upon it, since it was impossible to satisfy his love and he wished to attain to the highest degree. However, to show that to make this declaration authoritatively belonged to Him only, Christ said, 'Before the cock crows,' that is, 'now.' Indeed, that time was not far away, for He was conversing

---

5 John 21.15.
6 However, according to John's account, Christ said this later on in the Supper; cf. John 15.13.

with them at an unusually late hour of the night and the first and second watch had passed.[7]

'Let not your heart be troubled.' He said this because it was probable that on hearing Him they were greatly disturbed. For, if their leader, who was so much on fire with love, was told that he would deny Christ three times before cock-crow, it is reasonable to suppose that they would expect some great catastrophe to happen, sufficient to overcome even their unyielding souls. Therefore, since it was likely that because of these reflections they also were frightened, see how He reassured them by saying: 'Let not your heart be troubled.' By the first part of this statement He proved the power of His Godhead, because He knew what they had in their inmost soul and revealed it.

'You believe in God, believe also in me,' that is, 'All fearful things will pass away. For, faith in Me and in My Father is more powerful than all things that may come upon you and will not permit any evil to prevail over you.' Then He added: 'In my Father's house there are many mansions.' Just as He cheered Peter in his trouble of heart by saying: 'Thou shalt follow later,' so also He suggested this hope to them. In order that they might not think that the [other] pronouncement was made for him only, He declared: 'In my Father's house there are many mansions. Were it not so, I should have told you. I go to prepare a place for you.' That is, 'because that place which receives Peter will also receive you.' In that place, indeed, there is a great abundance of mansions, and it cannot be said that they are in need of being made ready.

Moreover, because He had said: 'Thou canst not follow me now,' in order that they might not think that they were cut off forever, He added: 'That where I am, there you also may be. I have such great concern with regard to this matter that I would have already taken it in hand, if it had not

7 That is, it was nearly midnight.

previously been placed in readiness for you.' He thus showed that they ought to be of good heart and have faith.

Next, in order that He might not seem to be speaking as if to delude them, but that they might believe that His words were true, He added: 'And where I go you know, and the way you know.' Do you see how He gave them proof that what He said was not mere empty show? Moreover, He said this because He was aware that their souls were seeking this information. Peter, to be sure, had said what he did, not to gain information, but so that he might follow Christ. But when he had been rebuked and Christ Himself had shown that what for the moment seemed an impossibility was actually possible,[8] and when the apparent impossibility had awakened a desire for more concise knowledge, to fulfill this desire He said to them: 'And the way you know.'

Just as, after saying: 'Thou wilt deny me,' though no one uttered a word, penetrating to the thoughts in their hearts, He said: 'Do not be troubled,' so also in this place, after saying: 'You know,' He revealed the desire in their thoughts and Himself gave them an opening for a question. However, while Peter had uttered the words, 'Where art thou going?' because of the abundance of his tender affection, Thomas spoke out of fear: 'Lord we do not know where thou art going; we do not know the place.' He meant: 'and how can we know the way leading there?' Moreover, notice with what respectfulness he spoke. For he did not say: 'Tell us the place,' but: 'We do not know where thou are going.' Indeed, before this they had all burned to know this. For, if the Jews were perplexed on hearing Him even though they wanted to be rid of Him, much more did those desire to know it, who wished never to be separated from Him. Therefore, though out of respect they hesitated to question Him, they did put

---

8 Namely, that the disciples would be able to follow Him.

the question, both because of their great affection and because of their anxiety.

What, then, did Christ reply? 'I am the way, and the truth, and the life. No one can come to the Father but through me.' Why, therefore, on being asked by Peter: 'Where art thou going?' did He not reply: 'I am going to the Father, but you cannot come now'? Why, on the contrary, did He entangle them in a net of so many words by multiplying questions and answers? It was with reason that He did not make this statement to the Jews, but why not to the Apostles?

To be sure, He had said, both to them and to the Jews, that He came forth from God[9] and that He was going to God, and on this occasion He said it more clearly than before. However, He did not speak as clearly to the Jews. For, if He had said: 'You cannot come to the Father, but through me,' they would have thought this vanity on His part, but by being enigmatic He cast them into perplexity.

'Yet why did He speak as He did to His disciples, and to Peter, too?' you will ask.

He knew Peter's great impulsiveness and that because of it he would be disposed to be more troublesome. Therefore, He spoke enigmatically to make him stop and think. But when He had succeeded in what He wished, by means of His lack of clarity and His enigmatic way of speaking, then He once again made His meaning clear. For, since He had said: 'Where I am, you cannot come,' He added: 'In my Father's house there are many mansions'; and again: 'No one comes to the Father but through me.'

Thus, He did not wish to say this to them from the outset, so as not to cast them into greater distress, but when He had heartened them, then He said it. For, because of His rebuke to Peter, He had caused them great distress; giving way to

---

9 Cf. John 8.42.

fear that they might hear the same words, they were the more downcast.

'I am the way.' This is the proof that 'No one comes, but through me,' while the words, 'and the truth, and the life,' are the proof that these statements will be fulfilled without exception. 'If I am the Truth, then nothing is false on My part, and, if I am also the Life, not even death itself will be able to prevent you from coming to Me. Besides, if I am the Way, you will not be in want of a guide; and if I am the Truth, there is nothing false in what I have said; and if I am the Life, even though you die you will receive the fulfilment of My words.'

Accordingly, they comprehended the idea of 'the Way' and assented to it, but they were in doubt about the rest, though not daring to voice their perplexity. Still, they took great comfort from the idea of 'the Way.' He meant: 'Well, then, if I am in control of bringing men to the Father, you will come there, without a doubt. Indeed, it is not possible to come by any other way.'

Now, since He had previously said: 'No one can come to me unless the Father draw him,' and again: 'If I be lifted up from the earth, I will draw all things to myself,'[10] and now again: 'No one comes to the Father but through me,' He was proving His equality to His Father.

'But how is it that, after saying: "Where I go you know, and the way you know," He went on to say: "If you had known me, you would also have known my Father. And henceforth you will know him and you will have seen him"?'

By no means was He contradicting Himself, for they did know Him to be sure, but not as they ought. They did indeed know God, but not yet the Father, for the Spirit, who came upon them afterwards, provided them with the knowledge of all this. Further, what He meant was some such thing as

10 John 6.44; 12.32.

this: 'If you knew My essence and dignity, you would also know that of the Father. And henceforth you will know Him, and you have seen Him' (the former in future, the latter at present), that is, 'through Me.' Moreover, by 'sight' He meant knowledge by means of the understanding. For we can both see and fail to know persons whom we actually see, but we cannot both know and fail to know [at the same time] persons whom we know. That is why He declared: 'And you have seen him,' just as Scripture says: 'as he has been seen by angels also.'[11] Even though His very essence was not, of course, seen, it said that He 'has been seen,' clearly meaning 'seen' in such a way as it was possible for the angels to see.

Now, He spoke in this way in order that you might learn that he who has seen Him also knows His father. Yet, they beheld Him, not in His pure essence, but clad in the flesh. And in another context also He called knowledge 'sight,' as when He said: 'Blessed are the pure of heart, for they shall see God.'[12] By 'pure' He meant not merely those who are innocent of immoral conduct, but those who are free from all sin, for every species of sin places a stain on the soul.

Let us, then, do everything so as to cleanse away the defilement of sin. First of all the laver of baptism cleanses it; afterwards, there are many and various other methods. For, since God is merciful, He has granted us, even after baptism, manifold means of being freed from sin, the foremost of which is that of almsgiving. For Scripture says: 'Sins are purged away by almsgiving and faith.'[13]

By almsgiving I do not mean that which is the fruit of unjust dealing, for this is not almsgiving, but cruelty and mercilessness. Indeed, what profit is there in stripping one man to clothe another? For the deed must take its beginning

11 Cf. 1 Tim. 3.16.
12 Matt. 5.8.
13 Cf Eccli. 3.33.

from mercy, but that is mercilessness. In fact, even if we give
away all our possessions obtained from other men, it is of
no benefit to us. Zacchaeus is a proof of this, since he declared
at that time that he would propitate God by giving fourfold
what he had defrauded.[14] On the contrary, we who have
robbed of amounts impossible to estimate think that by
giving a little we propitiate God, not realizing that in reality
we are angering Him more. Tell me, if you please, if you
brought to the altar of sacrifice a dead ass, already putrefying,
which you had dragged from the crossroads and streets, would
not all men stone you to death as impious and abominable?
Therefore, what if I should prove that the sacrifice which is
the fruit of robbery is more abominable than that, what kind
of defense shall we obtain? For, let us suppose that some
article of value has been obtained by fraud, is it not more
malodorous than a dead ass? Do you wish to learn how great
the stench of sin is? Listen to the Prophet saying: 'Noisome
and festering are my sores.'[15]

On the one hand, you beg God by your words to forget the
evil actions you do, while you yourself, by your deeds of
rapine and greed, cause Him to remember them continually,
as you place your sinfulness on the altar. Actually, this is not
your only offense, but also something more serious than this,
namely, that you are defiling the souls of the saints. For the
altar is a stone, and is consecrated, but the saints always bear
Christ Himself about with them; and do you dare to offer
there anything taken from such a corrupt source?

'No,' you reply, 'not this money, but some other.'

Stuff and nonsense! Do you not know that, even if merely
a drop of injustice falls into a large amount of money, the
whole is defiled? Thus, even as someone by casting filth into
a spring of pure water causes it to become altogether

---

14 Cf. Luke 19.8.
15 Ps. 37.6.

polluted, so also any unjust gain that enters into wealth makes all of it reek with the stench which comes from it. And so, then, while we wash our hands on entering a church, do we no longer cleanse our heart? Surely our hands will not utter a word? It is the soul that produces words; God gazes down upon it. If it is defiled, cleanliness of body is of no advantage. Indeed, what benefit is it if you cleanse your hands exteriorly while inwardly you have soiled ones? For the grave evil—and one that undermines all virtue—is this: that we are scrupulous about little things and completely neglect the important ones. Thus, to pray with unwashed hands is a thing of no consequence, but to pray with conscience uncleansed is the worst of all evils.

Listen to what was said to the Jews who were much concerned about such exterior purification: 'Wash thy heart from wickedness. How long shall hurtful thoughts abide in thee?'[16] Let us also wash our hearts, not with filth, but with pure water; with almsgiving, not with covetousness. First, get rid of rapine, and then give example of almsgiving. 'Let us turn from evil and do good.'[17] Remove your hands from greed and bring them thus to almsgiving. But if we defraud one group with these same hands, even though we do not clothe others with what has been wrested from them, we shall not, even so, escape punishment. For the matter that we use for propitiation becomes matter for our complete undoing. Indeed, it is better not to show pity at all than to show pity in this way. For example, it was better for Cain not to have offered sacrifice at all.[18]

But, if the man who brought too small an offering angered God, how will the one who offers the property of others fail to anger Him? 'I have said,' He will declare: ' "Thou shalt

---

16 Jer. 4.14.
17 Cf. Ps. 36.27.
18 Cf Gen. 4.4,5.

not steal," and do you pay Me honor with stolen goods? What do you think? That I am pleased with such?' Therefore He will address to you the words: 'Do you think unjustly that I will be like yourself? I will reprove you and will draw up your sins before your eyes.'[19]

However, may no one of us hear such words, but after practicing almsgiving with no defects, and with our lamps brightly gleaming, may we enter the bridal chamber thus, by the grace and mercy of our Lord Jesus Christ. Glory be to Him forever and ever. Amen.

Homily 74 (John 14.8-15)

'Philip said to Him, "Lord, show us the Father and it is enough for us." Jesus said to him, "Have I been so long a time with you, and you have not known me, Philip? He who sees me sees also the Father." '[1]

The Prophet said to the Jews: 'Thou hadst a harlot's forehead, thou who hast been utterly shameless towards all men.'[2] In all likelihood he could with justice address these words, not merely to that city,[3] but also to all those who brazenly look truth in the face without recognition. For, when Philip said to Christ: 'Show us thy Father,' Christ replied: 'Have I been so long a time with you, and you have not known me, Philip?' Notwithstanding this, there are some who, even after these words, divorce the Son from the Father.

But what closer relationship do you seek than this one? For, there are some who, by reason of this statement, have caught

---

19 Cf. Ps. 49.21.

1 John 14.8,9.
2 Cf. Jer. 3.3.
3 Jerusalem.

the malady of Sabellius.[4] However, let us disregard both the latter group and the others—since they fall into opposite extremes of error—and let us examine the exact meaning of what was said.

'Have I been so long a time with you, and you have not known me, Philip?' He asked.

'What, then? Are you the Father about whom I am inquiring?'

'Not at all,' He replied. That is why He did not say: 'You have not known Him,' but: 'You have not known Me.' The point that He was making clear above all else was that the Son is nothing other than what the Father is, though continuing to be Son in His Person.

But whence did Philip come to ask this question?

Christ had just said: 'If you had known me, you would also have known my Father,' and He had often said this to the Jews. Peter frequently had asked Him, as also had the Jews: 'Who is thy Father?' Furthermore, Thomas had asked Him, too, but no one had learned anything explicit, and they were still perplexed at His words. Therefore, when Philip himself asked: 'Show us thy Father,' he added: 'and it is enough for us; we are looking for nothing more,' so that he might not seem offensive and as though carping at Him, along with the Jews.

Yet Christ had just said: 'If you had known me, you would also have known my Father,' and He was revealing His Father through Himself. Philip, on the contrary, reversed the order and said: 'Show us the Father,' as if he already knew Christ adequately. However, Christ did not allow him to remain in error, but set him upon the right road by instructing him to learn of the Father through Him. But Philip wanted to see Him with these eyes of the body, perhaps because he had heard that the Prophets had 'seen' God.

---

4 Sabellius, a third-century heretic who taught that the Deity is one Person; see art. 'Monarchians' in *Catholic Encyclopedia*.

However, Philip, that was merely a humble way of speaking. That is why Christ said: 'No one has at any time seen God.'[5] And again: 'Everyone who has listened to the Father, and has learned, comes to me.' 'But you have never heard his voice, or seen his face.' And in the Old Testament: 'No man will see my face and live.'[6] What, then, did Christ reply here? He said reprovingly: 'Have I been so long a time with you, and you have not known me, Philip?' Moreover, He did not say: 'You have not seen Me.' but: 'You have not known Me.'

'Yes, I certainly do know You,' Philip meant, 'so why should I want to learn about You? At this time I am asking to see Your Father, yet You say to me: "Have you not known me?" What connection, then, has this with my question?'

A very close connection, to be sure. For, since He is what the Father is, though He remains the Son, with good reason does He direct you to His Father in Himself. Next, to distinguish the Persons He said: 'He who sees me sees also the Father,' lest anyone might say that Father and Son are the same Person. For, if He were the Father. He would not have declared: 'He who sees me, sees Him.'

But how is it that He did not say to him: 'You are asking the impossible and what is not within the province of man, for this is a power that I alone have'? He did not say this, because Philip had declared: 'It is enough for us,' as though He knew Christ. Therefore, He showed him that not even he had really seen Him. For, surely, He would have seen the Father, if he had been able to see the Son. For this reason He asserted: 'He who sees me sees also the Father. If someone sees me, he will also see Him.' And what He meant is something like this: 'It is not possible to see either Me or Him.' Philip indeed was seeking for the knowledge gained

---

5 John 1.18; the words, however, are actually those of the Evangelist.
6 John 6.45; 5.37; Exod. 33.20.

by seeing; and, since he thought he had so seen Christ, and wished also to see the Father in this way, Christ showed him that actually he had not even seen Him.

Moreover, if someone should say that in this place 'sight' means 'knowledge' I will not contradict even him. For He meant: 'He who knows me, knows the Father.' However, He did not say this, but in the desire to stress the fact of His consubstantiality He asserted: 'He who knows my essence knows also that of the Father.'

'Now, what is this?' you will say. 'I do not understand you, for he who knows creation also knows God.' Yet, though all men know creation and see it, they do not all know God.

On the other hand, let us see what it was that Philip was seeking to behold. Surely it was not the wisdom of the Father? Surely not His goodness? By no means; but, actually, whatever it is that God is: His very essence.

Therefore Christ replied to this request: 'He who sees me.' Now, he who sees creation does not also see the essence of God. But 'If anyone sees Me, he does also see My Father,' He declared. Moreover, if He were of another essence, He would not have said this. But, to use a somewhat crude illustration: no one who is ignorant of what gold is can see what it is by looking at silver, for the nature of one thing does not appear in another.

That is why Christ did well to rebuke Philip by saying: 'Have I been so long a time with you? Have you enjoyed the benefit of such excellent instruction; have you seen miracles performed with authority, and all the marks proper to the Godhead, and things which the Father alone could do: sins forgiven, secret thoughts revealed, death taking flight, a creature actually being made from earth[7]—and have you not known me?'

---

7 Referring to the cure of the blind man whose eyes Christ restored by using clay.

Indeed, because He had been clad in the flesh, for this reason He said: 'Have you not known me? You have seen the Father. Do not seek to see more, for in Him you have seen Me. If you have seen Me, do not inquire further, for in Me you have known Him. Do you not believe that I am in the Father?' That is: 'I am revealed in His essence. The words that I speak to you I speak not on my own authority.' Do you perceive their exceedingly close intimacy and proof of their unity of essence?

'But the Father dwelling in me, it is he who does the works.' How is it that He began by speaking of words and passed on to deeds?' Indeed, the natural conclusion was for Him to say: 'It is He who speaks the words.' However, He here was referring to two things: both His teaching and His miracles, or else He spoke in this way because His words also were deeds.

'How is it, then, that it is the Father who does them? Elsewhere, to be sure, He said: "If I do not perform the works of my Father, do not believe in me;"[8] how is it, then, that He here declares that it is His Father who does them?'

To show this same thing, namely, that there is no difference between the Father and Son. And what He meant is this: 'The Father would not have done one thing and I, another.' In another place, indeed, it is both He and His Father who work, when He says: 'My Father works even until now, and I work.'[9] In the other statement He proved that there is no distinction between Their works and here also He showed that Their works are the very same.

And if, on face value, the words show humility, do not wonder at the fact. It was after first saying: 'Dost thou not believe,' that He then made this statement, to show that He

8 John 10.37.
9 John 5.17.

couched His words in this way for the sake of bringing Philip to believe. For He was dwelling in their hearts.[10]

'Do you believe that I am in the Father and the Father in me?' On the one hand, on hearing of 'the Father' and 'the Son' you ought to seek for nothing more in proof of Their close relationship in Their essence. But if, on the other hand, this were not sufficient to show Their equality and consubstantiality, you would also learn it from Their works. Moreover, if the words: 'He who sees me sees also the Father were spoken of Their works, He would not have said further on: 'Otherwise believe because of the works themselves.'

Next, to show that not only could He do these works, but also others much greater than these, He continued in exalted terms. For He did not say merely: 'I can perform yet greater works than these,' but something much more remarkable. He declared: 'I can even grant to others to perform still greater works than these. Amen, amen, I say to you, he who believes in me, the works that I do he also shall do, and greater than these he shall do, because I am going to the Father.' That is: 'In future the working of miracles is your prerogative because I am going away.'

In the next place, when He had finished what the discussion demanded, He declared: 'Whatever you ask in my name, you will receive, and I will do this that the Father may be glorified in me.' Do you perceive how once more it was He Himself who was the doer? For He asserted: 'It is I who will do this.' Further, He did not say: 'I will ask my Father,' but 'in order that the Father may be glorified in me.'

Now, before this, to be sure, He had said: 'God will glorify him in himself';[11] here, on the contrary, He Himself will glorify the Father. For, when it is apparent that the Son can do great things, He that begot Him will be glorified .

But, what is the meaning of 'In my name'? As the Apostles said: 'In the name of Jesus Christ, arise and walk.' For He

10 Hence, knew their inmost thoughts.
11 John 13.33.

Himself gave them power to perform the miracles which they worked. 'And the hand of the Lord was with them.'[12]

'That I will do,' He declared. Do you perceive His autonomy? Does He Himself perform the miracles worked by others, while He is not powerful enough to accomplish what is done by Himself, but receives power from His Father? Who, indeed, could say such a thing?

'Why, then, did He relegate this statement to second place?'[13]

To confirm His first statement and to show that what He had said before was said out of condescension to their weakness. And the words, 'I am going to the Father,' have this meaning: 'I shall not perish, but ever remain in My own rank, and I am in heaven.'

Moreover, He said all these things to encourage them. For it was probable that, as they did not yet understand about the Resurrection, they would consider His words sad tidings. Therefore, because of His all-embracing solicitude for them, He promised that they also would perform for others such good works as He had been performing, by this assurance proving that He would always remain with them, and that He not only would remain with them, but would display still greater power.

Let us, then, follow Him and take up our cross. Even if there is no persecution at hand, there is opportunity for another kind of death. 'Mortify therefore your members which are on earth,' Scripture says.[14] Therefore, let us quench the fire of lust; let us slay anger; let us destroy envy. This is a 'living sacrifice.'[15] This sacrifice does not end in the ashes of the funeral pyre; nor is it dispersed in smoke; nor does it

---

12 Acts 3.6; 11.21.
13 That is, He first mentioned the miracles to be performed by others through faith in Him, and only afterwards declared that He Himself would do whatever was asked in His name.
14 Col. 3.5.
15 Cf. Rom. 12.1.

need wood or fire or sword. It has the Holy Spirit as fire and sacrificial knife.

Making use of this sacrificial knife, cut out of your heart what is superfluous and does not belong there. Remove what interferes with your sense of hearing. For, disorderly impulses and evil desires have the habit of preventing the entrance of God's word. I say this for, when the desire for wealth stands in the way, it does not permit you to hear the teaching about almsgiving. When envy is present, it becomes an obstacle to instruction about charity. Again, some other disorderly tendency assails the soul in turn and makes it still more apathetic towards everything.

Well, then, let us do away with our evil desires. I say this for it is sufficient to will it, and all of them will be snuffed out. Yet, I beseech, let us not be of the opinion that the love of wealth has a despotic power over us, but let us realize that the tyranny lies in our own love of ease. There are many, of course, who assert that they do not know what wealth is, for this desire is not one rooted in our nature. Our natural tendencies, to be sure, were implanted in human nature long ago and even from the beginning; but for a long period of time even the existence of gold and silver was unknown. From what source, then, did this desire for them grow so strong? From vainglory and excessive love of ease.

In fact, some of our desires are necessary ones, others are natural, while others are neither of these. For example: those desires which destroy the principle of life if they remain unfulfilled, are natural and necessary, like the desires to eat and drink and sleep; whereas carnal desire is natural, but not necessary, for there are many who do not satisfy this, yet do not die. But the desire for wealth is neither natural nor necessary, but superfluous. And if we wish, we need not accept its domination. As a matter of fact, even Christ, who in speaking of virginity said: 'Let him accept it who can,' did not speak thus of money. On the contrary, what did He say? 'Everyone who does not renounce all that he possesses is not worthy of Me.'[16] He exhorted them to practice the latter renunciation which was easy to do, while He merely left to their choice the renunciation of the other desire which prevails over many men.

Well, then, why do we deprive ourselves of all defense? For, the man who is vanquished by the more compulsive passion will not suffer much punishment. But he who has been worsted by the weaker one will be deprived of all excuse. What shall we reply when He says: 'You saw me hungry and you did not give me to eat?'[17] What excuse shall we have? Shall we plead our poverty as completely exonerating us? But we are not more poverty-stricken than that widow who by putting in two oboli[18] put in more than all.

Indeed, God will demand not how great was the amount of our contribution, but the measure of our good will, and this is evidence of His solicitude for us. Let us, therefore, in admiration of His mercy, make the offering we have it in our power to make, in order that, after securing the abundant mercy of God, both in this life and in the life to come, we may be able to enjoy the blessings promised to us, by the grace and mercy of our Lord Jesus Christ. Glory be to Him forever and ever. Amen.

---

16 Matt. 19.12; cf. Luke 14.33.
17 Cf. Matt. 25.42.
18 Cf. Luke 21.1-4. In the Greek New Testament the coins are called λεπτά, ('mites'). For a brief but informative summary of the kinds and the value of coins current in Palestine in the time of Christ, see the Glossary in the Confraternity New Testament, s.v. 'Money.'

Homily 75 (John 14.15-30)

'If you love me, keep my commandments. And I will ask
the Father and he will give you another Advocate to dwell
with you forever, the Spirit of truth whom the world cannot
receive, because it neither sees him nor knows him.'[1]

At all times it is works and deeds we need, not vain display
in word. For, it is easy for a person to make promises, but not
as easy to carry them out. Why, indeed, do I say this? Because
there are many at present who say that they fear and love
God, while they give example of the opposite in their deeds.
God, on the contrary, seeks for the love that is evidenced by
deeds.

That is why He said to His disciples: 'If you love me, keep
my commandments.' For, since He had said: 'Whatever you
ask, that I will do,' in order that they might not think that the
mere asking was enough, He added: 'If you love me.' He
meant: 'Then I will do what you ask.'

But because, on hearing: 'I am going to the Father,' it was
likely that they were troubled, He declared: 'The fact that
you are troubled at these words does not mean that you love
Me, but your love is proved by your obedience to My words.
I have given you a command to love one another: that you
should do to one another as I have done to you. Your
obedience to these words and your submission to the Beloved
prove your love.

'And I will ask the Father and he will give you another
Advocate.' Once again the statement is one of humble tenor.
It was probable that, because they did not yet rightly know
Him, they would miss that companionship with which they
had grown so familiar: His conversation, His presence in the
flesh, and would receive no consolation if He were absent.
Therefore, what did He say? 'I will ask the Father and he

---

1 John 14.15-17.

will give you another Advocate'; that is, 'Another like Me.'

Let those afflicted with the disease of Sabellius[2] blush for shame, and likewise those who do not have the proper opinion of the Holy Spirit.[3] And they should be discomfited, for the marvel of His statement is this: that with one blow it has felled heresies that teach doctrines diametrically opposite. For by saying 'another' He showed His distinction of Person; and by saying 'Advocate,' He showed the sameness of Their essence.

'But why did He say: "I will ask the Father"?'

Because, if He had said 'I will send,' they would not have believed in the same way, and at the moment what He was striving to achieve was this: that He should be believed. Later, to be sure, He would Himself declare that it was He Himself who sent Him, in the words, 'Receive the Holy Spirit.'[4] Here, however, that He might make His words seem credible to them, He said that He would ask the Father.

'Since John said of Him: "Of his fullness we have all received," how is it that He receives from another what He has? And again: "He will baptize you with the Holy Spirit and with fire."[5] But how much greater was His power than that of the Apostles, if He was going to ask the Father to give the Spirit to others, inasmuch as the Apostles are frequently to be seen doing this, even without prayer? And if the Spirit is sent by the Father in answer to Christ's prayer, how is it that the Spirit Himself descends at times of His own accord? Furthermore, how can the Spirit be sent by another, when He is everywhere present, and "divides to everyone according as He wills," and says with authority: "Set apart for me Saul and Barnabas"?'[6]

---

2 That is, those who support the erroneous belief that there is but one Person in God.
3 See art. 'Pneumatomachi' in *Catholic Encyclopedia*.
4 John 20.23.
5 John 1.16; Luke 3.16.
6 1 Cor. 12.11; Acts 13.2.

Though these ministers were engaged in the service of God, He summoned them with authority to His own works, not because He was calling them to a different work, but to show His power.

'What, then, is the meaning of "I will ask the Father"?' you will say.

He said it to show the time of the coming of the Spirit. For, when He had purified them by His sacrifice, then the Holy Spirit would descend upon them. Yet why did He not come upon them while Jesus was still with them? Because the Sacrifice had not yet been offered up. But, when at length sin had been destroyed, and they themselves were being sent into danger and were preparing for the contests, it was necessary for the Anointer to come.

'But why did the Spirit not come immediately after the Resurrection?'

In order that, when they were imbued with an ardent desire for Him, they might receive Him with much love. For, as long as Christ was with them, they were not in distress. But when He had gone away, they would welcome the Spirit very eagerly, because they had been made destitute and were in a state of great fear.

'He will dwell with you.' This means that not even after death will He depart. But in order that, on hearing 'Advocate,' they might not conceive the notion that there would once again be another Incarnation, and that they might not expect to behold Him with their eyes, to set them right He said: 'Whom the world cannot receive, because it does not see him. For he will not be with you as I am, but he will dwell in your very souls.' This indeed is the meaning of 'He will be in you.'

Further, He called Him 'the Spirit of truth,' thus making reference to the types found in the Old Testament. 'That he may dwell with you.'

'What is the meaning of "may dwell with you"?'

The meaning He Himself had when He said: 'I am with you.'[7] In addition, He was also implying something else, namely: 'He will not undergo the sufferings which I shall endure, nor will He ever go away. Whom the world cannot receive, because it does not see Him.'

'What is that, please? Was He, then, actually one of the things that can be seen?'

By no means. On the contrary, Christ here meant mental vision. Indeed, He added 'and does not know him,' for He was accustomed to use the term 'sight' with reference to precise knowledge. For, since sight is more penetrating than the other senses, He frequently referred to clear knowledge under that figure. Moreover, in this place He called the wicked 'the world,' thus at the same time consoling the Apostles by endowing them with a special gift.[8]

See how very sublime His words about the Spirit were! He said: 'He is another like Me.' He declared: 'He will not leave you.' He asserted: 'He is coming to you alone, even as I have done.' He said: 'He will dwell with you.' However, not even by these words did He dispel their sadness, for they were still seeking Him and His companionship. Accordingly, to cure them of this, He said: 'I will not leave you orphans; I will come to you.'

He meant: 'Do not be afraid. It is not because I shall be separated from you forever that I have said that I am sending another Advocate. Nor is it because you will no longer see Me that I have said that He will dwell with you. And I say this for I Myself also will come to you. I will not leave you orphans.' In fact, it was because He had begun by saying: 'Little children,' that He here also said: 'I will not leave you orphans.'

---

7 Matt. 28.20.
8 The power of knowing and receiving the Holy Spirit.

Accordingly, at the beginning He had asserted: 'You will come where I am going,' and 'In my Father's house there are many mansions.' However, in this place, inasmuch as that time was far distant, He gave them the promise of the Spirit. But, because they were ignorant of the real meaning of His words, they were not sufficiently heartened by them, so He said: 'I will not leave you orphans.' Indeed, they particularly needed this reassurance.

However, the words, 'I will come to you,' seemed to imply that He would be present with them. Therefore, lest they seek once more for the same kind of presence—as they had done before—notice that He did not simply state the fact, but spoke in riddles. For, after saying: 'Yet a little while and the world no longer sees me,' He added: 'But you see me.' It was as if He said: 'I will come to you, though not in the same way as before, when I was always present with you every day.'

Moreover, in order that they might not say: 'How is it, then, that You said to the Jews, "From this time forth you will not see me"?' He answered this objection by saying: 'I will come only to you, as also will the holy Spirit.'

'For I live, and you shall live. The cross, therefore, will not separate us forever, but will place Me in eclipse for a brief time only.' It seems to me that He meant not merely the present life but also the time to come. 'In that day you will know that I am in my Father, and you in me, and I in you.' Therefore, the part of this statement referring to the Father is asserted of His essence, while what He said with reference to the Apostles is indicative of their union with God and of the aid they derived from Him.

Do you ask: 'How is this reasonable, pray?'

How, then, is the contrary reasonable? For great, even infinite, is the difference between Christ and His disciples.

Furthermore, even if the same words are used of both, do not wonder at that. For Scripture is often accustomed to employ the same words, applied both to God and to men, though not in the same sense. Thus, when we are called gods and sons of God,[9] the expression, though used both in regard to us and in reference to God, does not have the same potency for both. Moreover, the Son is called the image and glory of God. And so are we, but there is a great difference. And again: 'You are Christ's, and Christ is God's,'[10] but Christ is not God's in the same way as we are Christ's.

However, what is the meaning of His words? 'When I rise from the dead,' He meant, 'you will know that I am not separated from the Father, but I have the same power as He, and that I am always with you, since events will loudly proclaim the assistance which I impart to you: when your enemies are vanquished, when you preach with eloquence, when difficulties are removed from your midst, when your apostolate flourishes from day to day, when all men acquiesce and give way to the doctrine of holiness. As He has sent me, I also send you.'[11] Do you perceive that not even here has the expression[12] the same force? For if we accept it as having the same meaning for both, the Apostles will be in no wise different from Christ.

'But why did He say: "In that day you will know"?'

Because it was then that they would see that He had risen and was present with them; it was then that they would learn the true faith. Great indeed is the power of the Spirit, who taught them all things.

'He who has my commandments and keeps them, he it is who loves me.' In truth, it is not enough merely to have them, but we also need to observe them carefully. But why did He repeatedly say the same thing to them, as: 'If you love me,

---

9 Cf. Gal. 3.27.
10 1 Cor. 3.23; cf. 11.7; Col. 1.15.
11 John 20.22.
12 That is, the word 'send.'

keep my commandments'; and: 'He who has my commandments and keeps them'; and: 'if anyone hears my word and keeps it, he it is who loves me. He who does not hear my words, does not love me.'

I think that He was referring indirectly to their grief. He had taught them many truths about His death, for He had said: 'He who hates his life in this world keeps it unto life everlasting,' and, 'He who does not take up his cross and follow me is not worthy of me,'[13] and He was also going to say still others. In reproof of them, therefore, He said: 'Do you think that it is out of love that you are grieving about My departure? A proof of love would be, rather, not to be sad.' And it was because He wished to establish this fact with finality that He summarized His discourse by returning to it. For, 'If you loved me,' He declared, 'you would rejoice that I am going to my Father.'

'As it is, however, you endure the prospect of this with fear. But to be so disposed toward death is not the attitude of those who are mindful of My commandments, for you must be crucified if you really love Me. And I say this for My words urge you not to be afraid, because of those who kill the body. My Father loves men who are not thus afraid and I do also. And I will manifest myself to them.'[14]

Then Judas[15] said: 'How is it that thou art about to manifest thyself to us?' Do you see that their souls were oppressed by fear? For he was disquieted and troubled, and thought that he was going to behold Christ in a dream, as we see the dead [when He manifested Himself]. Listen, therefore, to what He said in order that they might not conceive this suspicion: 'My Father and I will come to him and will make our abode with him.' It was as if He said: 'As My Father reveals Himself, so do I, also.'

---

13 John 12.25; Matt. 10.38.
14 Cf. Matt. 10.28.
15 Not Iscariot, but the brother of James the Less; see Jude 1.1.

Moreover, it was not only by this means that He dispelled that suspicion, but also by saying: 'We will make our abode with him,' for this does not happen in dreams. And please notice that the disciple was troubled and did not dare to say in so many words what he wanted to say. For he did not say: 'Woe is me, that you are departing this life and are going to appear to us, as the dead do.' On the contrary, he did not speak thus, but said: 'How is it that thou art about to manifest thyself to us, and not to the world?' Accordingly, Christ replied: 'I find you deserving of this because you keep My word.'

Now, the reason why He predicted future events as He did was in order that when they should see Him afterwards, they might not think Him an illusion. Furthermore, lest they think that He would appear to them in the manner I have described,[16] He also mentioned the reason for His manifesting Himself to them, namely: 'because you keep My commandments.' And He stated, too, that the Spirit also would manifest Himself in this way.

Now if, despite the fact that they had been with Him so long a time, they did not yet readily accept the idea of that existence after the Resurrection—or, rather, they could not even conceive of it—what would have been their reaction if He had revealed it to them in all its glory from the start? And that is why He partook of food with them:[17] that they might not think that what they saw was a ghost. In fact, they did think this, when they beheld Him walking on the water,[18] even though His very appearance was clearly evident and He was not far distant. Therefore, what notion would they not have conceived if, without being prepared for it, they had

---

16 That is, as a vision in a dream.
17 During His first apparition to the Eleven after the Resurrection; see Luke 24.36-43.
18 Cf. Matt. 14.26.

beheld Him risen, after seeing Him arrested and lying in His shroud? Therefore, He continually spoke to them of the fact that He would appear to them, and why and how He would appear, in order that they might not think that He was a ghost.

'He who does not love me does not keep my words. And the word that you have heard is not mine, but that of him who sent me. Hence, he who does not listen to these words not only does not love Me, but also does not love my Father. For if hearing my commandments is a proof of love, and if these commandments are also my Father's, then he who hears them, loves not the Son only, but also the Father.'

'Then how can the word be Yours and also not Yours at the same time?'

This means: 'I utter not a syllable without my Father, nor do I say anything at all of My own, not in conformity with His will.

'These things I have spoken to you while yet dwelling with you.' Now, the meaning of these teachings was not clear to them, and some they did not understand at all, while they were at least in doubt about most of them. Therefore, in order that they might not once again become troubled, and that they might not say: 'What commandments?' He freed them from all anxiety by saying: 'But the Advocate, whom the Father will send in my name, he will teach you. Perhaps my words are not clear to you now, but he will teach their meaning clearly.'

However, the words 'yet dwelling with you' imply that He was about to go away from them. In order that they might not be dejected, He then said that, as long as He Himself remained with them, the Spirit would not come, nor would they be able to comprehend anything great or sublime. Moreover, He said this to them to prepare them to bear up nobly under the trial of His departure, because it would be productive of great blessings for them. And He continually referred to Him as the Advocate,[19] because of the afflictions then besetting them.

Therefore, because they were disturbed on hearing even these things—as they thought of the troubles, the warfare, His departure—see how He once more attempted to soothe them by saying: 'Peace I leave with you,' all but saying: 'What harm do you suffer from worldly care, as long as you are at peace with Me? This peace, indeed, is not such as the world's. For outward peace is often dangerous and vain and of no help to those who possess it, whereas the peace that I give is the kind that causes you to be at peace with one another, and this makes you stronger.'

However, since He had once again said: 'I leave,' and these were the words of one on the point of departing, and this was enough to disturb them, for this reason He again said: 'Do not let your heart be troubled, or be afraid.' Do you see that they were afflicted partly by love, partly by fear? 'You have heard me say to you, "I go away to the Father and I am coming to you." If you loved me, you would rejoice that I am going to the Father, for the Father is greater than I.' Now what joy would this bring them? What consolation?

What, then, do the words mean? They did not yet understand about the Resurrection, nor did they as yet have the opinion of Him that was befitting His dignity (how, indeed, could they, when they did not even grasp that He would rise from the dead?), but they did regard the Father as great. Therefore He said: 'Even if you are afraid for Me because you think I am not powerful enough to protect Myself, and if you have no confidence that I shall see you again after the crucifixion, still, on hearing that I am going to the Father, you ought to rejoice at length, because I am going

---

19 Or 'consoler'; see Confraternity *Commentary* 343.

to One who is greater and who can therefore solve all difficulties. You have heard me say to you . . .'

Why did He add this?

'I am so sure of future events,' He meant, 'that I even foretell them; thus, I have no fear. Therefore, I have told you this[20] and the events to follow it, before it comes to pass, that when it has come to pass you may believe that I am God.' It was as if He said: 'You would not know it, would you, if I did not say so? But I would not say it, unless I were sure of it.'

Do you perceive that the statement is one of humble tenor? And I say this for, when He said: 'Dost thou suppose that I cannot entreat my Father, and he will furnish me twelve legions of angels,'[21] He was answering a suspicion in the minds of His hearers. For, no one could claim, even if he were very much demented, that Christ could not help Himself, but needed angels to rescue Him. On the contrary, it was because they esteemed Him only as Man that He said: 'twelve legions of angels.' Yet He merely asked them a question, and cast them prostrate on the ground.[22]

But, if someone should assert that the Father is 'greater' in so far as He is the begetter of the Son, we shall not contradict this.[23] However, this, to be sure, does not cause the Son to be of another substance. And what He meant was something like this: 'As long as I am here, it is reasonable for you to think that we are in danger. But if I go away to

---

20 'I am going to the Father.'
21 Matt. 26.53.
22 Cf. John 18.4-6.
23 Christ's words, 'The Father is greater than I,' are predicated of His human nature, according to the opinion more acceptable to present-day Scriptural exegesis. The explanation offered here by St. John Chrysostom—that the Son has His divine nature from the Father and that the Father may be said to be greater in that sense—has been approved by some other Church Fathers as well. See Confraternity *Commentary* 344-345.

the Father, be sure that we are safe, for no one will be able to prevail over My Father.' Now He addressed all this, of course, to the weakness of His disciples. 'I Myself indeed have complete confidence and account death as nothing.'

That is why He said: 'I have told you before it comes to pass.' He meant: 'But since you cannot yet accept my statement about these matters, I shall bring the Advocate to you from the Father whom you esteem as powerful.' Then, after He had heartened them, He once again spoke of sorrowful things. 'I will no longer speak with you, for the prince of this world is coming, and in me he has nothing.'

By 'the prince of this world' He meant the Devil, and was calling evil men 'this world.' He does not rule over heaven and earth, because he would upset everything and destroy it, but he rules over those who have surrendered themselves to him. Therefore, He calls him prince of the darkness of this world, again calling the evil deeds performed here 'darkness.'

'What, then, will the Devil destroy You?'

'Not at all, for in Me he has nothing.'

'How, then, will they put You to death.'

'Because I will it and that the world may know that I love the Father. For I am not subject to death,' He meant, 'nor am I in the Devil's power, but I am submitting to these sufferings because of My love for the Father.'

Furthermore, He said this that He might once more stir up their courage, and that they might learn that it was not against His will, but freely willing it, that He came to this suffering, and in scorn of the Devil. Indeed, it was not enough to have said once: 'Yet a little while I am with you,' but He repeatedly referred to this sad theme, with good reason, until He should make it readily accepted by them, interjecting into it, besides, information that was salutary for them to know.

Therefore, at one time He said: 'I go away and I am

coming to you'; and: 'That where I am, there you also
may be'; and: 'Thou canst not follow me now, but thou
shalt follow later; and: 'I am going to the Father'; and:
'The Father is greater than I'; and: 'I have told you before
it comes to pass'; and: 'I shall not suffer because I must,
but because of my love for the Father.' He spoke thus so that
they would realize that His Passion was not a destructive or
a harmful thing, if actually both He who loved the Father
very much, and the Father who was beloved by Him, willed
it so. Accordingly, therefore, though introducing a judicious
admixture of these consoling facts, He also spoke repeatedly
of the sad things as well, to train their understanding.

Now I say this for He spoke to console them when He
said: 'He will dwell with you' and 'It is expedient for you.'[24]
Indeed, it was on this account that He said innumerable
things of the Spirit in anticipation of His coming: 'He will
be in you,' and: 'The world cannot receive Him,' and: 'He
will bring all things to your mind,' and: 'Spirit of Truth,'
and: 'Holy Spirit,' and: 'Advocate,' and: 'It is expedient
for you.' He said this that they might not be dejected, thinking that there would be no one to protect and help them.
Moreover, He asserted that it was expedient for Him to leave
them, to teach them that the Spirit would make them spiritual
men.

Indeed, let us see that this has actually taken place. For,
after receiving the Spirit, men who had been fearful and
trembling precipitated themselves into the midst of dangers
and were ready to face the sword, and fire, and wild beasts,
and the sea, and every sort of punishment. Further, men who
were simple and unlettered discoursed with such eloquence
as to astonish their hearers. For, the Spirit transformed them
into instruments of steel instead of clay, and gave them wings,
and did not permit them to quail before any human agency.

---

24 John 14.17; 16.7.

Truly that grace is such that, if it finds discouragement, it dispels it; if it finds evil desire, it consumes it; if it finds fear, it casts it out; in fine, it does not permit the man who shares in it to be merely human, but causes him, as if transported to heaven itself, to contemplate all things there. That is why no one of those who came under its sway claimed anything as his own, but they were continuing in prayer 'with gladness and simplicity of heart.' To be sure, the Holy Spirit particularly requires this. For 'the fruit of the Spirit is joy, peace, faith, kindness.'[25]

'Yet spiritual men also are often sad,' you will object.

Yes, but their sadness is sweeter than joy. Cain, indeed, was saddened, but his was the sadness of this world.[26] Paul, also, was saddened, but his was sadness according to God.[27] In truth, everything that is spiritual has a very great reward; just as everything worldly has the worst of punishments. Let us, therefore, attract to ourselves the invincible aid of the Spirit, by keeping the commandments, and we shall be not inferior to the angels. For it is not because they are incorporeal that they are as they are (indeed, if this were so, no incorporeal being would be evil), but free will is completely responsible for everything. Therefore, among incorporeal beings, some have been found worse than men and even beasts; and, among those possessed of bodies, some have been found better than incorporeal beings. Certainly, all the just men have accomplished whatever righteous deeds they have to their credit, even while dwelling on earth and possessing bodies. For they have lived on earth as pilgrims and strangers, and dwell in heaven as citizens.

Well, then, do not say: 'I am impeded by the flesh; I can-

---

25 Gal. 5.22,23; cf. Acts 2.46.
26 That is, he was downcast out of envy of his brother; see Gen. 4.5-7.
27 That is, his sadness was prompted by zeal for the glory of God, and not caused by sinful or worldly considerations; see, for example, Rom. 9.1-5; Gal. 6.14.

not win out or take on myself efforts to acquire virtue.' Do not thus accuse your Creator. For, if the flesh makes it impossible to possess virtue, the fault is not ours. However, the company of the saints have shown that in reality it does not make this impossible. The nature of the flesh did not prevent Paul, for instance, from becoming such a saint as he became, or Peter from receiving the keys of heaven. Further, Henoch, though possessed of the flesh, was taken by God and seen no more. Thus Elias, also, was snatched up to heaven, together with his flesh; and Abraham, together with Isaac and the latter's son, though they possessed the flesh, shone forth resplendent. Furthermore, Joseph in the flesh overcame that brazen woman.[28]

Yet, why do I speak of the flesh? For, if you place bonds on it, there is no harm done. 'In truth, even if I am bound,' said Paul, 'yet the word of God is not bound.'[29] Still, why do I speak merely of chains and bonds? Add both imprisonment and bolts, but, even so, these do not become a hindrance to virtue. It was thus, indeed, that Paul instructed us in the faith. For, iron is not a restraint on the soul, but fear is, and the desire for possessions, and the innumerable passions. These bind us even if the body has been set free.

'But these passions are spawned by the body,' you will say.

These words of yours are pretense and deceitful evasion. For, if the passions were brought forth by the body, all men would remain in subjection to them. Just as it is not possible to escape from weariness, and sleep, and hunger, and thirst, because they belong to our nature, so also, if the passions were such, they would not allow anyone to be free from their despotic rule. But if, in fact, many do escape from them, it is quite clear that such imperfections proceed from a sluggish soul.

---

28 Cf. Gen. 5.24; 39.7-12; 4 Kings 2.11.
29 2 Tim. 2.9.

Let us, then, put a stop to this, and let us not accuse the body, but let us place it in subjection to the soul, in order that, with it held in control, we may obtain everlasting blessings, by the grace and mercy of our Lord Jesus Christ. Glory be to Him forever and ever. Amen.

Homily 76 (John 14.31-15.10)

'Arise, let us go from here. I am the true vine, you are the branches, and my Father is the vine-dresser.'[1]

A lack of spiritual understanding makes the soul weak and ignoble, just as being well instructed in heavenly doctrine makes it great and noble, for, if it does not benefit by the instruction given it, it is weak, not by nature, but by choice. In fact, when I see man, at one time bold, becoming craven at another, I maintain that this behavior is not a defect inherent in his nature, for the qualities inherent in his nature are invariable. Again, when I see those who were just now craven becoming suddenly bold, I once more draw the same conclusion, and ascribe all to their free choice.

The disciples also were cowardly before they gained the spiritual understanding they needed, and were deemed worthy of the gift of the Spirit; later, however, they became bolder than lions. And Peter, who had not been able to endure the taunts of a little maid, was crucified head downward, and was scourged, and, though exposed to perils without number, did not hold his tongue. On the contrary, he endured his sufferings as if they were but a dream, so freely did he speak out—not, however, before the crucifixion. Therefore Christ said: 'Arise, let us go from here.'

'Why did He say that, may I ask? Was He unaware of the hour when Judas would approach? Or else was He afraid that

---

1 John 14.31-15.1.

Judas would come there and arrest them and that those who were plotting against Him would approach before He had completed that noblest of His instructions?'

Perish the thought! Thése notions are far removed from His exalted dignity!

'Well, then, if He was not afraid, why in the world did He take them away from there? Why did He not finish His discourse, and then bring them to the garden that was so well known to Judas? Moreover, even if Judas were present, could He not have blinded His opponents' eyes, as He had done even when He was not present? Why, then, did He depart from the supper room?[2]

He was giving His disciples a short respite. And He was doing this for it was likely that, because they were in a place that was easy of access, they were fearful and apprehensive, both because of the time and by reason of the place. And this was so for it was the dead of night and it was impossible for them even to pay attention to what He was saying. On the contrary, they could only be continually distracted by thoughts of those who were on their way to them. And especially was this true because the discourse of the Master caused them to expect fearful things. For, 'Yet a little while,' He said, 'and I will not be with you, and the prince of this world is coming.'

Because, on hearing such words as these, they became deeply disturbed as if they were going to be captured almost at once, He therefore brought them to another place, so that, thinking they were in safety, they would at last listen to Him without trepidation. And this was necessary for they were about to hear teachings of great import. That is why He

---

2 Whether Christ actually suited the action to the word and left the cenacle at this point is a question that has occupied exegetes down to our own day. St. John Chrysostom's interpretation, though reasonable enough on the whole, does not account for the implication to the contrary in 18.1. See Confraternity *Commentary* 345.

said: 'Arise, let us go from here.' Then He went on to declare: 'I am the vine, you are the branches.'

'What did He wish to imply by the parable?'

That it is not possible for anyone to have life if he does not pay attention to Christ's words, and also that the miracles that would later take place would be performed through the power of Christ.

'My Father is the vine-dresser.'

'What is this, then? Does the Son need assistance?'

Perish the thought! For this illustration does not mean that. In fact, see how very carefully He developed the parable. He did not say that the root profits by the care of the vine-dresser, but the branches. Furthermore, in this context He made mention of the root in no other connection than that they might learn that nothing can be done without His power and that they must be united to Him by faith as the branch is to the vine.

'Every branch in me that bears no fruit the Father will take away.' Here He was referring by implication to conduct, to show that it is not possible to be in Him without works. 'And every branch that bears fruit he will cleanse,' that is, will give it the benefit of much care. Even though in reality the root needs care before the branches do—to be dug around, to be dressed—He said nothing at all of it here, but confined Himself to the branches. He was showing that He Himself was sufficient to Himself, while His disciples were in need of much assistance from the vine-dresser, even if they were of very excellent virtue. That is why He said: 'The one that bears fruit he will cleanse.'

The other one, indeed, since it is without fruit, cannot be in the vine, while this one, since it bears fruit, is rendered more fruitful. Now, one might say that this statement was made with reference to the persecutions that were at that time about to descend on them. For the words, 'He will

cleanse it,' mean 'will prune it,' an operation which makes
the branch more fruitful. By this He showed that their trials
would make them stronger.

Next, in order that they might not inquire into the
underlying meaning of these statements, and lest He should
once again cast them into a state of anxiety, He assured
them: 'You are already clean because of the word that I
have spoken to you.' Do you see how He was calling their
attention to the fact that He takes care of the vines? For He
meant: 'I have cleansed you,' although, to be sure, He
had previously pointed out that the Father does this. However, there is no difference between the operation of Father
and Son.

'And now you must do your part in this.'[3] Then, in order
to show that actually He had no need of their co-operation,
but that, on the contrary, it was to benefit them that He
urged this, He added: 'As the branch cannot bear fruit of
itself, so neither can he who does not abide in me.' Thus, lest
they become estranged from Him because of their fearfulness,
He bolstered up their souls that were being unnerved by
fear, and bound them closely to Himself, and held out to
them fair hopes for the future. For the root abides, but it is
the lot of the branches to be taken away or to be allowed to
remain. Therefore, after urging us on from both motives—
both reward and punishment—He particularly stressed the
need of our co-operation.

'He who abides in me, and I in him.' Do you see that the
Son contributes no less than does the Father to the care of
the disciples? The Father, to be sure, cleanses them, but the
Son keeps them in Himself. Now, to abide in the root causes
the branches to bear fruit. For, even if the branch is not
pruned, if it abides in the root it bears fruit, though not as
much as it ought. On the contrary, the branch that does not

---

3 That is, 'Abide in me.'

abide in the root bears no fruit at all. Nonetheless, it is clear that the cleansing of the branch is the work of the Son, also, and likewise that abiding in the root is attributable to the Father who begot the Root.

Do you perceive that all has a common origin: both the cleansing of the branch and the profiting by the power derived from the root? Therefore, the loss [for him who does not abide in the vine] is great: even the inability to do anything.[4] However, He did not make the punishment consist merely in this, but He made the word embrace more. For 'he shall be cast outside,' He said, no longer enjoying the cultivation of the vine-dresser, 'and will wither.' That is, if he did possess any part of the root, he is dispossessed of it; if he had any grace, he is stripped of it and is bereft of all help and life from that source. And what is the final step? 'He will be cast into the fire.' Quite different, however, is he who abides in Him.

Next, He showed what 'abiding in Him' means by saying: 'If my words abide in you.' Do you see that it was with reason that I asserted before this that He looks for the proof of our words in deeds? For, after saying: 'Whatever you ask I will do,' He added: 'If you love me, keep my commandments.' Here, likewise: 'If you abide in me, and if my words abide in you, ask whatever you will and it shall be done to you.' Moreover, He said this to show that those who were conspiring against Him were the branches that would burn, while the disciples would bring forth fruit.

Well, then, after dispelling the fear that they felt toward His opponents, and after showing them that they themselves would be unconquerable, He declared: 'In this is my Father glorified, that you may become my disciples, and may bear much fruit.' By these words He made His statements credible.

---

4 'Without me you can do nothing.'

For, if the bringing forth of fruit redounds to the glory of the Father, He will not neglect His own glory.

'And may become my disciples.' Do you see that it is he who bears fruit who is His disciple? And what is the meaning of 'In this is my Father glorified?' That is, 'He rejoices when you abide in Me, when you bear fruit.'

'As my Father has loved me, I also have loved you.' Here at length He spoke in more human fashion, for what is spoken as if between men has an effectiveness of its own. Indeed, since He chose even to die, and, though we were slaves, and foes, and enemies, considered us worthy of such great honor as even to bring us up to heaven, how great a measure of love He displayed! Then, 'If I love you, take courage; if your bearing fruit is the glory of the Father, do not suspect anything evil of this.'

Next, in order that He might not cause them to be downcast, see how He once again heartened them. 'Abide in my love, for you are in control of this.' But how will this be? 'If you keep my commandments,' He said, 'as I also have kept my Father's commandments.' Once again His words were uttered in human fashion. For, of course, the Lawgiver was not going to be subject to commandments. Do you perceive that here, also, as I always say, He used this manner of speaking because of the weakness of His listeners? He addressed many of His words to their suspicious reasoning and by all of them showed the disciples that they were in safety and that their foes would perish, and that they had gained possession of all that they possessed from the Son, and that if they should give evidence of a pure life no one of them would ever perish.

Moreover, notice how authoritatively He spoke to them. For, He did not say: 'Abide in the love of the Father,' but, 'in my love.' Next, lest they might say: 'When You have made us hateful to all men, then You abandon us and depart from us,' He pointed out that He was not abandoning them, but remained as closely united to them as the branch is to the vine. On the other hand, lest they become lazy through overconfidence, He made it clear that virtue could be lost if they should slacken in their practice of it.

Next, lest by seeming to limit this matter to Himself He might rather dispose them to fall away [when they witnessed His Passion and death], He said: 'In this is my Father glorified.' Everywhere, indeed, He showed His own and His Father's love for them. Therefore, it was not the affairs of the Jews that were the Father's glory, but those things which the disciples were going to receive. Then, lest they might say: 'We have fallen from the Father's favor, we have been abandoned and have become deserted and stripped of all things,' He said: 'Look at Me; I am loved by My Father, but nevertheless I shall endure the sufferings that now lie before Me. Well, then, I am not forsaking you either, nor am I leaving you because I do not love you. For, if I am slain and yet do not count this a proof of not being loved by the Father, you ought not to be disturbed either. If you abide in My love, these evils will lack power to harm you in proportion to your love.'

Therefore, since love is a great and invincible force and not merely something expressed in words, let us manifest it in our deeds. Christ won us over when we were His enemies; now that we have become His friends, let us remain so. He has made the start; let us at least follow. He does not love us for His own profit (for He is not in need of anything); let us at least love Him for our own advantage. He loved His foes; let us at least cherish our friend. Yet how readily we now do the opposite! Every day God is blasphemed through us by robberies, by avarice.

Now, perhaps some one of you will remark with good reason: 'Every day you preach about covetousness.'

Would that it were possible to speak of it every night also! Would that I might follow you in the marketplace and at table. Would that wives and friends and children and servants and husbandmen and neighbors, and the very pavement and walls might be able to shout forth this word that we might then cease for at least a little while. This contagion has seized upon the whole world, and the great tyranny of mammon possesses the souls of all men. We have been redeemed by Christ and become the slaves of gold. We proclaim the rule of one Master and obey another. Moreover, we listen with eagerness to whatever the latter ordains and on his account forget everything: race, friendship, nature, laws. No one looks to heaven; no one thinks of the life to come.

However, a time will come when there will be profit in none of these specious reasonings. For, 'In the nether world who gives you thanks?'[5] Scripture says. Gold is desirable and gives us much pleasure and causes us to be esteemed, but not so much as heaven does. For, many men both despise and hate the rich man, but they respect and esteem the man who lives a life of virtue.

'But the poor man is an object of ridicule, even if he be virtuous,' you will say.

However, he is not so among men, but among fools; therefore, you ought not to heed this. For, if asses should bray in disapproval, and crows should caw in disparagement, but all the wise should approve us, we would not spurn this audience to look to the cries of unreasoning beasts. I say this for those who hold the present life in esteem are like crows and worse than asses.

Besides, if an earthly king should show approval of a man, he would make no account of the vulgar crowd, even if they should all ridicule him. But, if the Lord of the universe praise

---

5 Ps. 6.6.

you, will you seek the praises of beetles and gnats besides? This, indeed, is what these men are in comparison with God; or, rather, not even this, but whatever is more vile than these creatures. Why do we spend our time in the mud? How long shall we choose sluggards and gluttons for our audience? They can be good judges of gamblers, drunkards, those who live for their belly; but they cannot even conjure up in sleep the concept of virtue or of vice.

Furthermore, if someone should jeer at you because you do not know how to construct drainage ditches, you would think it of no moment, but would even laugh at the one who charged you with inexperience of the kind. But, when you wish to practice virtue, do you set up as arbiters of your actions those who have no knowledge of virtue? That is why we never excel in that art. For we entrust our affairs, not to experts, but to ignoramuses. And the latter assess them, not according to the rules of the art, but according to their own ignorance.

Wherefore, I beseech you, let us despise the vulgar crowd; or, rather, let us not desire praise, or money, or riches, and let us not regard poverty as an evil. Let us adopt this attitude, for poverty is our instructor in prudence, patience, and all true wisdom. Lazarus, for instance, lived in poverty, and received the crown of eternal life.[6] Jacob desired to obtain only bread.[7] Joseph came to be in utter poverty and not only was a slave, but even a prisoner, and therefore we esteem him the more. Moreover, we praise him not so much when he distributed the grain as when he lived in the prison; not when he wore the diadem, but when he wore chains; not when he sat on the throne, but when he was plotted against and sold.[8]

---

6 Cf. Luke 16.20-22.
7 Cf. Gen. 42.2.
8 For these events in the well-known history of Joseph, see Gen. 37-50.

Therefore, reflecting on all these things and on the crowns that are fashioned for us by means of these trials, let us not esteem riches and honor and pleasure and power, but poverty, and chains, and bonds, and patience practiced for the sake of virtue. The end of the former, in truth, is full of trouble and confusion and they are coterminous with the present life; while the fruit of the latter is heaven and the blessings in heaven which the eye hath not seen nor the ear heard.

May it be the lot of all of us to obtain these by the grace and mercy of our Lord Jesus Christ. Glory be to Him forever and ever. Amen.

Homily 77 (John 15.11-16.4)

'These things I have spoken to you that my joy may abide in you, and that your joy may be made full. This is my commandment, that you love one another as I have loved you.'[1]

All good things receive their reward when they come to the proper end, but, if they are cut short prematurely, shipwreck is the result. Now, the ship laden with incalculable cargo does not profit from a long voyage if it does not succeed in arriving at the harbor, but is sunk in the middle of the sea. On the contrary, the more numerous the toils it undergoes, the greater the resulting loss in the end. So it is, also, with souls when they lose heart for the completion of their toils and grow despondent in the midst of their trials. And that is why Paul said that glory and honor and peace lie in store for those who run 'by patience in good works.'[2]

Accordingly, this is the disposition that Christ was now building up in His disciples. He had received them and they

---

1 John 15.11-16.4.
2 Cf. Rom. 2.7-11.

had rejoiced on His account, but the Passion then impending
and His ill-boding words would cut short their joy. Therefore,
after He had spoken words of encouragement to them, He
said: 'These things I have spoken to you that my joy may
abide in you, and that your joy may be made full': that is,
'that you may not be cut off from me, that you may not stop
short in the race. You have rejoiced in Me—and rejoiced
very much—but now sadness has come upon you. Therefore
I am casting this out, that your joy may persist to the end.'
Thus He pointed out that their present circumstances should
evoke, not grief, but joy. 'I have seen that you were taking
offense at my words. I did not condemn you for it; I did not
say: "Why do you not remain true to me?" But I spoke
words calculated to bring you consolation. I wish to keep you
in this disposition always: in the same love. You heard about
the kingdom; you rejoiced. Therefore, I have said these
things to you that your joy may be made full.'

'This is my commandment, that you love one another as
I have loved you.' Do you perceive that the love of God is
interwoven with ours, like a kind of cord binding it together?
That is why Christ at one time spoke of two commandments;
at another, one. For it is not possible for him who is receptive
to the love of God not to possess the other kind of love.[3] In
one place Scripture says: 'On this depend the Law and the
Prophets.' And in another: 'Whatever you would that men
should do to you, even so do you also to them; for this is the
Law and the Prophets.' Also: 'Love is the fulfillment of the
Law.'[4] This He was saying here, too. If abiding with Him
is the result of our love of Him, and our love of Him is
manifested by keeping His commandments, and the commandment is that we love one another—therefore, our love
for one another results in abiding in God.

---

3 Love of neighbor.
4 Cf. Matt. 22.40; 7.12; Rom. 13.10.

Moreover, He did not merely say that we should have love for one another, but even revealed the manner in which we should do this; namely, 'as I have loved you.' Once again He was pointing out that His very departure from them was motivated, not by coldness, but by love, 'so that I ought rather to be admired for it, since I am laying down my life for you.' However, He nowhere said this in so many words, but previously, in describing the best of shepherds,[5] and also here, in heartening them and pointing out the greatness of His love[6] and revealing Himself to them as He is, He said it tacitly.

'But why did He extol love at every opportunity?'

Because it is the mark of His disciples; it is the force that unites them in the practice of virtue. And that is why Paul also said such great things of it,[7] since he was a true disciple of Christ and had had experience of it.

'You are my friends. No longer do I call you servants, because the servant does not know what his master does. You are my friends, because all things that I have heard from my Father I have made known to you.'

'How is it, then, that He later said: "Many things I have to say to you, but you cannot bear them now"?'[8]

By the words, 'all that I have heard from my Father,' He intended no other meaning than that He was saying nothing in opposition to the Father, but only His Father's teachings. And, since it seems to be especially a sign of friendship, if one discloses secrets, 'You are deemed worthy even of this degree of friendship,' He declared. However, when He said 'all,' He meant 'as much as you ought to hear.'

Next, He revealed another proof of friendship, and no

---

5 Cf. John 10.11-18.
6 That is, 'Greater love than this no one has, that one lay down his life for his friends.
7 Cf. 1 Cor. 13.
8 John 16.12.

ordinary one. What, then, was this? 'You have not chosen me,' He said, 'but I have chosen you'; that is, 'I have eagerly sought for your friendship.' Furthermore, He did not stop here, but even declared: 'I have appointed you'—that is, 'I have planted you—that you should go'—that is, 'that you should spread out' (He was still using the metaphor of the vine) 'and bear fruit and that your fruit should remain.' If the fruit remains, much more will you. For He meant: 'I have not merely loved you but also have given you the greatest blessings by causing your branches to spread out everywhere in the world.'

Do you perceive in how many ways He showed His love? By disclosing secrets; by taking the initiative in seeking eagerly for their friendship; by bestowing great benefits upon them; by enduring the sufferings which He then experienced for their sake. And after this He indicated that He would remain always with those who were going to produce fruit. For they would need to enjoy His assistance and, thus fortified, would bear fruit.

'That whatever you ask the Father in my name he may give you.'

'Yet, the deed belongs to the Person of whom the request is made. And if the request is to be made of the Father, how is it that it is the Son who actually fulfills it?' In order that you may learn that the Son is not inferior.

'I have spoken these words to you that you may love one another'; that is: 'It is not to reproach you that I am saying that I lay down my life for you, or that I have taken the initiative in seeking you out, but to persuade you to friendship with Me.'

Next, because it was difficult, and hard to bear, to be persecuted by many men, and to be reviled, and this was sufficient to depress even a lofty soul, Christ arrived at the subject of persecution only after having, for this reason, paved the way by countless references. For, after He had soothed their souls, He then approached the matter, giving abundant evidence that these sufferings would take place for their benefit, just as did the other things which He had pointed out to them.

Just as He had declared that they ought not to grieve, but even to rejoice, 'because I am going to the Father' (since He was doing this, not to abandon them, but actually out of very great love for them), so here, likewise, He pointed out to them that they ought to rejoice and not to be sad. Furthermore, notice how He managed this. He did not say: 'I know that the ordeal is a grievous one, but bear it for My sake, since you are suffering on My account.' Not yet, indeed, would this explanation be sufficient to hearten them. Therefore, He passed it by and presented another.

What, then, was this? That persecution would be evidence of virtue already acquired. And that it was the contrary which ought to worry them: 'You ought not to be troubled because you are now hated, but only if you should be loved by the world.' It was this, indeed, that He was implying by the words, 'If you were of the world, the world would love what is its own. So that if you were loved, it is very clear that you would be providing proof of your evil character.'

Next, since this persecution had not taken place, though He was foretelling it, He again continued: 'No servant is greater than his master. If they have persecuted me, they will persecute you also.' He was pointing out that they would be imitators of Him especially in this respect. For, as long as Christ was still in the flesh, the world manifested hostility towards Him, but, when He had departed from them, the enmity transferred to them in turn. Then, because they were so few in number, when they were in consternation at the prospect of being the target of the hostility of so many men, He cheered their souls by declaring that being hated by them is particularly cause for rejoicing: 'For thus you will share with me in my sufferings. Therefore, you ought not to be disturbed, for you are not better than I, as I even said in anticipation of this: "No servant is greater than his master." '

In the next place, He mentioned a third reason for consolation, namely, that, when His disciples were being insulted, the Father also was. For He said: 'All these things they will do for my name's sake, because they do not know him who sent me'; that is, 'They are insulting Him also.'

In addition, to debar these from pardon, and also to set forth another reason for consolation, He said: 'If I had not come and spoken to them, they would have no sin,' pointing out that they would be guilty of wrongdoing in what they did both to Him and to His disciples.

'Why, then, did You bring us to such great wrongs? Did you not foresee the hostility and the hatred?'

For this reason He again said: 'He who hates me hates my Father also,' predicting no light punishment for them by reason of this. Since they repeatedly alleged that they were persecuting Him in the Father's interest,[9] He said these words to deprive them of this pretext. 'Indeed they have no excuse: I have provided them instruction by My words and I added to this the example of My deeds, according to the prescription of Moses who bade all men to obey Him who did and said such things, when He should bring them to righteousness and perform very great wonders.' Moreover, Moses specified that He would not merely work miracles, but such miracles as no one else worked. And they themselves testified that this was fulfilled in Christ when they said: 'Never has the like been seen in Israel,' and: 'Not from the beginning of the world has it been heard that anyone opened

---

9 That is, on the ground that He was breaking the Sabbath, and also because He said that God is His Father.

the eyes of a man born blind.'[10] Such were their sentiments also with regard to Lazarus, and all His other deeds of the kind. Likewise, the way in which He worked miracles [astonished them], since everything about it was new and different.

'Why, then,' someone asks, 'will they persecute us as well as You?'

'Because you are not of the world. If you were of the world, the world would love what is its own. He was recalling to them the words which He had also spoken before this to His own brethren.[11] On that occasion, however, He spoke somewhat restrainedly, lest He might give offense; here, on the contrary, He revealed all.

'Still, how is it clear that it is for this reason that we are hated?'

'Because of what happened to Me. For, which one of My words or deeds gave them a pretext for not receiving Me, may I ask?'

Next, since their conduct must astound us, He told the reason for it: that is, their wickedness. Furthermore, He did not even stop at this, but also went on to mention the Prophet, pointing out that he had foretold this of old and said: 'They have hated me without cause.'[12] Now, Paul likewise did this. For, since many men wonder why the Jews did not believe, he cited Prophets who foretold this of old and who made it clear that the reason for their incredulity was their malice and pride.[13]

'What, then? If they have not kept Your word, therefore they will not keep ours. If they have persecuted You, there-

10 Matt. 9.33; John 9.32.
11 Cf. John 7.7.
12 Ps. 68.5; 34.19.
13 Cf. Heb. passim.

fore they will persecute us, also. If they have seen such miracles as no one else has performed, if they have heard such words as no one else has spoken, and have not profited by this, if they have hated Your Father and have hated You with Him, why have You embroiled us in this?' someone might ask. 'How shall we obtain a hearing? And who of our fellow men will pay attention to us?'

Accordingly, see what sort of consolation He went on to mention, lest they be disturbed by these reflections. 'When the Advocate has come, whom I will send you, the Spirit of truth who proceeds from the Father, he will bear witness concerning me. And you also bear witness, because from the beginning you are with me.' He will be trustworthy, for He is the Spirit of Truth. That is why Christ called Him, not 'the Holy Spirit,' but 'the Spirit of Truth.'

Moreover, the words, 'who proceeds from the Father,' mean that He has precise knowledge of all things, as He Himself also said of Himself: 'I know where I came from and where I go,'[14] and there also He was speaking on the subject of truth. 'Whom I will send.' See, it is no longer the Father only, but also the Son who sends.

'And you also are reliable witnesses, you who are with me, since you have not heard your teachings from others. Now, the Apostles gained confidence from these words and said: [by us witnesses, designated beforehand by God,] 'who ate and drank with Him.'[15] And the Spirit bore witness that these words were not uttered to curry favor.

'These things I have spoken to you that you may not be scandalized,' that is, when you see many men without faith, while you are undergoing terrible sufferings. 'They will expel you from the synagogues.' Indeed, they had already agreed that if anyone should confess Christ he would be excluded

14 John 8.14.
15 Acts 10.41.

from the synagogue. 'Yes, the hour is coming for everyone who kills you to think that he is offering worship to God. And so they will try to accomplish your murder as a righteous deed, pleasing to God.'

Next, He once again went on to give them encouragement. 'And these things they will do because they have not known the Father nor me. It suffices for your consolation that you endure these sufferings for my sake and that of the Father.' Here He was again recalling to them a beatitude that He had proclaimed at the start of His public life: 'Blessed are you when men reproach you, and persecute you, and, speaking falsely, say all manner of evil against you, for my sake. Rejoice and exult, because your reward is great in heaven.'[16]

'These things I have spoken to you, that when the time for them has come you may remember them, and so by means of them you will believe that the rest of my teachings are also true. For, you will not be able to say that to flatter you I said only those things that would win your favor, or that my words were those of a deceiver. Indeed, if anyone were going to deceive you, he would not make predictions of this kind to you, since they are apt to influence you to change your purpose. Accordingly, I have made these predictions for this reason: that the events might not come upon you unexpectedly and completely confuse you; and also for another reason, namely, that you might not say that I did not foresee that these things would take place. Therefore, remember that I told you.'

Now, He said this for the Jews would ever disguise their persecution of them by malicious pretexts, driving them out as if they were a corrupting influence. However, this did not disconcert the disciples since they had heard of these things beforehand and knew why they were suffering them. In truth, the reason why they were taking place was enough to

---

16 Matt. 5.11,12.

hearten the disciples. That is why He repeatedly reviewed
it by saying: 'They have not known me,' and 'They will do
this because of me,' and 'for my name's sake,' and 'because
of the Father,' and 'I have first borne these sufferings,' and
'They will dare to do these things for no just reason.'

Let us also reflect on these words in our trials, when we
have something to suffer from evil men. Let us look 'towards
the author and finisher of our faith'[17] and consider that our
sufferings come from men of no account and are borne both
for the sake of virtue and for His sake. For, if we keep these
facts in mind, all things will become easy and tolerable.
Indeed if a man who suffers for his loved ones even glories in
it, what account will a man make of terrible sufferings, if he
bears them for God's sake? If Christ Himself for our sake
sake called a most shameful experience, the cross, 'glory,' how
much more ought we to adopt this attitude. In fact, if we can
thus despise sufferings, much more can we despise money and
covetousness.

Well, then, when we are going to suffer anything unpleasant we ought to think, not of the hardships involved, but
of the crowns to come. Just as traders consider not merely
the seas, but also the profits they will obtain, so we also
ought reflect on heaven and confidence in God. And if it
appears desirable to be greedy, consider that Christ does not
wish it, and it will at once seem undesirable. Again, if it is
burdensome to give to the poor, do not concentrate your
thoughts on the cost, but at once transfer your attention to
the harvest to come from the sowing. When it is difficult to
refrain from the love of another's wife, think of the crown
that will be won by the effort and you will easily endure the
difficulty. For, if the fear of men averts us from evil enter-
prises, much more should the love of Christ.

Virtue is difficult to acquire. But let us modify our view

17 Heb. 12.2.

of it by the greatness of the promise of future rewards. Virtuous men, to be sure, even without these, regard virtue as beautiful of itself, and therefore they seek it and practice it because it is pleasing to God, and not for the sake of a reward. They hold chastity in great esteem, not because they will escape punishment if they do so, but because God has commanded it. However, if a man be somewhat weak, let him keep the rewards in view.

Let us act in this way also with regard to almsgiving, and let us take pity on our fellow men; let us not neglect those wasted by hunger. For, is it not strange behavior for us to take our place at table, amid gaiety and luxury, while we hear others passing through the streets moaning, and do not go to the aid of anyone who is moaning, but even become annoyed at him and call him an imposter? What is it you are saying, my man? Does anyone devise a fraud for the sake of one loaf of bread?

'Yes, he does,' you will declare.

Well, then, let him be especially pitied for this. For this reason particularly, let him be set free from want. But, if you are unwilling to give to him, at least do not insult him; if you are unwilling to rescue him from shipwreck, do not force him into the abyss. Indeed, when you drive away the poor man who comes to you, be mindful who it is that will be coming as a suppliant to God. 'With what measure you measure,' Scripture says, 'it shall be measured to you.'[18] Think how he goes off, after being rebuffed: head bent low, grieving, because besides his poverty he has also received the blow of your affront. For, if you regard begging as a curse, consider how great a disturbance it creates when the beggar receives nothing, and goes off offended. How long shall we be like wild beasts and ignore our nature itself because of covetousness?

18 Matt. 7.2.

Many groan at my words, but I wish them to show this mercy, not now only, but forever. Think, if you please, of that day when we shall stand before the tribunal of Christ, when we shall seek for mercy, and Christ, leading them forth into the midst, will say to us: 'Was it for the sake of one loaf or one obol that you caused such great disturbance to these souls?' What shall we say? And what defense shall we make?

For, in testimony that He will bring them forward, also, listen to what He said: 'As long as you did not do it for one of these least ones, you did not do it for me.'[19] In the end it is not they who will address us, but God who will rebuke us in their behalf. When the rich man saw Lazarus, Lazarus to be sure, said nothing to him, but Abraham spoke in his behalf. Thus it will be, also, with regard to the poor whom we now treat with scorn. For we shall not then see them holding out their hands in a pitiable manner, but they will be at rest. We, on the contrary, shall take on their role—and would that it were the role only and not something much harder to bear, namely, punishment. The rich man, indeed, did not there long to be filled with crumbs, but wasted away and was grievously tormented. Furthermore, he heard: 'Thou in thy lifetime hast received good things, and Lazarus evil things.'[20]

Let us not, then, have great esteem for wealth. This will be the cause of punishment for us if we do not take care, just as poverty will be for us a source of refreshment and peace if we do take care. And this is so for we even free ourselves of our sins if we endure it uncomplainingly, and also obtain much favor from God.

Well, then, let us not always seek for security here in order that we may actually enjoy security there. On the contrary, let us undertake works for the sake of virtue, and let us do

---

19 Matt. 25.45.
20 Cf. Luke 16.24.

away with superfluous things. Let us not seek for more, but expend all our possessions on the needy. Indeed, what excuse shall we have when He Himself promises heaven to us, and we give Him not even a loaf? What excuse, when He makes his sun rise on you and furnishes you with the service of all creation, while you do not even give Him a garment, or share your dwelling with Him?[21]

Why do I mention merely the sun and material creation? He has given His Body to you, and His precious Blood, and do you not even provide Him with a drink of water?

But you did give it to Him once?

This, however, is not showing mercy, for, as long as you have anything that you do not share, you have not yet done all you should. The virgins, to be sure, had oil with their lamps, but not enough.[22] Accordingly, even if you were giving to the poor from your very own goods, you ought not to be so sparing; but since you are in actual fact dispensing the goods of the Lord, why are you niggardly? Do you want me to tell you the cause of this brutishness? Those who amass their possessions through covetousness also shrink from almsgiving, for he who learns how to make his money in this way does not know how to spend it.

How, indeed, could a man, all prepared to commit robbery, change his mind to do just the opposite? How, in truth, will he who seizes upon other men's possessions be able to bestow his own possessions upon another man? Now, I say this for a dog that has grown accustomed to feeding upon flesh meat is no longer able to guard the flock; therefore, the shepherds even destroy dogs of this sort. Let us refrain from such food lest we ourselves also suffer this fate. I say this for those who are responsible for the death of the poor from hunger are feeding on flesh.

---

21 Cf. Matt. 5.45.
22 Cf. Matt. 25.9.

Do you not see how God has apportioned all things to us in common? In fact, if He has permitted some to be poor in this world's goods, He has also permitted this for the consolation of the wealthy, that they may be able to be rid of their sins by giving alms to the poor. But you have been cruel and brutal even in this. From this it is clear that, if you had jurisdiction over more weighty matters, also, you would have caused murders without number and would have shut off the light and all life from men. Lest this happen, Providence has thwarted your insatiable desire, at least in those matters.

But, if you are bothered by hearing these things, I am much more so, on seeing them take place. How long will you be rich, and that man poor? Until evening—and no later than that. For life is so short, and everything so presses on us at each moment, that the whole of life is considered to be but a brief hour. Why do you need bursting treasuries and numbers of slaves and stewards? Why not have heralds of your almsgiving without number? Your treasury certainly utters no sound, but even attracts many thieves. The treasuries of the poor, on the contrary, will mount to God Himself, will make the present life sweet, will free you from your sins, and will bring glory to you from God and honor from men.

Why, then, do you begrudge yourself such blessings? For by your benefactions to the poor you will not only benefit them, but yourself as well, and still more effectively. For them, to be sure, you will set the affairs of this life in order, while for yourself you will store up, beforehand, glory and a secure haven in the life to come.

May we all attain this by the grace and mercy of our Lord Jesus Christ. To Him be glory and power forever. Amen.

Homily 78 (John 16.5-15)

'These things, however, I did not tell you from the beginning, because I was with you. And now I am going to him
who sent me, and no one of you asks me, "Where art thou
going?" But because I have spoken to you these things,
sadness has filled your heart.'[1]

The tyranny exercised over us by despondency is a strong
one. We need great courage if we are to persevere in resisting
this emotion, and if, after deriving from it what profit we can,
we are to refrain from indulging in it to excess—for, actually,
it does have some usefulness. When we or other men commit
sin, only then is it salutary to give in to sadness. But when we
meet with misfortune in human affairs, then sadness has
no efficacy.

Therefore, as despondency was taking hold of the disciples,
since they were not yet perfect, see how Christ set them right
by a rebuke. Before this, to be sure, they had asked Him
questions without number. (Peter, for instance, had said:
'Where art thou going?' and Thomas: 'We do not know
where thou art going, and how can we know the way?'
and Philip: 'Show us thy Father.')[2] Yet these men now, on
hearing: 'They will expel you from the synagogue,' and 'They
will hate you,' and 'Everybody who kills you will think that
he is offering worship to God,'[3] were so downcast that they
were struck dumb for the moment, and said nothing to Him.
Therefore, reproaching them with this, He said: 'These
things I did not tell you from the beginning, because I was
with you. And now I am going to him who sent me, and no
one of you asks me, "Where art thou going?" But because I

---

1 John 16.5,6.
2 John 13.36; 14.5,8.
3 Cf. John 15.19.

have spoken to you these things, sadness has filled your heart.'

A terrible thing indeed, a terrible thing is uncontrolled sadness, and it leads to spiritual death. That is why Paul said: 'Lest perhaps such a one be overwhelmed by too much sorrow.'[4]

' "These things I did not tell you from the beginning," Christ said. But why did He not tell them from the beginning?'

That no one might declare that He said them by conjecturing from what often happens.

'Yet why in the world did He begin to discuss a matter likely to give rise to such great dissatisfaction?'

He meant: 'I knew these things from the beginning, and it was not because of not knowing them that I did not say them, but because I was with you.' Moreover, He was speaking in human fashion once again, as if He said: 'Because you were in safety, and while it was possible for you to ask questions whenever you wished, and because all the hostility was directed only at Me, it would have been superfluous to tell you these things in the beginning.'

'But did He not tell this? After He had called the Twelve, did He not say: "You will be brought before governors and kings, and they will scourge you in their synagogues"?[5] How is it, then, that He said: "I did not tell you from the beginning"?'

Because He had foretold scourgings and arrests, but not that their death would seem so desirable to the Jews that it would be even considered worship of God. This, indeed, more than anything else, was capable of terrifying them: namely, the fact that they were to be brought to judgment as impious and pernicious. Besides, we may mention that other fact,

---

4 2 Cor. 2.7.
5 Matt. 10.18,17.

also: that on the previous occasion He told them the sufferings they would endure from the Gentiles, while here He
added to these the sufferings to be inflicted by the Jews,
speaking in greater detail, and He informed them that this
was close at hand.

'And now I am going to him who sent me, and no one
of you asks, "Where art thou going?" But because I have
spoken to you these things, sadness has filled your heart.'
Even this was no small consolation to them: that He was
aware of their excessive sadness. For they were frightened out
of their wits by the anguish they felt at the thought of His
departure, and by the prospect of the fearful things to come
upon them (since they did not know whether they would
endure them courageously).

'Why did He not, then, tell them these things afterwards,
when they had been granted the privilege of receiving the
Spirit?'

So that you might learn that they were already very
strongly confirmed in virtue. For if, when they have not yet
been deemed worthy of the Spirit, they do not turn away
from Christ, though completely overcome by sadness, think
what they will be like when they enjoy the advantage of
possessing grace. Indeed, if on hearing these things at that
later time they had borne it well, we should have attributed
it all to the Spirit. But now all their behavior is the fruit of
their character and disposition, and is a clear proof of their
love for Christ who was testing their will, unassisted as yet by
the Holy Spirit.

'But I speak the truth to you.' See how He again offered
them consolation. For He meant: 'I am not saying what will
please you, but, even if you are saddened ten thousand times
over, you must hear what it is to your advantage to hear.
My presence is surely what you desire, but it is quite the
opposite—My absence—that is to your advantage. Moreover,

it is characteristic of one who has his friends' interests at heart not to spare them with regard to what is advantageous to them, and not to lead them away from what is good for them.

'For if I do not go,' He declared, 'the Advocate will not come.' What have they to say here, who do not properly esteem the Spirit? Is it 'expedient' for the Lord to go away and for a servant to come instead? Do you perceive how great the dignity of the Spirit is?[6]

'But if I go, I will send him to you.' And what is the advantage of this? 'When he has come he will convict the world.' That is, 'They will not do these things with impunity if He comes. What has already taken place, to be sure, is enough to confute them. But, when these other things also are achieved through Him—namely, more perfect teachings and greater miracles—they will be much more surely condemned, since they will see such things being done in My name, and thus the proof of My Resurrection will be still more certain. At present, to be sure, they can speak of "the Son of the carpenter, whose mother and father we know,"[7] but, when they see death dissolved, malice worsted, lameness cured, demons driven out, the ineffable ministry of the Spirit, and all these things taking place by invoking Me, what will they say? The Father has indeed borne witness to Me and the Spirit likewise will bear witness. Though He has borne witness even from the beginning, He will do this now, also.

Furthermore, the words, 'He will convict the world of sin,' mean: 'He will deprive them of all defense and will show that their transgressions are inexcusable. And of justice, because I go to the Father, and you will see me no more,' that is, 'I

---

6 That is, that He is equal to the Son and therefore equal to the Father. For a summary of the heresies denying this doctrine, see art. 'Pneumatomachi' in *Catholic Encyclopedia*.

7 Cf. John 6.42.

have given the example of a blameless life. And my going to the Father is an evidence of this. For, since they were continually charging that He was not of God, and therefore they maintained that He was a sinner and a transgressor of the Law,[8] He meant that the Spirit would deprive them even of this pretext for condemning Him. 'For, if the supposition that I am not of God proves that I am a transgressor of the Law, when the Spirit proves that I have gone to the Father, and not for a time only, but to abide there (for the words "You will see me no more" clearly have this meaning), what will they say then?'

Notice that their evil suspicion was completely dispelled by these two statements. For the performing of miracles is not the work of a sinner (a sinner, to be sure, is not capable of performing miracles), nor is it the mark of a sinner to be forever with God. 'So that you can no longer assert that this man is a sinner, or that He is not from God.'

'And of judgment, because the prince of this world has been already judged.' Here He was once more directing the discussion to the subject of justice, in declaring that He had worsted His opponent. But if He were a sinner He could not have beaten him, since not even a just man is powerful enough to do that. 'Those who will trample on him in time to come will know that he has been condemned through Me, since they will have clear knowledge of My resurrection. This is an acomplishment which, of course, implies that I am his conqueror because he was unable to hold Me fast by death. Therefore, inasmuch as they have been saying that I have a devil and am a seducer, they will be shown hereafter that these opinions, also, are untenable. For I would not have gotten the better of him if I were subject to sin; actually, however, he has been condemned and cast out.'

'Many things yet I have to say to you, but you cannot bear

---

8 See, for example, John 9.16-34.

them now. Therefore it is expedient for Me to depart if, when I have gone, you will then be able to bear them.'

'Now, what is this? Is the Spirit greater than You? Will He dispose us to bear what we cannot bear now? Is His power greater and more perfect than Yours?'

'No, this is not the case, for the words He will utter will be Mine.'

That is why He asserted: 'He will not speak on his own authority, but whatever he will hear he will speak, and the things that are to come he will declare to you. He will glorify me, because he will receive of what is mine and will declare it to you. All things that the Father has are mine.'

Now, He had said: 'The Spirit will teach you, and will recall things to your mind and will comfort you in your distress,' functions which He Himself had not performed. And He had declared: 'It is expedient that I depart and that He come,' and also: 'You cannot bear to hear some things now but you will be able to do so then,' and 'He will guide you to all truth.' Therefore, lest they think, on hearing these words, that the Spirit was greater than He, and thus descend into the lowest degree of impiety, He said: 'He will receive of what is mine,' that is: 'Whatever I say He also will say. And when He speaks, He will not speak on his own authority, and will say nothing contradictory, and nothing exclusively His and distinct from my words.'

Accordingly, just as when He said of Himself: 'I speak not of my own authority,' He meant that He made no assertion apart from the Father and made no statement of His own, exclusive of the Father or contradictory to Him, so it was also with regard to the Spirit. Further, the words: 'He will receive of what is mine' mean 'of what I know, of My knowledge. For My knowledge and that of the Spirit are one.'

'And will declare to you the things that are to come.' He

was cheering them up, for the human race is eager for nothing so much as for knowledge of the future. Indeed, they were continually asking Him about it: 'Where are you going? What is the way?' Thus, to relieve them of this anxiety He said: 'He will foretell everything to you,' so that it may not come upon you unexpectedly.

'He will glorify me.' How? 'He will communicate His power in My Name.' For it was because they would perform greater miracles when the Spirit had come, that He said: 'He will glorify me,' once again drawing attention to Their equality.

'What did He mean by "all the truth"? And I ask this for He even testified to this very thing, namely, that the Spirit would teach us all the truth.'

Christ Himself, indeed, because He was clad in the flesh, and because it did not seem best to speak of Himself: both by reason of the fact that they did not yet know clearly of His resurrection and were too imperfect as yet; and also by reason of the Jews: lest they think they were punishing Him as a transgressor of the Law, had kept to His policy of not saying anything great of Himself and of not making any open deviation from the Law. And when the disciples had finally been cut off from the Jews, and the latter were at length out of the way, and many were on the point of believing and of being absolved from sin, and there were others who were speaking of Him, He still with good reason did not speak of His own greatness.

'So that it is not because of My ignorance that I refrained from saying what I should have told you,' He meant, 'but because of the weakness of My listeners.' And that is why, after He had said: 'He will teach all the truth,' He added: 'He will not speak on his own authority.' For, in testimony that the Spirit does not need instruction, listen to Paul saying: 'Even so, the things of God no one knows but the

Spirit of God.'[9] Therefore, just as the spirit of the man knows [the things of a man][10] without learning them from another, so also the Holy Spirit 'will receive of what is mine'; that is, 'will speak in complete agreement with my words. All things that the Father has are mine. Therefore, since these are mine, and the Spirit will speak from the things that are the Father's, He will also speak from mine.'

'But why did He not come before Christ had departed?'

Because He could not come, since the curse had not yet been lifted, the original sin had not yet been forgiven, but all men were still subject to the penalty for it. 'Therefore,' He said, 'that enmity must be destroyed and you must be reconciled to God, and then you will receive that gift.'

'But why did He say: "I will send him"?'

That means: 'I will condition you to receive Him.' For how can He who is everywhere present be 'sent'? And, in addition, He was also pointing out the distinction of the Persons. Moreover, He spoke in this way for these two reasons: first—because they were finding it hard to be separated from Him—to persuade them to cling to the Spirit; and, second, that they might cherish the Spirit. Christ Himself also, to be sure, could have accomplished these things, but He conceded the power to work miracles to the Spirit in order that they might learn His dignity. As the Father could have altered the course of human affairs,[11] but it was the Son who did so, that we might learn His power, this is the case here also with the Spirit.

That is also why the Son was made flesh by delegating to the Spirit the performing of this work; and also to silence the tongues of those who make this evidence of ineffable mercy an occasion of impiety. For, when they claim that the Son was

---

9 1 Cor. 2.11.
10 That is, his own thoughts.
11 By becoming the Redeemer of mankind.

made flesh because He was inferior to the Father, we inquire of them: 'What, then, would you say about the Spirit? He did not assume flesh, yet you will not, I suppose, say that He is greater than the Son on that account, or that the Son is inferior to Him?'

That is also why the Trinity is invoked at baptism. I say this for the Father is capable of doing the whole thing, as also is the Son, and likewise the Holy Spirit. But, since no one is in doubt about the Father, though there was doubt about the Son and the Holy Spirit, They were brought into the rite of initiation in order that, by Their participation in the dispensing of those ineffable blessings, we might also realize Their common dignity.

Furthermore, in clear testimony that of Himself the Son has those powers which He exercises in collaboration with the Father in baptism—as also has the Holy Spirit—listen to the following texts. For He said to the Jews: 'That you may know that the Son of Man has power on earth to forgive sins'; and again: 'That you may become sons of light' and 'I give them everlasting life.' Then afterwards[12] He said: 'That they may have life, and have it more abundantly.' Moreover, let us òbserve the Spirit also doing this same thing.

'Where can we see this?'

'The manifestation of the Spirit,' Scripture says, 'is given to everyone for profit.' Well, then, if He produces this effect, much more does He forgive sins. And again: 'It is the Spirit that gives life,'[13] and: 'He will bring to life [your mortal bodies] because of his Spirit who dwells in you.' And: 'The Spirit is life by reason of justification.' And again: 'If you are led by the Spirit, you are not under the Law. For you have not received a spirit of bondage so as to be again in

---

12 Actually before: John 10.10; cf. Mark 2.10; John 12.36; 10.28.
13 1 Cor. 12.7; John 6.64.

fear, but you have received a spirit of adoption as sons.'[14]
Furthermore, they performed all the miracles which they
worked at that time by the Spirit who had come. And in
writing to the Corinthians Paul said: 'But you have been
washed, but you have been sanctified in the name of our
Lord Jesus Christ and in the Spirit of our God.'[15]

Accordingly, since they had heard many things about the
Father, and had seen the Son doing many things, but had
no clear knowledge as yet about the Spirit, it was He who
worked the miracles and thus brought them to knowledge of
Him in its fullness.

However, lest He might be suspected to have some superiority for that reason (as I have just said), Christ therefore
declared: 'Whatever he will hear he will speak, and the
things that are to come he will declare to you.' If this is not
the reason for the statement, is it not absurd to be saying that
He would only then[16] hear it, and that He would hear it on
account of those becoming His disciples? For He would not
even then know it, according to you, were it not for His
hearers. Yet what could be more unfair than this statement?

Besides, what is it that He would hear? Is it not He who
said all these things by the Prophets? For, if He was going
to instruct them about the destruction of the Law, this
teaching had already been given; or about Christ and His
Godhead and about the Incarnation—these teachings, too,
had already been imparted. What, indeed, was He going to
say still more clearly afterwards?

'And the things that are to come he will declare to you.'
In these words especially He was showing the dignity of the
Holy Spirit, because it is in particular the prerogative of God
to foretell the future. However, if He should get this knowl-

---

14 Rom. 8.11,10,15; Gal. 5.19.
15 1 Cor. 6.11.
16 That is, after the Resurrection.

edge from others, He would be no better than the Prophets. Here, on the contrary, Christ was making it clear that it is impossible for the Spirit to give utterance to any knowledge other than that in exact agreement with God's.

Furthermore, the words, 'He will receive of what is mine,' either mean 'of the grace which came into My flesh' or 'of the knowledge which I also have,' not as though He were in need of it, or as if obtaining knowledge from another, but because His knowledge is one and the same as that of the Son.

'Yet, why did He say it in this way and not otherwise?'

Because they did not yet know the doctrine about the Spirit. Therefore He was making one thing only His concern: namely, that the Spirit might be believed and welcomed by them and that they might not take offense. To be sure, He had said: 'One only is your Master, the Christ.'[17] Therefore, lest they think that if they believed in the Spirit they did not have faith in Christ, He said: 'My teaching and His are one, and He Himself also will draw on the same source for His teaching as I. Accordingly, do not think that His teachings are different; and I say this for His teachings are Mine and contribute to My glory. For the Father, the Son, and the Holy Spirit have one will.'

Moreover, He expressed a desire for us to imitate this unity in the words: 'That they may be one, even as thou and I are one.'[18] For, nothing can be compared with unity and harmony, since the individual man, when united with others, becomes multiple. If two men, or ten, are united in spirit, the individual is no longer alone, but each one of them becomes tenfold, and you will find the ten united as one, and in each one the ten. And if they have an enemy, because he is attacking not one man, but, as it were, ten, he will be

17 Matt. 23.10.
18 John 17.12.

vanquished. For he is struck, not by one sword-edge only, but by the ten.

Is the individual without resources? However, he is not in want, for in the greater part, namely, in the nine, he is well off, and the needy part—the lesser one—is completely protected by the larger part which is well off. Each one of these men has twenty hands, and twenty eyes, and just as many feet. He sees, not only with his own eyes, but also with those of the rest; he walks, not only with his own feet, but also with those of the rest; he works, not only with his own hands, but also with those of the others. He has ten lives, for not only does he himself care for his own, but those others also take care of him. Moreover, if there should be a hundred men in the group, the same thing will once again be true and their strength will have been proportionately increased.

Do you perceive the excellence of charity: how it makes the individual man invincible and many times more significant than he is? Do you see how the man can be in many places at the same time? How the same man can be both in Persia and in Rome?

What nature cannot do, charity can. For part of him will be here, the other, there; or, rather, the whole will be here and the whole, there. Therefore, if he has a thousand friends, or two thousand, think to what extent his power will once again exceed its former bounds. Do you see how charity multiplies a man's strength? For this is a remarkable thing: to make the one man a thousand strong.

Why, then, do we not procure this power and place ourselves in safety? This is better than any power or wealth; it is better than health; it is more valuable than light itself; it is the foundation of happiness. To what end do we restrict our charity to one or two?

Moreover, learn about the matter from its opposite. Suppose that a man has no friend—a condition of utter madness

—(for the fool will say: 'I have no friend');[19] what sort of life will such a man live? Even if he be wealthy ten thousand times over, even if he live in opulence and luxury, even if he be possessed of advantages without number, he is actually destitute and stripped of everything.

With regard to friends, on the contrary, the case is not so, but even if they be poverty-stricken they are better off than the wealthy. Further, the things which a man does not venture to say in his own behalf his friend will say for him. The favors which he cannot obtain for himself he will be able to obtain through his friend—and much more than these—and thus we shall have in our friends a means of profit and safety. For, it is not possible to suffer harm if protected by such guards as these. Indeed, the bodyguards of the king are not as watchful as friends are. The former show vigilance through constraint and fear; the latter, through kindness and love—and this is a much more compelling force than fear. Moreover, the king fears his guards, while this man places greater confidence in his friends than in himself, and because of them he fears none of his foes.

Well, then, let us deal in this merchandise:[20] the poor man, that he may have consolation for his poverty; the rich man, that he may be safely in possession of his wealth; the ruler, that he may govern securely; the subject, that he may have well-disposed rulers. This is the basis of kindliness; this is the foundation stone of gentleness. For even among wild beasts, those which do not gather in herds are savage and fierce. That is why we dwell in cities and have meeting places: that we may associate with one another. Moreover, Paul enjoined this upon us when he said: 'not forsaking our assembly.'[21] Indeed, nothing is worse than solitude, whether

---

19 Cf. Eccli. 20.17.
20 That is, charity.
21 Heb. 10.25.

we refrain of our own accord from associating with others or are deprived of their company.

'What, then, of the solitaries,' you will ask, 'and those who have taken up their abode on the mountain peaks?'

Not even these are without friends; they have indeed fled from the turmoil of the market places, but have many companions closely bound to one another by the bond of charity. Moreover, it was to accomplish this result that they withdrew from society. For, since competition in wordly affairs causes much contention, withdrawing from the midst of them for this reason, they cultivate charity with great care.

'But, if a man should live alone, how could he also have friends without number?' you will ask.

I for my part think that men should know how to dwell with one another, if possible. However, let the advantages of friendship outlined above remain unchallenged for the present. It is not one's location, indeed, that makes one's friends. The solitaries surely have many admirers; and these would not admire them if they did not love them. Furthermore, they themselves in turn pray for the whole world, and this is a very great proof of friendship. Therefore, at the Mysteries, also, we embrace one another in order that, though we are many, we may be one. And in the case of the uninitiated, we pray in common with them, making invocation for the sick, and for the fruits of the earth both of land and of sea.

Do you see all the power of charity? In prayers? In the Mysteries? In exhortations? It is the cause of all blessings. If we hold it with care, we shall both administer the affairs of this life well and attain to the possession of the kingdom. May we all obtain this by the grace and mercy of our Lord Jesus Christ. Through Him and with Him glory be to the Father, together with the Holy Spirit, forever and ever. Amen.

Homily 79 (John 16.16-33)

' "A little while and you shall see me no longer; and again a little while and you shall see me, because I go to the Father." Some of his disciples therefore said to one another, "What is this he says, 'A little while'?" ' etc.[1]

When a soul is in sorrow and overwhelmed by sadness, nothing is more likely to depress it still further than continually hearing gloomy words. Why in the world, then, after Christ had said: 'I am going away and 'I will no longer speak with you,' why did He keep returning to the same subject by saying: 'A little while and you shall not see me' and 'I go to him who sent me?'[2] For, when He had heartened them by His words about the Spirit, then He once more caused their spirits to sink. Why, then, did He do this?

He was testing their mettle and making it more true, and conditioning them that by repeatedly hearing sad things they might bear His departure with fortitude. When they had reflected on it as depicted by His words, they would later bear it in actual fact with equanimity. Moreover, on closer scrutiny, there is consolation in the very fact that He said: 'I go to the Father.' For these words made it clear that He would not perish but that His death would simply be a kind of metamorphosis.

Furthermore, He gave them additional consolation in that He did not say merely: 'A little while and you shall see me no longer,' but added: 'A little while and you shall see me.' Thus He showed that He would return, and that His departure would be for a brief time only, and that His presence with them would be everlasting.

However, they did not understand this. Therefore, with good reason someone might wonder how it was that, though

---

1 John 16.16,17.
2 See, for example, John 14.28-30.

they had often heard these things, they were as much perplexed as if they had heard nothing. How is it, then, that they did not understand? Either because of their sadness, as I for my part think—for it drove His words from their minds —or else because of the obscurity of what was said. And therefore it seemed to them that He was setting forth two contradictory things, though actually they were not contradictory.

'If we shall see You,' they said, 'where will You go? But if You go, how shall we see you?' That is why they declared: 'We do not know what he is saying.' They knew, to be sure, that He was going away, but they did not understand that He would come to them after a little while. For this reason, accordingly, He even rebuked them because they did not grasp the meaning of what He said.

Because He wished to fix firmly in their minds His teachings about His death, what did He say? 'Amen, amen, I say to you that you shall weep and lament,' which was true of His crucifixion and death, 'but the world shall rejoice.' Indeed, because they did not wish Him to die, they were quick to hasten back to the belief that He would not die, and when they then heard that He was going to die, they were bewildered, not knowing what in the world was the meaning of 'a little while.' Therefore, He said: 'You shall weep and lament, but your sorrow shall be turned into joy.'

Next, after pointing out that sorrow is followed by joy, and that sorrow will bring forth joy, and that sorrow is short-lived, while joy is eternal, He continued with an illustration drawn from earthly experience. And what did He say? 'A woman about to give birth has sorrow.' Now, He was making use of a comparison frequently employed by the Prophets, also, when they compared their sufferings to the excessive pain of birth pangs.[3] What He meant is something like this:

---

3 See, for example, Isa. 13.8; Jer. 4.31; Osee 13.13; Mich. 5.9.

'Suffering as keen as birth pangs will take possession of you. However, the pain of childbirth becomes a cause of joy.' At the same time He was confirming His teaching about the resurrection and pointing out that His departure from them was like leaving the womb for the bright light of day. It was as if He said: 'Do not be surprised that I am bringing you by such sorrow to what is profitable for you, since a mother, too, in the process of becoming a mother undergoes suffering followed by great joy.'

Here He was also implying a mystical meaning, namely, that He Himself paid the penalty for sin by the birthpangs of His death and caused the new man to be regenerated by that means. Furthermore, He did not say merely that the anguish of childbirth passes away, but that the woman no longer even remembers it, so great is the joy she feels. Thus will it be also with the saints.

Yet actually the woman does not rejoice because of the fact that a man has come into the world, but rather because a child has been born to her. For if it were for the former reason, nothing would prevent women who have never given birth from feeling the joy of motherhood because of another woman's giving birth to a child.

'Why, then, did He speak in this way?'

Because He was using the illustration merely to this end: to show that sorrow is ephemeral, while joy is everlasting; also, that death is a transforming to life and the profit therefrom is comparable to the great one derived from birth pangs. Still, He did not say 'that a child is born,' but 'that a man is born.' Here, indeed, it seems to me that He was indirectly referring to His own resurrection, and also to the fact that by the pangs of His sufferings He was going to be brought forth, not to death, but to His kingdom.[4] That is why

---

4 See His words to Pilate: 'For this was I born, etc.' (John 18.33-38).

He did not say: 'That a child is born to her,' but 'that a man is born into the world.

'And you therefore have sorrow now but I will see you again, and your sorrow shall be turned into joy.' Next, to make it clear that He would die no more, He said: 'And no one shall take it from you. In that day you shall ask me nothing.' Once again, by these words He was establishing nothing else but that He was from God. 'Then indeed you will at last know all.'

'But what is the meaning of: "You shall ask me nothing"?'

'You will not need a mediator, but it will be enough to mention my name only and you will receive all things. Amen, amen, I say to you, if you ask the Father anything in my name.' He was pointing out the power of His Name, since, indeed, without being seen or asked, but merely by being named, He would cause them to win approval from the Father.

'When did this actually happen?'

When they said: 'Have regard to their threats and grant to thy servants to speak thy word with all boldness and to work miracles in thy name.'[5] And the place where they were was shaken.

'Hitherto you have not asked anything.' By these words He was pointing out once again that it was truly of advantage to them for Him to go away, if until then they had asked nothing, but when He had gone they would receive everything for which they asked. 'When finally I am no longer with you, do not think you have been abandoned. My name will be for you a source of greater confidence.'

Therefore, since His words were somewhat obscure, He said: 'These things I have spoken to you in parables. The hour is coming when I will no longer speak to you in parables. There will be a time when you will know all things clearly.' He meant the time after the Resurrection. 'Then I

---

5 Cf. Acts 4.29-31.

will speak to you freely of the Father.' And this transpired for He was with them for forty days and conversed with them, eating with them, and discussing matters pertaining to the kingdom of God.[6]

'At present, to be sure, since you are fearful, you do not pay attention to My words. Then, on the contrary, when you have seen Me risen from the dead, and when you are in My company, you will be able to learn all things with assurance because the Father Himself will love you, since your faith in Me will have become firm. And I will not ask the Father—your love for Me will be sufficient to win His favor, because you have loved Me and have believed that I came forth from God. I came forth from the Father and have come into the world. Again I leave the world and go to the Father.' Now, His words about the Resurrection did not, as it happened, cheer them, nor did it help to hear afterwards: 'I came forth from God and I am going to Him.' So, He kept reiterating this. He assured them on the one hand that their faith in Him was well founded, and, on the other, that they would be in safety. Accordingly, it was with good reason that they had been bewildered when He had said: 'A little while and you shall not see me and again a little while and you shall see me,' but now they were no longer so.

'But what is the meaning of: "[In that day] you shall ask me nothing"?'

'You will not say: "Show us the Father" and "Where art thou going?"[7] because you will know all knowledge and the Father will have the same attitude as I towards you.' He was causing them to derive consolation particularly from the knowledge that they would be on friendly terms with the Father.

---

6 Cf. Acts 1.3,4.
7 John 14.8; 13.36.

Therefore, they said: 'Now we know that thou knowest all things.' Do you perceive that He had evidently replied in conformity with what they were secretly thinking? 'And dost not need that anyone should question thee'; that is: 'You knew what was bothering us before You heard it, and You calmed our trouble when You said: "The Father loves you because you have loved me." ' After so many proofs and such great evidence, they only then said: 'Now we know.' Do you perceive how spiritually immature they still were?

Next, since they said 'Now we know' as if they were doing Him a favor, He declared:[8] 'You have need of much more than this in order to arrive at perfection. You are by no means perfect as yet. Therefore, you will now betray Me to My enemies, and so great a fear will overcome you that you will not even be able to withdraw from Me in company with one another.[9] However, I shall suffer no damage from this.'

Do you see how condescending His language is once again? Indeed, He even reproached them with their continual need for Him to condescend to their lowliness. For, when they said: 'Behold, now thou speakest plainly and utterest no parable and for this reason we believe in thee,' He showed that now, when they declared their belief, they actually did not believe, and He did not give credence to what they were saying. He made this reply to turn their thoughts to another occasion.[10]

But once again for their sake He added the words: 'The Father is with me,' for He wished them to have this knowledge at all times. Next, to show that in saying these things He had not yet given them perfect knowledge, but

8 Cf. John 16.31-32.
9 'You will be scattered, each one to his own house.'
10 When, that same night, despite this profession of faith, they would abandon Him to His enemies.

also so that their thoughts might not make them rebellious (for it is probable that they still were thinking on a human plane and reasoned that they would enjoy no assistance from Him), He said: 'These things I have spoken to you that in me you may have peace'; that is: 'that you may not drive Me from your thoughts, but may receive Me with welcome.'

Well, then, let no one force these words into a preconceived pattern of his own, for they were spoken for our consolation and for love of us. 'Indeed, when you endure such sufferings as I have mentioned,' He meant, 'your troubles will not come to an end, but as long as you are in the world you will have affliction: not only now when I am betrayed, but also afterwards. However, lift up your hearts, for you will suffer no serious harm. Indeed, since the Master has overcome His enemies, the disciples ought not to be troubled.'

'But how, pray, have You overcome the world?'

'I have already said that I have cast its prince down below.[11] Furthermore, you will know it later, when all men give way to you and obey you.'

Now, it is possible for us also to be conquerors, if we wish, by observing the Leader of our faith, and treading the path which He Himself has cut for us. Thus, not even death will overcome us.

'What, then,' you will say, 'shall we not die?'

Yes, you will, for it is clear from this very fact that it will not overcome you. Surely the wrestler will be famous, not when he does not grapple with his opponent, but when, after grappling with him, he is not worsted. Well, then, because we come to grips with death we are not therefore merely mortal, but we are immortal because of our victory

---

11 Cf. John 14.30; 16.11.

over it. For we should be mortal if we remained forever in its power.

Therefore, just as I could not call those animals endowed with the longest life immortal, even though they remain for a long time untouched by death, so also when a man is going to rise again after death he is not mortal, even though laid low by death. Indeed, if a man should blush for a little while, tell me, please: shall we then say he is always red?

'By no means, for the condition is not permanent.'

If someone should become pale, shall we call him jaundiced?

'By no means, for the affliction is only temporary.'

Well, then, you will not call him mortal who comes for a short time under the dominion of death. If we did so, we should also call those who are asleep 'dead,' for they have died, so to speak, and are inactive.

'But death corrupts the bodies of the dead?'

And what of that? For it does not do so that they may remain in a state of corruption, but that they may become better.

Let us, then, overcome the world; let us hasten to immortality; let us follow after our King; let us set up a trophy for Him; let us despise the pleasures of the world. Moreover, there is no need of toils; let us transfer our soul to heaven, and the whole world has been conquered. If you do not desire it, it has been vanquished; if you ridicule it, it has been worsted.

We are strangers and travelers. Let us not be saddened, then, by any trial at all. Indeed, suppose that you who were of an illustrious native land, and descended from renowned ancestors, came to some far distant land, and were known to no one and had with you no servants or wealth. In this case, if someone insulted you, you would not be troubled

by it, as you would if you suffered this at home. For the
clear knowledge that you were in a strange and foreign
land would persuade you to bear everything patiently:
not only being despised, but also hunger and thirst and any
other suffering whatsoever.

At the present time also, consider the fact that you
actually are a stranger and a traveler, and let nothing in
this alien country trouble you. And I say this for you have
a city, the Architect and Builder of which is God. Moreover,
your very sojourn here is brief and passing. Let him who
wishes to do so, strike, insult, defame. We are in a foreign
land and live wretchedly.

A grievous thing it is, to be sure, to have this suffering in
one's native land at the hands of one's fellow citizens; then
there is the greatest infamy and disgrace. However, if one
is where he has no acquaintance, he undergoes everything
patiently. For insult assumes greater proportions from the
intent of those offering the insult. For example, if someone
who knows that a prince is a prince insults him, then the
insult is a bitter one; but if he insults him, thinking him a
private citizen, he cannot affect the one who actually suffers
the insult.

Accordingly, let us also follow this line of reasoning.
Certainly those who insult us do not know what we are,
namely, that we are citizens of heaven, enrolled in our
native land on high, and fellow choristers of the Cherubim.
Well, then, let us not be sad; let us not regard insult as
insult. If they recognized us, they would not offend us.

On the contrary, they consider us worthless and of no
account?

Well, then, let us not ourselves regard this as an insult.
For, I ask you, if a certain wayfarer, having outstripped
his servants, sat down for a little while in an inn to wait for
them, and then the inn-keeper, or some other wayfarer,

ignorant of his identity, should begin to rant and rail at him, surely he would laugh at the other's ignorance, would he not? Or rather, would he not enjoy the mistake? Would he not make sport of the matter, as if someone else were being insulted?

Let us also act in this way. And I say this for we are sitting in an inn waiting for our fellow travelers on this road. When we are all finally together, then they will know whom they are now insulting. Then they will hang their heads; then they will say: 'This is he whom we who are fools had in derision.'[12]

Let us console ourselves, then, with these two considerations: namely, that we are not really being insulted (for they do not know who we are), and that if we desire to avenge the wrong, they will pay a most severe penalty for it later. However, may no one of us have such a cruel and inhuman desire!

'Then, what if we should be insulted by our fellow countrymen? This would indeed be a heavy trial.'

Nay, rather this would be a mere trifle.

'How in the world is that?'

Because we do not endure it in the same way when we are insulted by those we love as by those whom we do not know. In fact, we frequently have this to say to buoy up the spirits of those who suffer insult: 'The person who has hurt you is your brother; so bear it bravely.' 'He is your father'; or, 'he is your uncle.' And if the name of 'brother' or of 'father' shames you into meek endurance, much more should I be able to say this of him who is more closely akin to you than these. For we are not merely one another's brothers, but even members of one another and one body. Moreover, if the name of brother disconcerts you, much more should that of 'member.' Have you not heard of the

---

12 Cf. Wisd. 5.3.

worldly proverb which says that we must keep their short-comings with our friends? Have you not heard Paul saying: 'Bear one another's burdens'?[13]

Do you not observe people who are in love? For I am compelled, since we cannot draw an illustration from your experience, to have recourse to that well-known example. Moreover, Paul also did this when he spoke as follows: 'Furthermore, we had fathers of our flesh to correct us, and we reverenced them.'[14] Or, rather, what he said to the Romans is even more to the point: 'As you yielded your members as slaves of uncleanness, and iniquity unto iniquity, so now yield your members as slaves of justice.'[15] Therefore, we also have the courage to keep to this illustration.

Well, then, do you not see how great afflictions paramours endure—because they are consumed with passion for harlots —when they are slapped, beaten, ridiculed, and how they bear with a conceited mistress when she spurns them and offers them insults without number? Nevertheless, if they but once see some sign of sweetness or gentleness, every-thing is all right with them, everything from the past is a bygone, and everything is now borne with equanimity: whether poverty or sickness, or anything else of the kind. For they regard their lives as happy or miserable according to whether they have a mistress who is well disposed towards them. Moreover, they do not discern human honor or dis-honor, but, even if someone insults them, they endure it all easily because of the pleasure and happiness they derive from being with her. Moreover, if she rails at them, and even if she spits in their face, they consider that they are being pelted with roses in suffering this.

Now what wonder that they feel as they do about her?

13 Gal. 6.2.
14 Heb. 12.9.
15 Rom. 6.19.

I say this for they think that her house is the most splendid of all, even if it be made of mud and falling to ruin. Yet why do I speak of the walls of the house? For, on seeing the very localities where they spend their time in the evening, they are thrilled.

At this point, however, permit me in what follows to speak like the Apostle. Even as he said: 'As you yielded your members as slaves of uncleanness, so yield your members as slaves of justice,' so I also speak in the same way: As we have loved these women, let us love one another, and then we shall think we have nothing terrible to endure. Yet why do I speak of one another merely? Let us love God in this way. Do you shudder because I am asking for as great a measure of love for God as we show for a harlot? However, I shudder because we do not even show that much.

So, if you please, let us continue the discussion, even if what we say is very painful to hear. The beloved woman promises nothing of worth to her lovers but dishonor, and shame, and opprobrium. For, the fact of consorting with a harlot causes this relationship to be ridiculous, shameful, dishonorable.

God, on the contrary, promises heaven and the blessings of heaven, and makes us His sons, and brothers of the only-begotten Son. Furthermore, during your lifetime He has provided you with countless gifts, and, when you die, resurrection. In addition, He promises that He will give so many blessings that they cannot even be imagined and will make us more esteemed and more venerated.

Then, too, that harlot forces them to squander all their possessions for their ruin and destruction, while God bids us to sow for heaven and gives the hundredfold and life everlasting. Again, she uses her lover as a slave, giving orders more harsh than those of any tyrant, while God says: 'No longer do I call you servants, but friends.'[16]

Do you see the excessive evils in the one instance, and the blessings in the other? What, therefore, are the consequences? Many men are solicitous for the interests of this woman, and eagerly obey whatever demands she makes, and forsake home, and father, and mother, and friends, and wealth, and patronage, and permit all their affairs to fall into neglect and want. Frequently, on the other hand, we do not choose to spend even a third part of our possessions for the sake of God—or, rather, for our own sake—but when we see a hungry man we ignore him, and spurn a naked one and do not even pass a word with him.

But, if the harlot's lovers see so much as her serving-maid —even a foreign one—they stand in the middle of the market place, and converse with her, as if proud and honored, rolling out copious tides of verbiage. Moreover, they regard their whole life as nothing for her sake, despise rulers and sovereignty (as those who have experienced this affliction well know), and they are more grateful to her when she gives them orders, than to others when they act as their slaves. Is it not with good reason that there is a hell? Is it not with good reason that there are punishments without number in store?

Well, then, let us be on our guard, and let us give to the service of God as much as, or at least a half as much as those others devote to the harlot—or even a third as much. Do you perhaps shudder again? I ask you this for I, too, shudder. However, I do not wish you to shudder only at my words, but also with regard to your actions. Actually, our hearts are filled with compunction while in this place, but on leaving it we put all this aside. Therefore, what profit is gained?

Moreover, if it is necessary to spend money elsewhere

---

16 John 15.15.

than in church, no one complains of his poverty, but when a man is smitten, he even borrows money to give. Yet, if we mention almsgiving here, they allege to us children, and wife, and home, and care of their household as excuses—and other pretexts too numerous to list.

'But there is great pleasure to be had there,' you will say.

Yes, and that is the thing for which I lament and weep. What, then, if I should show that there is greater pleasure to be had here? For there, shame, and contumely, and extravagance detract not a little from the pleasure; and likewise, quarreling and enmity. Here, on the contrary, it is quite different. Indeed, I ask you what is a match for the pleasure of sitting here to await heaven and the kingdom there, and the splendor of the saints, and life without end?

'But these things are merely expected, while those others are actually experienced,' you will say.

What kind of experience? Do you want me to tell you of pleasures actually experienced here, also? Reflect on how much freedom you enjoy, and how you fear no one. Since you are living virtuously, you do not tremble because of an enemy, a conspirator, a sycophant, a competitor, a rival in love, a jealous man, poverty, sickness, or any other human cause. There, on the contrary, even though there are ten thousand things according to your wish, and riches stream upon you as if from a fountain, bitter competition with rivals, and scheming and trickery, will make your life the most wretched of all those who are plagued by these troubles. In fact, if that despicable and voluptuous woman entices, war must be set in motion at her pleasure. Therefore, this condition is harsher than death ten thousand times over, and more intolerable than any punishment.

Here, on the contrary, there is nothing like this. For Scripture says: 'The fruit of the Spirit is: charity, joy, peace,'[17] never quarreling or ill-advised expenditure of money, or reproach accompanying the expenditure. Moreover, if you give an obol, or bread, or a cold drink, you will receive much gratitude. Nothing will cause you to worry or to be distressed, but everything will be such as to make you highly esteemed and altogether above reproach.

What defense, therefore, shall we have, what pardon, if we despise these things and give ourselves over to the opposite, and thus of our own accord cast ourselves into the furnace of burning fire? Wherefore, I beseech those who are suffering from this disease to retrieve themselves and restore themselves to health and not permit themselves to fall into despair. Furthermore, that well-known prodigal son was in a much more serious plight than these, but, when he returned to his father's house, he was restored to his former place of honor and even appeared to be esteemed more than his brother who had always lived uprightly.[18]

Let us also imitate him, and returning to our Father, however late it is, let us break away from that captivity and restore ourselves to freedom, in order that we may also enjoy the kingdom of heaven by the grace and mercy of our Lord Jesus Christ. Glory be to Him and to the Father, together with the Holy Spirit, forever and ever. Amen.

Homily 80 (John 17.1-5)

'These things Jesus spoke; and raising his eyes to heaven, he said, "Father, the hour has come! Glorify thy Son, that thy Son may glorify thee." '[1]

---

17 Gal. 5.22.
18 Cf. Luke 15 *passim*.

1 John 17.1-5.

'Whoever carries out the commandments and teaches them,
he shall be called great in the kingdom of heaven,'[2] Scripture
says, and very rightly so. For it is easy to teach true wisdom in
word, but to exemplify the words by one's deeds is the
part of a great and noble soul. Therefore, in speaking of
forbearance, Christ put His words into practice before them,
and told them to follow that example.

That is also the reason why, after this exhortation, He
turned to prayer; namely, to teach us to take refuge in God
in our trials, and to spurn everything else. Because He had
said: 'In the world you will have affliction,' and thus had
disturbed their souls, He calmed them again by His prayer,
for they still regarded Him as a man. Moreover, it was for
their instruction that He said this prayer, just as it had been
in the case of Lazarus when He specifically told the reason
[for His prayer to the Father]; namely, 'Because of the
people who stand round, I spoke, that they may believe that
thou hast sent me.'[3]

'Yes,' you will say, 'but it was right for Him to do so in
the case of the Jews, but why was it appropriate in the case
of the disciples?'

Even in the case of the disciples it was needful. For since,
even after such great proofs of His divinity, they said merely:
'Now we know that thou knowest all things,' they were most
especially in need of being confirmed in their faith. Besides,
the Evangelist did not refer to His action as a prayer, but
what did he say? He asserted: 'He raised his eyes to heaven,'
and he meant that Christ's words were a colloquy with His
Father, rather than a petition.

Moreover, if elsewhere he did actually speak of prayer,
and represented Him at one time bowed on His knees, and at
another time raising His eyes to heaven, do not be disturbed.

2 Matt. 5.19.
3 John 11.42.

By means of these references we are taught perseverance in our petitions so that, when we are standing erect, we may look upward, not only with the eyes of our body, but also with those of our understanding; and likewise so that when we bend our knees, it will be with contrite hearts. Indeed, Christ came, not only to reveal Himself, but also to teach ineffable virtue. And it was necessary for Him to teach, not merely by His words, but also by His deeds.

Well, then, let us listen to what He said in this instance. 'Father the hour has come! Glorify thy Son, that thy Son may glorify thee.' Once more He was pointing out to us that it was not against His will that He was going to the Cross. For how could this be against His will, if He was praying for it to take place, and was calling His sufferings 'glory'—not only the glory of Him who is crucified, but also that of His Father? And indeed it turned out that way, for not the Son only, but also the Father, actually was glorified. Before the Cross, certainly, not even the Jews knew Him, for Scripture says: 'Israel hath not known me';[4] while after the Cross the whole world flocked to Him.

Next, He spoke of the manner of this glorification and how He would glorify Him: 'Even as thou hast given him power over all flesh in order that all thou hast given him may not perish.' For it is giving glory to God when one unfailingly does good.

'But what is the meaning of "Even as thou hast given him power over all flesh"?'

He was pointing out, meanwhile, that the teachings contained in His preaching were destined, not for the Jews only, but also were to embrace the whole world and He was laying the first foundations of the calling of the Gentiles. For, since He had said: 'Do not go in the direction of the Gentiles,' but afterwards was going to say: 'Go, and make

4 Isa. 1.3.

disciples of all nations,'[5] He was now pointing out that His Father, also, wished this.

This, to be sure, gave great offense to the Jews, and to the disciples as well. For not even after this did they take kindly to the idea of being united with the Gentiles, until they had received instruction from the Spirit. I say this for even then the Jews took no little offense at the prospect. Therefore, despite the very impressive revelation of the Spirit, Peter, on coming into Jerusalem, with difficulty succeeded in escaping censure when he spoke of the matter of the sheet [let down from heaven by its four corners].[6]

'But what is the meaning of: "Thou has given him power over all flesh"?'

Shall I ask the heretics: 'When, then, did He receive this power? Was it before He created them, or after that?'

'It was after the crucifixion and resurrection, to be sure, that He Himself spoke of it. At that time, as you know, He said: "All power has been given to me. Go, and make disciples of all nations." '[7]

What, then? Did He not have power before over His own works? Notwithstanding the fact that He had created them, did He not have power over them after He had made them? Yet He Himself appears to have been doing all things, even in times of old: both punishing some as sinners, and reforming others who turned from sin (for Scripture says: 'I will not hide from my servant Abraham what I am going to do'),[8] and honoring still others for living uprightly.

Then, did He have power at that time, and had He lost it at this time, and did He regain it? Now, what kind of devil would claim that this is true?

---

5 Matt. 10.5; 28.19.
6 Cf. Acts 11.
7 Matt. 29.18,19.
8 Cf. Gen. 18.17.

But, if His power was the same both then and now ('As the Father raises the dead and gives them life, even so the Son also gives life to whom he will,' He said), what is the meaning of His words? He was about to send them to the Gentiles. Therefore, lest they might think this an innovation because He had said: 'I was not sent except to the lost sheep of the house of Israel,'[9] He was pointing out that His Father, as well as He, willed the salvation of the Gentiles.

Further, if He uttered this statement in very humble language, it is by no means strange. By speaking thus He not only edified them at that time, but also those to come afterwards. And, as I have said, by this excessive humility He always shows convincingly that His words were scaled to the weakness of His hearers.

But what is the meaning of 'over all flesh?' For in actual fact not all men believed. Yet, as far as His mission was concerned, all could have believed. And, if they did not heed His words, the fault was not that of the Master, but of those who refused His teachings.

'In order that to all thou hast given him, he may give everlasting life.' Now, if here, also, He spoke in somewhat human fashion, do not be surprised. He did this for the reasons mentioned, and also because He was always on guard against attributing greatness to Himself, because this vexed his listeners, since nothing out of the ordinary was in evidence about Him for the moment.

Of course, when John was speaking on his own, he did not write thus, but brought his words to a more sublime level when he said: 'All things were made through him, and without him was made nothing'; and 'He was Life' and 'He was Light' and 'He came unto His own.' He did not say that Christ did not have power unless He had received it, but that He even gave to others 'the power of becoming sons of

9 Matt. 15.24.

God.' Moreover, Paul likewise declared that He is equal to God.[10]

He Himself, however, petitioned in somewhat human fashion: 'In order that to all thou hast given him, he may give everlasting life. Now this is everlasting life, that they may know thee, the only true God, and him whom thou hast sent, Jesus Christ.' He said 'the only true God' to differentiate Him from the gods that do not exist. And He did so because He was about to send them to the Gentiles. However, if they did not agree to this, but on account of the word 'only' should deny that the Son is true God, pursuing this reasoning further, they would also deny that He is God at all. I say this for He said: 'You do not seek the glory which is from the only God.'[11]

What, then? Will the Son not be God? But, if the Son is God, and if He is Son of the Father who is called 'the only God,' it is very evident both that He is true God, and Son of Him who is called 'the only true God.' Why, when Paul said: 'Or I only and Barnabas,'[12] surely he was not rejecting Barnabas? By no means, for 'only' is used to set him apart from others. Yet, if He is not true God, how is He 'the truth'? For generally 'the truth' surpasses 'the true.' Why, may I ask, do we say that a man is not true man? Do we not say this when [the creature] is not a man at all? Thus, if the Son is not true God, how is He God? Moreover, how does He make us gods and sons, if He is not true God? However, I have discussed these matters in greater detail elsewhere; let us therefore continue with the text that follows this one.

'I have glorified thee on earth.' He said 'on earth' with good reason, for the Father was already glorified in heaven, both with the glory that was His by nature, and also because

10 John 1.3-12 *passim;* cf. Phil. 2.6.
11 John 5.44.
12 1 Cor. 9.6.

He was worshiped by the angels. Therefore, He was not speaking of that glory which was proper to God by His very nature (for He continued to have that glory even if no one glorifies Him), but He meant that glory which is His by reason of the worship given Him by man. Accordingly, the words 'Glorify me' also have such a meaning.

Moreover, in order that you may learn that He did mean this kind of glory, listen to His next words. 'I have accomplished the work that thou hast given me to do.' Yet His work was still in its beginning; or, rather, it had not yet begun. How, then, could He say: 'I have accomplished'? He meant either: 'I have done everything that was incumbent on Me'; or He was speaking of what was going to take place as already accomplished; or else, as is most probable, He meant that all had already been accomplished by anticipation because the root of the blessings to come had been set in place, and solely by means of it fruits would inevitably follow; and also that He would be present at those events that were to take place after this and would assist in them.

Therefore He was once again speaking out of condescension for His listeners when He said: 'that thou hast given me.' For if He had actually waited to hear and to learn His work, this would derogate greatly from His glory. Indeed, it is clear from many texts that He came to His task of His own volition; for example, when Paul said: 'He loved us so much that he delivered himself up for us.' Also: 'He emptied himself, taking the nature of a slave.' And again: 'As the Father has loved me, I also have loved you.'[13]

'Do thou, Father, glorify me with thyself, with the glory that I had with thee before the world existed.' Now, where is that glory? For, granted that He was with good reason without glory in the eyes of men because of His being clad in the flesh, why did He seek to be glorified with God? What,

13 Cf. Eph. 5.2; Phil. 2.7; John 15.9.

then, did He mean here? His words concerned the Incarnation, since His human nature had not yet been glorified, nor did it as yet enjoy incorruptibility, nor share in the royal throne. That is why He did not say 'on the earth,' but 'with thyself.'

We also shall enjoy this glory in our own measure, if we are watchful. That is why Paul said: 'Provided we suffer with him that we also may be glorified with him.'[14] Therefore, since such great glory is available to us, those who act as their own enemies by laziness and torpor are deserving of infinite pity. Even if there were no hell, they would be most wretched of all because, though they could reign and be glorified with the Son of God, they are depriving themselves of these blessings.

Indeed, if it were necessary to be slain, or to die ten thousand deaths, or to give up ten thousand lives and just as many bodies every day, ought we not to endure such great sufferings for the sake of obtaining such great glory? In actual fact, however, we do not even despise our wealth, though we shall later be deprived of it, even if we are unwilling. We do not despise our riches, though they remain in this world and are not our own. For we merely have the management of things that are not our own, even if we inherit them from our ancestors.

However, since in reality hell is in store, and the worm that dieth not, and unquenchable fire, and gnashing of teeth, how shall we bear these, may I ask? Why are we not clear-sighted, but instead waste all our resources in daily strife and struggles and senseless discussions; feeding the earth, fattening our bodies, and taking no care of our souls; making no account of necessary things, but taking great thought for superfluous and vain matters? We build elaborate tombs, and purchase costly houses, and trail along with us crowds of

---

14 Rom. 8.17.

all sorts of servants; we deliberate about different overseers: placing officials in charge of fields, houses, money—and officials in charge of these officials—but we do not confer about our desolate soul.

Now, what will be the end of all this? Do we not have only one stomach to fill? Do we not have only one body to clothe? Then, why this undue bustle about business matters? What in the world is it? And why do we divide up the soul which we have been allotted and tear it into pieces for the administering of such matters, conjuring up a harsh slavery for ourselves?

He who needs many things is a slave of many things, even if he seems to be their master. For the master is indeed a slave of his servants, and introduces another, more binding kind of servitude. He is a slave in a different way, since he does not dare to venture into the market place, or the bath, or the field, without his servants, while they, on the contrary, frequently go around everywhere without him. However, he who appears to be master does not dare to go forth from his house if his slaves are not with him. If he merely steps outside the house alone, he thinks he will be an object of ridicule.

Perhaps some may laugh at me for saying these things, but for this reason they would be deserving of infinite pity. In fact, to show that this is slavery, I should like to ask you some questions. Would you like to be in need of someone to move morsels of food to your mouth, or to bring the cup to your lips? Do you not consider that this dependence upon others would be pitiful? Furthermore, if you always needed crutches in order to walk, would you not consider yourself pitiable and most wretched of all because of this? Well, then, you ought to feel that way at present, also. For it makes no difference whether a man endures this dependence because of men or because of irrational things.

But, tell me, are not the angels different from us in this: that they do not need as many things as we do? Well, then, the less we need, the closer we approach to them; the more things we need, the closer we sink to the level of this fleeting life. Moreover, to discover that this is so, ask the aged what sort of life they regard as blessed: the one in which they have possessed empty power over these things, or that of their present state when they are detached from them. Indeed, it is because of this that we have invoked their testimony: namely, because those who are in the flush of youth do not perceive the heavy weight of this slavery.

Similarly, consider the case of those who are stricken with fever. When they are very thirsty they drink many draughts and need many, but when, on returning to health, they are free from the consuming thirst, they consider themselves blessed. Do you perceive that in every instance it is a pitiable thing to be in need of many things, and it is far removed from true wisdom? It is ever-increasing servitude and consuming desire.

Well, then, why do we of our own accord cause this wretchedness to grow in ourselves? Tell me, please: if it were possible for you to dwell without roof or walls and not suffer harm thereby, would you not rather choose this? Why, then, do you increase the evidences of your weakness? Do we not consider Adam blessed for this reason: that he was in need of nothing, neither dwelling or even clothing?

'Yes,' you will say, 'but actually we have been placed in a condition where we do need things.'

Why, then, do we even add to our needs? If, indeed, not a few men dispense with many things, even those regarded as necessities (I mean slaves, and mansions, and money), what excuse should we have if we should exceed the bounds of what we actually need? The more numerous the possessions with which you surround yourself, the more completely you become enslaved. For, the more numerous the things of which you are in need, the more you circumscribe your freedom. Complete freedom, in truth, is to be in need of nothing at all; the next degree is to have few needs, a degree of freedom which the angels especially possess, and also those who imitate them. Moreover, consider how praiseworthy it is for men to do this even while remaining in their mortal bodies.

Indeed, Paul meant this when he wrote to the Corinthians: 'But I spare you that,' and, in order that such as these might not 'have tribulation of the flesh.'[15] The reason why money is so called[16] is that we may use it according to our need, not that we may keep it and hoard it, since this is not to possess it, but to be possessed by it. For, if we should be bent on ascertaining how we may make our wealth increase, not how we may enjoy it according to our need, the order of things is reversed and it has taken possession of us, not we, of it.

Well, then, let us rid ourselves of this harsh slavery, and let us become free sometime. Why are we contriving manifold and innumerable bonds for ourselves? Is not the bond imposed by your nature sufficient for you, as well as the necessary limits of your life, and the swarm of troubles without number? Notwithstanding these, do you fashion yet others for yourself and shackle your feet with them? Will you ever reach heaven and be able to stand on that lofty height?

Indeed, a desirable thing it is, a desirable thing, I say, for a man to sever these cords and be able to reach the City above, since other hindrances are also so great. In order that we may overcome them all, let us embrace poverty.[17] For thus we shall likewise attain to everlasting life by the grace and mercy of our Lord Jesus Christ. Glory be to Him, forever and ever. Amen.

---

15 That is, the worries and troubles of this world; cf. 1 Cor. 7.28.
16 χρήματα: 'things that one uses or needs.'
17 That is, the poverty of detachment from superfluous possessions.

Homily 81 (John 17.6-13)

'I have manifested thy name to the men whom thou hast given me out of the world. They were thine, and thou hast given them to me, and they have kept thy word.'[1]

The Son of God is said to be the Angel of Great Counsel[2] because of His many other teachings, but especially because He revealed His Father to mankind. That is why He now said this: 'I have manifested thy name to the men.' For, after saying: 'I have accomplished thy work,' He then went on to explain this statement by telling what sort of work it was.

Yet the name of God had already been manifested, to be sure. I say this for Isaias had declared: 'You have sworn by the true God.'[3] However, as I have often said, and now repeat, even if it had been made manifest, it was clearly evident to the Jews only, and not even to all of them. But now He was speaking of the Gentiles. Moreover, not only did He make this clear, but also that they knew God as the Father. It is not the same thing, of course, to know that He is the Creator as to know that He has a Son. And Christ 'manifested His name' both by word and by deed.

'Whom thou hast given me out of the world.' Just as He had previously said: 'No one can come to me unless he is enabled to do so by my Father' and 'unless my Father draw him.'[4] so it was in similar vein that He here said: 'Whom thou hast given me.' Yet He had declared that He Himself is the Way. From this it is clear that He was making two points by His words in this instance, namely, that He was in complete harmony with Father, and that it was the Father's will for them to believe in His Son.

---

1 John 17.6.
2 Cf. Isa. 9.6. (Septuagint).
3 Cf. Isa. 65.16.
4 John 6.66,44.

'They were thine, and thou hast given them to me.' Here He desired to teach them that He was very much beloved by the Father. For it is quite clear that He actually did not need to receive them, because He Himself had created them and it was He Himself who unceasingly provided for their needs. How, then, did He receive them? In a different sense, as I have said, and this statement testified to His oneness with the Father.

Moreover, if anyone wants to place a merely human interpretation on it, and accept it in its literal meaning, in that case the disciples will no longer belong to the Father [after the Son has received them]. For if, when the Father had them, the Son did not have them, it is clear that when He gave them to the Son He Himself relinquished His dominion over them—and something still more strange likewise follows from this. For it will be discovered that when they were with the Father they were imperfect, but when they came to the Son then they became perfect. Yet it is ridiculous even to say such things.

What, then, did He really mean by this statement? That it was granted to them by the Father to believe in the Son. 'And they have kept thy word. Now they have learned that whatever thou hast given me is from thee.' How have they 'kept thy word'? 'By believing in Me and not paying any attention to the Jews.' For He had said: 'He who believes in Him has set his seal that God is true.'[5]

Some, to be sure, word the text this way: 'Now I know that whatever thou has given me is from thee,' but this would not be logical. For how could the Son be ignorant of what belonged to the Father? As a matter of fact, however, He was speaking of the disciples. For He meant: 'From the fact that I have said these things they have learned that whatever Thou has given me is from thee. I have nothing

---

5 Cf. John 3.33.

alien, nothing of My own, apart from Thee.' For it is what is specially characteristic of a person that makes him seem alien in other respects.[6] 'Therefore, they have learned that whatever I teach is Thine: both doctrine and laws.'

And how have they learned it? 'By My words, for it is by means of them that I have been teaching. Moreover, not only have they learned this, but also that I came forth from Thee,' for by the Gospel He continually strove to convey this knowledge.

'I pray for them.'

'What are You saying? Are You instructing the Father as if He were ignorant of their needs? Are You speaking to Him as if to a man who lacks knowledge? Well, then, what is the meaning of this apparent separation?'

Do you perceive that His prayer had no other purpose than that they might learn His love for them? For he who gives not only what he himself possesses, but also intercedes with another to do the same, shows greater love.

'What, then, is the meaning of "I pray for them"?'

'Not for the world do I pray,' He said, 'but for those whom thou hast given me.' He kept repeating 'thou hast given me,' that they might learn that this was the Father's will.

Next, since He had frequently said: 'They are thine, and thou hast given them to me,' lest anyone suppose that His sovereignty was but recently acquired and that they had just now been received by Him, what did He say to dispel this evil suspicion? 'All things that are mine are thine, and thine are mine; and I am glorified in them.' Do you see the equality of Father and Son? For, lest on hearing 'thou hast given me,' you might think that the disciples were now being removed from the sphere of the Father's power, or that

---

6 That is, if the Son had some distinctive characteristic not possessed by the Father, this would be enough to destroy Their perfect unity.

previous to this they had been outside the Son's power, He refuted both these ideas by speaking as He did.

It was as if He said: 'When you hear, "Whom thou hast given Me," do not think that they are thus placed outside the Father's power for the things that are Mine are His. And when you hear: "They are Thine," do not think that they are outside My power, for the things that are His are Mine.' Hence, the words 'Thou hast given' were used only for the sake of condescending to the weakness of His listeners. For the things that the Father has are the Son's and the things that the Son has are the Father's.

Now, this cannot be said of the Son merely as Man, but only in so far as He has a nature greater than that of a man,[7] for it is clearly evident to all that what belongs to the lesser nature belongs also to the greater, but the opposite is not the case. However, in this context He matched strophe with antistrophe,[8] and the antistrophe clearly reveals the equality of the Son with the Father. To make this clear He also said elsewhere: 'All things that the Father has are mine,'[9] referring to knowledge. But He said 'thou hast given me,' and other statements of the kind, to point out that He did not come in opposition to the Father, and draw them to Himself, but received them as His own.

Next He set forth the reason and the proof by saying: 'And I am glorified in them,' that is, either 'because I have power over them' or 'because they will glorify Me, since they believe in You and in Me, and they will glorify Us alike.' But, if He was not glorified in them in the same way as the

---

7 That is, it can be predicated of His divine nature, but not of His human nature, taken by itself. The Benedictine editor notes a textual difficulty here and points out that St. John Chrysostom's meaning seems to be that, while it can be said of Christ as God that He became Man, was crucified, and suffered, it cannot be said of Christ, considered only as Man, that He is equal to the Father.

8 'All the things that are mine are thine, and thine are mine.'

9 John 15,16.

Father, the things that the Father has would not be His, for no one is glorified in things over which he has no power.

'But how is He glorified in the same way as the Father?'

They all died for His sake in the same way as for the Father's; and they preached Him just as they did the Father; and just as they declared that all was done in the Father's name, so also that it was done in the name of the Son.

'And I am no longer in the world, but these are in the world,' that is, 'Even when I am not visible in the flesh, I am glorified through these men.'

'But why in the world did He say repeatedly: "I am not in the world"; and "Since I am leaving them, I commend them to you"; and "When I was in the world I guarded them"? For, if one should take these statements literally, many strange contradictions would follow. How could it be reasonable for Him to say He was not in the world, yet that, since He was departing from it, He was commending them to the care of another? Indeed, these were like the words of a mere man who was leaving them forever.'

Do you not see that He conversed with them for the most part in human fashion, and according to their understanding, since they thought that they derived greater safety from His presence? That is why He said: 'When I was present, I kept them.'

'Still, did He not say: "I will come to you" and "I am with you even to the consummation of the world"?[10] How is it that He now spoke as if about to be cut off from them?'

In doing so, as I have said, He was speaking according to their understanding, in order that they might relax a little on hearing Him say this and commend them to the care of His Father. Since, though they heard many words of encouragement from Him, they were not convinced, He finally addressed Himself to the Father, to prove His affection for

10 Matt. 28.20.

them. It was as if He said: 'Because thou art summoning me to thyself, place them in safety. For I am coming to thee.'

'What are You saying? Can You not protect them?'

'Yes, of course I can.'

'Why, then, are You speaking in this way?'

'That they may have My joy made full,' that is, 'That they may not be troubled, since they are as yet imperfect.' Furthermore, by saying these words He made it clear that He said everything as He did, for the sake of their peace and joy, even though His discourse seemed to be quite the opposite.

'Now I am no longer in the world, but these are in the world.' This was indeed their idea of the situation; therefore, for the moment He catered to their weakness. For, if He had said: 'I will protect them,' they would not have believed Him. That is why He said: 'Holy Father keep them in thy name,' that is, 'by thy aid.'

'While I was in the world, I kept them in thy name.' Once again He was speaking as Man and as a Prophet, since He nowhere appears to have done anything in the name of God.

'Those whom thou hast given me I guarded; and not one of them perished except the son of perdition, in order that the Scripture might be fulfilled.' Elsewhere, also, He had said: 'I shall lose nothing of what thou hast given me.'

'Yet, not only did the son of perdition perish, but many others afterwards. How it is, then, that He could say: "I shall lose nothing"?'

He meant: 'I shall not lose anything as far as My part is concerned.' To make this clear He said in another place: 'I will not cast him out.'[11] That is: 'He will not be lost through My fault, though I neither force him nor, on the other hand, abandon him. But, if he goes away from Me of his own accord, I shall not compel him by force to return.

---

11 Cf. John 6.37,39.

'But now I am coming to thee.' Do you perceive that His words now are couched in rather human language? Hence, if someone is disposed to detract from the Son because of them, he will also detract from the Father. In fact, notice that from the beginning, on the one hand He appears to be informing the Father and giving Him a commission. Informing, as when He said: 'Not for the world do I pray.' Commissioning, as when He said: 'I guarded them up till now, and not one perished.' And: 'Do thou, then, keep them,' He urged. And again: 'They were thine, and thou hast given them to me.' And: 'While I was in the world, I kept them.' However, the explanation that applies to all these statements is that He was adapting His words to their weakness.

Moreover, when He had said: 'Not one of them perished except the son of perdition,' He added, 'in order that the Scripture might be fulfilled.'

'What Scripture did He mean?'

That which foretold many things of Him. It was not, of course, for this reason that a man did perish, namely, that the Scripture might be fulfilled. We have already discussed this matter in detail before this,[12] and stated that this is the method characteristic of Scripture, namely, to relate things that turn out according to its predictions, as if it were the cause of this. Yet we must examine everything with care, both the manner of the one speaking and also his statement, and the laws of Scripture as well, unless we are to reason falsely, for, 'Brethren, do not become children in mind.'[13]

Now, we ought to apply this text not only to the matter of understanding Scripture aright, but also to the question of striving to live rightly. I say this for small children do not desire valuable things, but, generally, admire worthless ones. For they are delighted when they see chariots, and horses,

12 See *Homilies,* Vol. I (in this series) 228-230.
13 1 Cor. 14.20.

and the charioteer, and wheels, all made of clay. But, if they should see a king seated in a golden chariot, and a yoke of white mules, and a great deal of ornamentation, they do not even turn to watch them. Again, if they receive dolls made of the same material,[14] they dress them up as brides, while they do not even look at brides that are actually real and beautiful. Moreover, they react similarly in the case of many other things.

This is the kind of behavior many men are even now displaying. For, when they hear of the things of heaven, they do not pay attention, but, like the children, they are excited over everything made of clay, and so are lost in admiration of earthly riches. They esteem glory and pleasure in the present life, even though these things are as much toys as those, while heavenly things are productive of real life and glory and rest. However, just as children cry if deprived of their playthings and cannot even desire the real thing, so it is with many who appear to be men. That is why Paul said: 'Do not become children in mind.'[15]

Do you love earthly wealth, may I ask—not the riches that remain with you, but only childish toys? Then, if you should see someone admiring a coin made of lead and bending down to pick it up, would you conclude that his poverty is great, while you collect things still less valuable than this and count yourself among the wealthy? Yet how is this logical? On the contrary, we declare that that man is wealthy who despises all things present. For no one, no one will choose to scorn these things as of little worth—silver, gold, and the rest of the array—unless he has a desire for things of greater worth, just as no one scorns the lead coin unless he is in possession of a gold one.

Well, then, when you see a man despising the whole

---

14 That is, clay.
15 1 Cor. 14.20.

world, consider that he is doing so for no other reason than because he has his gaze fixed on a greater world. Thus, the farmer also despises a few grains of wheat when he is looking forward to a greater harvest. But if, though our hope is uncertain of fulfillment, we yet condemn our possessions to destruction, much rather ought we do this in the case of an expectation that is sure to materialize. Therefore, I beg and beseech, do not punish yourselves, and do not deprive yourselves of the treasures from above by holding on to mud, or by bringing your ship into the harbor, laden only with straw and chaff.

Let anyone who wishes to do so, talk about us; let him find fault with the continual repetition of my warnings; let him call us silly, disgusting, annoying; we shall not cease frequently admonishing you about these matters, and often quoting gently to all of you that saying of the Prophet: 'Redeem thou thy sins with alms and thy iniquities with works of mercy to the poor, and suspend them from thy neck.'[16] Do not do this today and stop tomorrow. And I say this for this body is in need of daily food. So also is the soul; or, rather, much more so. And unless it is well nourished it becomes weaker and more sluggish. Let us not neglect it, as it is perishing and being strangled. It receives many wounds every day from lust, anger, sloth, profanity, revenge, envy. Well, then, we must apply remedies to it. Now, almsgiving is no trifling remedy, since it can be applied to every wound. Indeed, 'Give alms,' Scripture says, 'and all things will be clean to you'[17]—alms, not rapine, for what is given out of rapine does not remain, even if you give it to the needy. It is the almsgiving which is free from all injustice that makes all things clean.

It is better than fasting and sleeping on the ground. Even

16 Dan. 4.24.
17 Cf. Luke 11.41.

though those practices are more difficult and demand more exertion, almsgiving is more profitable: it enlightens the soul, enriches it, makes it noble and beautiful. The fruit of the olive does not strengthen athletes as effectively as this olive oil invigorates those engaging in the contest of piety. Let us, then, anoint our hands, that we may raise them staunchly against the foe.

He who is concerned with showing pity to the needy will, similarly, quickly refrain from covetousness. He who perseveres in giving to the poor will, similarly, quickly refrain from anger and will never be puffed up by pride. For, just as when a physician is continually caring for the wounded he is readily inspired with sober reflections, as he observes the plight of human nature in the misfortunes of other men, so also if we engage in giving assistance to the poor we shall readily become truly wise. We shall not admire wealth or consider the possessions of this life important, but will despise them all. Rising above them to the heights of heaven, we shall with ease attain to the everlasting blessings by the grace and mercy of our Lord Jesus Christ. Glory be to Him and to the Father, together with the Holy Spirit, forever and ever. Amen.

Homily 82 (John 17.14-26)

'I have given them thy word; and the world has hated them, because they are not of the world, even as I am not of the world.'[1]

When we are persecuted by the wicked, though we are virtuous, and are treated scornfully by them because of our pursuit of virtue, let us not be troubled or find it hard to bear. For virtue is so constituted of its very nature that it

---

1 John 17.14.

generally evokes hatred on the part of the wicked. Indeed, since they are envious of those who strive to live uprightly, and because they think they are providing an excuse for themselves, if they can defame the good, they both hate them as exponents of conduct opposite to their own, and make every effort to dishonor the way of life of their rivals.

However, let us not be saddened, for this is a proof of virtue. That is why Christ said: 'If you were of the world, the world would love what is its own.' And elsewhere, again, He said: 'Woe to you when all men speak well of you.'[2] That is likewise why He here said: 'I have given them thy word; and the world has hated them.' Once more He was mentioning this as a reason for their deserving to be the object of much solicitude on the part of His Father. He meant: 'They have been hated because of You and Your word; consequently, they should rightly enjoy the benefit of all the care of Your providence.

'I do not pray that thou take them out of the world, but that thou keep them from evil.' Once again He was elucidating His meaning; once again He was making it clearer. By this statement He was unmistakably pointing out that His concern for them was very great, since He was interceding so anxiously in their behalf.

'Yet He Himself had declared that the Father would do anything they themselves should ask.[3] How is it, then, that He was here making intercession for them?'

For no other reason, as I have said, than to show His love. 'They are not of the world, even as I am not of the world.'

'Why, then, did He say elsewhere: "The men whom thou hast given me out of the world, were thine"?'

In the latter instance He was speaking of their human

2 John 15.19; Luke 6.26.
3 Cf. 16.23,24.

nature, while in the other He was referring to evil-doing.[4]
Moreover, He was delivering a long discourse in praise of
them, saying in the first place that they were not of this
world; next, that the Father Himself had given them,
and that they had kept His word, and that they were objects
of hatred on this account. Furthermore, do not be troubled
because He said: 'Even as I am not of the world.' For the
expression 'even as' does not here imply complete identity.
Just as when He used the expression 'even as' with reference
to Himself and the Father, Their complete equality was in-
timated because Their nature is the same, so, when He used
it with regard to Him and us, the abysmal difference between
us is implied, because there is a great, even infinite, difference
between the two natures. If 'He did no sin, neither was deceit
found in his mouth,'[5] how could the Apostles be placed on
an equality with Him?

'Then, what is the meaning of the words: "They are not
of the world"?'

'They have something else in view; they have nothing in
common with earth, but have become citizens of heaven.'
By these words, also, He was showing His love, since He was
praising them to His Father and commending them to Him
who had begotten Him. Moreover, in saying 'Keep them'
He did not mean merely freedom from danger, but was referring also to their perseverance in the faith. And that is
why He added: 'Sanctify them in thy truth; make them holy
by giving them the Spirit, and true doctrine.' Just as when
He had said: 'You are clean by reason of the word that I
have spoken to you,'[6] so He now also said the same thing:
'Instruct them; teach them truth.'

'Yet He said before that it was the Spirit who would do
this. How it is, then, that He now asked it of the Father?'

---

4 That is, by the phrase 'of the world.'
5 Isa. 53.9; Peter 2.22.
6 John 15.3.

That you might once again learn Their equality. For, certainly, true teachings about God sanctify the soul. Moreover, do not be surprised if He spoke of sanctification effected by the word. To show that He was referring to doctrine, He added: 'Thy word is truth,' that is, 'There is nothing false in it; all His words must be completely fulfilled.' He also made it clear that there is nothing purely figurative, nothing purely material in His word, as Paul, too, said of the Church that Christ sanctified her by means of the word. For he also knew that the word of God cleanses souls.[7]

Now, it seems to me that the words 'Sanctify them' have another meaning, namely: 'Set them apart for the word and preaching.' That is again clear from what follows: 'Even as thou hast sent me into the world,' He said, 'so I also have sent them.' Paul, too, declared this: 'Entrusting to us the message of reconciliation.'[8] For, the Apostles also took possession of the world for the same reason as that for which Christ came. But the expression 'even as' here once again carries no implication of equality between Christ and the Apostles (for how could men be sent in any other way than as Christ was?). And He was accustomed to speak even of the future as if it had already taken place.

'And for them I sanctify myself, that they also may be sanctified in truth.'

'What is the meaning of "I sanctify myself"?'

'I offer sacrifice to Thee.' Now, all sacrifices are called 'holy,'[9] and things that are consecrated to God are called 'holy' in a special way. Indeed, since of old sanctification was prefigured in the lamb, and now it was not merely in figure but in truth, He therefore said: 'That they also may be sanctified in thy truth. I say this for I consecrate them to

---

7 The reference here is to baptism; cf. Eph. 5.26.
8 2 Cor. 5.19.
9 That is, 'sanctified.'

thee and offer them to thee.' He asserted this either because
their Head was to become a Victim or because they themselves also would be immolated. For Scripture says: 'Present
your members a living, holy sacrifice' and 'We are looked
upon as sheep to be slaughtered.'[10] Thus, without death He
was making them a sacrifice and oblation.

Indeed, it is quite clear from the words that follow that in
saying 'I sanctify myself' He was indirectly referring to His
immolation. 'Yet not for these only do I pray, but for those
also who through their word are to believe in me.' In fact,
since He did die in behalf of these and had said: 'For them
I sanctify myself,' lest anyone might think that He did this
for the Apostles alone, He added: 'Yet not for these only do
I pray, but for those also who through their word are to
believe in me.'

By these words He once more raised their spirits by pointing out that there would be many disciples. For, since He
had made what they had considered their singular privilege
common to many, He consoled them again by making it
clear that they would be responsible for the salvation of the
rest. So, after treating of their salvation and of sanctification
by faith and sacrifice, finally He spoke on the subject of harmony and concluded His discourse with this. As He had
begun with it, He came to an end with the same topic.

He had opened by saying: 'A new commandment I give
you,'[11] and here: 'That they may be one, even as thou,
Father, in me and I in thee.' Once again the expression
'even as' does not imply complete equality on their part,
for such a thing was not possible for them, but it means:
'as far as is possible for men.' It is just as when He said:
'Be merciful even as your Father is merciful.'[12]

'What is the meaning of "in us"?'

---

10 Cf. Rom. 12.1; Ps. 43.23.
11 John 13.34.
12 Luke 6.36.

'In their faith in Us.' For, since nothing gives all men such grave offense as dissension, He brought it about that they should all be one.

'What is that, then? Did He really accomplish this?' you will ask.

Yes, He did accomplish it very well. For, all those who believe through the Apostles are one, even though some have become separated from them. Indeed, this defection was not hidden from Him; more than that, He even foretold it, and pointed out that it resulted from human depravity.

'That the world may believe that thou hast sent me.' He had begun His discourse, then, with this idea when He said: 'By this will all men know that you are my disciples, if you love one another.'[13]

'Yet, how would the world believe because they were one?'

'Because Thou art a God of peace,' He meant. 'Then, if they keep to the same precepts as their Teacher, those who hear will know the Master by reason of the disciples; but if they are in strife with one another, other men will deny that they are disciples of a God of peace. And if I am not peaceful, they will not acknowledge that I have been sent by Thee.' Do you perceive how to the very end He gave proof of His complete harmony with the Father?

'And the glory that Thou hast given Me I have given to them—that is, by My miracles, by My teachings, and that they may be of one soul. For glory even greater than miracles consists in this: that they be united. Indeed, just as they marvel at God because there is no dissension, no strife, in that divine nature, and this is Its greatest glory, so let these disciples also be outstanding in this respect,' He declared.

'Yet, how is it,' you will say, 'that He asked the Father to give this favor to them, though He said that He Himself gave it?'

---

13 John 13.35.

Whether He spoke of miracles, or of harmony, or of peace, it clearly was He Himself who had granted them these things. From this fact it is evident that the request was made of His Father for the sake of consoling them. 'I in them and thou in me.'

'How did He give his glory to them?'

By being in them and having the Father with Him so that He joined them together. Elsewhere, however, He did not speak thus,[14] for He did not say that the Father came through Him, but that He and the Father would come and 'make their abode with him.'. By the latter statement He refuted the suspicious reasoning of Sabellius[15] and by the former, that of Arius.[16]

'That they may be perfected in unity, and that the world may know that thou hast sent me.' This He said repeatedly, to show that peace can draw men to Him more effectively than miracles. For, just as strife causes men to disperse, so harmony causes them to unite.

'And that I have loved[17] them even as thou hast loved me.' Here again the expression 'even as' means being loved in so far as man can be loved, and that His giving Himself in their behalf is a proof of His love.

Well, then, after saying that they would be safe, that they would not be overcome, that they would be sanctified, that many would believe through them, that they would enjoy great glory, that not only did He Himself love them, but also the Father, He finally began to speak also of the things

---

14 Cf. John 14.23.
15 Sabellius denied the distinct personality of the Father and of the Son, a truth which these words of Christ attest (John 14.23).
16 That is, 'Even as we are one: I in them and thou in ,me." The consubstantiality of the Father and the Son is thus affirmed, a truth which the teachings of Arius contradict.
17 Both the Greek New Testament and the Confraternity translation have the second person singular here: 'thou hast loved.' The first person singular (ἠγάπησα), used by St. John Chrysostom, has a strong manuscript tradition. See Merk 376, annotation on John 17.23.

destined to come after their departure from this life: of the rewards and crowns in store for them. For He said: 'Father, I will that where I am, they also whom thou hast given me may be with me.' And this, accordingly, was what they were seeking when they repeatedly asked: 'Where art thou going?'[18]

'What are You saying? Will You receive this favor by asking for it, and have You not yet obtained it? How is it, then, that You could assure them: "You shall sit on twelve thrones"?[19] How is it that You made still other promises greater than this?'

Do you not see that He was phrasing all He said with a view to condescending to their weakness? For how else could He say: 'Thou shalt follow later?'[20] In fact, He said this for the sake of strengthening and confirming Peter's love.

'In order that they may behold my glory which thou hast given me.' Once more this is a proof of His complete harmony with the Father, more sublime than the previous ones (for He added: 'before the creation of the world'), but also displaying some condescension to their weakness, for He specified: 'my glory which thou hast given me.' However, if this be not the explanation, I should like to ask those who deny it: 'Is not the giver considered superior to the one who receives his gift?' After having first begotten Him, then, surely He did not give Him His glory later, permitting Him to be without glory until then? Yet, how could this be reasonable? Do you perceive that the expression 'hast given' really means 'hast begotten'?

'But, why did He not say: "In order that they may share my glory," instead of: "in order that they may behold my glory"?'

18 For example, John 13.36.
19 Matt. 19.28.
20 John 13.36.

Here He was implying that all true rest[21] consists in this: namely, beholding the Son of God. And, of course, this will cause them to be glorified. Paul, too, said this: 'We all, with faces unveiled, reflecting as in a mirror the glory of the Lord.'[22] Just as those who behold the sunbeams and enjoy the benefit of very clear atmosphere derive pleasure from their organ of sight, so also, in the hereafter, our sight will cause us even greater pleasure. However, at the same time He pointed out that the Vision we shall see is not what can be seen with bodily eyes, but a certain awesome Being.

'Just Father, and the world has not known thee.' What does this mean? What connection has it with the foregoing? Here He was indicating that no one knows God except those who know the Son. What He meant is something like this: 'I should like all men to be of this class, but they have not known Thee, even though they can find no fault with Thee.' Indeed, this is the meaning of the words, 'Just Father.' Here He seems to me to be saying this out of disappointment because they were unwilling to come to the knowledge of Him who is so good and so just.

In fact, since the Jews had said that they knew God, but Christ did not know Him, He was striking out against this when He declared: 'Thou hast loved me before the creation of the world,' and He was thus offering His defense against the accusations of the Jews. For, how could He be opposed to the Father if He had received glory from Him, if He had been loved by Him before the creation of the world, if He wished them to be witnesses of the Father's glory? 'Well, then, what the Jews claim is impossible, namely, that they themselves know Thee, but I do not know Thee. On the contrary, the opposite is true: I know Thee, but others have not come to the knowledge of Thee.

---

21 That is ,the 'eternal rest' of the life to come.
22 2 Cor. 3.18.

'And these have known that thou hast sent me.' Do you perceive that He was indirectly referring to those who said that He was not from God and that He was summing up everything in this statement? 'And I have made known to them thy name, and will make it known.'

'Yet You say that perfect knowledge comes from the Spirit.'

'Yes, but the things that are the Spirit's are Mine. In order that the love with which Thou hast loved Me may remain in them, and I in them. For, if they learn who Thou art, then they will know that I am not separated from Thee, but exceedingly beloved by Thee, both Thy true Son and one with Thee. And when they are persuaded of this, as they must be, they will also carefully guard their faith in Me and their strong love for Me. And when they love Me as they ought, I will remain in them.'

Do your perceive how He brought His discourse to a beautiful close by ending it with love, the mother of all blessings? Let us, then, believe in God and love Him, that it may not also be said of us: 'They profess to know God, but by their works they disown him.' and again: 'He has denied the faith and is worse than an unbeliever.'[23]

For, when the latter comes to the aid of slaves, and kinsmen, and foreigners, while you do not even care for those who belong to the same family as you, what will your excuse finally be when God is blasphemed and insulted on your account? Indeed, consider how many opportunities God has given us of doing good. 'Take pity on this one as your kinsman, that one as your friend, this as your neighbor, the other as your fellow citizen, this one as a human being,' He says. However, if none of these holds you in check, but you break all ties, listen to Paul saying that you are 'worse than an unbeliever.' This is because, even though the unbeliever

---

23 Tit. 1.16; 1 Tim. 5.8.

has heard nothing about almsgiving, or about the things of heaven, he has surpassed you by showing charity, whereas you who have been commanded to love your very enemies regard the members of your household as enemies and spare your money rather than their bodies.

On the one hand, the money that is spent will suffer no loss, but your brother, neglected, will perish. What madness it is, therefore, to be sparing of money but unsparing of one's kindred! Whence has this passion for wealth come in upon us? Whence comes this mercilessness and cruelty?

Suppose that someone, as if seated in the highest part of a theater, should look down upon the whole world; or rather, if you please, let us concern ourselves for the moment with a single city. If someone, then, seated on a high point of vantage should be able to observe all human affairs, think how much stupidity he would discover, what great floods of tears he would pour forth, how much that is ridiculous he would find to laugh at, how much that is hateful he would hate. For we do such things as are worthy of ridicule, and of the charge of folly, and of tears, and of hatred.

This fellow raises dogs in order to hunt wild beasts, while he himself declines into a state of ferocity. Another feeds asses and bulls, that he may use them to move building stones, while he pays no attention to men who are wasting away with hunger. Moreover, he spends gold lavishly that he may cause men to be fashioned out of stone,[24] while he completely neglects real men who are becoming petrified as a result of ill-treatment.

Another collects golden tiles[25] and covers over his house walls with great solicitude, but he sees the bodies of the poor naked, and remains unmoved. Furthermore, these plan new garments to add to the ones they already have, while that

24 That is, by a sculptor.
25 Apparently for mosaic work.

man cannot even cover his very body which is without clothing.

Again, in the law courts, one will consume one; another, another. One spends money on harlots and hangers-on; another on actors and dancers; still another on elaborate dwellings and on purchases of land and buildings. Once more, this one counts his interest and also his compound interest; another jots down notes in his tablets, replete with many a murder, and he does not enjoy rest even by night, preoccupied as he is with doing harm to other men. When day dawns, one goes to his unjust profit-making, another to his licentious extravagance, others to their peculation.

Great is the zeal shown for useless and even forbidden pursuits, but there is no thought at all of the ones that matter. Those who judge have the name of judges, but actually they are thieves and murderers. If one examines law suits or wills, in either case he will again discover, even here, ten thousand wicked deeds: frauds, thefts, schemes. Moreover, there is plenty of time for all these, but no thought at all of spiritual things; on the contrary, all darken the door of the church merely to look in.

This, however, is not what is required, but we need good works and a pure intention. If you spend the entire day on your personal gain and then come to church and mumble a few words, not only have you not been pleasing to God, but you have actually angered Him more. If, indeed, you wish to reconcile the Lord to you, show Him the evidence of your deeds: become acquainted with the debris of misfortunes; take note of the naked, the hungry, those suffering injustice. He has created for you countless ways of loving your neighbor.

Let us not deceive ourselves, then, by living empty and purposeless lives. And let us not be unsympathetic towards others because we are now in good health. On the contrary, remembering that often when we have fallen ill and have come to the last extremity, we have practically died because of fear and expectation of the life to come, let us suppose that we have once again met with the same misfortune, and let us feel the same fear, and so become better men henceforth, because, certainly, our present actions deserve immeasurable condemnation.

Now, some men in the law courts are like lions and dogs; some in the market place are like wolves; some there are who live a life of leisure, but these do not even use their leisure as they ought, and spend all their free time in the theater and its evils. Moreover, there is no one at all who disparages these practices, while there are many who emulate them and are vexed because they cannot equal them. Hence, this group must also be punished, even though they do not actually carry out these evil purposes. For 'not only do they do these things, but they applaud others doing them.'[26] I say this for their desires are just as corrupt as those evil deeds, and from this it is clear that it is possible to be punished even because of an evil intention alone.

Every day I say these things, and I will not stop saying them. For, if some do listen to me, it will be worth while. However, even if there be no one who pays attention to me now, you will hear these truths at that time when it will be of no profit to you to listen, and you will then blame yourselves for not having done so before, while we shall be free from guilt.

Howevtr, I hope not only that we shall not have this excuse to make, but that you will even be our boast before the tribunal of Christ, that we may together enjoy the blessings of heaven by the grace and mercy of our Lord Jesus Christ. Glory be to Him and to the Father, together with the Holy Spirit, forever and ever. Amen.

---

26 Rom. 1.32.

Homily 83 (John 18.1-36)

'After saying these things, Jesus went forth with his disciples beyond the torrent of Cedron, where there was a garden into which he and his disciples entered.'[1]

Death is an awesome thing, and one that inspires great fear—not, however, to those who have knowledge of the true wisdom from above. The man who has no clear understanding of the life to come, but considers death as a kind of annihilation and end of life, with good reason shudders and is afraid, under the illusion that it means passing on to a state of non-existence. We, on the contrary, who by the grace of God have learned the mysteries and secrets of His wisdom, and who consider death merely as a transition, have no reason to tremble at it. We ought to rejoice and be of good heart, because, leaving behind this ephemeral life, we are going to another, much better and brighter, and one that is without end.

It was to teach us this lesson by His example that Christ went to His Passion, not by compulsion or by necessity, but willingly. 'Jesus spoke these words,' the Evangelist declared, and went forth beyond the torrent of Cedron, where was a garden into which he and his disciples entered. Now Judas who betrayed him also knew the place, since Jesus had often met there together with his disciples.' He started out in the middle of the night, and crossed a river, and went directly to the place familiar to His betrayer in order to make the task of His opponents easier, and to free them from all difficulty. Besides, He was showing His disciples that He was going to His Passion willingly, for this fact was sufficient to give them very great courage. So, He went into the garden, as if into a prison.

'After He had said these words to them.'

---

1 John 18.1.

'What do you mean? He had just finished the discourse in which He was conversing with His Father, and, so, had been praying. Why, then, do you not say that after finishing His prayer He went to the garden?' Because His words were not really a prayer but were uttered for the sake of the disciples.

'And His disciples also entered the garden.' He had so effectually freed them from fear that they no longer held back, but even proceeded right into the garden. Yet, how was it that Judas went there? And from what source did he gain his information when he came there? From his coming there it is clear that Christ had spent the night many times out of doors. For, if He ordinarily passed the night in a dwelling, Judas would not have gone to seek Him out in that lonely spot, but to His lodgings, expecting to find Him sleeping there.

However, in order that on hearing the word 'garden' you might not conclude that He was in hiding, the Evangelist added: 'Judas knew the place,' and not merely that, but also: 'He had often met there with his disciples.' He did this for He frequently held meetings with them in private to talk with them of important matters and those which it was not right for others to hear. These conferences took place, for the most part, on hilltops and in gardens, as He always sought out a place free from distractions so that the minds of His listeners might be better able to concentrate.

Judas, then, taking the cohort, and attendants from the chief priests and Pharisees, came there.' Now, the latter had often on other occasions sent to arrest Him, but had not been able to do so. From this it is clear that at this time He gave Himself up of His own accord. And how did they persuade the cohort to accompany Judas? They were soldiers and so would undertake to do anything for money.

'Jesus therefore knowing all that was to come upon him,

went forth and said to them, "Whom do you seek?"' That is, He did not wait to learn this from them when they reached Him, but spoke and acted with assurance, as one who knew all these things.

'But why did they come armed if they intended merely to arrest Him?'

They feared His followers, and it was for this reason, also, that they approached at an untimely hour of the night.

'And he went forth and said to them, "Whom do you seek?" They answered him, "Jesus of Nazareth."'

Do you perceive His insuperable power and how He stood in their midst and blinded them? For the Evangelist has made it clear that darkness was not responsible for the question, since he mentioned that they also had lanterns. And, even if there were no lanterns, they ought to have recognized Him at least by His voice. Besides, even if they were in doubt, how could Judas, who had been continually in His company, have any doubt? I say this for he himself was also standing with them, yet knew Christ no more than they, but fell to the ground with them. Now, Jesus brought this about to make it clear that not only were they unable to arrest Him, but that they could not even see Him when He was in their midst, unless He Himself permitted.

'He asked them again, "Whom do you seek?"' Oh, what stupidity! His words cast them to the ground yet not even thus were they converted, though they had experienced the effect of such great power, but once again they returned to the same subject. Then, when He had brought to fulfillment all things incumbent on Him, He finally gave Himself up and said to them: ' "I have told you that I am he." Now Judas, who betrayed him was also standing with them.'

Do you notice the restraint shown by the Evangelist, how he did not revile the traitor, but simply related the incident and concentrated his efforts on showing one thing, namely, that everything took place according to the will of Christ? Next, He forestalled the objection of anyone who might say that it was He Himself who brought them to this deed by giving Himself up and clearly showing them the way to do it. On the contrary, it was after He had used every possible means calculated to deter them, at the moment when they were persisting in evil-doing and had no excuse, that He gave Himself up and said: 'If, therefore, you seek me, let these go their way,' thus, up to His last hour showing His love for them.

He meant: 'If, indeed, you want Me, do not include these men in this. See, I am giving myself up.' That the word which He said might be fulfilled: 'Of those [whom thou has given Me] I have not lost one.' Actually, however, in this passage He was referring not to this loss—that of death—but to that other in eternity. But the Evangelist accepted it as referring also to the present life.

Someone may wonder how it was that they did not arrest the disciples along with Him, and slay them, especially since Peter roused their anger by what he did to the servant. What held them in check? Nothing else than the Power that had cast them prostrate on the ground. Accordingly, it was to make it clear that what took place happened, not according to their will, but by the power and consent of Him who was arrested, that the Evangelist added: 'That the word which he said might be fulfilled, "Not one of these has been lost." '

Whereupon, Peter, emboldened by Christ's words and by what had already taken place, took up arms against the aggressors.

'But how is it,' you will ask, 'that he who had been directed not to have a wallet, not to have two tunics, had a sword?'[2]

It seems to me that, because he feared the very thing that happened,[3] he had prepared for it just before this. And if you object, 'How is it that he who had been directed not even to give a blow[4] now became a murderer?' I reply that he had been enjoined not to defend himself, but here he was defending not himself but his Master. Besides, the disciples were not by any means perfect and without defect. If you wish to see Peter in pursuit of perfection, look at him afterwards when he was wounded and endured it meekly, and when he bore countless painful sufferings with calm resignation.

Now, Jesus here worked a miracle, both to teach us that we must do good to those who injure us and also to reveal His power to us. Therefore, He restored the ear to the servant and said to Peter: 'All those who take the sword will perish by the sword.'[5] Here, also, He acted as He had done at the washing of the feet, putting a check on his impetuosity by a reproof. Moreover, the Evangelist divulged the name of the servant since the incident was a very important one, not only because Christ performed a cure, but because He healed a man who was an enemy and was going to strike Him a little later, and also because He held in check the hostility that might have been stirred up against the disciples by this deed. And it was also for the following reason that the Evangelist gave the name: that it might be possible for those who read it at that time to make inquiry and ascertain whether the miracle actually had taken place. Moreover, it was not undesignedly that he mentioned the right ear, but it seems to

---

2 Cf. Matt. 10.10.
3 Namely, that Christ would be attacked by His enemies.
4 Cf. Matt. 5.39.
5 Matt. 26.52.

me that he wished to say that the Apostle just missed be-
heading the man when he attacked him.

However, Jesus not only checked the disciples by threatening him, but also encouraged him by other words, and said:
'Shall I not drink the cup that the Father has given me?'
He was pointing out that what was taking place was not
brought about by the power of His enemies, but by His own
will. And He was making it clear that He was not an enemy
of God, but was obedient to His Father unto death.

Then, at length, Jesus was taken prisoner and they bound
Him and brought Him to Annas. Why to Annas? Gleefully
they were parading their triumph as if erecting a trophy.
'For he was the father-in-law of Caiphas, and it was Caiphas
who had given the counsel to the Jews that it was expedient
that one man should die.' Why did the Evangelist again
remind us of the prophecy? To make it clear that these
things took place for our salvation. Besides, truth is of such
surpassing excellence that even its enemies proclaim it. In
order that his hearers might not be troubled on learning of
Christ's bonds, he recalled that well-known prophecy to
mind: that His death was salvation for the world.

'Peter was following, and so was another disciple.' Who
was the other disciple? The author of this Gospel himself.
And why did he not mention himself? When he leaned upon
the bosom of Jesus, with good reason he then concealed his
identity, but why did he do so now?

For the same reason. I am of this opinion for here he was
also relating a thing greatly to his credit, namely, that when
all had run away he himself continued to follow Jesus.
Therefore, he concealed his identity and placed Peter before
himself, but he was forced to mention himself, as well as
Peter, that you might learn that he was giving a more
accurate account than the others did, of the events in the
courtyard, since he was actually inside. Yet, notice how he

deprecated what redounded to his praise. For, lest anyone might say: 'How is it that when all had fled this man went even farther inside than Simon?' he said: 'It was because he was known to the high priest,' so that no one would admire him because he accompanied Christ inside, nor would anyone spread abroad his praises for his courage.

The marvel, on the contrary, was that of Peter because, though he was so fearful, he went even to the courtyard, when the rest had fled. Accordingly, his going there proceeded from his love of Christ, but his not going inside stemmed from his anguish of mind and fear. Indeed, it was for this reason that the Evangelist recorded these details: to pave the way for making an excuse for his denial of Christ. He mentioned the fact that he himself was known to the high priest, not as if it were something to his credit, but, since he had said that he alone went in with Jesus, in order that you might not conclude that the action had a lofty motive, he explained the reason. Moreover, he made it clear by what he said next that Peter also would have gone in, had he been permitted. For, when [John] went out and directed the portress to bring him in, Peter did enter at once.

'But why did John himself not bring him in?'

Because he was completely preoccupied with Christ and so was staying close to Him. That is why he bade the woman to bring him in.[6] Accordingly, what did the woman say?

'Art thou not also one of this man's disciples?'

And he said: 'I am not.'

What are you saying, Peter? Did you not declare, just a little while ago, 'Should it be necessary even to lay down my life for You, I will do so'? Well, then, why does it happen that you cannot even bear up under questioning of the portress? It is not a soldier who is asking the question, is it?

---

6 According to the Greek New Testament and the Confraternity translation, it was John himself who conducted Peter inside.

Or one of those who have just arrested Christ? It is merely a portress asking a casual question, and her manner of asking is not even impertinent. For she did not say: 'Are you a disciple of that deceiver and scoundrel?' but 'of this man' and this was the question of a sympathizer, rather than of a fault-finder.

Peter, however, could not endure any questioning at all. Actually, the words, 'Art thou not also,' were spoken because of the fact that John was inside; hence, the woman was addressing Peter kindly. Yet he did not realize that at all, and did not understand: not when questioned the first time, or the second, or even the third, but only when a cock crowed. Moreover, not even this brought him to complete realization of his sin until Jesus looked accusingly at him.[7] In fact, Peter continued to stand warming himself with the servants of the high priest, while Christ was imprisoned within, bound. We mention this, not in disparagement of Peter, but to show the truth of what Christ had said.[8] 'The high priest therefore questioned Christ concerning his disciples and his teaching.'

Oh, what hypocrisy! Though he had heard Him preaching in the Temple and teaching openly, now he said he wished to learn His teaching. Since they were unable to bring any charge against Him, they asked about His disciples: where they were, perhaps, and why He had brought them together, what His purpose was, and on what terms they followed Him. Moreover, the high priest said this with the air of implying the accusation that Christ was an insurgent and rebel, and that no one else paid any attention to Him except only those disciples, as if He were an evil-doer.

---

7 Cf. Luke 22.61.
8 That is, in predicting his infidelity; cf. especially Luke 22.31-34.

What, then, did Christ do? He said in reply: 'I have spoken openly to the world, not in private to my disciples; I have taught openly in the temple.'

What's that? Did He say nothing in secret? Yes, He did, but not in the way that these men thought: out of fear and to plot rebellion. On the contrary, He spoke in secret when what He said was beyond the comprehension of the multitude.

'Why dost thou question me? Question those who have heard me.' He answered thus, not because He was seeking to have His teachings corroborated, but to show that He was secure in the confidence that everything He had said was true. This He had declared in the beginning of His public life: 'If I bear witness concerning myself, my witness is not true,'[9] and He was hinting at this on this occasion, also, when He wished to establish the trustworthiness of His testimony to Himself beyond question. For when the high priest referred to His disciples as if they were His only pupils, what did He say? 'Do you ask me about my teachings? Question my enemies, those who plot against me and bind me fast; let these speak.' Indeed, it is an indisputable proof of the truth of what a man says, when he calls on his foes as witnesses to his words.

What, therefore, did the high priest reply?

Though he ought to have instituted this inquiry, he did not do so, but 'one of the attendants who was standing by gave Him a blow' as He said these words. What deed could be more rash than this? Shudder, ye heavens, be astonished, O earth, at the long-suffering of the Lord and the arrogance of His slaves. Yet, what was it that He had said? It was not, indeed, as if refusing to speak that He asked: 'Why dost thou question me?' but in the desire to remove all pretext for

---

9 John 5.31. That is, is not accepted as true by the Jews. See Homily 40, Vol. I 403-405.

their arrogance. Yet, when He was struck for saying this, though He had the power to smite, and obliterate, and do away with all things, He did nothing like that, but uttered words calculated to destroy all their ferocity.

He said: 'If I have spoken ill, bear witness to the evil,' that is, 'If you have any fault to find with My words, show what it is: but, if you have none, why do you strike me?' Do you see that the trial was full of confusion and ill-will and spite and disregard for law? The high priest had questioned Him hypocritically and treacherously; Christ had answered straightforwardly and respectfully. What, then, should have followed? Either to refute or to accept what He said. However, this was not what happened, but the attendant struck Him a blow.

Thus, it was not a court of justice that was in session, but a lawless and tyrannical assembly. Thereupon, since there was nothing further to be accomplished in this manner, 'they sent him bound to Caiphas. But Peter was standing and warming himself.' Alas, what torpor now held the hot-headed and impetuous disciple in check as Jesus was being led away! Moreover not even after this was he moved, but continued to warm himself, that you may learn how great is the weakness of human nature, when God leaves it to itself. And so, when he was once more questioned he repeated his denial.

Then 'A relative of the attendant whose ear Peter had cut off, said, "Did I not see thee in the garden," ' since he was indignant at Peter's deed. Not even the mention of the garden caused him to remember what had happened there, and the tender love that Christ had there displayed by those words of His, but he put all these thoughts out of his mind by reason of his fear.

But why in the world did the Evangelists all universally record this denial of Peter? It was not to condemn the disciple for this, but in the desire to teach us how great an evil it is not to place one's confidence completely in God, but to trust to oneself. And as for you—marvel at the solicitude of the Master, and how, even though under arrest and bound, He was deeply concerned for His disciple, and by a glance raised him up from his fall, and moved him to tears.[10]

They led Him, then, from Caiphas to Pilate. This took place in order that the multiplicity of judges might attest the tortuous trial of Truth, even though they were unwilling to bear witness to this. 'Now it was early morning.' Before cock-crow He was led to Caiphas, and in the early morning to Pilate. By these details the Evangelist showed that, though He was questioned all during half the night, He was not convicted; therefore Caiphas sent Him off to Pilate. However, leaving the details of the trial before Caiphas to the other Evangelists to relate, he himself told of what followed.

Now, notice the ridiculous behavior of the Jews. Though they had arrested an innocent man, and were bearing weapons, they did not enter the praetorium, 'that they might not be defiled.' Yet, I ask you, what sort of defilement was incurred by entering a court room where wrong-doers were justly punished? They who paid tithes on mint and anise[11] did not consider that they were defiled by becoming murderers, but thought that they defiled themselves by merely entering the court of Pilate.

Moreover, why did they not put Him to death, instead of leading Him to Pilate? Most of their power and authority had been cut off since their affairs were under control of the Romans. Besides, they feared lest they might be punished later if they were accused by him. But what is the meaning of 'that they might eat the passover?' Christ Himself, to be sure, had kept the Passover on the first day of the azymes. Therefore, the Evangelist meant the whole festival by the

---

10 Cf. Luke 22.61.
11 Cf. Matt. 23.23; Luke 11.42.

word 'passover'; or else he meant that they were then observing the Passover, while Christ had done so a day ahead,
keeping His own actual immolation for the Day of Preparation, the day when the Passover really took place in olden
times.

To resume: these men were bearing weapons, which was
not allowed, and, though they were bent on bloodshed, they
had scruples about the place, so they summoned Pilate to
come out to them. As he came forth he said: 'What accusation do you bring against this man?'

Do you see that he was free from their envy and ambition?
For, on seeing Christ bound and led to him by such men as
these, he considered that the grounds for accusation were
not clear. Hence, he asked the question, meaning that it was
a strange thing that they themselves, on the one hand, seized
the right to try Christ, but then entrusted to him the passing
of the sentence, without a trial. What reply, then, did they
make?

'If he were not a criminal, we should not have handed
him over to thee.' Oh, what nonsense! Why are you not
specific about His wrongdoing, but merely hint at it? Why
do you not give proof of the wrong?

Do you perceive that they were always evading frank
accusation and actually had nothing they could say? Annas
had asked Him about His teaching and, when he heard His
reply, sent Him to Caiphas. When the latter had himself
questioned Him again and had found out nothing, he sent
Him away to Pilate. Pilate said: 'What accusation do you
bring against this man?' Yet not even here did they have
anything to say, but used evasions once again. Wherefore, he
himself, at a loss what to do, said: ' "Take him yourselves,
and judge him according to your law." The Jews, then, said
to him, "It is not lawful for us to put anyone to death." And
they said this that the word of the Lord might be fulfilled

which he said, signifying by what death he was to die.'

Now, how is this indicated by the words: 'It is not lawful to put anyone to death'? The Evangelist said this, meaning either that Christ was going to be slain not only for their sake but also for the sake of the Gentiles, or that it was not permissible for the Jews to sentence Him to crucifixion. And when they said: 'It is not lawful for us to put anyone to death,' they were speaking merely with reference to that time of the year.[12] Besides, Stephen, who was stoned to death, proves that they did execute the death penalty, even though they did so in another way.

However, they desired to crucify Christ, in order that they might make a spectacle of even the manner of His death. Now, Pilate, wishing to be rid of this bothersome business, did not submit Him to a long trial. Going inside again, he questioned Jesus and said: ' "Art thou the king of the Jews?" Jesus answered: "Dost thou say this thyself, or have others told thee this?" '

Why did Christ ask this question? Because He wished to expose the wicked purpose of the Jews. Pilate, to be sure, had heard this from many people, and since the Jews made no specific charge, in order not to prolong the inquiry, he decided to bring out into the open what they were continually discussing. Besides, when he had said to them: 'Judge him according to your law,' because they wished to intimate that His crime was not solely against Jewish law, they declared: 'It is not lawful for us, for he has not offended against our law, but the charge is one pertaining to the general welfare.' Therefore, Pilate, conscious of this, said, as if he himself were about to be imperiled: 'Art thou the king of the Jews?'

It was not, then, because Christ was in need of information that He replied with His question, but it was because He wished the guilt of the Jews to be exposed by Pilate that

12 That is, the paschal time.

He said: 'Have others told thee?' Making their guilt clear, Pilate replied: 'Am I a Jew? They own people and the chief priests have delivered thee to me. What hast thou done?' By these words he wished to clear himself.

In short, since Pilate had asked: 'Art thou the king?' Jesus was saying, to reprove him: 'You have heard this from the Jews. Why do you not investigate their charges more searchingly? They say that I am a criminal; ask them what crime I have committed. However, you do not do this, but merely trump up charges. Do you say this of yourself or from another source?'

When Pilate had heard this, he was unable to answer Him at once, but merely took refuge in the conduct of the crowd, saying: 'They delivered you to me. Therefore I must ask what you have done.' What, then, did Christ reply? 'My kingdom is not of this world.' He was elevating Pilate's thoughts, since he was not very wicked—not like the Jews—and He wished to show him that He is not merely man, but God and the Son of God.

'If my kingdom were of this world, my followers would have fought that I might not be delivered to the Jews.' He was dispelling the fear that Pilate had been entertaining until now, namely, the suspicion that He had designs on his power.

Is His kingdom not of this world, then? Yes, of course it is.

How is it, therefore, that He said it is not? He did not mean that He does not hold sway in this world, but that He has His sovereignty also from on high and that it is not mere human power, but much greater and more brilliant than that.

'But, if it is greater, how is it that He was taken prisoner by human power?'

This happened by His own will; He gave Himself up. However, for the moment He did not reveal this, but what did He say? 'If I were of this world, my followers would have fought that I might not be delivered up.' By these words He was pointing out the weakness of our earthly kingdom because its strength lies in its followers, while the heavenly kingdom is sufficient to itself and not in need of anyone.

The heretics, basing their claims on this passage, allege that He is independent of the Creator.[13] What, then, of the words, 'He came unto his own?' And what of the words, 'They are not of the world, even as I am not of this world?'[14] Thus, He says that His kingdom is not from here, not to deprive the world of His providence and overlordship, but to show, as I have said, that His kingdom is not a human one, nor is it transient.

What, then, did Pilate say? ' "Thou art then a king?" Jesus answered, "Thou sayest it; I am a king. This is why I was born." ' Well, then, if He was born a king, all His other attributes are also innate and He has nothing which He has received [from anyone else]. So that when you hear: 'As the Father has life in himself, even so he has given to the Son also to have life in himself,'[15] place no other interpretation on this than that it means His eternal generation, and similarly with reference to the other passages. 'And I have come for this reason: to bear witness to the truth,' that is, 'that I may say this very thing, and teach it, and convince all men of it.'

And you, O man, on hearing these things and seeing your Lord driven in fetters from place to place, have no esteem for the present life. Is it not a strange thing, indeed, if Christ has undergone such great sufferings for your sake, whereas you frequently cannot even bear up under harsh words? But

---

13 The Manichaeans; see art. 'Manichaeism' in *Catholic Encyclopedia*.
14 John 1.11; 17.14.
15 John 5.26.

He, on the one hand, was spat upon, whereas you adorn your-self with fine apparel and rings, and, if you do not meet with words of approval from all men, you consider life not worth living.

Yes, He was insulted, endured jibes, and mocking blows against His face, while you wish to receive honor at all times and cannot bear the dishonor received by Christ. Do you not hear Paul saying: 'Be imitators of me as I am of Christ'?[16] When someone ridicules you, then, remember your Lord, that they bowed the knee to Him in mockery, dishonored Him both in word and deed, and showed great hypocrisy toward Him. However, He not only did not reciprocate, but even gave back the opposite, namely, gentleness and kindness.

Let us also imitate Him, for in this way we shall be able to remain unharmed by every kind of insult. For it is not the one who offered insult, but the weak character who is troubled by insults, who makes the scoffing effective and causes it to give pain. If you are not troubled, you are not insulted. The pain of such suffering comes, not from those who inflict it, but from those who regard it as suffering. Why, indeed, are you troubled at it at all? If you are insulted unjustly you particularly ought not to grieve at this, but rather to be sorry for the one who wronged you. And if you have been justly affronted, you have much less cause for complaint.

Just as, if someone calls you a rich man when you are actually poor, the flattering words are nothing to you, but the praise is, rather, absurd, so if someone says what is not true by way of insult, the opprobrium in turn is nothing in your eyes. Furthermore, if the consciousness that the insult is deserved lays hold of you, do not be troubled at the words, but amend your actions. I say this even with regard to things that are truly insults.

However, if someone should pass insulting remarks about

---

16 1 Cor. 11.1.

your poverty or humble birth, this is again merely ridiculous. The ignominy belongs, not to him who hears these insults, but to him who utters them, since he does not know how to place the true value on things.

'But when these insults are uttered before many people who are in ignorance of the truth, the hurt is too great to bear,' you say.

On the contrary, this is particularly easy to bear, since your audience is composed of witnesses who praise you and show you approval, while despising and ridiculing your adversary. For it is not the man who justifies himself, but he who remains silent that is admired by those who are truly wise. And even if there be no truly wise person among those present, pay no attention to your critic all the more for this reason, and find your satisfaction in your heavenly audience. There, all will praise you and applaud and approve you. Moreover, one angel makes up for the whole world. Yet why do I speak merely of the angels, when the Lord Himself will sound your praise?

Let us school ourselves by these reflections. For it is not a fault for a man to remain silent when insulted; on the contrary, it is blameworthy when the man who has been insulted strikes back. If it were a fault to bear such words in silence, Christ would not have said: 'If someone strike thee on the right cheek, turn to him the other also.'[17] Therefore, if someone says what is not true, let us pity him also for this, because he is drawing on himself the punishment and vengeance meted out to those who have spoken against others, and he is becoming unworthy even to read Scripture. For 'to the wicked man God says: "Why do you recite my statutes, and profess my covenant with your mouth? You sit speaking against your brother."'[18]

---

17 Matt. 5.39.
18 Ps. 49.16,20.

But if he says what is true, even so he is to be pitied. The Pharisee, to be sure, spoke the truth, but he, too, did his hearer no harm; on the contrary, he even helped him. However, he deprived himself of blessings without number, wrecking his future by this public confession.[19] Hence, in either case,[20] that man [who insults you] is the one who suffers injury, not you. On the other hand, if you control yourself, you derive a twofold gain: both causing God to be propitious toward you because of your silence, and also strengthening your self-discipline, taking occasion from the words of your adversary to amend your deeds and making no account of the praise of men.

I say this for it has grieved us to see that many men have been in open-mouthed admiration of worldly glory. So, if we wish to be truly wise, we shall have the conviction that worldly glory is nothing. Let us learn this, therefore, and, reflecting on our own faults, let us gradually effect their correction: this one in the present month, the other in the following month, and let us mark out another for ourselves to correct after that one. Thus, as it were, mounting step by step, let us reach heaven by a Jacob's ladder. I say this for it seems to me that by that well-known vision Jacob's ladder was a figure of this, namely, the ascent through virtue, little by little, by which it is possible to ascend from earth to heaven, not by steps apparent to the senses, but by the emending and correcting of one's habits.

Let us, then, set out on this journey and ascent in order that we may reach heaven and enjoy all the good things there, by the grace and mercy of our Lord Jesus Christ. Glory be to Him, forever and ever. Amen.

---

19 Cf. Luke 18.9-14.
20 That is, whether he tells the truth or lies.

Homily 84 (John 18.37-19.15)

'This is why I was born, and why I have come into the world, to bear witness to the truth. Everyone who is of the truth hears my voice.'[1]

Patience is a wonderful virtue. It places the soul in a calm harbor, as it were, sheltering it from the billows and winds of evil. Christ has taught us this virtue at all times, but especially now when He is being subjected to trial and forcibly driven from one place to another. I say this for, when brought before Annas, He replied with great gentleness, and everything He said in answer to the attendant who struck Him was calculated to dispel the mist of his pride. Moreover, when He went from there to Caiphas, and then to Pilate, spending the whole night in these 'trials,' He demonstrated His meekness throughout.

When they declared that He was a malefactor, yet were unable to prove it, He stood silent. But when He was asked about His kingdom, then He replied to Pilate in order to instruct him and conduct him to higher thoughts. However, why in the world did Pilate not conduct the inquiry in the presence of the Jews, but in private, going into the praetorium? It was because he dimly suspected His greatness and wished to get accurate information about everything, undistracted by the noisy protests of the Jews.

Next, when he asked: 'What hast thou done?' Jesus did not reply to this, but instead answered the question uppermost in Pilate's thoughts, namely, regarding His kingdom. He said in reply: 'My kingdom is not of this world'; that is, 'I am a king, but not the kind you suspect. On the contrary, I am a much more illustrious one.' Both by these words and by those that follow He was making clear that He had done nothing evil. For by saying: 'This is why I was born, and

---

1 John 18.37.

why I have come, to bear witness to the truth,' He was pointing out that He had done nothing evil. Then He declared:
'Everyone who is of the truth hears my voice.' and by these
words was trying to persuade Pilate to join the number of
those who were receptive to His teaching. He meant: 'If a
man is of the truth and desires it, he will listen to Me with
undivided attention.' So strongly, indeed, did He attract
Pilate by these brief words that the latter rejoined: 'What is
truth?'

However, for the moment he hurried on to the issue re-
quiring immediate attention. He was conscious that it would
take time to explore this question, and he wished to rescue
Christ from the onslaught of the Jews. Therefore, he went
outside, and what did he say? 'I find no guilt in him.' Now,
mark how prudently he spoke. He did not say: 'Since He
has done wrong and is worthy of death, show leniency to
Him on account of the festival.' On the contrary, he first
absolved Him of all guilt, and then indicated that, even if
they were unwilling to let Him go free because of His in-
nocence, He was more than deserving that they show Him
favor by allowing Him to benefit by the festival time. Therefore, he added: 'You have a custom that I should release
someone at the passover;' then, ingratiatingly: 'Do you wish,
therefore, that I release the king of the Jews?' They all then
cried out: 'Not this man, but Barabbas!'

Oh what an accursed decision! They lay claim to those
who are like themselves and they set free the guilty, while
they decree punishment for the innocent One; indeed, this
has been their custom from olden days. Please notice, on the
other hand, the love shown them by the Lord throughout
all this.

'Pilate had Him scourged,' perhaps in the desire to exhaust
and appease the Jews' wrath. For, since he had been unable
to set Him free by his previous efforts, he was striving to halt

the dreadful deed at least at this point. Thus, he now had Him scourged and permitted the rest to be done, namely, to put on Him the purple garment and the crown of thorns, so as to calm their anger. Therefore, he brought Him forth to them, crowned with thorns, in order that, on seeing the insults that had been inflicted on Him, they might have their ill-will satisfied and be purged of its poison.

'Yet, how is it that the soldiers did these things, if it was not by command of the governor?'

To curry favor with the Jews, because even from the start it was not by his orders that they set out against Him during the night, but rather to please the Jews, since they would dare anything for the sake of money. However, despite so many and such trying sufferings Christ stood silent, just as He had done at the trial, and He made no reply.

But do not, I beg you, merely listen to this, but keep it ever in your mind, and when you see the King of the world and of all the angels made the sport of the soldiers by their words and actions, and bearing it in silence, imitate Him yourself by your deeds.

Because Pilate had called Him 'the king of the Jews' they then even put on Him a caricature [of kingship] to ridicule Him. Next, bringing Him out, he said: 'I find no guilt in him.' Accordingly, Christ came forth, wearing the crown of thorns, yet not even then was their anger extinguished. On the contrary, they kept crying out: 'Crucify him! Crucify him!' Thereupon, Pilate, seeing that all was in vain, said: 'Take him yourselves and crucify him.' From this it is clear that he had permitted the previous outrages in order to endeavor to exhaust their mad passions. 'For,' he said, 'I find no guilt in him.'

Notice in how many ways the judge pronounced Him guiltless, as he repeatedly absolved Him of the charges against Him. However, nothing of this had any effect on those dogs. I say this for the words, 'Take him and crucify him,' indicate that he was disclaiming responsibility for the deed and telling them to do something that they had no right to do. Of course, they themselves had brought Christ to him in order that the crucifixion might be the result of a verdict pronounced by the governor, but just the opposite happened; He was, rather, acquitted by the verdict of the governor.

Next, since they had been discomfited, they said: 'We have a Law and according to our Law he must die, because he has made himself Son of God.'

How is it, then, that when the judge said: 'Take him yourselves and judge him according to your law,' you replied: 'It is not lawful for us to put anyone to death,' while here you have recourse to the Law? Moreover, notice the charge: 'He has made himself Son of God.' Is it a crime, I ask you, for one who performs the deeds of the Son of God to say that He is Son of God?

What did Christ do next? He remained silent, even while Pilate and the Jews were exchanging these remarks, thus fulfilling that prophecy: 'He shall not open his mouth.' By His humility His judgment was removed.[2] Then Pilate was afraid, on hearing that He had made Himself Son of God. He feared lest what He said might be true, and so he himself might seem to have done wrong. The Jews, on the contrary, though they had obtained knowledge of this fact from both His deeds and His words, did not shudder with fear, but wished to destroy Him for the very reason for which they ought to have prostrated before Him.

Therefore Pilate no longer asked: 'What hast thou done?' Shaking with fear, he now began to conduct the investigation on a spiritual plane, and said: 'Art thou the Christ?'[3] But

---

2 Isa. 53.7-8.
3 According to the Greek New Testament and the Confraternity translation, the words of Pilate here were: 'Where art thou from?'

Jesus gave him no answer, for, because Pilate had heard: 'This is why I was born and why I have come' and, 'My kingdom is not from here,' he ought to have resisted the Jews and saved Christ. However, he failed to do so and yielded to the pressure of the Jews.

Next, since they were confuted on every issue, they changed the subject and resorted to a political charge by declaring: 'Everyone who makes himself king sets himself against Cæsar.' Therefore Pilate ought to have investigated carefully whether Christ was in fact attacking the sovereign power and attempting to oust Cæsar from his throne. However, he did not make a detailed inquiry into this point. That is why Christ made no reply to him, since He knew that Pilate was asking pointless questions. Besides, because His deeds testified for Him, He did not wish to win out over His foes verbally and to speak in His own defense. Thus He proved that it was by His own will that He came to this ordeal.

Accordingly, when He remained silent, Pilate said: 'Dost thou not know that I have power to crucify thee?' Do you see how he was passing judgment on himself? For, if all power was in your hands, why did you not set Christ free when you found no guilt in Him? Therefore, when Pilate had pronounced this implicit accusation against himself, Christ then said: 'He who betrayed me to thee has the greater sin,' to show him that he, too, was guilty of sin.

Furthermore, to put down his pride and to dispel his blindness, He said: 'Thou wouldst have no power at all, were it not given thee.' He was making it clear that his office had been given him, not by accident or even by the vote of the majority, but this had been arranged by a mystical power.[4] But, in order that on hearing: 'Were it not given thee,' you might not think that Pilate was free from all blame,

---

4 That is, the providence of God.

He therefore added: 'He who betrayed me to thee has the greater sin.'

'Yet, if it was actually given [from above] neither he nor they would be blameworthy.'

In vain do you say this, for the word 'given' here means 'permitted,' as if He said: 'These things have been allowed to take place, but you are not on that account free from guilt.' By these words Christ terrified Pilate and gave a clear defense of Himself. Therefore, 'Pilate was looking for a way to release Him.'

'But the Jews again cried out, "If thou release this man, thou art no friend of Cæsar."' For, since they had accomplished nothing by bringing charges based on the Law they treacherously turned to secular laws and said: 'Everyone who makes himself king sets himself against Cæsar.' Now, just where was this usurpation evident? And whence can you prove it? By His purple robe? By His diadem? By His apparel? By His soldiers? Did He not always go about unattended, in company with His twelve disciples, observing the proper moderation in His use of all things: food, and clothing, and dwelling?

But, Oh, what shamelessness and ill-timed caution! Pilate, thinking that he would be risking his future, if he should take no notice of these words, went forth as if to try the case (for his seating himself makes this clear), but without making any investigation of the charge at all, he handed Christ over to them, in the hope that this would disconcert them. In proof that this was his motive in doing so, listen to what he said: 'Behold your king!' And when they cried: 'Crucify him,' he again added: 'Shall I crucify your king?' But they shouted: 'We have no king but Cæsar.'

They were deliberately laying themselves open to punishment. Therefore, God also gave them up, because they themselves first cast themselves off from His providence and protection. Moreover, since they unanimously disavowed His rule over them, He permitted them to be ruined in accordance with their own expressed wish.

Yet, their words could have exhausted their anger at last. However, they feared lest He might again gather the people about Him if He were released, and they motivated all their actions by this consideration. A frightful force, indeed, is ambition, frightful and capable of destroying one's soul. That is why they never listened to Him at all. On the contrary, Pilate, as a result of hearing only a few words, wished to release Him, while the Jews persisted in their attack, crying: 'Crucify him!'

'Yet, why in the world were they trying to have Him put to death in that way?'

This was a very ignominious kind of death. Therefore, lest some honorable memory of Him might afterwards persist, they were striving to bring Him to a disgrace that was even accursed, not realizing that the truth is exalted by obstacles. In proof that they did indeed suspect that He would be held in honor, listen to what they said: 'We have heard how that deceiver said, "After three days I will rise." '[5] Therefore, they were making prodigious efforts, throwing everything topsy-turvy, so as to spoil His subsequent reputation, and they kept shouting continually, 'Crucify Him!' since the undisciplined mob was swayed by the corrupt influence of its leaders.

Let us not merely read of these things, but let us also keep them in our thoughts: the crown of thorns, the purple cloak, the reed, the buffets, the blows on the cheeks, the spitting, the ridicule. These, indeed, are sufficient to curb all our anger, if we continually ponder them. If we are mocked, if treated unjustly, let us keep on saying: 'No servant is greater

---

5 Matt. 27.63.

than his master.'[6] Let us also recall the things said by the
Jews, furious utterances, as when they even declared: 'Thou
hast a devil,' and 'Thou art a Samaritan,' and 'By Beelzebub he casts out devils.'[7]

Truly it was for this reason that He endured all these
sufferings, namely, that we might walk in His footsteps and
that we might bear up under scoffing, the kind of insult that
stings most of all. Notwithstanding this fact, He not only
bore scoffing patiently, but even exerted every effort to save
those who were inflicting these sufferings on Him and to free
them from the punishment in store for them. Now, I say
this for He even sent the Apostles to effect the salvation of
these men. In truth, you hear them declaring: 'We know
that you acted in ignorance,' and by this means drawing
them to repentance.[8]

Let us also imitate this. For nothing pleases God so much
as loving our enemies and doing good to those who treat
us meanly.[9] When someone abusively insults you, do not
harbor resentment against him, but against the Devil who
is tempting him to do this. Vent your wrath on him, but
pity the man who is tempted by him. For, if lying comes
from the Devil, showing anger to no purpose is much more
from that source. When you see someone making fun of you,
reflect that it is the Devil who is tempting him. Scoffing does
not belong to Christians. He who has been bidden to mourn,
and who has heard: 'Woe to you who laugh,'[10] and who
nevertheless insults us, derides us, and nurses the fire of his
anger is worthy, not of being insulted by us, but of being
pitied, since Christ was moved even at the thought of Judas.

Let us, then, put all these considerations into practice by our

---

6 John 13.16.
7 John 7.20; 8.48; Luke 11.15.
8 Acts 3.17.
9 Cf. Matt. 5.44-46.
10 Luke 6.25.

deeds. If we do not perform them rightly, to no purpose and in vain have we come into the world, or, rather, we have come for the sake of evil. Faith is not enough to bring us into the kingdom; on the contrary, even because of it, those who live bad lives can be most severely condemned. For, 'He who knows the will of his master and does not fulfill it, will be beaten with many stripes.'[11] And again He says: 'If I had not come and spoken to them, they would have no sin.'[12] What defense shall we have, then, we who are within the royal palace and who have been deemed worthy to penetrate into the Holy of Holies, and who have been made sharers in the mysteries that free us from sin, if we become worse than the pagans who have had no share at all in these privileges?

Indeed, if pagans have practiced such an exemplary philosophy of life for the sake of worldly glory, how much more ought we to practice every virtue for the sake of fulfilling the will of God? In actual fact, however, we do not even despise money; they, on the contrary, often have made little account of their own lives, and in time of war have given over their children to the insane fury of the demons, and thus have despised their own nature for the sake of demons, while we do not even despise silver for the sake of Christ. We do not despise anger for the sake of pleasing God, but are rotten with apathy, and our condition is no better than that of fever-stricken patients. Even as they are on fire, completely possessed by their affliction, so also are we, suffocating, as it were, from a kind of fire. We are completely incapable of refraining from our unbridled passion, as we feed the flame both of anger and of avarice.

Therefore, I am ashamed and astonished on seeing some among the pagans despising wealth, while all of us have

11 Cf. Luke 12.47.
12 John 15.22.

a frenzied desire for it. For, even if we should discover some among us who, do scorn it, yet they are caught in the toils of other passions, namely, anger and envy, and it is a difficult thing to find conduct that is completely free from vice.

Now, the reason for this is that we do not strive to take the remedies available in the Scriptures, and we do not read them carefully, with compunction and contrition and remorse, but merely casually, whenever we have time. Therefore, since a great deal of debris accumulates from worldly affairs, it buries everything and, if there is any gain, destroys it. For, if a person who has a wound, after applying a remedy, should not carefully fasten it on, but should allow it to fall off, and should expose himself to water and dust and parching heat and the countless other things which are liable to aggravate the sore, he will derive no benefit from the treatment—not, however, because of the inefficacy of the remedy, but because of his own laziness.

This frequently happens to us also when we give our attention briefly to the divine revelations, but then at once fix our thoughts without ceasing on worldly matters. Thus, all the seed sown is stifled and becomes unproductive. Therefore, in order that this may not take place, let us keep studying the Scriptures for a little while; let us look up to heaven, and then let us turn our gaze downward to the monuments and tombs of the departed. Let us do so, for the same end awaits us, also, and frequently the inevitable departure itself will be upon us before the evening of life has come.

Well, then, let us get ready for this journey. We should do so for we need many provisions, since there is much burning heat on the way, much aridity, much loneliness. It is not possible to stop at an inn for awhile, it is not possible to buy anything, if one does not take from here everything he needs. Listen, indeed, to what the virgins said: 'Go to those who sell.' But when they went, they did not find any oil. Listen to what Abraham said: 'Between us and you is a gulf.'[13] Listen to what Ezechiel said about that day: 'Not Noe and Job and Daniel shall deliver their sons.'[14]

However, may we not hear these words, but, having taken provisions from here sufficient for eternal life, may we confidently behold our Lord Jesus Christ. Glory, power, honor, be to Him and to the Father, together with the Holy Spirit, now and always and forever and ever. Amen.

Homily 85 (John 19.16-20.9)

'Then Pilate handed him over to them to be crucified. And so they took Jesus and led him away. And bearing the cross for himself, he went forth to the place called the Skull, in Hebrew, Golgotha, where they crucified him.'[1]

Prosperity has a way of bringing about the downfall and complete dissolution of the unwary. Thus, the Jews, who from the beginning enjoyed the favor of God, repeatedly turned to the law of the kingdom of the Gentiles and when they were in the desert, after receiving manna, they kept recalling onions![2] In the same way, in this instance, also, they spurned the kingdom of Christ and called on that of Cæsar for support. Therefore, God in consequence set him up as king over them in accordance with their declaration.

Accordingly, when Pilate had heard these words,[3] he handed Christ over to them to be crucified—and was acting very illogically in this. For, though he ought to have investigated whether Christ had really tried to overthrow the

---

13 Matt. 25.9; Luke 16.26.
14 Cf. Ezech. 14.14,16.

1 John 19.16-18.
2 Cf. Num. 11.6.
3 'We have no king but Caesar.'

government, motivated by fear alone he tacitly consented to the charge, even though Christ, in anticipation of this, and to protect him from this blunder, had declared: 'My kingdom is not of this world.'[4] However, surrendering himself completely to the interests of this life, Pilate had no desire to do right to the point of heroism, though his wife's dream must have terrified him greatly. On the contrary, nothing influenced him for the better, nor was he moved at all by unworldly considerations, but handed Christ over to them.

Moreover, they placed the cross on His shoulders as if on one henceforth accursed. And they did so for they regarded the wood as an evil portent and could not bear even to touch it. Now, this was the case also in the Type [of the immolation of Christ], for Isaac carried the wood for the sacrifice. At that time, however, the sacrifice took place only in so far as being willed by the father (for it was a type merely), while now it was taking place in actuality, for it was the fulfillment of the type.

'And he came to the place called the Skull.' Some say that there Adam had died and lay buried, and that Jesus set up His trophy over death in the place where death had begun its rule. For He went forth bearing His cross as a trophy in opposition to the tyranny of death, and, as is customary with conquerors, He also carried on His shoulders the symbol of His victory. What matter that the Jews were here acting with an altogether different end in view!

And so they crucified Him, and with Him thieves, unwittingly fulfilling prophecy in this detail, also. Indeed, the very things which they did to revile Him were the ones that contributed to reveal the truth, in order that you might learn its power. I say this for the Prophet had foretold this circum-

---

4 John 18.36.

stance, also, from ancient times in the words: 'He was reputed with the wicked.'[5]

The Evil Spirit, of course, certainly wished to confuse the issue, but he did not succeed. There were indeed three crucified, but Jesus alone was glorified, that you might learn that it was His power that was in control of everything. Even though it was when the three were fastened to the cross that miracles took place, no one attributed anything of what took place to any one of the others, but to Jesus only. Thus, the strategy of the Devil was foiled and all recoiled upon his own head. I say this for one of the other two was saved. Not only, then, did He not diminish His glory by the crucifixion, but He even augmented it not a little. For, to convert the thief on the cross and conduct him to paradise was an achievement in no way inferior to that of splitting open the rocks.

'And Pilate also wrote an inscription,' at the same time to avenge himself on the Jews and to defend Christ. They had to be sure, delivered Him up as of no account, and had tried to strengthen this erroneous opinion of Him by associating Him with the thieves. Hence, that it might be impossible for anyone in future to impute evil charges against Him and to malign Him as a nobody and a malefactor, he silenced their tongues and the tongues of all who might wish to malign Him, by pointing out that they had risen up against their own king. And so he set the inscription in place, as if it were to serve as a kind of trophy, giving voice to a splendid message; both proclaiming His victory, and heralding His sovereignty, even though not in its universal sway. Moreover, he made this clear, not in one tongue only but in three languages. For, since it was likely that there were many of mixed race among the Jews, because of the festival, he inscribed the proclamation of the mad deed of the Jews in all their languages so that no would fail to be aware of

5 Isa. 53.12.

Christ's vindication. He did this for the Jews slandered Christ even when He was on the cross.

Yet, what harm has this inscription done to you? None. For, if He was just a mortal man, possessed of human frailty, and on the point of having His life snuffed out, why were you afraid of an inscription which declared that He was King of the Jews? Yet, what did they say? 'Say that He said this. For, as you put it, it is a label and a public declaration, but if "He said" be added, it will be a clear proof of His rashness and boastfulness.'

Pilate, however, was not moved by their argument, but persisted in his decision. Moreover, it was no trifling matter that was being thus disposed of, but an all-important one. The wood of the cross would be lost to view, since no one undertook to preserve it, both because of the influence of fear and because the faithful were then busily engaged with other pressing matters. But at a later date it would be sought for, and it is likely that the three crosses would be lying together. Hence, provision was being made that the one belonging to the Lord might not go unrecognized: first, because of the fact that it was lying in the middle place; and second, it was clearly evident to all because of the label, since the crosses of the thieves had no superscription.

Now, the soldiers divided His garments among themselves, but not His tunic. Notice how they frequently caused prophecies to be fulfilled by their wicked deeds. I say this for this detail had been foretold of old. Furthermore, even though there were three crucified, the prophecy was fulfilled only with reference to Christ. Why, indeed, did they not do this in the case of the other two, but only with regard to this One alone? Kindly notice, too, the exactness of the prophecy. The Prophet declared not only that they divided the garments among themselves, but also that they did not divide them.[6] Thus, the soldiers divided some of Christ's garments into parts, but they did not divide the tunic; on the contrary, they settled its possession by lot.

Moreover, the words 'woven from the top' do not occur undesignedly, but some say that an allegory is being pointed out by this means: namely, that the crucified One was not man merely, but also possessed His Godhead from above.

Some, however, say that the Evangelist was thus telling the kind of tunic this was.[7] Since in Palestine they join two strips and then weave their garments in one piece, John said: 'woven from the top' to indicate that it was this kind of short tunic. Besides, it seems to me that he said it to imply the ordinary quality of Christ's garments, and that, as in all other respects, so also in the matter of clothing, He sought the plain and simple type.

These things the soldiers did, while He Himself, though crucified, gave His Mother to His disciple's keeping, to instruct us to take every care of our parents, even to our last breath. When she came to Him at an inauspicious moment, He said: 'What wouldst thou have me do, woman?' and: 'Who is my mother?'[8] But here He showed great tenderness, and gave her into the keeping of the disciple whom He loved.

Once again John conceals his identity, out of humility, for, if he wished to boast, he would have set forth also the reason why he was beloved. He would have done so for it is likely that it was for some great and remarkable reason.

But why did He address no other word to John and give him no comfort in his grief? Because it was not the time for words of consolation. Besides, it was of itself no small thing that he was deemed worthy of such an honor as this, and thus received the reward for his fidelity.

6 Cf. Ps. 21.19.
7 See H. Leclerq, 'Tuniques sans coutures,' DACL 17 (1953) 2820-2824.
8 John 2.4; Matt. 12.48.

Notice, also, if you please, how He did everything with calmness, even though crucified: speaking to the disciple about His mother, fulfilling prophecies, holding out to the thief fair hopes for the future. Yet, before being crucified, He was observed to be sweating, in an agony, fearful. Why in the world was this? By no means did this occur by chance, by no means without a clear purpose. For, in the time before, the frailty of His human nature was demonstrated, while here the infinite extent of His power was being shown.

Besides, He was giving us instruction in both cases: even if we are greatly perturbed in anticipation of keen sufferings, not on that account to refuse to accept suffering, but when we actually enter upon our trial, then everything will be thought very easy and not hard to bear. Let us not, then, tremble at the thought of death. Naturally, our soul has a strong desire for life, but there lies within us the power to free it from these bonds and to weaken this attachment to life, or else to bind our souls by it and make it still more despotic.

Just as we have by nature the desire for sexual intercourse, but when we practice chastity we weaken the power of this urge, so is it also the case with regard to our desire for life. Indeed, just as God has implanted in us the desire for carnal intercourse for the sake of perpetuating our race by the generation of children, but without forbidding us to follow the higher way of continence, so also He has instilled the desire for life, forbidding us to take away our own lives, but not deterring us from maintaining an attitude of detachment from the present life.

Now, since we know these truths, we must carefully keep to the middle course: neither going to meet death by our own hand, even if we are enduring trials without limit, nor, on the other hand, drawing back and shrinking away when drawn to sufferings willed by God, but courageously making ready for the fray, setting greater store by the life to come than by the present one.

'There were women standing by the cross,' and the weaker sex at that time appeared the stronger, so completely were all things turned upside-down for the moment. And when Christ had confided His Mother to the disciple, He said: 'Behold thy son.' Goodness, what an honor! With what a great dignity He honored His disciple! Since He Himself was now departing, He entrusted her to the disciple to take care of. Because as His mother she would naturally be grief-stricken and need a protector, with good reason He placed her in the keeping of His beloved disciple. To him He said: 'Behold thy mother.' He uttered these words to unite them in love of one another, and therefore, as the disciple was aware of this, 'he took her into his home.'

Yet, why was it that He made no mention of any other woman, though others also were standing there? To teach us to give more to our mothers than to any others. For, just as we must not even recognize parents who act as an obstacle to us in spiritual affairs, so also when they do not hinder us in any way, we must give them everything that is their due and place them ahead of all others, in return for their bringing us into existence, in return for their care of us, in return for the numberless ways in which they have helped us.

By His consideration for His Mother here, Christ was also refuting the shameless teaching of Marcion,[9] for, if He were not born in the flesh, and had no mother, why was she the only one for whom He made such provision?

'After this Jesus, knowing that all things were accomplished,' that is, He knew that no part of the divine plan re-

---

9 Marcion (born c. 110) rejected the inspired history of the infancy, in fact any childhood of Christ at all; see art. 'Marcionites' in *Catholic Encyclopedia*.

mained as yet unfulfilled. The Evangelist endeavored in every way to show that this death was something new, if, in fact, every detail was controlled by the One who was dying, and death did not enter His body until He Himself willed it, and He willed it only after all had been fulfilled. That is why He had said: 'I have power to lay down my life and I have power to take it up again.'[10] Therefore, knowing that all things were now accomplished, He said: 'I thirst,' in this once again fulfilling a prophecy.

Now, please notice the callousness of the bystanders. For, even if we have innumerable enemies and have suffered irremediable harm from them, on seeing them dying we take pity on them. However, these men were not even then softened towards Him, and did not become more kindly because of what they saw, but rather were more savage, and increased their mockery. Offering Him a sponge soaked in wine, they gave Him a drink in the way in which they offered it to condemned criminals, since it was for this reason hyssop was employed in addition to the sponge.

'Therefore, when he had taken it, he said, "It is consummated!" ' Do you see that all was done calmly and authoritatively? Moreover, what follows also shows this. Since all things had been consummated, 'Bowing his head'— for it was not fastened to the cross—'he gave up his spirit,' that is, He expired. It is not after bowing the head that one expires ordinarily; here, however, it was just the opposite. For, it was not when He had expired that He bowed His head, as is the case with us, but, after He bowed His head, He then expired. By all these details the Evangelist made it clear that Christ Himself is Lord of all.

However, once again the Jews, who swallow the camel and strain out the gnat,[11] though they were in the act of

10 John 10.18.
11 Cf. Matt. 23.24.

performing such a brazen deed yet had scruples regarding the day. 'Since it was the Preparation Day, in order that the bodies might not remain upon the cross, besought Pilate that their legs might be broken.' Do you see how powerful truth is? By the very things which they were at pains to do, prophecy was fulfilled. For, by means of them a prediction unconnected with them received fulfillment itself, when the soldiers came and broke the legs of the others, but not those of Christ. Nevertheless, to please the Jews, they pierced His side with a spear, and now offered insult to His lifeless body.

Oh, what a brutal and accursed act! However, do not be disturbed, do not be dejected, beloved. For, the very things which they did for a wicked purpose became powerful champions of truth. There was indeed a prophecy which said: 'They shall look on him whom they have pierced.' And not this only, but also this brazen deed would become evidence to confirm the faith of future unbelievers, such as Thomas, and others like him.

Moreover, in addition to this, an ineffable mystery was also accomplished, for 'There came out blood and water.' It was not accidentally or by chance that these streams came forth, but because the Church has been established from both of these. Her members know this, since they have come to birth by water and are nourished by Flesh and Blood. The Mysteries have their source from there, so that when you approach the awesome chalice you may come as if you were about to drink from His very side.

'And he who saw it has borne witness and his witness is true,' that is: 'I have not heard about this from others, but I myself have seen it in person, so my testimony is true.' Undoubtedly so—because he was telling about an insult that had been inflicted. It was not something great and wonderful that he was narrating, that you might be suspicious of his word. On the contrary, he himself, to check the lying tongues of heretics, to predict the future Mysteries, and in consideration of the treasure lying hidden within them, gave an accurate account of what took place.

That well-known prophecy likewise was fulfilled: 'Not a bone of him shall you break.' For, even if this was spoken with reference to the lamb among the Jews, the type preceded for the sake of truth and was, rather, fulfilled in this event. Moreover, that is why the Evangelist cited the Prophet. Since he might not seem to be worthy of credence because he was repeatedly making reference to his own testimony, he summoned Moses to testify that this not only did not take place by accident, but that it had been foretold in writing from of old. This is the meaning of that famous prophecy: 'Not a bone of him shall be broken.'[12]

Again, he was strengthening belief in the words of the Prophet by his own experience. 'I have said these things,' he meant, 'that you may learn that there is a close relationship between the type and the truth.' Do you see how great an effort he made so that a thing that appeared disgraceful and likely to bring shame might, nonetheless, be believed? For the fact that the soldier inflicted an insult on the lifeless body of Christ was much worse than the fact that He was crucified.

'Notwithstanding this,' he meant, 'I have told this, and have told it with great care, that you might believe it.' Let no one, therefore, be incredulous; let no one cast aspersion on our words through shame. For the details which seem to be most ignominious of all are the ones that preach most eloquently of our blessings.

'After these things Joseph of Arimathea came, because he was a disciple—though not one of the Twelve, but perhaps one of the seventy. Thinking that the anger of the Jews had subsided for awhile because of the crucifixion, they ap-

---

12 Cf. Exod. 12.46; Num. 9.12.

proached without fear and took care of the burial. He came, then, and asked permission of Pilate, who granted it. Why, indeed, would he not? Nicodemus lent his assistance also and made it a lavish burial, for they still regarded Christ as merely man. Thus, they brought those spices which are most likely to preserve the body for a long while and not permit it quickly to become the prey of corruption, a procedure which indicated that they thought nothing out of the ordinary of Him, except that they were displaying very tender affection toward Him.

But how is it that none of the Twelve came: not John, not Peter, or any other of His chosen Apostles? Moreover, the disciple did not conceal this fact. If, indeed, someone should claim that it was because they feared the Jews, these men were just as likely to be hindered by that same fear; I say this for Nicodemus also had been 'a secret disciple for fear of the Jews,' the Evangelist declared. Yet, one could not say that he took part in the burial because he now scorned their power, but, in fact, he came despite his fear.

John, on the other hand, who had been present and had seen Christ as He expired, did nothing of the kind. Why is this, then? It seems to me that Joseph was one of the most prominent Jews (and this is clear from the lavishness of the funeral). He was well known to Pilate and for this reason obtained the permission. Moreover, he buried Him, not as a condemned criminal, but as is customary among the Jews, with lavish expenditure, as a great and illustrious man.

But, as they were pressed for time (for His death took place at the ninth hour, and then, since they had afterwards gone to Pilate and taken away the body, it is probable that evening overtook them, when it was not allowed to work), they placed Him in the tomb that was close at hand. The providence of God ordained that He be placed in a new

tomb where no one had as yet been buried, so that the
Resurrection might not be thought to have taken place in the
case of some other person who was lying there with Him,
and so that the disciples might be able to go there easily and
thus become eye-witnesses of what transpired, since the place
was near at hand—yes, and so that not only they would
be witnesses themselves of the burial, but even Christ's
enemies, also. For the placing of seals on the tomb and
stationing soldiers there as guards testified to the burial.
Indeed, Christ strove to have this clearly acknowledged no
less than the Resurrection. The disciples therefore took
great pains about the burial, so that they proved that He
had actually died.

All the time subsequent to this would certainly confirm
the Resurrection, but if His death had been in doubt and
were not very clearly evident, it would cast doubt upon the
account of the Resurrection. Furthermore, it was not merely
for these reasons that He was buried nearby, but also to prove
the falsity of the story about the theft of the body.

'Now on the first day of the week,' that is, on the Lord's
Day, at daybreak, 'Mary Magdalen came early and saw the
stone taken away from the tomb.' He had arisen while the
stone and the seals still lay on the tomb. But, since it was
necessary for the others also to be informed, the tomb opened
after the Resurrection, and in this way the event would gain
credence. It was this circumstance, in fact, that startled
Mary. She had very tender affection for her Master, and
therefore, when the Sabbath had passed she could not bear
to remain inactive, but went at crack of dawn, in the desire
to obtain some consolation from the place.

Now, when she saw the place and the stone taken away,
she did not enter, or stoop and look in, but ran to the disciples in great excitement. The thing that most concerned

her was this: she wished to learn what had become of Christ's body. I say this for the fact that she ran indicates this and her words prove it. She cried: 'They have taken away my Lord and I do not know where they have laid Him.' Do you see how she did not yet understand anything clearly about the Resurrection, but thought that the location of the body had been changed, so she told everything to the disciples as the situation appeared to her?

Moreover, the Evangelist did not deprive the woman of her extraordinary claim to fame, nor did he think it a disgrace to have first learned these things from a woman who had set out in the darkness of night. Thus, his honesty always gleams brightly everywhere in his Gospel.

Accordingly, when she had come and said these things, the Apostles on hearing them hurried with great eagerness to the tomb and saw the linen cloths lying there, a circumstance which was a sign that the Resurrection had taken place. For, if some persons had changed the location of the body, they would not have stripped the body in doing this. Or, if they had stolen it, they would not have taken the trouble to take the handkerchief from the head[13] and roll it up and put it 'in a place by itself.' How differently would they have done it? They would have taken the body just as it was.

Indeed, it was for this reason that John, anticipating this discussion, said that Christ was buried with a great deal of myrrh, because this would glue together the linen cloths on

---

13 'Handkerchief' is the Confraternity translation of the Greek σουδάριον. For arguments supporting the opinion that the word signifies rather the shroud of Christ, cf. P. Barbet, *A Doctor at Calvary* (New York 1953) 137-149.

the body as solidly as lead.[14] Further, when you would hear, also, that the handkerchief was lying in its own place, you would not follow the opinion of those who declared that the body was stolen. For the thief would not have been so foolish as to expend effort on such a trifling detail. For what reason, indeed, would he cast the handkerchief aside? And how would he escape notice as he did so? I say this for he probably would waste time on this and be detected because of this delaying.

But why in the world were the linen cloths lying there in one spot and the handkerchief .folded up in another? That you might realize that it was not the work of men in haste or agitation to put the cloths in one place and the handkerchief in another, and to fold the latter. Because of this fact the Apostles believed in the Resurrection. That is why it was after this that Christ appeared to them, since they were now disposed to believe because of what they had seen.

Notice here, also, the humility of the Evangelist as he testified to the carefulness of Peter's examination of the tomb. For, though John had arrived there first and had seen the linen cloths lying there, he did not investigate any further, but stood aside. But Peter eagerly went within and closely examined everything, obtained a more detailed view, and then John was summoned in to look. Entering after Peter, he, too, saw the grave clothes lying there and separated from each other. Certainly, to have separated them and to have placed this one in one spot, and the other, folded, in another,

---

14 The mixture of myrrh and aloes impregnated the shroud enfolding Christ's body, and would harden as it dried. These substances were used here for the purpose of temporary preservation only, because lack of time made it impossible to follow the Jewish burial customs of the day in their entirety. The Evangelists Mark and Luke note that, when the women came to the tomb on Easter morn, they were bringing aromatic spices, intending to wash, anoint, and dress the body properly. Cf. E. Levesque, 'Ebaumement,' *DB* 2 (1899) 1729; P. Barbet, *op. cit.* 140.

was the work of someone acting with careful deliberation and not that of someone acting hurriedly and haphazard.

Now, when you hear that the Lord rose from the dead without the covering of His shroud, cease from your foolishness regarding funerals. What meaning has this excessive and silly extravagance which inflicts great hardship on the mourners and is of no benefit to the departed but, if we must say so, is even harmful? For the lavishness of the burial has frequently been responsible for grave-robbing and has caused him who had been so carefully entombed to be cast out naked and unburied. But, O vainglory, what great despotism it exercises even in grief, what great folly!

Many men, of course, in order that the grave may not be robbed, cut short those thin linen cloths and fill them with many spices so that they become doubly useless to thieves, and have handed them over to the earth thus. Is this not the deed of madmen, the work of idiots: to make an ambitious display and then to make it vanish again?

'Yes,' they say, 'but we contrive all these devices so that all may remain in safety with the corpse.'

What, then, if the grave-robbers do not take this, will the moths and the worms not seize upon it? And more than that—if the moths and the worms do not take it, will time and decay not destroy it? However, let us suppose that neither grave-robbers, nor moths, nor worms, nor time, nor anything else consumes what lies there, but that the body remains incorrupt until its resurrection, and that these trappings stay new and fresh and intact, what benefit will the departed derive from them when the body arises in its nakedness, while these things remain here and give us no help at all in that dread accounting?

'Why, then,' you will ask, 'did Christ have an elaborate burial?' Be most careful not to compare His case with that of ordinary men, for the sinful woman even poured ointment on His sacred feet. However, if we must say a word regarding these matters: in the first place, these things were done by people who did not yet grasp the teaching about the Resurrection. It was for this reason that the Evangelist said: 'After the Jewish manner [of preparing for burial].'

Those who were doing this honor to Christ were not any of the Twelve; on the contrary, it was the latter who did not pay Him much external honor at all. The Twelve, in fact, did not honor Him by assisting at His burial, but by their own death and sacrifice and by risking danger for His sake. If the funeral was indeed honor, it was much less than what I have just mentioned. Besides, as I said, our present discussion is about the funerals of men; at that time it was the Lord to whom this lavish burial was accorded.

Moreover, that you might learn that Christ has no esteem for these things He said: 'You saw me hungry and you gave me to eat; thirsty, and you gave me to drink; naked, and you covered me'![15] Nowhere, however, did He say: 'You saw me dead, and you buried me.'

Now, I am saying these things, not to do away with burial —God forbid—but to put an end to extravagance and untimely ambition. 'Yet,' you will say, 'suffering and grief and sympathy for the departed inspire us to do these things.' But these trappings are not an expression of sympathy for the departed, but of vainglory. If you actually do desire to show your grief for the dead, I will show you another kind of burial, and will teach you how to put garments on him that will rise with him and will give him a splendid appearance. These are indeed garments not consumed by moths, or wasted by time, or stolen by grave-robbers. What kind are they, then? The covering of almsgiving.

This garment will rise with him, for the seal of almsgiving is on him. Those will be resplendent in these garments who

15 Cf. Matt. 25.35,37.

then hear 'You gave me to eat when I was hungry.' These are the things that make men illustrious, these make them famous, these place them in safety. Those others that are now in vogue are nothing else than food for moths and sustenance for worms.

I am saying this, not to forbid funerals, but I urge that these be conducted with moderation, so as to cover the body and not consign it naked to the earth. For, if it is prescribed for the living to have nothing more than their clothing, much more is this applicable to the dead.[16] The body of a dead man does not need clothing, as it did when alive and breathing. When alive, we need the covering of clothing both as protection against cold, and because of modesty. When dead, however, we need grave-clothes for none of these reasons, but merely lest the body might lie naked. Moreover, even better than our shroud, we have the earth as a very beautiful covering and one more suited to the nature of such bodies as ours. Well, then, if nothing superfluous ought to be sought for, where there are such great needs, much more is excessive display untimely where there is no such necessity.

'But those who view the funeral will laugh at it,' you object. Now, if there is someone present who laughs, you ought most especially not to make much account of anyone so very foolish. In reality, there are many who will rather feel admiration and will applaud our truly wise conduct. For, it is not this that deserves ridicule, but the things which we now do at funerals: weeping, mourning, burying ourselves with the departed. These things do indeed deserve ridicule and punishment.

To behave with true wisdom, on the contrary, both in these matters and in observing due proportion in grave-clothes, will surely win rewards and praises for us. All will commend us and will wonder at the power of Christ and

---

16 Cf. Matt. 10.9,10.

say: 'Heavens, how great is the strength of Him who was crucified! He has persuaded men, who are to die and perish, that death is not death; therefore, they do not act like men who are themselves to perish, but as if sending the dead ahead to a better abode. He has convinced them that this corruptible body of clay will be clad in the garment of immortality, more splendid by far than garments of silk and cloth of gold. For this reason, they do not take much trouble about the grave, but fix their thoughts on the really worthwhile burial: an exemplary life.'

These are the things they will say if they see us acting with true wisdom; but if, on the contrary they see us bent over with grief, playing the woman with tears, surrounded by a group of wailing women, they will ridicule and make fun of us, and condemn us on numberless counts, criticizing our excessive expenditure, our foolish efforts. I say this for we hear all men making these charges, and very rightly so.

What excuse shall we have if we richly adorn the body which is destined to be consumed by decay and worms, while we ignore Christ who is thirsty as He goes about, naked and friendless? Let us cease, then, from this senseless, exaggerated care of the dead. Let us us bury the departed in such a way as to be of benefit both to ourselves and to them to the glory of God. Let us make payment in their behalf of generous alms; let us send with them the best traveling expenses. If, in truth, the memory of illustrious men who have died has been of benefit to the living ('For, 'Scripture says, 'I will protect this city for my own sake and for David my servant's sake'),[17] almsgiving is of still greater benefit. This, indeed, this has even raised the dead, as when the widows stood about [Peter] showing how much Dorcas used to do while she was among them.[18]

17 4 Kings 19.34.
18 Cf. Acts 9.36-43.

Therefore, when a man is at the point of death, let his next of kin make the preparations for the funeral, and let him persuade the dying man to bequeath something to the needy. Let him send him to the grave with this kind of grave-clothes; let him also persuade him to leave Christ as his heir. For, if those who include kings in the list of their heirs leave boundless security to their kinsmen by so doing, consider what great advantage a man will derive, both for himself and for all who belong to him, if he leaves Christ as his heir, along with his sons. This kind of funeral is a beautiful one, and is of benefit both to those who remain on earth and to the departed.

If we have funerals of this kind, we shall be brilliantly adorned at the time of our resurrection; but, if we take care of the body and neglect the soul, we shall endure many fearful sufferings then and will incur much ridicule. For, the ignominy resulting from departing this life destitute of virtue is not small. The body that is cast out unburied is not as grievously shamed as the soul that then appears without virtue.

Let us clothe ourselves in this, let us cover ourselves with it, especially during all our time here. But if we have neglected it here, let us repair our negligence when we are dying; let us lay a strict charge upon our relatives to aid us after our death by almsgiving. Assisted by one another in this way, let us be altogether confident of our eternal reward by the grace and mercy of our Lord Jesus Christ. Glory, power, honor be to Him, together with the Father and the Holy Spirit, now and always and forever and ever. Amen.

Homily 86 (John 20.10-23)

'The disciples therefore went away again to their home. But Mary was standing outside weeping at the tomb.'[1]

How tender-hearted and inclined to sympathy is woman-kind! I am mentioning this that you may not wonder why in the world it was that, while Mary was weeping bitterly at the tomb, Peter displayed no such emotion. 'The disciples,' the Evangelist stated, 'went away to their home, while she remained standing there weeping.'

She did this because she was by nature very easily discouraged, and she did not yet understand clearly the doctrine of the Resurrection as the others did. On seeing the linen cloths, they believed that Christ had risen, and they went away to their home, mute with awe. Yet why did they not go away at once to Galilee, as they had been bidden to do before the Passion? Perhaps they were waiting for the rest to come, or else they were still in a state of great bewilderment. At any rate, they went away, while she remained standing at the spot.

Even the sight of the tomb was a great source of consolation, as I have said. Do you see that, the better to revive her courage, she leaned forward and tried to look at the spot where the body had lain? Therefore, she received no small reward for her great earnestness. For, it was the woman who first saw what the disciples had not seen: namely, angels sitting, one at the feet and the other at the head, in white, and with a manner radiating great brightness and joy. Since the woman was not sufficiently spiritual-minded to grasp the fact of the Resurrection from the grave-clothes, further evidence was added and she beheld angels sitting in bright array, so as to afford her gradual relief from the suffering caused by the empty tomb, and to give her consolation.

---

1 John 20.10,11.

However, they said nothing to her of the Resurrection, but led her on only by degrees to this teaching. She beheld their shining faces—out of the ordinary in their brightness; she beheld their splendid appearance; she heard a sympathetic voice. What did it say? 'Woman, why art thou weeping?' And by means of all these things, as if through a door gradually opening, little by little she was brought to an understanding of the Resurrection. Moreover, the way they were seated led her to question them, for they certainly appeared to know what had taken place. For this reason they were not sitting together, but separated from one another. Since it was not likely that she would venture to begin the inquiry herself, they led her to start conversing with them by asking her a question and also by the way they were sitting.

What reply, then, did she make? She spoke warmly and tenderly: 'They have taken away my Lord, and I do not know where they have laid him.' What are you saying? Do you not yet know about the Resurrection? Are you still thinking about the location of the body?

Do you perceive that she had not yet accepted this sublime doctrine? 'When she had said this she turned around.' But how was it logical for her to turn around, when she had just begun to talk with them and had not yet heard any information from them? It seems to me that as she said these words, Christ suddenly appeared behind her and startled the angels who, on beholding the Master, immediately showed by their attitude, by their gaze, and by their movements, that they were looking at the Lord. This awakened the curiosity of the woman and caused her to turn around.

He appeared to the angels, then, as He was,[2] but did not show Himself to the woman in the same way, so as not to awe her from the start by the sight. On the contrary, He appeared to her under a humble and ordinary guise. And it

2 That is, in His glorified body.

is evident from her words that she even thought He was a gardener. However, it was not desirable to lead so lowly a person as this woman suddenly to lofty considerations, but, rather, to do so gradually. Therefore, He in His turn asked: 'Woman, why are thou weeping? Whom dost thou seek?'

This implied that He knew what she desired to ask, and induced her to reply. Since the woman also was conscious of this, she did not yet mention the name of Jesus, but said, as if her inquirer knew about whom she was seeking information: 'If thou hast removed him, tell me where thou hast laid him and I will take him away.' Once again she was talking of placing and taking away and removing, as if the conversation concerned a corpse. That is, her words meant: 'If you have taken Him away from there out of fear of the Jews, tell me and I will take possession of Him.' What great good will and tenderness the woman showed! But her thoughts were not as yet fixed on the sublime. That is why He finally revealed His presence to her, not by the sight of Him, but by His voice.

Indeed, just as He was at one time recognized by the Jews, at another, unknown, even though actually present, so also, when He spoke, He made Himself known only when He wished. I say this for, when he said to the Jews: 'Whom do you seek?'[3] they recognized neither His face nor His voice until He wished them to do so. That is what also happened in this instance. He merely called her by name, to reproach and chide her because she persisted in these ideas of Him who was alive again.

But why is it that she now 'turned' and spoke to Him, if He was actually already conversing with her? It seems to me that when she had said the words, 'Where thou hast laid him,' she turned back to the angels to ask them why they had seemed so amazed, and then, when Christ called her by

3 John 18.7.

name, she turned toward Him again and from them, and He revealed Himself by His voice. For, when He called her 'Mary,' then she recognized Him. Thus, her recognition was brought about, not by the vision of Him, but by His voice.

Now, if some are inclined to ask: 'How do you know that the angels were struck with astonishment and that it was for this reason the woman turned around?' they will also inquire here: 'How is it evident that she touched Him and fell at His feet?' However, just as this is evident from the words, 'Do not touch me,' so also the other is implied in the fact that the Evangelist states that she turned around.

But why did He say: 'Do not touch me'? Some maintain that she was asking for a spiritual favor, since she had heard Him speaking of it to His disciples: 'If I go to the Father, I will ask him, and he will give you another Advocate.'[4]

Yet, how could she have heard Him say this, when she was not in the company of His disciples? Besides, such an interpretation as this is far removed from the meaning of this passage. Moreover, how could she be making a request, when He had not yet gone to the Father? What does it mean, then? It seems to me that she wished to enjoy His presence still, in the same way as before, and because of her joy at seeing Him, had no realization of His greatness, even though He had become much more excellent in bodily appearance. Thus, to lead her to abandon this notion and to refrain from addressing Him too familiarly (for He does not appear after this conversing so familiarly even with His disciples), He elevated her thoughts so that she would treat Him with a more reverential attitude.

Accordingly, if He had said: 'Do not touch me as you did before, because things are not the same now, and I will not associate with you in future in the same way as before,' it would seem somewhat harsh and boastful. But when He

---

4 John 14.3,16.

said: 'I have not yet ascended to my Father,' even though the words were without offense, they meant the same thing. By saying ' I have not yet ascended' He meant that He was going to do so without delay; and that, because He was on the point of departing and of ceasing to be among men any longer, she ought not to regard Him in the same way as before. Moreover, what follows makes it clear that this is so.

'Go to my brethren and say to them. "I ascend to my Father and your Father, to my God and your God.' Yet, He was going to do this only after forty days. How it is, then, that He said this? In the desire to uplift her thoughts and make her realize that He was actually going away to heaven. And the words, 'My Father and your Father' and 'My God and your God,' have reference to the Incarnation, just as the act of ascending belongs to His human body. For He was addressing these words to one who did not yet realize His true greatness.

'Is the Father His Father in one way, and ours in another, then?'

Of course He is. For, if He is the God of the just in a way different from the rest of men, much more truly is this so of the Son and of us. By saying 'Tell my brethren' He was pointing out the difference in their relationship, lest they conjure up some idea of His and their equality by reason of His other words. He Himself would indeed sit on the throne of His Father, while they would be allowed to stand near it. So that, even if He did become our brother as far as to become flesh, there is a great difference in dignity, and it is not even possible to say how great the difference is. Accordingly, she went away to tell the disciples about these things, so noble a thing is fidelity and devotedness.

But how is it that the disciples were not grieved because He was about to leave them, and why did they not say the same things as before? Before this they felt as they did, because

He was going to die, but now why would they be sad when He was risen from the dead? She reported both the vision of Christ and His words, and this was enough to give them consolation.

However, it was probable that the disciples, on hearing these things, would either refuse to believe the woman or, if they believed her, feel regret that He had not deemed them worthy of the apparition, even though He sent a message that He would appear to them in Galilee. Accordingly, in order that they might not be troubled by these thoughts, He did not allow even one day to pass, but induced them to desire to see Him, both because they saw the evidence that He had now risen and because they heard about it from the woman. Thus, when they were eagerly longing to see Him and were, besides, extremely fearful (and this very feeling made their desire even stronger,) late in the day He then stood in their midst and in a most astonishing way.

Now, why in the world did He appear to them in the evening? Because at that hour it was most likely that they were particularly fearful. But the marvel is: how is it that they did not think Him a ghost? This was remarkable for He entered despite the closed doors, and His coming was sudden. The chief reason was that the woman had greatly aroused their faith ahead of time, and then, too, He showed them the vision clearly and familiarly. Moreover, He did not come to them during the day, so that they might all be gathered together, for their consternation at the sight would be great. He did not even knock at the door, but stood suddenly in their midst and showed them His side and His hands. At the same time He calmed with His voice the stormy thoughts that began to seethe in their minds and said: 'Peace be to you,' that is, 'Do not be afraid.'[5] By these words He was recalling to them the words which He addressed to them before

5 Reminiscent of the incident of the storm at sea; cf. Mark 4.37-40.

the crucifixion: 'My peace I leave with you'; and again: 'In me you have peace. In the world you will have affliction.'[6]

'The disciples therefore rejoiced at the sight of the Lord.' Do you perceive that His words were being fulfilled in fact? For, before the crucifixion He had said: 'I will see you again and your heart shall rejoice, and your joy no one shall take from you.'[7] This He was now carrying out in deed. Furthermore, all these things moved them to more lively faith. For, since they had to wage unending warfare against the Jews, He often repeated the words: 'Peace be to you,' to give them consolation proportionate to the strife.

This was the first word He spoke to them after the resurrection (and therefore Paul frequently said: 'Grace be to you and peace').[8] To the women, however, He announced good tidings of joy, because of the fact that that sex existed in sorrow and had been afflicted with pain and distress as the first curse.[9] Therefore, it was appropriate for Him to announce peace to the men, because of their strife, and to the women joy, because of their sorrow. Having freed them from all sadness, He went on to speak of the victory achieved by the Cross, and this was peace.

Then, when He had removed all the hindrances, and had established the fact of His brilliant victory, and set everything right, He finally said: 'As the Father has sent me, I also send you. You will have no difficulty at all, both by reason of the events that have already taken place and also by reason of the fact that I who send you am of exalted dignity.' By His words He was uplifting their spirits, and giving indisputable proof that they could have confidence in Him, if they would undertake the task He was assigning.

---

6 Cf. John 14.27; 16.33.
7 John 16.22.
8 See for example, Rom. 1.7.
9 Cf. Gen. 3.16.

Moreover, He was no longer asking the Father to help them, but was giving them power by His own authority. 'For, He breathed on them and said: "Receive the Holy Spirit; whose sins you shall forgive, they are forgiven them; and whose sins you shall retain, they are retained." ' Like a king who, as he sends out governors, gives them power to imprison, and also to release from prison, so likewise, in sending the disciples, He endowed them with this power.

How it is, then, that He said: 'If I do not go He will not come,'[10] yet gave them the Spirit? Some say that He did not actually give them the Spirit at this time, but by breathing on them put them in the proper dispositions to receive Him. For, if Daniel was astounded on beholding an angel, what effect would it not have had on them when they received that ineffable grace, if He had not prepared the disciples themselves beforehand? That is why the Evangelist did not say: 'He said, "You have received the Holy Spirit," but, "Receive the Holy Spirit." '

However, one would not err in saying that at that time they did receive a certain spiritual power and grace—though not to raise the dead and to perform miracles, but to forgive sins, for the gifts of the Spirit are of various kinds.[11] Therefore, He added: 'Whose sins you shall forgive, they are forgiven,' to point out what kind of power He was giving them.

In that place, also, forty days later,[12] they received the power of miracles. Therefore, He said: 'You shall receive power when the Holy Spirit comes upon you and you shall be witnesses for me in Jerusalem and in all Judea,' and they did become witnesses by their miracles. This is so, for

10 John 16.7.
11 Cf. 1 Cor. 12.4-11.
12 The occasion when Christ said the words that immediately follow here, was forty days later, that is, just before the Ascension; cf. Acts 1.8. But the coming of the Holy Spirit and the gift of the power of miracles took place fifty days after the Resurrection.

ineffable is the grace of the Spirit and manifold are His gifts. Moreover, this took place that you might learn that the gifts and power of the Father and of the Son and of the Holy Spirit are one. What appears to be proper to the Father also belongs in reality to the Son and to the Holy Spirit.

'How is it, then,' you will say, 'that no one comes to the Son "unless the Father draw Him"?'

But this is shown to be true of the Son, also, for He said: 'I am the way; no one comes to the Father but through me.' And notice that the same thing is true of the Spirit, also. For 'No one can say, "Jesus Christ is Lord," except in the Holy Spirit.'[13] And again, we are told that Apostles have been given to the Church, at one time by the Father, at another by the Son, and at another by the Holy Spirit, so we see that the varieties of gifts belong to the Father and to the Son and to the Holy Spirit.

Let us, then, exert every effort so that we may be able to possess the Holy Spirit within ourselves, and let us hold in great honor those who have been entrusted with His power. Great indeed is the dignity of the priesthood. 'Whose sins you shall forgive, they are forgiven them,' He said. And therefore Paul declared: 'Obey your superiors and be subject to them,'[14] and regard them with the greatest esteem.

Now, you take care of your own affairs, and if you conduct them well, you will have no reckoning to give of the rest. The priest, on the contrary, even if he orders his own life well, but should not concern himself zealously about your interests, and those of all entrusted to his care, will depart with the wicked into hell. Yes, frequently, though not liable to punishment because of his own shortcomings, he goes to perdition because of yours, if he should fail to perform

---

13 John 6.44; 14.6; 1 Cor. 12.3.
14 Heb. 13.17.

every duty for which he is responsible. Therefore, since you are aware of the magnitude of their peril, show lively good will toward your priests. Paul was saying this indirectly when he declared: 'They keep watch for the sake of your souls,' and not merely that, but 'as having to render an account of them.' Therefore, they ought to enjoy great respect from you.

However, if you join the rest in disrespect toward them, neither you nor your affairs will prosper. For, as long as the pilot remains in peace of mind, the possessions of the passengers will be safe, but, if he is unnerved because they are insulting him and annoying him, he cannot be as vigilant and is unable to practice his skill in the same way, and involves the passengers in countless misfortunes, without meaning to do so. It is the same way with the priest, too: if he enjoys respect from you, he will be able to take care of your interests well; if, on the contrary, you are a source of trouble to your priests, thus weakening their hands, you will cause them to be easily overcome by the waves, even if they be very stalwart.

Remember what Christ said about the Jews: 'The Scribes and the Pharisees have sat on the chair of Moses. All things, therefore, that they command you, do.'[15] Now, however, it is possible to say, not 'The priests have sat on the chair of Moses,' but 'on the chair of Christ,' for they have received their teachings from Him. And for this reason Paul said: 'On behalf of Christ we are acting as ambassadors, God, as it were, appealing through us.'[16]

Do you not see that in the case of temporal rulers all men are submissive to them, even though they are often of nobler race, and superior in conduct and wisdom to those who are over them? Notwithstanding this, out of consideration for the one who appointed those in office, they consider these

15 Matt. 23.2,3.
16 2 Cor. 5.20.

differences of no account, but show respect for the decision of their king, no matter who the man is who receives the power to rule. Thus, where a man has made an appointment there is so much respect shown, but when God is the One who appoints, we despise the man chosen, insult him, keep aiming at him mean blows without number, and, though forbidden to sit in judgment even on our brethren, we sharpen our tongues against our priests.

Now, what excuse do these things deserve, inasmuch as we do not consider the beam in our own eye, while we carefully scrutinize the speck in the eye of the other?[17] Do you not know that by passing judgment in this way you are making the judgment more difficult for yourself?

Now, I am saying these things, not because I approve of those who are exercising their priesthood unworthily, but because I pity them very much and weep for them; yet I do not say, because of this, that it is right for them to be judged by those subject to them and especially by those of very low estate. For, even if their conduct be very blameworthy, if you mind your own affairs you will suffer no loss in those things that have been entrusted to the priest by God.

Indeed, He even caused speech to be uttered by an ass, and bestowed spiritual blessings by the agency of the seer, and acted in behalf of the disobedient Jews by means of the mouth of the animal and the impure tongue of Balaam.[18] Much more certainly, then, will He carry into effect all His designs in your behalf when you are charitable, even if the priests are very remiss, and He will send the Holy Spirit. For, the pure individual does not attract Him because of his personal purity; it is grace that effects everything. Scripture, to be sure, says: 'All things are for your sake, whether Paul,

17 Cf. Matt. 7.3; Luke 6.41.
18 Cf. Num. 22-24.

or Apollos, or Cephas.'[19] Whatever the priest has entrusted to him can be given only by God, and, however far human wisdom may reach, it always appears inferior to that grace.

Furthermore, I am saying these things, not in order that we may conduct our own life in a negligent manner, but lest, perchance, if certain of your superiors should fail to do their duty, you who are subject to them may be storing up punishment for yourselves [by finding fault with them].

Yet why do I mention merely priests? Not even an angel, or an archangel, can effect anything with regard to what is given by God, but Father and Son and Holy Spirit direct everything. The priest simply lends his tongue and furnishes his hand. This is so for it would not be right for those who have embraced the faith to suffer harm with regard to the symbols of our salvation because of the evil conduct of another.

Therefore, since we know these truths, let us fear God, and hold His priests in honor by showing them every mark of respect, in order that we may receive from God a great reward both for our own good works and for the reverence shown toward them—by the grace and mercy of our Lord Jesus Christ. Glory, power, honor be to Him, together with the Father and the Holy Spirit, now and always, and forever and ever. Amen.

---

19 1 Cor. 3.22.

Homily 87 (John 20.24-21.14)

'Now Thomas, one of the Twelve, called the Twin, was not with them when Jesus came. The other disciples therefore said to him, "We have seen the Lord." But he said, "Unless I see, I will not believe," ' etc.[1]

Just as it is an indication of gullibility to believe easily and carelessly, so to scrutinize and examine immoderately before believing is the mark of an obstinate will. That is why Thomas is blameworthy. For he refused to believe the Apostles when they said: 'We have seen the Lord,' not so much because he did not trust them, as because he considered the thing an impossibility—that is, resurrection from the dead. He did not say: 'I do not believe you,' but, 'Unless I put my hand into his side, I will not believe.'

How did it happen, then, that though all the Apostles were gathered in one place, he alone was not with them? It is likely that at that time he had not yet returned from the dispersion of the disciples that had recently taken place after the death of Christ. And when you see the disciple refusing to believe, reflect on the mercy shown by the Lord: how even for the sake of one soul He showed Himself with His wounds, and came so that He might save even the one soul, despite the fact that this one was more crass than the others. That is why he was seeking to have his faith substantiated by the least spiritual of the senses, and did not even believe his eyes. He did not say: 'Unless I see Him,' but, 'Unless I feel Him with my hands, lest what is seen be somehow a ghost.'

Even though the disciples deserved to be believed when they reported these things, and Christ Himself, also, since He had promised the Resurrection, nevertheless, when Thomas demanded more, Christ did not refuse it to him. Yet why did

---

1 John 20.24,25.

He not appear to him immediately, but only after eight days had passed? So that in the interval Thomas would be instructed by the disciples, and by hearing the same thing repeated would be inflamed with more ardent desire and become stronger in his faith afterwards.

'From what source had he learned that Christ's side was pierced?' He had heard it from the disciples.

'How is it, then, that he believed that, but did not believe the other story?' Because the latter was very strange and unusual. But please notice the honesty of the Apostles, and how they did not conceal the least details, neither their own actions nor those of others, but recorded them all with great truthfulness.

Jesus once again stood in their midst, but did not wait to be approved by Thomas, or to hear from him any such conditions as he had laid down for accepting the apparition as genuine. On the contrary, without Thomas' saying anything, He Himself forestalled him by fulfilling the desires he had expressed, thus proving that He was actually present when Thomas had uttered those words to the disciples. I say this for He used the selfsame words, though very reproachfully, and with the addition of an admonition for his future conduct.

After saying: 'Bring thy finger, and see my hands, and put thy hand into my side,' He added: 'and be not unbelieving, but believing.' Do you see that Thomas was hesitating because of his unbelief? However, this was before he had received the Spirit. Afterwards they no longer doubted, but were henceforth unhesitating in their belief.

But it was not only by these words that He reproved him, but also by His next words. For, when Thomas, now fully convinced, could breathe again and cried out: 'My Lord and my God,' Christ said: 'Because thou hast seen me, thou hast believed. Blessed are they who have not seen, and yet have believed.' This is indeed a proof of faith, namely, to accept what we have not seen. For, 'Faith is the substance of things to be hoped for, the evidence of things that are not seen.'[2] Moreover, Christ was here declaring that not only were His disciples blessed, but also those to come after them, who would believe.

'Yet,' you will object, 'the disciples did see Him and they believed.' However, they were not looking for any such evidence, but immediately accepted the doctrine of the Resurrection from the linen cloths, and before they had beheld His body they showed that their faith in Him was without reservation. Therefore, when someone now says: 'I wish I had lived at that time and had seen Christ working miracles,' let him remember: 'Blessed are they who have not seen, and yet have believed.'

But, one might understandably be puzzled as to how an incorruptible body could show marks of the nails and be capable of being touched by a mortal hand. However, do not be disturbed, for the phenomenon was an evidence of Christ's condescension. To be sure, a body so tenuous and unsubstantial that it entered through doors that were shut was entirely lacking in density. But Christ made His appearance as He did so that the Resurrection would be believed and so that they would know that it was He—the very one who had been crucified—and not someone else who had arisen instead of Him.

That is why He arose with the marks of the crucifixion still evident and it was for this reason that He partook of food. In fact, the Apostles repeatedly cited this as a proof of the resurrection and said: 'We who ate and drank with Him.[3] Therefore, just as when we saw Him walking on the waves, before the crucifixion, we did not say that body of His was of a nature different from our, so when, after the Resurrec-

2 Heb. 11.1.
3 Acts 10.41.

tion, we see that He still has His wounds, we do not say that He is, therefore, still mortal. It is for the sake of the disciple that He is making His appearance in this way.'

'Many other signs also Jesus worked.' Since this Evangelist told of fewer miracles than the others did, he mentioned that not even the others have told all, but only as many as were sufficient to win their listeners to believe. 'For if all of them should be written,' he said, 'not even the world, I think, could hold the books.'[4]

From this it is evident that it was not for reasons of ambition that they wrote what they did, but only that it might be of use. How, indeed, could men who omitted to mention many more things have written those they did tell, because of ambition?

'But why, then, did they not tell all of them?'

More especially because of the large number; besides, they were thinking of the obvious truth that the man who did not believe the ones mentioned would not believe if these were more numerous. On the other hand, the man who accepted them would need no more to confirm his faith.

In this passage, however, it seems to me that John was referring, for the moment, only to the miracles after the Resurrection, and that is why he said: 'in the sight of his disciples.' For, just as, before the Resurrection, it was necessary for many miracles to take place, that they might believe that Christ is the Son of God, so also, after the Resurrection, this was necessary that they might accept the fact that He had risen. Another reason, also, why John added: 'in the sight of his disciples,' is because Christ associated only with them after the Resurrection. And therefore He had said: '[Yet a little while] and the world no longer sees me.'[5]

Next, that you might learn that it was only these things

4 John 21.25.
5 John 14.19.

that took place for the sake of the disciples alone, John added: 'and that believing you may have everlasting life in his name.' Here He was addressing humanity in general, and making it clear that in writing the Gospel he was doing a favor, not to Him in whom we believe, but most of all to us ourselves. 'In his name,' that is, 'through Him,' for He Himself is the Life.

'After these things he manifested himself again to his disciples at the sea of Tiberias.' Do you see that He was not continuously with them, or as He had been previously? He appeared in the evening, and then disappeared; next, after eight days He appeared once again, and again disappeared; then, later, He appeared to them at the sea, and once more caused great awe.

But, what is the meaning of 'He manifested himself'? From this it is clear that He was not seen unless He permitted it, because henceforth His body was glorious and immortal. And why did he mention the place? To show that He had freed them from most of their fear, so that they now went out of the house and traveled about, everywhere. No longer did they remain shut up in the house, but they went to Galilee to avoid danger from the Jews.

Simon, then, went fishing. Because Christ Himself was not always with them, and the Spirit had not been given, and at that time they had not yet received their sacred mission and so had nothing to do, they returned to their trade. 'There were together Simon and Thomas and Nathanael, who had been called by Philip, and the sons of Zebedee, and two others.' Since they had nothing to do they therefore returned to fishing, and they did this at night because of being very fearful. At least, Luke recorded that they were very much afraid—though the occasion of which he was speaking is not this one but another.[6] Moreover, the other

---

6 Cf. Luke 24.37.

disciples followed, because they now felt closely bound to one another, and at the same time they wished to see the fishing and to put their leisure to good use.

When they were weary and discouraged, then Jesus appeared to them, yet refrained from making His identity clear at once, so that He might enter into conversation with them. Therefore, He said to them: 'Have you anything to eat?' For the moment He was speaking in human fashion, as if he were going to buy something from them. But as they replied that they had nothing, He bade them to cast the net to the right of the boat. And when they cast it they caught a large haul.

Now, in recognizing Him, the disciples Peter and John once again showed the traits peculiar to their respective characters. For, Peter was more ardent, John, more spiritual; Peter was more impulsive, John, more cautious. Therefore, John was the first to recognize Jesus, while Peter was the first to go to Him. They did so for the indications that it was He were no mere coincidences.

What were these signs? In the first place, the fact that the fishes they caught were so many; besides, the net was not torn; then, also, the fact that, before they landed, a fire had been prepared, and fish and bread were laid upon it. For He now did not start from something already existing in making these, as He had done before the crucifixion [in making the loaves and fishes,] according to some design of divine Providence.

As soon as Peter recognized Him, then, he cast everything aside—fish and nets—and girded himself. Do you see both his respect and his love? Even though they were only two hundred cubits away, he did not even wait for the boat to get to Him, but came to Him, swimming.

What did Jesus say, then? 'Come and breakfast.' And no one dared ask Him any questions. No longer, indeed, did they feel the same freedom towards Him; no longer were they as forward; now they did not even begin a conversation with Him, but in silence and great reverence and respect sat down and listened to Him attentively. For 'they knew that it was the Lord.' And therefore they did not ask: 'Who art thou?'

Moreover, when they saw that His appearance was different and very extraordinary, they were filled with wonderment and wished to ask something about it. However, fear, and the fact that they knew that it was not anyone else, but certainly He, checked their questioning, and they merely continued eating the things which He had made for them by exercising greater power than ever. Here He did not look up to heaven, or do those human things He did before, thus showing that those things also were done out of condescension to their weakness.[7]

But, because He did not stay with them constantly, or in the same way as before, the Evangelist declared: 'This is the third time that he appeared to them after he had risen from the dead.' And He bade them to bring some of the fishes, to show that what they had seen was not an illusion. Here, however, John did not say that He partook of food with them, though Luke said elsewhere of Him: 'He was eating with them.'[8] How this was done is not for us to say, for it took place in some very remarkable way, not because His nature now needed food but out of condescension to our human weakness, to prove the Resurrection.

---

7 A reference to the fact that on the occasion of the multiplication of the loaves and fishes, the Evangelist records that Christ did not create them out of nothing, but made use of the small quantity of loaves and fishes available, and miraculously increased the supply. Before performing the miracle He prayed. Cf. John 6.7-11. Likewise, before raising Lazarus, He looked up to heaven and prayed. Cf. John 11.41-42. See also Homilies 42 and 64. Vol. I 429-431; II 190-195, where the implications of these actions are discussed in detail.

8 Acts 1.4.

Perhaps on hearing these things you may become inflamed with love for Christ and call those men blessed who were actually in His company, and likewise those who will be with Him on the day of the general resurrection. Well, then, let us exert every effort so that we may behold that wonderful countenance of His. At present, to be sure, when we hear the Gospel, we are on fire with love, and we wish very much that we had lived in those days which He spent on the earth: so as to have heard His voice, and seen His face, and to have come to Him, and touched Him, and done some service for Him. Think, therefore, what it will be like to see Him, no longer in human shape or performing merely human actions, but guarded by angels, in His glorified body, as we ourselves also will be, gazing on Him and likewise enjoying the rest of the happiness which altogether defies expression.

Accordingly, I beseech you, let us so perform all our actions that we may not fail to obtain such glory as this. To obtain it is by no means difficult, if we desire it; or arduous, if we apply ourselves to it. For, 'If we endure, we shall also reign.'[9] What is the meaning of 'If we endure'? If we patiently bear tribulations and persecutions; if we walk the narrow path. The narrow path is unattractive by nature, but becomes easy when we choose to follow it, because of our hope for the future.

'For, our present light affliction, which is for the moment, prepares for us an eternal weight of glory that is beyond all measure; while we look not at the things that are seen, but at the things that are not seen.'[10] Let, us then, shift our gaze to heaven and let us be always thinking about and looking at what belongs there. For, if we are always preoccupied with it, we shall not have any affection for the joys of earth;

---

9 2 Tim. 2.12.
10 2 Cor. 4.17,18.

we shall have no difficulty in bearing sorrow. On the contrary, we shall laugh at these things, or anything resembling them. Consequently, we shall find it impossible to enslave ourselves to things of earth, or to feel uplifted because of them, if we keep our desires fixed only on heavenly joys, and keep our gaze leveled at that kind of love only.

Moreover, why do I say we shall not be troubled by the misfortunes of this life? Indeed, we shall seem not even to be aware of them in future. This, to be sure, is characteristic of love. Every day we think of those whom we love and who are not with us, but are absent. Truly, the despotism exercised by love is a strong one; it separates us from everything else and binds our soul fast to the object of our love.

If we love Christ in this way, everything belonging to this life seems but a shadow; everything seems an illusion and a dream. We, too, shall say: 'Who shall separate us from the love of Christ? Shall tribulation or distress?'[11] He did not mention money, or wealth, or beauty (for these things are altogether worthless and ridiculous, but he listed the things which seem burdensome to us, like hunger, persecution, death. These, too, he despised as nothing, while we alienate ourselves from our Life for the sake of money and shut ourselves off from the Light. Yet Paul preferred neither death, nor life, nor things present, nor things to come, nor any other creature, to his love for God, whereas, if we see a little gold, we burn with desire for it and tread His laws underfoot to get it.

But, if these things are not to be tolerated in theory, this is much more so in practice. For it is a deplorable fact that, though we shudder on hearing about these things, we do not shrink from doing them. On the contrary, we swear rash oaths, and commit perjury, and defraud, and exact usury, and have no regard for chastity, and refrain from earnest

---

11 Rom. 8.35.

prayer, and transgress most of the commandments, and show no consideration for our fellow members, all because of money.

The man who loves money will indeed be the cause of evils without number to his neighbor, and also to himself, along with him. I say this for he will easily give way to anger, and will revile him, will call him a fool, will swear, and perjure, and will not observe even the least commandment of the Old Law. Truly, he who loves gold will not love his neighbor. Yet we are commanded to love even our enemies because of our love for the kingdom of heaven. For, if we shall not be able to enter this kingdom, even though we have fulfilled the commandments of the Old Law, unless our justice exceeds theirs,[12] what excuse can they have who transgress even those commandments? He who loves money not only will not love his enemies, but will even treat his friends as enemies.

Yet, why do I say friends merely? In truth, those who love money have often ignored nature itself. Such a man does not know kinship; he does not keep social amenities in mind; he does not respect age; he has no friend, but is inimical to all men, and, above all, to himself, not only because he is destroying his own soul, but also because he is torturing himself with cares and toils and trials without number. Now, I say this for he will take on journeys, and enmities, and perils, and plots, and anything at all, merely to possess the root of all evil as his own and that he may have much gold to count up. What, then, could be more serious than this malady?

It is a heavy burden, for he deprives himself entirely of luxury and pleasure—for the sake of which men even commit many sins—and also foregoes glory and honor. He who loves money harbors countless suspicions of others, and there are many who are ready to accuse him of wrong-doing,

---

12 That is, that of the Scribes and Pharisees; cf. Matt. 5.20.

many who envy, slander, and plot against him. Those who
have been treated unjustly by him hate him because they have
been wronged. Those who have not been wronged by him fear
that they will and, because they sympathize with the victims,
show the same hostility towards him. Moreover, even those
who are greater and more powerful than he, because they are
resentful and indignant at his treatment of inferiors, yet envious of him, too, are likewise hostile and hate him. But why
do I speak merely of men? Truly, when a man has God war-
ring against him what hope can he have for the future? What
consolation? What refreshment?

The man who loves money will never be able to have the
use of it, but will be a slave and a guard, but not its master.
Since he is always striving to increase it, he will never be
willing to spend it, but will restrict himself and be more
poverty-stricken than any poor man, since he never has any
respite from his greedy desire. Yet money exists, not for us
to keep, but to use. And even if we should intend to store
it away for others, what occupation could be less profitable
than ours, since we labor busily in the effort to get together
all we can, merely in order to hoard it up, and thus prevent
its use in common?

But there is still another malady, no less serious than this
one. Some men, it is true, do bury their riches in the ground,
but others put them away in gluttony and voluptuousness
and excessive drinking, thus adding the punishment for their
licentiousness to that already incurred for their greed. Some,
too, make provision for parasites and flatterers; others, for
gambling and prostitutes; while others take care of still other
expenses of the kind, thus carving out for themselves innumerable paths leading into hell, and avoiding the straight
and narrow one that leads to heaven. Yet, the latter brings
not only a greater reward, but even greater enjoyment than
the others mentioned.

Indeed, the man who gives money to prostitutes will be ridiculous and disgraceful. He will have many struggles and but short-lived pleasure, or, rather, not even short-lived, because, no matter what he gives to these courtesans, they will give him no thanks. For 'a perforated container'[13] is the house of another.

Besides, that sex is rash and Solomon compared the love of a woman to the deep pit.[14] She calls a halt only when she sees that her lover has been stripped of all his possessions; nay, more, she does not even stop then, but decks herself out more elaborately and insults him in his humiliation, and draws ridicule upon him, and causes him so much misfortune that words are inadequate to describe it.

However, the pleasure of those who attain salvation is not like this, for here one does not have a rival in love, but all rejoice and are glad: both those who are well off and those who see that they are. No anger, no grief, no shame or ignominy beset the soul of such a man. On the contrary, he has great peace of conscience and great hope for the future; also, bright glory and abundant esteem, and, more valuable than all these, the approval of God and promise of security from Him. He has not even one obstacle to overcome, no suspicion, but a calm harbor and complete tranquility.

Therefore, keeping all this in mind, and balancing real pleasure against licentiousness, let us choose that which is better, in order that we may also obtain the blessings of the life to come, by the grace and mercy of our Lord Jesus Christ. Glory and power be to Him, forever and ever. Amen.

13 A proverbial expression. The allusion is to the futile task of the Danaids; see E.L. Leutsch and F.G. Schneidewin, *Paroemiographi Graeci* 1 (Gottingen 1841) 33; *Homilies* I 339 n. 14.
14 Cf. Prov. 23.27.

Homily 88 (John 21.15-25)

'When, therefore, they had breakfasted, Jesus said to Simon Peter, "Simon, son of John, dost thou love me more than these do?" He said to him, "Yes, Lord, thou knowest that I love thee." '[1]

There are many virtues which can make us pleasing to God and cause us to appear illustrious and worthy of esteem, but the one that more especially wins favor from on high is loving concern for the welfare of our neighbor, an office which Christ now asked of Peter.

When they had finished eating, 'Jesus said to Simon Peter, "Simon, son of John, dost thou love me more than these do?" He said to him, "Yes, Lord, thou knowest that I love thee." He said to him, "Feed my lambs." '

Now, why in the world did He pass over the other Apostles, and speak to this one about these matters? He was the chosen one of the Apostles, the mouthpiece of the disciples, and the head of the band. That is why Paul also came, on that later occasion, to make inquiries of him rather than of the others.

At the same time, also, Christ entrusted to Peter the primacy over his brethren to show him that in future he must have no fear, because his denial had been completely forgiven. Moreover, He did not bring up the denial at all, or find fault with him for what had happened, but said in effect: 'If you love Me, assume responsibility for your brethren and now show to them the ardent love which you have always displayed towards Me and in which you have gloried. And for the sake of My lambs lay down that life which you used to say you would lay down for Me.'

Then, after being questioned about his love for Christ once, and again a second time, when he had called on

---

1 John 21.15.

Christ as a witness who knew the secrets of his heart, he was thereupon questioned a third time also, and so was greatly disturbed. Fearing, a repetition of what had happened before (for, because he was overconfident at that time, he afterwards was overcome), he therefore once more turned to Him for support. By saying: 'Thou knowest all things,' he meant: 'Thou knowest the past and the future.'

Do you see how he had become a better and a wiser man, now no longer boasting and contradicting? Indeed, it was for this reason that he was greatly disturbed: 'Lest I think I love you, though in reality I do not, just as I had many boastful thoughts before, and was overconfident, and later was overcome by temptation.'

Moreover, three times Christ asked the question and three times gave the same injunction, to show how greatly He esteemed the office of caring for His own lambs, and that to perform this task was most of all a proof of his love for Him. And after speaking to him of his love for Him, Christ foretold to him also the martyrdom that he was going to suffer, to show him that it was not because He did not trust Peter that He spoke as He did, but on the contrary, because He did trust him very much. Moreover, in the desire to show Peter what would be a proof of his love for Christ and also to instruct us about the way in which we must especially love Him, He therefore said: 'When thou wast young thou didst gird thyself and walk where thou wouldst. But when thou art old, others will gird thee and lead thee where thou wouldst not.'

Now, Peter really did wish and desire this, and that is why Christ made this revelation to him. He had said on many occasions: 'I will lay down my life for thee,' and, 'Even if I should have to die with thee, I will not deny thee!'[2] Therefore Christ granted him what he desired.

---

2 John 13.37; Matt. 26.35.

'Then, what is the meaning of "where thou wouldst not"?' He was referring to the feelings of our human nature, and the tendency to self-preservation on the part of the flesh, and meant that the soul unwillingly becomes separated from the body. So that, even if the will was strong, the flesh was weak, despite this.

No one, indeed, lays his body aside without a struggle, since God has ordained this designedly, as I have said before, so that there would not be many self-inflicted deaths. Even though this is the case, the Devil has yet succeeded in caus-ing this to be done, and has driven innumerable men to cliffs and pits. Hence, if the desire of the body for life were not so strong, many would hastily put an end to their life because of some chance indisposition. Accordingly, the words, 'Where thou wouldst not,' refer to the feelings of nature.

How is it that, after saying: 'When thou wast young,' He added: 'When thou art old'? By this He meant that Peter was not young at that time—for actually he was not—but still not yet an old man, but one in the prime of life. Why, then, did He recall to him his previous life? To make clear to Peter His standard of values. For, in the eyes of the world the young man is considered useful, while the aged man is held of no use. 'In what concerns Me this is not so,' He meant, but when old age comes, then nobility shines more brilliantly, manly virtue becomes more evident, unimpeded by youthful passion.'

Moreover, he said this, not to frighten him, but to arouse him, since He knew Peter's love for Him and that he had been feeling this noble emotion strongly for a long time. At the same time, too, He was revealing to him the way he would die. Because Peter had always wanted to be in peril for His sake, 'Take courage,' He was saying, 'for I will satisfy your desire in this way, so that in your old age you must undergo these sufferings which you did not have in your youth.'

Then, for the inspiration of his audience the Evangelist added: 'Now this he said to signify by what manner of death he should glorify God.' He did not say 'he should die,' but 'he should glorify God,' that you might learn that to suffer for Christ is glory and honor for the sufferer.

'And having spoken thus,' the Evangelist declared, 'he said, "Follow me." ' In these words He was once again referring indirectly to His solicitude for Peter and to the fact that He was on terms of intimate friendship with him. And, if someone should say: 'How is it, then, that it was James who received the bishop's chair in Jerusalem?' I would make this reply: that Christ appointed this man, not merely to a chair, but as teacher of the world.

Thereupon, 'Turning round, Peter saw following them the disciple whom Jesus loved, the one who, at the supper, had leaned back upon his breast.' So Peter said: 'Lord, and what of this man?' Why did the Evangelist recall to us that leaning back on Christ's breast? He was recalling it, not undesignedly or by chance, but to show how completely at ease Peter was with Christ after his denial. At the time of the Last Supper he did not dare to question Christ, but turned this task over to the other. He had now been entrusted with the primacy over his brethren. Hence, he not only did not depend on the other disciple to act as intermediary for him, but he even sought for information himself from the Master, on behalf of the other. And it was John who remained silent, while he was the one who spoke to Christ.

Moreover, here he showed the affection he had for the other, for Peter loved John very much. Later events also made this evident and it is revealed both throughout the Gospel and also in the Acts.

Since Christ had predicted great things of him, then, and had entrusted the world to his care, and had foretold his martyrdom, and had shown that his love was greater than that of the others, in the desire to have John share in all this, Peter said: 'What of this man? Will he not travel the same road with us?' On that other occasion, because he was unable himself to ask the question, he caused John to do it for him. Similarly, now, to make return to him, and supposing that John wanted to ask about his own affairs, but did not now have the courage, he took it upon himself to ask.

What, then, did Christ reply? 'If I wish him to remain until I come, what is it to thee?' Since Peter had spoken out of his very deep affection for John and because he was unwilling to be separated from him, Christ said: 'If I wish him to remain, what is it to thee?' to point out to him that however greatly he might love, he did not surpass His love. By these words He was teaching us not to be perturbed, not to be restlessly seeking reasons for anything, beyond the fact that it is His will Because Peter was always impulsive and ready to ask such questions, Christ made this reply to check his enthusiasm once again, and to teach him that he ought not to go too far in his zeal.

'This saying therefore went abroad among the brethren,' that is, the disciples, 'that that disciple was not to die. But Jesus had not said to him: "He is not to die," but rather: "If I wish him to remain until I come, what is it to thee?" '

He meant: 'Do not think that I have the same plans for both of you.' And He was telling Peter this because the personal affection of the two disciples for one another was now no longer fitting. Since they were about to take upon themselves the guardianship of the world, henceforth they ought not to be engrossed in one another; in fact, this could prove very harmful to the world. Therefore, He was saying to him: 'You have been entrusted with a mission; look after it, perform it, fight and struggle for it. What if I do indeed wish for him to remain here? You look after, and take care of, your own affairs.'

Moreover, please notice, in this passage, also, the Evangelist's modesty. For, in telling the conclusion the disciples drew from Christ's words, he corrected it because they did not grasp what He meant. 'Jesus did not say,' he declared, "He is not to die," but, "If I wish him to remain." This is the disciple who bears witness concerning these things and who has written these things, and we know that his witness is true.'

Why in the world was it that, though none of the other Evangelists did this, he alone made a statement of this kind and for the second time testified in his own favor, though this would probably give offense to his audience? What, then, is the reason? It is said that he was later in coming to the task of writing, under the direction and inspiration of God. That is why he repeatedly drew attention to the love of Christ for him, thus hinting at the reason for which he felt impelled to begin to write. Moreover, he kept recalling it for this reason: to show that his work was trustworthy and to make it clear that he was moved by love in coming to this task. 'And I know,' he declared, 'that what he says is true. However, if many still do not believe, it is possible for them to acquire faith from the following fact.' What one? The one that he next mentioned.

'There are, however, many other things that Jesus did,' he said; 'but if every one of these should be written, not even the world itself, I think, could hold the books that would have to be written. From this it is evident that in writing I was not currying favor. Though there were so many things that could have been written I did not even tell as many as the other Evangelists. On the contrary, I omitted most of these and exposed, instead, the plotting of the Jews, the

stoning, the hatred, the insults, the reviling, and revealed
how they called Christ a demoniac and seducer. It is very
clear, therefore, that if I did all this, I was not trying to
curry favor.'

Indeed, someone who was trying to curry favor ought to
have done quite the opposite: concealing uncomplimentary
details, making much of those that lend distinction. Therefore, since he wrote what he did with great certainty, he did
not hesitate to cite his own testimony, challenging his audience to examine the items, one by one, and to test the truth
of the events. Now, it is customary with us, when we think
we are telling something very true, not to refuse to give our
own testimony. If this is our practice much more would it
be that of one who was writing, under the inspiration of the
Spirit, what the rest of the Apostles also said when they
preached: 'We are witnesses ourselves of what we are saying,
and so is the Spirit, whom God has given to those who obey
him.'[3]

Furthermore, John was an eye-witness of what he wrote,
and did not even abandon Christ when He was crucified,
and he was entrusted with the care of His mother, facts
which are all proofs of Christ's love for him and that he had
accurate knowledge of everything. But do not doubt and be
curious if he has said that the number of miracles performed
was so great. On the contrary, reflecting on the ineffable
power of the One who performed them, accept with faith
what is said. For it is as easy for Him to do what He wishes
as it is for us to speak—in fact, much easier. Indeed, it is
enough for Him to will it, and everything is at once accomplished.

Let us, then, pay close attention to the words of the
Evangelist, and let us never cease reading and studying them,
for we gain more profit from them by unceasing study. By

---

3 Acts 5.32.

this means we shall be able to purify our lives; by this means, to cut out the thorns. Sin and concern for the interests of this world are indeed thorns: bearing no fruit, and very troublesome. And just as the thorn, however it is held, pierces him who is holding it, so also, in whatever way you hold to the things of this life, they will give you pain if you cling to them and cherish them.

Spiritual things, however, are not like that, but resemble a kind of pearl: whatever way you turn it, it pleases your eyes. For example, someone has engaged in almsgiving; not only is he buoyed up by the hope of the life to come, but he also rejoices in the blessings of this life, ever in good spirits, and accomplishing everything with great ease. He has vanquished his evil passions and, before reaching the kingdom of heaven, has already begun to enjoy the happiness found there, since he is approved and admired, by his own conscience first of all.

Moreover, every good work has this effect, just as a man's conscience likewise punishes wicked deeds in this life, even before he gets to hell. If you think of the future life after you commit sin, you become very fearful and tremulous, even if no one punishes you; if you think of the present life, you realize that you have many enemies and live in a state of suspicion, and will be able henceforth not even to look directly at those who have injured you, or, rather, who have not really injured you. Indeed, we do not enjoy as much pleasure from our sins as we do discomfort: while our conscience keeps reproaching us from within, men pass sentence on us from without; God is angry with us, hell is reaching out to receive us, our thoughts give us no rest. Sin is a heavy weight, to be sure, heavy and burdensome, and more difficult to bear than any leaden weight. The man who feels this weight will be unable to look upward, even a little, however callous he may be. Thus it was with Achab. Even though he was extremely impious, because he felt this weight, he began to walk with his head bent down, contrite and thoroughly wretched. Therefore, he put on sackcloth, and shed fountains of tears.[4]

If we also do this and repent as he did, we shall make expiation for our offenses as Zaccheus did, and we shall obtain pardon.[5] Just as in the case of tumors and ulcers, if one does not first stop the fluid that is oozing out and aggravating the sore, whatever remedies he applies, his efforts are all in vain, since the root of the evil has not been checked. So, if we also do not restrain our hand from greed and thus prevent this evil inflow of riches, even if we give alms, we do it all in vain. Covetousness, overtaking what has been cured by this means, sweeps it away and destroys it, and makes the evil worse than before.

Let us, then, stop defrauding, and let it be thus that we give alms. But, if we unnecessarily expose ourselves to falling, how shall we be able to keep our balance? I say this for, if a man is on the point of falling down and someone pulls him up from above (as almsgiving does), while another person begins forcefully pulling on him from below, nothing more advantageous would result from this struggle than for the man to be torn asunder.

Therefore, that this may not happen to us and that, while covetousness is weighing us down from below, almsgiving may not forsake us and depart, let us lighten ourselves and let us fly upward. Then, having been made perfect by ridding ourselves of evil deeds and by the accomplishing of the good works that are everlasting, we may obtain the eternal blessings by the grace and mercy of our Lord Jesus Christ. Glory, power, honor be to Him, together with the Father and the Holy Spirit, now and always, and forever and ever. Amen.

---

4 3 Kings 21.27.
5 That is, by almsgiving; cf. Luke 19.1-10.

INDEX

INDEX

481

Apostles, 1: 117, 177, 210, 296, 388, 479, 481; 2: 38, 128, 198, 207, 304, 339, 389, 437, 442
apprenticeship, 2: 118
Arianism, 1: 121, 187; 2: viii, 392
arteries, 1: 243; 2: 91
article, definite, 1: 21, 50-51, 71, 146, 154, 178, 187
athlete, 1: 263
attachment, to earthly goods, 2: 373, 384-385, 425
avarice, 1: 265-266, 413-414, 483; 2: 32-33, 130-131, 203-205, 373, 396, 468

Balaam, 2: 206, 456
baptism, of John the Baptist, 1: 71, 113, 151, 157-158, 163, 165, 278-279
baptism, sacrament of, 1: 11, 100, 246-248, 251-256, 260-262, 339, 352-354; 2: 56, 288, 346, 435; deferment of, 1: ix, 175, 249; triple immersion, 1: 247
Barabbas, 2: 418
Barnabas, 2: 301, 371
beasts, of burden, 2: 396
beatitudes, 1: 329; 2: 130
begging, 2: 334
Bethabara, 1: 162
Bethany, 1: 162; 2: 168, 209, 217
Bethlehem, 1: 196-197; 2: 25, 39
Bethsaida, 1: 352
bile, 1: 244
birds, 1: 124

birth, spiritual regeneration, 1: 238-240, 242-248, 251-257
Bishop, of Constantinople, 1: xii; of Jerusalem, 2: 6, 473
blasphemy, 1: 360, 361
blindness, 1: 118, 220
blood, 1: 244
bones, 1: 244
books, 1: 105, 319-320
Bosom of the Father, 1: 141-147
Bread of Life, 1: 452-453, 465-466
brethren, of Christ, 2: 5-6
building, method of, 1: 74
burial, customs, 2: 184; of Christ, 2: 437-438; spices used in, 2: 437, 439-440

Caesarea, 1: 92
Cain, 1: 129, 366-367; 2: 290, 313
Caiphas, 2: 205-206, 404, 409, 417
'can' meaning 'will,' 1: 378-379, 381; 2: 3, 72-73, 239
Cana, 1: 346
Canaanite woman, 1: 115, 215, 300; 2: 147
Capharnaum, 1: 224, 345, 347, 425, 437, 440, 475
captivity, of Jews, 2: 202
cartilage, 1: 243
catechumen, 1: 248
centurion, 2: 169
charioteers, 1: 320; 2: 116

482

charity, virtues of, 2: 277-281, 326-327, 349-351, 395-396, 466
chastity, 1: 356; 2: 163, 187, 432
cherubim, 1: 111, 135, 143
childbirth, 1: 341; 2: 353-355
children, 1: 5, 24, 27, 43-44, 86, 242; 2: 262, 384
Christ, as God, 1: 33-35, 38, 117, 130, 202, 236, 253, 289, 453; 2: 4, 6, 9, 15, 17, 25-27, 48, 90-91, 228, 371, 380, 412, 420-421, 432, 450, 461; as Judge, 1: 249, 269-272, 297, 338, 385, 392-393, 401, 459; 2: 49, 228, 244-245; as King, 2: 413, 417-422, 429-430; as Man, 1: 34-35, 152, 163, 197, 202, 206, 252-253, 304-305, 380, 432, 463; 2: 4, 14-15, 24-27, 182-183, 229-230, 380, 382, 432, 437, 446-448; as Messias, 1: 187, 326; as Redeemer, 1: 72-73, 84, 109, 177, 262-265, 269, 344, 471; 2: 354, 424, 433-434; Blood of, 1: 469; 2: 336, 435; Body of, 1: 468-469; 2: 336, 'coming' of, 1: 269, 341; conception of, 1: 252; death of, 2: 433-434; see also crucifixion; humility; Incarnation; Lamb; Passion; Resurrection; Son of God
Christians, 1: 170, 171; 2: 179, 233; name of, 1: 191
Church, the, 1: xvi, 176, 284, 325; 2: 133, 435

church, 1: 24, 106, 310; 2: 61-62, 116, 119, 189-190, 364-365, 397
circumcision, 2: 21-22
Communion, Holy, 1: 150, 468-469, 471, 473, 484; 2: 146-147, 336, 435
company, evil of bad, 2: 103-104
confession, 1: 79
consubstantiality, 1: 20, 48-52, 63-64, 72, 77-78, 389; 2: 51, 68, 70, 158, 194, 243-244, 294-296, 310
continence, 2: 188, 298, 432
courts, of law, 2: 397
covetousness, 1: 86; 2: ix, 74-75, 131, 211-215, 321-324, 336, 365-366, 478
creed, of Christians, 1: 171
cross of Christ, identification of, 2: 430
crowning with thorns, 2: 419
crucifixion, of Christ, 1: 117, 262; 2: 221, 274-275, 353-354, 368, 411, 418-420, 423, 428-435

dancers, 1: 184-185, 320, 434-435; 2: 2, 116
Daniel, 1: 111, 113, 119, 142, 336; 2: 453
David, 1: 82, 113, 127, 136, 141, 169, 196, 210, 303, 336, 373, 396, 411; 2: 3, 30, 40, 58, 235
death, 1: 68; 2: x, 176-178, 399, 426, 432, 444
Debbora, 2: 161

Dedication, feast of, 2: 152
departed, help for, 2: 177, 445
despondency, 2: 338, 352
detachment, from earthly goods, 1: 53, 192, 432-433, 447-448, 484-485; 2: 63, 226-227, 375-376, 384-385, 465
Devil, 1: 49, 76, 80, 94-95, 114, 158, 185, 221-222, 248, 320, 321, 366, 469; 2: 3, 71-74, 231-233, 241, 311, 424, 429, 472
dictatorship, 2: 201-202
disciples, of Christ, 1: 175, 230, 232-233, 280-281, 304-305, 328, 333, 425, 436, 467; 2: 7, 121, 167, 218-219, 222, 260, 277, 390; of John the Baptist, 1: 179, 280-286
Docetae, 1: 107
dogs, hunting, 2: 396; sheep, 2: 336
dolls, 2: 384
Dorcas, 2: 444
dropsy, 1: 368

earth, an element, 1: 245
education, of young, 1: 27-29, 43-44, 242; 2: 260
Egypt, 1: 122, 450, 469; 2: 88, 159
Elcana, 1: 33
Elias, 1: 111, 154; 2: 314
Eliseus, 1: 111, 428; 2: 93
Elizabeth, 1: 113, 166
Empedocles, 2: 225

entertainment, public, 1: 170, 184, 320
envy, 1: 93-94, 151, 286, 365-367; 2: 3, 7, 14, 76, 83-85, 202-203
Ephrem, 2: 208
eremitical life, 1: 286; 2: 351
Esau, 1: 366
Eunomius, Bishop of Cyzicus, 1: 158, 187
Evangelists, honesty of, 1: 169-170; 2: 6, 182, 289, 292-293
evil, nature of, 1: 356; 2: 88
example, good, 2: 53
eye, 1: 23; 2: 90-91
Ezechiel, 1: 119-120, 142, 169, 411; 2: 84, 87, 245, 427

faith, 1: 75, 239-240, 271, 322, 344, 347-352, 362, 456, 464, 476, 478; 2: 28, 38, 53, 56, 65, 92, 100, 121, 185-187, 317, 388, 395, 452, 460; not sufficient without works, 1: 102, 297-298, 394; 2: 187, 233, 425
faithful, the, 1: 243
farmer, 1: 120, 192
fasting, 1: 80
fate, belief in, fallacious, 1: 459
father, 1: 24, 348
fever, 1: 347-350
fisherman, 1: 13
food, moderation in, 1: 220, 428; preoccupation about, 1: 304, 333-334

484

forbearance, 1: 400-401; 2: x, 10-
11, 264-268, 424, 414-416
forgiveness, of sin, 1: 79, 239,
268-269, 400-401; 2: 67-68, 288-
291, 416, 453
fortitude, in suffering, 2: 333,
413-416, 432-433
fraud, 1: 421; 2: 148, 234, 289-
291, 397
funerals, 2: x, 174-178, 441-445

Gabriel, 1: 113
Galilee, 1: 12, 194, 204, 300, 345,
424; 2: 3, 25, 47
Gamaliel, 1: 282
Gentiles 1: 90-93, 300-306; 2: 31,
136-137, 218, 220-221, 368-369,
370, 411
Giezi, 2: 212
gluttony, 1: 220, 431, 448-449
Gnosticism, 2: 187, 223
God, existence and attributes of,
1: 20, 30-31, 34, 36, 46-48, 51,
58, 63, 65, 84-85, 96, 108, 114-
115, 143-146, 264, 268, 353,
389, 390, 410-411; 2: 89, 294,
301
gold, 1: 9, 100, 484; 2: 75, 131,
148, 162-163, 213, 294, 322,
384, 396, 466-467
Golgotha, 2: 428
gout, 2: 242
grace, sanctifying, 1: 81, 100,
101-102, 134-136, 312; 2: 32,

36-38, 340, 353-354, 456-457
grave-robber, 2: 146, 149, 441
Greeks, 1: 16; 2: 186, 224-225

harlots, 1: 184-185, 266; 2: 145-
147, 189, 362-365, 469
heart, 1: 243
heaven, 1: 87, 118-119, 160, 251,
311, 401, 414; 2: 23, 74, 94-96,
203, 205, 226, 228, 324, 360,
465, 468
hell, 1: 94, 96, 118-119, 130, 185,
249, 265, 267, 286, 311, 368,
414; 2: 10-11, 23, 142, 188,
190, 204-205, 373, 454, 468,
477; gehenna, 1: 60, 351
Henoch, 2: 314
heretics, 1: 404, 412; 2: 49-50, 80,
223, 369-370, 413
Herod, 1: 122
HE WHO IS, 1: 146
home, woman's influence in, 2:
160-164
homily, 1: xv, xvii, 23, 110, 119
honey, 1: 8, 85
'hour,' of Christ, 1: 212-215; 2:
7, 55, 168, 221, 229
humility, of Christ, 1: 36-37, 125,
190, 257, 259, 261, 330, 380,
387, 389-390, 397-399; 2: 12,
17, 19-20, 27, 50, 59-60, 137,
140, 149, 191-196, 200, 237-238,
246, 252-257, 262, 297, 310-311,
320, 344, 357, 367, 372, 381-
382, 393, 460, 463-464

485

husband, influence of wife on, 2: 160-164, 249-250

idolatry, 1: 134, 196, 212-213
immortality, of soul, 2: 174-179, 186, 359-360, 444
Incarnation, 1: 34-35, 44-45, 52, 72, 99, 106-109, 299, 374, 463; 2: 4, 12, 195, 373
Isaac, 1: 190, 256, 427; 2: 81, 314, 428
Isaias, 1: 122, 127, 142, 147, 411; 2: 235, 238, 239, 241

Jacob, 1: 83, 142, 190, 301-303, 309, 313-315, 326; 2: 160, 235, 323, 416
James the Greater, St., 1: 13; 2: 270
James the Less, St., 2: 6, 473
jaundice, 1: 220
Jeremias, 1: 122, 411; 2: 245
Jericho, 1: 373
Jerusalem, 1: 122, 224-225, 324, 352, 425; 2: 24, 201, 205, 208, 217, 277, 369; Bishop of, 2: 6, 473
Jews, hostile to Christ, 1: 38, 72, 82, 88-89, 91, 99, 121, 168, 210, 233, 280-286, 290, 300, 302-303, 306-309, 313, 316-319, 322-327, 342-344, 346, 361, 363, 372, 375, 382, 389, 404-412, 449, 462; 2: 3, 7-8, 12-13, 17-22, 24-29, 55, 66-74, 76-82, 100, 106-

115, 140-142, 150, 152-159, 180, 205-208, 215, 235-237, 276-277, 286, 292, 332, 339-340, 367-369, 394, 409-413, 417-423, 429-430, 434-435; as a nation, 2: 31, 40, 66, 207, 221, 236, 277, 423, 427; priests and rulers of, 2: 14, 24, 28, 46, 102-103, 134, 212, 215, 242, 423; High Priest, 2: 206-207, 406
Job, 1: 119, 369, 468; 2: 161
John the Baptist, St., 1: 70, 73, 75, 113, 121-126, 130-132, 151-158, 161-169, 173-180, 278-286, 288-293, 296-299, 406-409, 420; 2: 49, 158-159
John the Evangelist, St., 1: 4-5, 12-13, 15-18, 328-330; 2: 3-4, 269-273, 279, 404-406, 431, 433, 437, 439-440, 463-464, 473-476
Jordan River, 1: 161, 178-179, 251, 278, 408, 410; 2: 93, 158
Joseph, St., 1: 195, 463, 477
Joseph, son of Jacob, 1: 366; 2: 147, 266-277, 314, 323
Joseph of Arimathea, 2: 436-437
Josephus, 2: 207
Josue, 1: 190
Judas, 1: 329; 2: 210-212, 251, 255, 259-262, 263-265, 269-274, 315-316, 382, 399-401, 481-482
Judas, associate of Theodas, 2: 124, 127-128
Jude, St., 2: 7, 306-307
Judea, 2: 152

Judith, 2: 161
judges, 2: 22, 397
judgment, general, 1: 338, 340, 458-461; particular, 1: 110, 265, 384, 413-414, 435, 485; 2: 145, 335

king, 1: 11, 70, 100, 112, 243, 353, 472; 2: 32, 218, 232, 322, 453
kinsmen, of Lord, 1: 210

Lamb, type of Christ, 1: 138, 164, 177, 436
law, civil, sanctions of, 1: 96; natural, 2: 298
Lazarus, 2: 165-174, 180-200, 209, 216-217, 394-395
Lia, 1: 190
life everlasting, 1: 21, 52, 65-67, 171, 447-448. 474-475; 2: 78, 172, 287
Light, the, 1: 21, 52, 65-67, 72-73, 81, 271-272; 2: 47-48, 53, 93, 236, 244
liver, 1: 243
Lot, 1: 460
love, of neighbor, 1: 401; 2: 242, 321, 325, 349-351, 363, 391, 395-397, 424, 470
Luke, St., 1: 13, 44-45, 153, 169, 205, 207, 347; 2: 30, 165, 208, 462, 464
lying, 2: 71-72, 277-278

magi, 1: 113, 115, 167
mange, 2: 189
Manichaeans, 1: 216, 463; 2: 413
manna, 1: 450-451, 465-466
Marcellus of Ancyra, 1: 78
Marcion, 1: 429; 2: 4, 224, 433
Mark, St., 1: 44-45; 2: 219
marriage, 1: 176, 186-187, 284-285; 2: 160-164, 249-250; infidelity in, 2: 187-190; of Cana, 1: 204-219
Martha, 1: 444-445; 2: 165-174
Mary, Mother of God, 1: xviii, 44, 113, 204-209, 252-253; 2: 62-63, 431, 433
Mary, St. Paul's helper, 2: 161
Mary Magdalen, 2: 165-174, 180-181, 210-211, 438-439, 446-450.
Matthew, St., 1: 44-45, 115, 124-126, 162-163, 347, 360, 374, 377, 424, 438, 466; 2: 165, 183, 217
meals, time for, 1: 178
medicine, 1: 140
membranes, 1: 243
Michael, Archangel, 1: 113
miracles, 1: 114, 167, 205-206, 233, 349, 362; 2: 5, 28, 216, 278-279, 461; Cana, 215-219; cure of man born blind, 2: 85-91; daughter of Jairus, 1: 362; Lazarus, 2: 165-174, 197-200; lepers, 1: 361; loaves and fishes, 1: 429-431; paralytic at Bethsaida, 1: 352-360
Moabites, 2: 84

487

money, 2: 376; as root of all evil, 2: 397, 466-469

mortification, of senses, 2: 297-299

mosaics, 2: 396

Moses, 1: 34, 57-58, 62, 82, 111-113, 121, 130, 136-138, 142, 146-148, 169, 183, 194-195, 302, 326, 329, 396, 411, 419-421, 426, 439-440, 450; 2: 19-22, 51, 87, 112-113, 125, 329

Mysteries, the, 1: 150, 473, 484; 2: 351, 435

Mystical Body, 1: 149-150, 186; 2: 131, 189, 248-249, 468-469, 207-208, 242, 348-349, 361-362, 391, 435, 450

murderers, 2: 146, 149

Naaman, 2: 93

Nabal, 2: 161

Nabuchodonosor, 2: 206

Nahum, 2: 204

Nathanael, 1: 188, 194-199, 201-204, 317, 322, 476; 2: 39, 462

Nazareth, 1: 196, 346; 2: 39

nerves, 1: 243; 2: 92

Nicodemus, 1: 234-244, 252-257, 264, 269, 275-276, 308, 314-315, 322, 394, 467, 476; 2: 45, 437

Noe, 1: 119, 384, 460; 2: 266

occupations held in low esteem, 1: 100, 305; 2: 116

olive, 1: 241

organs, 1: 243

Osee, 1: 122; 2: 241

pagans, 1: 14, 17, 22, 170, 273; 2: 42, 175, 224-225, 279-280, 425; games of, 1: 3, 139; letters of, vs. Christian, 1: 27; 2: 186

Palestine, aridity of, 1: 215

Parables, cockle, 1: 204, 335; Good Shepherd, 2: 124-130, 133-140, 155-156; hours in the day, 2: 168; king's son, 1: 97; marriage feast, 1: 102-103; Pharisee and the Publican, 2: 416; prodigal, 2: 366; rich man and Lazarus, 1: 339; 2: 335, 427; sheep and goats, 1: 338; sower, 1: 10, 25, 119-120, 173, 240-241; unmerciful servant, 1: 129, 400; 2: 143, 267; the vine, 2: 317-321, 327; vineyard, 1: 91; 2: 59; virgins, 1: 102, 231, 241; 2: 32, 53-54, 143, 336, 426; widow's mite, 2: 94

paradise, 1: 251, 355, 358

paralysis, 1: 220, 347, 370-371

paramour, 2: 362-365

parents, love for, 1: 207; 2: 431, 433

passions, 1: 26; 2: 314

Passion, of Christ, voluntarily endured, 1: 52, 116, 263-265; 2: 138, 235, 312, 325

Passover, 1: 425; 2: 5, 208-209, 409-410

488

patience, virtue of, 2: 360-361; 417

Paul, St., 1: 23, 25, 35-36, 42-43, 49-50, 62, 64-65, 69, 78, 89-94, 97-98, 115, 120, 128, 134, 139, 144, 148-149, 151, 158, 172, 180, 186, 191, 201, 212, 229, 239-240, 247, 251-252, 258, 261, 263, 268, 285, 294-295, 322, 324-325, 338-341, 359, 366-369, 378, 384, 397-400, 412, 417-418, 422, 429, 434, 444, 460, 462, 469, 471, 481, 495, 498; 2: 6, 25-26, 36, 45, 56, 67, 83, 90, 93, 98, 104-105, 122, 134-135, 137, 140, 148, 150, 187, 212, 222, 240, 244, 246-247, 250, 270-271, 279, 313-314, 324, 326, 331, 339, 344, 347, 350, 362-363, 371-372, 376, 384, 389, 394, 414, 452, 454-456, 466; Saul, 2: 301

Paul of Samosata, 1: 45, 81, 164, 393; 2: 4

Pentecost, feast of, 1: 352

people, 1: 39, 41

persecution, 2: 328, 330-333

Persia, 2: 95, 152

Persis, 2: 161

Peter, St., 1: 34-35, 83, 92, 180, 188-190, 202, 214, 230, 299, 329, 438, 480-482; 2: ix, 36, 185, 254-257, 269-270, 274, 279-287, 292, 314-315, 338, 369,

393, 402-409, 437, 440, 462-464, 470-474

Pharao, 2: 83, 206, 240

Pharisees, 2: 28, 43-48, 100-103, 201-202, 219-220, 251

Philip, St., 1: 188, 193-199, 214, 329, 349, 425; 2: 220, 291, 338, 462

phlegm, 1: 244

physician, 1: 368

Pilate, 1: 278; 2: ix, 409-413, 417-423, 429-430, 436-437

Plato, 1: 14, 16, 18; 2: 186

poverty, 1: xvi, 2: 63, 132, 323, 335, 376

Powers, choir of angels, 1: 135, 143

prayer, 1: 350-351, 355; 2: 351, 367-368; of Christ, 1: 429-430; 2: 196-200, 367-368; Lord's, 1: 441

preaching, 1: 24-27, 120, 212, 222

pride, 1: 94, 158-160

priesthood, 2: x, 454-457

Priscilla, 2: 161

prisons, 2: x, 144-150

prophecy, 1: 127, 189; 2: 238

Prophet, the, 1: 154, 462; 2: 382

prophets, 1: 83, 89, 93, 119, 143, 148, 177, 255-256, 261, 290, 325, 335-337, 396, 428, 464; 2: 36-37, 79, 347-348

Providence, 1: 373-374, 478

purification, 1: 215

purse-snatchers, 2: 146
Pythagoras, 1: 14, 16, 17; 2: 186, 225

races, 1: 105, 320; 2: x, 116
Ramathaimsophim, man of, 1: 31, 33
Red Sea, 1: 439-440
remarriage, 2: 190, 258
Resurrection, of Christ, 1: 117, 230; 2: 56, 222-223, 233, 235, 307-308, 354, 359, 438-441, 446-454, 458-462, 464
resurrection, of body, 1: 171, 311, 392-395, 454-455, 458-461, 474-475; 2: 172-174, 222-223, 441, 445, 465
revenge, 2: 40-42
rest, eternal, 2: 394
rhetoric, 1: xvii, 18, 335
robbers, 2: 20
Romans, 2: 201, 205-206

Sabbath, 1: 28, 106, 226, 363-365, 372, 374-375, 409, 419; 2: 17-22, 59, 100-102, 106-108, 216, 236
Sabellius, 1: 78, 389; 2: 292, 301, 392
salvation, 1: 210, 324, 333-334, 344; 2: 253
Samaria, woman of, 1: 115, 174, 188-189, 306-345, 404, 451; 2: 79, 147

Samaritans, 1: 300-303, 322-327, 334-338, 342-344, 346-347
Samson, 1: 190
Samuel, 1: 83
Sara (Sarai), 1: 190, 238
Satan, 1: 312; 2: 118, 272; see also Devil
scabies, 2: 104
Scripture, Holy, 1: xvi, 74, 104, 141, 183, 202, 293-295, 319-320, 324-325, 336, 351-352, 359, 403, 412, 415, 426, 473; 2: xi, 23, 35-36, 61-63, 96, 98, 106, 115, 124, 159, 224, 239, 241, 252, 265, 278, 304-305, 383, 426, 476; linguistic usage peculiar to, 1: 127; 2: 88-89, 167, 238, 383; quotations from, or references to, individual books:
Acts of the Apostles, 1: 13, 34, 35, 65, 83, 92, 97, 115, 166, 247, 282, 300, 444, 445; 2: 124, 127, 185, 198, 212, 297, 301, 313, 331, 355, 356, 369, 424, 444, 460, 464, 476
Amos, 1: 109, 196, 433
Apocalypse, 1: 141, 470
Colossians, 1: 62, 63, 65, 144, 172, 263, 289, 400, 461; 2: 212, 297, 305
1 Corinthians, 1: 6, 36, 60, 64, 65, 98, 100, 120, 134, 148, 149, 151, 191, 195, 222, 239, 240, 245, 262, 294, 295, 338, 359, 366, 367, 368, 397, 422, 424,

490

493

494